The Apostles

A Personal Biography

As Channelled To Shontara

About the Author

I was born in Brisbane 1957 under the fire sign of Aries; which makes me enthusiastic and determined. My name, Shontara, means 'The Rose of Love'. And this is my purpose – to give love unconditionally to all, whenever they need it and to make people laugh and feel good about themselves.

My favourite free time pursuit has always been photography and in my twenties, I'd often dream of becoming the next Steve Parish. Today, I also relax by involving myself with Tai Chi, doing tapestries, creating wedding stationery and graphic design. I can also be found 'chilling out' in front of the TV.

My expertise falls in three main areas of equal importance. One is energy healing, using the vibration of pure sound to release all manner of illness and pain; cancer in particular. The second is writing. Thirdly, I am passionate about teaching spiritual self awareness. I achieve the first by utilising my voice and the latter two by using the skills built up over many years of training, learning and personal experience.

I can be whoever people want me to be, without compromising my true self. I am unlimited and accepting. Because I believe in miracles, all things are possible.

Published in Australia by Sid Harta Publishers Pty Ltd,
ACN: 007 030 051
23 Stirling Crescent, Glen Waverley, Victoria 3150 Australia
Telephone: +61 3 9560 9920, Facsimile: +61 3 9545 1742
E-mail: author@sidharta.com.au

First published in Australia 2009
This edition published 2009
Copyright © Shontara 2009
Cover design, typesetting: Chameleon Print Design

The right of Shontara to be identified as the Author of the Work has been asserted in accordance with the Copyright, Designs and Patents Act 1988.

The information in this book is based on the author's personal experiences and opinions. The publisher specifically disclaims responsibility for any adverse consequences which may result from use of the information contained herein.

All rights reserved. No part of this publication may be reproduced, stored in a retrieval system, or transmitted, in any form or by any means without the prior written permission of the publisher, nor be otherwise circulated in any form of binding or cover other than that in which it is published and without a similar condition being imposed on the subsequent purchaser.

Shontara
Apostles, The
ISBN: 1-921642-12-2 EAN13: 978-1-921642-12-8
pp642

Dedication to

*All the Angels in Heaven,
as well as those placed firmly upon this Earth.*

*With God's blessing, I have a whole army of them,
144,000 and more.
All standing behind and around me,
guiding, protecting and inspiring me,
to take the next step without fear.*

*Besides which, my heart is big enough,
to embrace the whole Universe.*

Contents

Foreword 3

Introduction 5

Part 1 – The Original Twelve

Matthew   Originally known as Levi and who wrote
the Gospel of Matthew 13
Fear of Abandonment 27
Roses 43
Affirmations 48

Peter   Originally known as Simon Peter and
brother of Apostle Andrew 49
Fear of Illness 71
Cleansing My Aura 84
Affirmations 85

Sim(e)on   A Zealot who pledged to drive out the
Romans 87
Fear of The Unknown 103
Moving into the Unknown 117
Affirmations 118

Judas   Betrayed Jesus to the Romans and looked
after the Apostles Money 119
Fear of Not Having Enough Money 139
Cave of Abundance 153
Affirmations 155

Thomas	His name means 'twin'	157
	Fear of Being Powerless	173
	You are the Source of all Power	194
	Affirmations	195
James	Brother of Apostle John and son of Zebedee	197
	Fear of Spirit	215
	Introduction to Your Spirit Guide	235
	Affirmations	238
John	Brother of Apostle James and son of Zebedee	239
	Fear of Being Judged	257
	The Last Judgement	271
	Affirmations	273
Bartholomew	Also known as Nathanael	275
	Fear of Persecution	301
	Ancient Chinese Proverb	322
	Affirmations	323
Philip	He introduced Bartholomew to Jesus	325
	Fear of Being Alone	343
	I Am the Rose of Love	359
	Affirmations	360
Andrew	Brother of Simon Peter	361
	Fear of Failure	377
	Two Seeds	397
	Affirmations	398
Lebbaeus	Whose surname was Thaddaeus	399
	Fear of Rejection	417
	The Plum	434
	Affirmations	435

James	The son of Alphaeus	437
	Fear of Death	453
	Fly Free Tonight	476
	Affirmations	478

Part 2 – And Then There Was More

Matthias	He was chosen as an Apostle after the death of Judas	481
	Fear of Feelings	497
	Forgiveness Visualisation	515
	Affirmations	517
Paul	Originally known as Saul	519
	Fear of Abuse	533
	Invocation Prayer	553
	Affirmations	554

Part 3 – Our Friends

Luke	A Greek speaking doctor who wrote the Gospel of Luke	557
Mark	Wrote the Gospel of Mark, as largely told to him by the Apostle Peter	573
Timothy	Son of a Jewish Christian mother and a Greek father	593

Part 4

A Spiritual Journey Towards World Peace	613
Affirmations	623

I have returned and I am of flesh, blood and bone.

*And as such, I openly walk amongst you,
yet you don't fully recognise my face.*

You look in partial recognition but still you do not see.

*One day very soon, in terms of manmade time,
you will once again stand and feel secure in my Light.*

*This is where I can reveal my Truth to you and
while in this sacred space,
you will come to know who you are and the future role
you have to play in helping the whole of mankind
ascend to great and unexpected heights.*

Foreword

I am overjoyed to be able to recommend the writing of Shontara, a very remarkable woman whose faith could put many of us to shame.

Shontara is one of the most interesting characters I have ever met. She is a teacher, an eloquent speaker, a healer, a brilliant writer but most of all, she is a mystic. A mystic, out of whose firsthand experience of the living God, have been born some striking insights into the truth. Notably, this is apparent in her teachings on the subject of what happens to the soul after death. The God which is revealed in this book is an all embracing love that unites the whole of creation into one indivisible whole.

This mystical vision is not a psychological anomaly; rather it is a purer state of being. Humanity only fails to experience this because they have been led to believe that they themselves are separate from God; when in fact, God is their very essence.

This book, as indeed all mystical treatises, is designed to dispel this illusion of separateness. The Apostles that we meet through the direct contact of Shontara's greater vision are no plastic saints. They are real, full, understanding and humane, whose experiences with the Christ is as relevant today as it was in the first Century. The benefit of receiving these teachings afresh through the abilities given to Shontara is that they represent a pure teaching unfettered by institution or dogma.

At this time in our history, many people are inquisitive

to learn more about the Christ, his Apostles and their true mission and message. This has come about through recent discoveries of ancient texts, at places like Qumran and the Nag Hammadi Library; Codexes such as the **'Gospel of Judas'** and works of fiction like Dan Brown's **'The Da Vinci Code'**.

It is my hope that Shontara's work, which bridges the gap between these works, will lead others to a greater understanding and further them on their path to personal liberation. This book is one that I found utterly refreshing. In some ways, this is the most original book that I have come across recently.

It should be of great value to many, putting some profound truths in a simple, joyful and practical way. I hope it will have wide circulation and bring blessings to all.

The Most Reverend Ian Adrian (DD RSJ)
Bishop of Australia
The Reformed Catholic Church

Introduction

It has been requested from Spirit that I act as a clear and perfect channel, through which they, the Twelve Apostles, and others, could express themselves, by utilising the written word. I don't know about the perfect bit but their individual voices were clearly heard and understood.

You might well ask why they chose me. This is a good question and it is one that I too have asked myself many times in the past. As you read on, you may think I am big noting myself. I'm not and I hope it doesn't come across like that. I am just stating what was, although I can't prove it to you. I'm also forcing you to use your own intuition to decide for yourself whether what I speak of is fact or fiction. That decision must be made by you. Whether you accept or reject the following information, this is your choice.

For those of you who have not yet had the pleasure of reading my first publication, **'The Angel Within'**, let me explain that approximately 2000 years ago, in the time of Jesus, I lived as a man whose name was Shontara. Incidentally, my name means 'The Rose of Love'. I know it may not sound masculine but this is the truth, as I know it. I earned my living by being a goldsmith. I was quite skilled, talented and quite imaginative with my craft. I also made the cup which was used at the Last Supper and which was later used to catch the Blood of Christ.

This same cup was initially given as a gift to Matthew from me as a sign of my friendship and respect that I felt for him. Matthew later passed it on to Jesus for his use, with my blessing and permission. A short time before the Last Supper, I added a deep red ruby in the centre of the cup, especially for that occasion. It was square cut but was inserted at an angle which created a diamond effect.

My occupation then had nothing to do with why they chose me today. Once upon a time (and no, this is not a fairytale), I had a close friendship with Matthew the Disciple; well before he ever knew Jesus. As you know, Matthew and the others became a follower of the teachings of Jesus and later spread the word of God across the lands. Matthew was well educated. He came from a wealthy family background, while I did not. In that way, we were like chalk and cheese but this did not bother us. We grew up together and he taught me how to read and write. We were inseparable. We were like blood brothers. When Matthew became a Disciple and later an Apostle, I became not only his trusted friend and confidante, but I had another major role to play in Matthew's life; as his scribe and travelling companion.

I have done all this before and more, although not in quite the same way as I am experiencing it today. It's rather ironic and funny but now I understand why I have become such a prolific writer and because of this unique friendship in that lifetime that I shared with Matthew and the others, this is why they chose me to relay their personal message.

Please, don't believe for one minute that I have exclusive rights to Jesus and the Twelve, or any other highly evolved Spirit entity. This is far from the truth. You have this same ability and they invite you to call out their name; to visualise their faces and to talk with them in the same way that I have done. They would like to share themselves around to as many people as they can. As do the Archangels. They are there for all of us, as is God.

In short, I have had the opportunity to live, touch, breathe and speak with each one of the 'inner circle of men', their travelling companions, their wives and family members. This, of course, includes the great man himself as well. Jesus was so charismatic, intense and powerful and he exuded a sense of inner strength. He portrayed all this and more, in a gentle and approachable way. Jesus would either become your best friend or hated enemy. It depended greatly upon the perspective of the one who was listening.

You might ask, am I a good listener? I would say yes, although my husband John would point out that I am a far better talker. Perhaps this is true to a certain extent (and what woman doesn't relate to that?) but I can listen when needed.

I have now explained why they chose me but I haven't yet explained what their purpose is in doing so. They believe it is time for people, like you and me, to be reawakened to the Truth. Little has been written about their personal lives and that is what this book is all about. It looks at each man separately and collectively; where they speak of their fears, their very human inadequacies and joys, their highs and lows, as well as how some of them died and their impressions about their death.

Many well educated and so-called Christian people have placed Jesus the man and his Twelve Disciples, upon a far too high pedestal for too long; where they have all become unreachable and not quite real in today's society. You could say this book is similar in purpose, in part, to that popular TV show **'This Is Your Life'**.

I certainly haven't been shown everything and I don't yet have all the answers to the mysteries of the Universe but I know the memories are there, not just for me to access but for you too.

As you continue reading and evaluating, you will notice that everything is written in the first person. That is, each one of them has had an opportunity to speak for themselves. They share a little of their past and a lot about their philosophy on life. This book is not just about their lifetime experiences as the Apostles and followers of Jesus but it's also a great book of prophecy – for you and for me; yet you won't see any grandiose predictions. They are much more subtle than that.

This is their story, not mine, even though I was personally involved with each of their lives. Listen to their voices carefully and make your own judgements. Read between the lines if you have to, put some of their ideas into practice and above all, be your own person and remain happy with the identity that you alone have created for yourself. Don't try and be like another.

Please read our book with an open heart and mind. For the majority of those who come across it, you will experience a gut feeling and know that what has been spoken about is their Truth. While sceptics may read it and disbelieve all of what is said. Jesus, too, had many sceptics who would try and get in his way but do you think that stopped him? No, and it won't stop me from doing what I need to do.

If you're a sceptic, I say to you, enjoy it regardless and read it in the same way that you would if it was a good fiction novel and I hope you at least like the characters that have been created. I am not here to preach or force you to believe. Our purpose is to help you let go of your fears and inspire you to go beyond your self-imposed limitations.

Before I finish, I must reiterate that I don't have exclusive rights to the Twelve, Jesus, the Dalai Lama, Buddha, St Germaine or any other great prophet, religious or spiritual leader. They are there for all of us who wish to listen. Don't be afraid to put up your hand to ask a question. Without questions, how can we ever expect to learn?

They have had other incarnations since the one they were most famous for and the language used is not of that time period. It is spoken, using today's terminology, so it then becomes readable and easy to understand and digest.

God bless and I hope that many happy hours and days are spent, spellbound by the contents shared within the pages of this book.

Yours truly, from one to another, with love
SHONTARA and **THE TWELVE APOSTLES**

Part 1

The Original Twelve

MATTHEW

My eyes adore you and I

Accept the Blood of Christ, which will help me to wipe away all

Tears of sorrow, fear and pain.

The Master is with me, as well as the Twelve, therefore I drink from the

Holy Grail, which is God's precious gift to me. I will

Endeavour to fulfil my destiny to the best of my ability,

With the sign of the Cross, emblazoned upon my forehead.

One of the places that I travelled to after the death of Jesus was Tibet. Shontara was my lifelong friend and companion. Thanks to my father, I was well educated and could easily read and write. As a young boy, I became Shontara's teacher/mentor and taught him how to read and write. When later in life I became an Apostle of Jesus, Shontara then became my scribe and travelling companion. I loved my food and possessed a wicked sense of humour. To look at me, you could compare me to a huge, friendly and furry bear or gentle giant. I once had a great love, but lost it.

The village had a real community spirit but there is a certain amount of dissention in the ranks. There was much uncertainty in regards to the government of the day. Many were waiting for a sign of better things to come. Many just wanted to forget about their everyday problems. They placed their faith in an outside force. The village life of trading and gossip was a place of escape for many people. Life was difficult. You had to be careful when it came to declaring where and in whom one placed their faith. The city walls had many ears and the windows had big eyes to take note of all the comings and goings. Trust no-one. Betrayal was in the air, even amongst good friends.

I felt great sorrow at seeing so much sadness and uncertainty around me. Quite often, I felt powerless to intervene in the life of so many. Perhaps it was not my business to do so anyway. Where is the line defined between helping and interfering? Everyone will be different. Sometimes it is difficult to discern where that line is.

I have reached a crossroad. Which way do I go? I ask myself on a constant basis. I suffer from a certain amount of fear, doubt and indecision. What would my Master and Lord have done? I would often ask myself this, after his death. But I cannot be him, as he can never be me. I am an individual who has been given the free will to choose which path I wish to follow. Nothing about the future is set in stone. There can never be any guarantees of success down the track.

I learnt not to expect too much from other people and situations but on the other hand, I demanded so much from myself. I had a reputation to uphold. I wanted to be always seen as a man of honour and I tried so hard not to disgrace myself in the eyes of my God, or of my family. To try and continually live up to the expectations of others can be tiring and frustrating to say the least. I would find solace by sitting upon my favourite rock which could be found just outside the city gates and stare up at the moon shining its light upon me. I would imagine that I was receiving a blessing, as the moonbeams caressed and soothed my soul. I wrote many poems and love songs as well.

I was affectionate and loved nothing more than to give great big strong hugs, something that the recipient could not easily forget. Quite often, I would laugh uproariously in their ear, to loosen them up a bit, although it didn't always have the desired effect; which was primarily for them to be happy and not take life and all its problems too seriously. Even when sharing the word of God, I would put it in such a way that people could relate it back to their own personal experiences and feel on a soul level, the Truth that is being spoken.

There was much singing around an open fire, as well as sharing and listening to stories. I may not necessarily have had a bath every day but made sure that upon awaking and before retiring at night, I washed my hands, feet and face. This became like a religious ritual for me; a time of great cleansing and purification of the physical body and the soul.

You could say that I was a bit of a night owl. I could be found many times late at night at home or in my makeshift tent if travelling, pouring over some ancient script, avidly reading away by the light of my oil lamp. Sometimes, I would write letters home which I would then give to a messenger to deliver. This delivery service could, quite often, take many months before the intended person would receive it. My script was neat but small.

I was a good cook and a man of independent means. The woman I chose to love that lifetime died young, under tragic circumstances, fairly early in our relationship. She bore a son to me but he also died. I blamed myself for this happening. After that, I swore I would never become so attached or dependent upon anyone again. I figured this would bring me a lot less heartache and disappointment. That may sound selfish and cynical but that didn't stop me from being happy for my close friends who had successful partnerships with others. I would never persuade anyone against the sanctity of marriage. This is what God wants for each one of us. I chose to walk a solitary path, although I still had many friends – both male and female. I also had myself, I had Jesus and I had my life. What more could one ask for?

I was bitten often by the wanderlust bug; therefore dedicating a large portion of my time to travelling from town to town spreading the Word, suited my purposes well. I would have to say I must have incarnated with some strong Gypsy blood flowing through my veins.

From my early boyhood days, I had always walked with a

slight limp. I was in no pain and it caused me no trouble. My left leg just happened to be shorter than the right. Some people noticed but most did not. This affliction never stopped me from fulfilling my destiny to the best of my ability.

I didn't relish the idea of people looking at me and I didn't like to be the centre of attention. But how else was I able to pass on God's knowledge and wisdom to others? This personal dislike for recognition was mentally put on the backburner in order for me to get my message across. I wasn't one to allow fear to control my actions.

Sometimes I would doubt and not know what to say and where to begin. But I need not have worried because when I opened my mouth, the words poured forth. My God was with me, using me as his channel. I was not the only one, God used in this way. I felt honoured and deeply humbled to have been trusted enough and chosen to help the cause of Jesus. I always tried my best never to let him down – which I didn't – but that didn't stop me from feeling strongly at times, that I had indeed failed to fulfil a specific task given. I was sometimes my own worst enemy.

At every opportunity I got, I would love to watch the sea from a nice safe distance upon the shore. That great expanse of water unnerved me at times, especially when on top of it and when there was no way I could avoid hopping into a boat; again I would swallow my fear and pray for the good Lord to protect me for yet another day. I much preferred to have my two feet planted firmly on solid ground.

I grew a vegetable patch behind where I lived. Whilst travelling, I commissioned another to look after the plants for me. Had an excellent green thumb and, considering the condition of the soil, was more successful in growing plants, which was a miracle in itself. I shared much with the village but made sure I never went without. I needed this body, so it would be a smart move on my part to feed it properly with all the nutrients I needed to lead a full, active and sometimes stressful and frustrating lifestyle.

I died by drowning but this is not what the official records said. I had a high fever and was suffering from delirium, hallucinations and body tremors. I was as weak as a kitten. In my semi conscious state, late one night, my detractors/enemies snuck in and half dragged and pushed me to my death. There was a nearby body of water where they threw me in and held my head down. I struggled but was unable to continue, due to lack of strength and not through lack of trying.

Those precious few moments when I was able to hold my head above water, I attempted to scream in order to attract attention to myself but no-one came. After I took my last breath, they swiftly removed my body, placed it back in my bed, dried me off to the best of their ability and left me. It was late the following morning before they found my body. No questions as to cause of death were raised. To the big majority, it was an unfortunate incident. My enemies were clever at hiding behind the cloak of authority in order to protect themselves from being seen as guilty.

I should thank them because in a sort of a way, they did me a huge favour. I did not suffer for too long and throughout my underwater ordeal, I continued to see the great love that I had lost. Now I can join her. Is that so selfish of me? She had always been waiting beyond the misty veil that separated us both in a physical but not spiritual sense.

As a young boy, I would spend many hours playing in the dirt and with a stick; I would create many different abstract designs and symbols. It was a most pleasant way to pass the time. I had two older brothers who could also read and write. My father had the necessary standing, means and authority in the community to ensure that all of his sons received a good education. He wanted them to do well in life and not have to struggle.

I was a finicky and fussy eater when young but as I grew older and much wiser, I began to appreciate food for food sake, no matter what it was. I felt no guilt or shame in eating my fair share. Although, when sharing a meal with others, I always made sure that everyone had plenty or at least had what they wanted.

Jesus passed on to the Twelve and that of course includes me, many different healing techniques. A broad range of medicine was needed to apply, as people are all so different and because of this, certain people would be attracted to certain healing modalities. The laying on of hands and the use of plants were two very common and well accepted forms of healing.

Healing with the mind and using the higher power of the God within were also very effective tools. This was shown to us. It was his gift and he wished for us all to continue and expand upon what he did. He knew at times, we would be separated for various reasons, so each of us needed to take that skill and pass it on.

Nothing is truly new. It was already there in existence, lying dormant within. All that was needed was to find the right teacher to bring it to the surface and further enhance it with his own personal power.

To have faith, on both the part of the healer and the one being healed, is all important. It is not absolutely essential for a cure to take place as not everyone is a believer and may not be convinced of its authenticity, until of course, they experience it for themselves; but it is most helpful under the circumstances.

While growing up as a young boy and living with my parents and brothers, I was allocated certain chores inside and outside the home. Some I liked and some I disliked intensely. We would always help our neighbours and all the women were expected to look after one another's children, if the situation arose, where it was deemed necessary. I regarded myself as being blessed to have such an extended and supportive family. The children I played and swam with (although tentatively, because I naturally did not like the water), I regarded them all to be my brothers and sisters, no matter how young or old they were.

I would give my mother flowers on a consistent basis, in appreciation for all she did for me and who willingly shared with an open heart, her knowledge and wisdom, from a woman's perspective. I greatly admired her strength and sense of humour. She was always laughing, even when confronted by difficult people and situations. She always found some glimmer of hope to hold on to. There must always be a silver lining to every golden situation. These qualities rubbed off on me to a certain extent but I always regarded my mother as being a natural expert in this field, whereas I felt that sometimes I had to work on it. When I started to earn my keep, I donated a portion of what I received back into the family. This was my duty to do so and one which I had no hesitation in doing.

Many times, I was beaten within an inch of my life. I would lay there mortally and spiritually wounded, trying so hard to forgive those people who did this to me and I can honestly say it was sometimes difficult to forgive. People can become hostile if you appear to be different to them and because of the type of things I talked about were so thought provoking and evoked great change in an individual's life, I became a target for abuse – sometimes verbal but quite often it was more on a physical level. It took some getting used to but it was all part and parcel of the job I did. These days, one would demand danger money. Why do people have to get so irate and upset about things? I never stopped them from doing their job, so why do it to me?

I tried to blend in to whichever community I found myself in, in order not to create rough waves for myself. I made an effort to have no class distinctions. We are basically all the same – both men and women. We all come from the same higher force and we are all God's children. As such, we should all have the freedom and right to shine brightly, in whichever way we choose. God gives us this freedom but man steps in like some clumsy giant and insists upon interfering with the spiritual and personal growth of another human being. I had no expectations of another person changing their life simply as a result of what I said. This was not part of the plan and it was certainly none of my business to force change upon some unwilling participant.

If I was successful and change occurred, of course I was happy for them but I didn't lose any sleep over it if nothing transpired. The only expectation I had was about what I personally did and how I felt about things. I was constantly re-evaluating and was determined to find better ways to improve things for myself if I was not at first successful in achieving my goal. Although sometimes I must admit, I could occasionally become my own worst enemy but at other times, I was my own best friend.

With my line of work, that is while sharing about Jesus and the word of God, I was forced sometimes to be discerning before I said anything too damaging and on occasion, I would have to keep my mouth shut. This I found to be very difficult and most disconcerting.

The Twelve of us led a somewhat dangerous lifestyle and as such, much of our work was done under cover out of necessity, depending upon the attitude and belief system of the town's majority. We had to fit in. We were only visitors, while travelling or as some would say, "do as the Romans do" and this is what we did.

I was a good mathematician. I loved playing with numbers and as I was a tax collector before I became a full time Apostle; this occupation was ideal for me. I had a job to do and I was only carrying out the law of the land. Whether I believed it to be a fair system or not, I was well looked after and appreciated by those I was in service to.

Numbers, in a spiritual and metaphysical sense, always fascinated me from a young age. There is indeed something magical about certain numbers and when put together in a particular way, can create miracles that humans would never have thought possible. Think about the Seven Wonders of the World and how they came into existence.

In ancient times, there was Noah's Ark that was built to very precise specifications, as was the Ark of the Covenant and the great pyramids of Egypt. This was done for both a practical and metaphysical reason. Many seek answers from just the stars above for how and why these great pieces of work came into being but one must also look to the Earth for answers. The answer to the puzzle lies with both Mother Earth and Father Sky. They were both equal partners in the overall equation of things. Another example is the Glastonbury Zodiac in England that lay uncovered for centuries, until the day that man learnt how to fly with artificial wings.

The numbers 9, 7 and 3 in particular (and multiples thereof), have an energy pattern all of their own and can bring about outstanding results. This is why certain days were considered to be more important than others in the calendar year for many reasons; ranging from harvesting and sowing of crops to carrying out grand religious ceremonies, initiations and rituals.

Today, people have lost touch with this reality. Many understand about numerology in the way it is presented to the world today but this is just an edited and watered down version. It is just a mere tip of the iceberg and like its namesake, much is left hidden and covered and is deceptively dangerous if used by the wrong people.

In the years to come, certain people will be reawakened to this information, which will be used to benefit mankind on a world wide scale. It is too powerful for the general populace at large to comprehend its true reality and power at this time. Man's attitude must first change sufficiently enough and consistently, towards that desire to find enlightenment and who are not afraid to take action. There are many thinkers and talkers but alas, not so many doers.

We didn't just do physical healings. We did healings for spiritual and emotional problems as well. Quite often, we never needed to be with the person who required our help. Much work was also done while sleeping, which is a most pleasant way of doing business. Direct laying on of hands could become draining on our energy, especially if we were a little bit distracted about our own personal issues.

In those early days, as a grown man and when I was first chosen to be with Jesus, it was a whirlwind time of great personal healing and study. Here was someone I could relate to and he had the ability to say things that I needed to hear.

Mentally, I posed a question and not wanting to take up too much of his valuable time, sometimes I would leave these words unspoken. Many times, often soon after, he would speak the answer out loud. We all felt that when he was speaking to us as a group, it was like each lesson was designed specifically for each separate individual. We were all similar in stature and attitude but there were differences, mainly pertaining to our separate and individual fears and doubts.

Jesus was a very patient and compassionate man; laid back, most times, and did not like to rush things. He made sure that we all understood what he was saying. He never got tired of having to repeat himself. Jesus spent time with us as individuals as well – just the two of us. On these occasions, it wasn't always as teacher and pupil. It was like two friends spending time together because they enjoyed the company of each other. Even though he was a man of great power, he was a man in the same way that we were.

Other than his inner circle of followers, which we were for a time (and this includes our travelling companions as well and all our respective partners and family members), he sometimes didn't know who to turn to if seeking comfort. Many times he would, as the Australian Aboriginals would say, "go walkabout". He would use this valued and much needed time away from us to re-energise himself with God's love and power. Often, he would come back to the group as a changed man – a man filled with renewed inner peace, contentment and purpose.

And as Jesus was not one to sit on any information that would provide empowerment and enlightenment to another, he was more than eager to share with us his experiences and what he had learnt about himself whilst away on these self-imposed sabbaticals.

Before he left, he always chose one of us to tell exactly where he was going and where he could be found if absolutely necessary. The one he chose to give this information to needed to keep it to themselves. It was an issue of faith and trust. We never betrayed that trust, except once, but that situation was preordained and Jesus reluctantly knew of it well ahead of time. Judas was only following out God's instructions and this is why Jesus could forgive Judas for his betrayal. We were warned but didn't want to accept or listen to the facts of the situation. We didn't want to think bad thoughts about one of our own.

When it came to pass and Judas was exposed as being a traitor, we went into shock. How could this happen? But it had to. It was God's will and because of this, there was much inner conflict and anger at this time because, from our point of view, it was all so unfair. We were only human; we were unable to see the big picture from a spiritual point of view.

Fear of Abandonment

Some people believe that abandonment and rejection is the same thing. They are similar in their own individual ways but as you advance further into this book, you will discover there are differences. So what are some of the situations where you may feel abandoned? The first could be when a parent dies, whether that is expected or not. As a young child and sometimes even as an adult, you will feel abandoned because you can't follow them to the place where they are going.

You are left alone to guard against possible disaster, which you thought was your parent's role before but no more. It's time to sink or swim. That is why it is so important never to take them, or any other, for granted or assume they will be there at your beck and call 24 hours a day, 7 days a week, 365 days a year. Even God deserves a bit of a holiday, so why not your parents as well? The same can be said when we later grow up and experience the death of a partner we have loved so much.

To say goodbye is the hardest thing. I know. And mixed in with this all encompassing emotion of grief which is only natural, we will feel angry and cheated – angry at them, our parents, partner or friend, and/or angry at God for allowing it to happen. And you inwardly scream 'How dare you abandon me at my time of need and in my darkest hour. I need you here, not there'. You then live the rest of your days longing for yesterday. By doing so, you have stood still.

As long as you feel abandoned, you can no longer advance. Many people are caught up in the sticky and unbreakable web of their past and can't escape. The more they struggle and live in yesterday, the more trapped they will become and sooner or later, this is when they will come face to face with the killer spider from hell that represents their fears, all rolled into one. Some won't be able to cope. Some will find ways to cope by suppressing what they feel, thinking they have let go, but the opposite is true – they are holding on to it tighter than ever before and by doing this brings it so much closer to them that causes great pain and emotional distress.

In fact, they bring it so close to themselves that they can no longer see what's them and what's not. And because it is such a familiar sight, smell and sound in amongst the horror of it all, this fear still has an odd sense of comfort about it. "Better the devil you know than the devil you don't". For myself, I would choose neither of these two options and give a big "thumbs down" to cohabitating and dining with the Devil. Not only that, it's bad for the digestion. But for you, if you are living these feelings of abandonment today and have been for a long time and where you long for yesterday (sounds like a Beatles song, doesn't it?), take a definite step in the opposite direction.

Step outside your comfort zone. Don't be afraid to experience life in a different way. You can reach those greener pastures but you can't if you choose to live only in a memory, which incidentally you can't do 100% of your time. It's not real. It may feel pleasant in the short run but rest assured someone in your physical environment will drag you back to the moment, albeit kicking and screaming. Your memories and dreams can only ever be a temporary fix to a much bigger and deep seated problem. Even though your heart may be heavy, learn to deal with today with a clear and open mind. Don't dull your senses just because you don't like what you are feeling.

The perception of abandonment needs to be nipped in the bud quickly, before it gets out of hand. If allowed to blossom fully without any sort of trimming, pruning or cutting, it will hurt more.

Don't put off tomorrow what you can do today. If you choose to do nothing, then nothing can ever change and you would have drifted through life like a rudderless ship, simply because you have no anchor. The person you have depended upon for your survival no longer physically exists and they represented your anchor. But I say be your own anchor and drive your own ship. You will always have some direction then.

Look to the stars and allow their light to guide you through the dark and stormy nights because believe it or not, the darkness cannot last forever; as day always follows night and where the sun comes out to play which warms and strengthens your heart, but only if you let it.

So when else could you feel abandoned? Some people think that Moses was abandoned by his mother when she placed him in the basket and set him afloat down the Nile but look what great things later happened to him and all of what he achieved as a result of taking that single journey down the river. What appears to be a terrible act on behalf of a mother was a blessing in disguise for Moses. Later, he and his mother made their peace, as he found out she was concerned only for his long term safety and welfare.

And so it is today with some mothers who, due to circumstances beyond their control, let go of their babies for adoption. Are you an adopted child? If yes, do you feel abandoned, cheated and angry at your biological mother you never knew while growing up? Perhaps you have found each other again and perhaps not but either way, can you forgive? Do you understand what lay behind your mother's decision? How do you feel about those people who adopted you and accepted you as one of their own? Did they tell you or did you find out by accident? Are you any worse off for being adopted? This last answer I don't believe you can answer because the past cannot be relived in a different way.

When looking back in time, all we can do in the present is to make assumptions about what could have been but who is to say these conclusions are correct. You just can't tell. Should a woman who gave up her baby, for whatever reason, be condemned for life and labelled forever with the tag of a bad and evil mother? What of the daughter if she later lives out her mother's fate? Would the daughter, who hated her mother for giving her away feel the same if she too found herself in the same position as her mother had those many years before? I don't think there would be, no change of heart. The daughter would understand, even though she may not wish to believe it.

How can one judge another harshly if the one accusing makes the same mistake or decision as the accused? The attitude being – what's okay for me is not okay for her! This is called being hypocritical and having double standards. But most hypocrites, deep down feel guilt and blame themselves, for they know the truth and they don't like other people poking and prodding them to admit out loud to others the lie that they have been living. Double standards truly stink like dead fish and have been the cause of much heartache and despair.

But what of the adopted son? How do they feel, especially when they grow up? Do they strongly disagree with adoption, believing there is no excuse why a mother should abandon her child?

What if his future wife or girlfriend finds themselves pregnant to this man but says she wants to give their child up for adoption or to have an abortion? How will he react? Will he withdraw in disgust, become physically violent; verbally browbeat his woman until she sees the error of her ways, leaves her in peace to make her own decision or simply agrees with her wholeheartedly? This will all depend upon his own earlier child experience and upbringing with his adopted parents.

If the wife/girlfriend decides to let go of their child, will the man then feel abandoned, cheated and angry at her for taking away his right to become a father? What rights does a man have when we talk about adoption or abortion? Can we fight back through the court system or should we accept what the woman wants? Only you, as a man involved in this situation, can decide what is right for you, in the same way as a woman too must do what she feels is right for her. But who is more right than the other? And what about the rights of the unborn child?

The whole subject of adoption and abortion is a three way street, although some believe it is only one way, with no side exits to divert you. It can get extremely messy for all concerned, emotionally and financially. I would say follow your heart and be happy to live with the consequences of your actions; guilt free and blameless. Relationships can be torn apart but they can also be mended. If they can't, was it ever meant to be in the long term?

And let's face it, some women are not born or meant to be mothers. This doesn't mean to say they are bad people, because as women they still have a lot to contribute to society but not in the traditional sense and no woman, man or child should ever be put into a position where they are made to feel guilty for following their own heart rather than being led by the hearts of others. Should you abandon all your dreams just to keep everybody else happy?

And then there is divorce. Both the partner and child, who do not agree with the split, will feel abandoned. It comes as a rude awakening and other than feeling angry, they can quite often blame themselves for this sad and sorry mess so seek to find fault within. They will analyse and dissect the situation until the cows come home but still they will not have advanced one step towards understanding the truth.

Some children and spouses don't have a problem in dealing with this separation. In fact, they could be breathing a collective sigh of relief and this is okay too, especially where domestic violence has played a major role in the breakdown of that particular family unit.

Abandonment doesn't necessarily need to start at the end of a relationship. It can, on those rare occasions, happen at the beginning but more often than not it begins somewhere in the middle and when it does begin, the person who has to live with the fear of possible abandonment, may go into a protective hard shell of self-denial. To accept the truth would be too heartbreaking, so they choose to hide their head in the sand. It's so much safer there, where you are left to your own devices to create your own sights and sounds. They may be pleasant or they may be distressing but they are still your thoughts and you are the only one who can live with it.

No-one can truly appreciate, understand, feel or see what's inside your head, or heart, except yourself. This is why you will often cry out loud in pain for everyone to hear, 'no-one understands me' or alternatively you will plead 'no-one ever listens to me' and these two statements will more than likely be correct. But is this any reason for you to judge others for their ignorance and selfishness? They need your patience and forgiveness. Don't reject another simply because they have abandoned you. Humans were not designed to live alone.

The world's populace was created for love and companionship, yet quite often we have abused this sacred privilege. Why do you think there are so many teenage suicides happening in today's society? Suicide victims have increased those feelings of abandonment to such an extent, where it painfully and slowly suffocates the life force out of them. Rather than prolong this particular form of abandonment torture, they end their life by their own hand. Sadly sometimes, they choose to take another down with them and that then becomes a murder suicide, simply because they felt all alone yet in reality, this may not have been the truth but because their fear was so strong, that's all they could see.

Any love that came towards them would immediately be deflected, as the one who felt abandoned wouldn't perceive it as being love. They would become suspicious and think it was a trick to entrap them. Love would appear as a form of control and for the victim of suicide, to be under someone else's control, power or authority would be a fate far worse than mere physical death. So why not die right here and now? No-one can hurt or abandon me ever again then. By believing in this philosophy or attitude means they are actually abandoning themselves as people. They become their own worst enemy yet they would disagree quite vehemently because to them, they are being their own best friend by taking themselves out of a life filled only with misery, heartache and despair. If that's all they have to look forward to, they'd prefer to opt out now and try again for something better next time but there are no guarantees for them or for us.

Because you chose not to learn your spiritual lessons by ignoring them and hoping they would go away this lifetime, it could be a thousand times worse next time round. Are you willing to take that risk? Don't let the feelings of abandonment from others totally ruin your life because if you do, you and not they, become responsible for your own premature demise and knowing this, can you live with that?

Initially, I talked about the death of a parent or partner but what of that of a young child or baby? This can be considered to be the worst tragedy of all and what of those left behind? How can they possibly survive with such a burden on their shoulders and a heart that continually weeps blood? It is extremely difficult.

Most times, death can come swiftly and unexpectedly. They may die as a result of natural causes, they may die in an accident or they may be physically abused that leads to their death which would then be considered as either murder or manslaughter, depending upon the circumstances. Personally, I think the last case scenario would be the most distressing to live with, as it makes no sense. I guess, neither does death by illness to some people but somehow, the existence of a disease is easier to accept.

Death at the hands of a complete stranger, relative or trusted family friend goes against everything that God ever stood for. The parents and surviving family members are left to struggle alone, or at least they feel they are alone.

There can be feelings of guilt or blame on their part. A mother may feel she should have been there to protect her child, so she would blame herself and believe she is a bad mother. If the mother was in attendance watching on, this would make matters so much worse in her mind and would feel a large measure of guilt for not doing anything to stop it from happening. But sometimes there are limits and you, as a parent, sibling or friend, can only ever do your best under these most tragic of circumstances.

If you yourself were physically bound helpless and gagged, what could you do, except to pray that if death has to pay your child a visit, to please make it quick? To believe that our helpless babies or young children suffered prolonged pain and fear is, in itself, a torture too much to bear.

Hate, in this instance, is understandable and can be created within our hearts almost instantaneously. Sometimes the hate that fills us is so bitter and vile; you can actually taste it in your mouth. But once this monster has been unleashed into society and into the family home, it becomes an unstoppable force; like an escaped evil genie from its bottle that can consequently wreak havoc upon everyone that gets in its way, both guilty and innocent alike.

Perhaps the guilty deserve to feel guilty but what of the innocent victims of your child's death? Is it really fair to blame them, or yourself, as well? The desire to accuse someone of this tragedy will be strong and if the guilty party is not brought to trial, where do you unleash all that hate? You certainly don't need to absorb it into your body but you don't need to lash out at those closest to you either. Why destroy a perfectly good relationship or friendship because of your need to blame or hate another? This too does not make sense. Stop and think for a moment and ask yourself – 'Would my precious baby be happy to see me now, destroying the very person or people that were important to him or her?'

When you have the answer to that question, you'll then know what you need to do and that is to forgive yourself and others for being unable to protect your child from the Angel of Death. I know you don't like that word, forgiveness, as it doesn't seem to quite fit with this situation. But please try and then hold on to the treasured memories that you and your child have shared together; even if only briefly in human terms. And never feel abandoned by them. God and your baby are still both there with you in Spirit, keeping you warm at night, if you only let it be.

Hate will only kill you too. Dying at your own hand will serve no real meaning because your life's purpose has not yet been accomplished. This is why you have been spared. The one who has died so early in years and so tragically has completed theirs. Just because their time was brief, doesn't mean it was ever wasted. It is what they have left behind in your heart that counts; that is their love, laughter and presence. These young ones were already Angels when they arrived to teach us some valuable lessons about ourselves and as Angels; they needed only to stay a short amount of time, otherwise your lesson could not have been learnt as effectively.

I know you don't want to hear that and you may regard this reality as being cruel and unjust for all concerned but from your child's perspective, safe in their new Spirit home, it is not. This is where they belong, which one day will become your home but only in Divine timing and not in yours. Please accept that you have not been abandoned. You are merely being watched over, loved and protected by your Angel on a different level. Remember this always if you can, for I tell not a lie.

Sometimes, we feel that even the church has abandoned us, even if God has not. For some people, what church life can offer is essential to them living a life filled with purpose. Regardless of whatever religion you choose to follow, if you get caught out doing or saying that which is considered the wrong thing, you could find there is a high price to pay, as there is no true freedom in orthodox or dogmatic religions of today. It only appears that there is.

In regards to some religiously fanatical groups that follow the commandments, rules or credo to the letter in a strict and rigid fashion, it can be extremely difficult for its parishioners to adhere to these guidelines all the time, especially when they don't agree with that which has been set down for them; they may consider them to be quite archaic and have nothing to do with the way life is today. If the church, temple, synagogue, mosque or any other place of worship remains inflexible, they can cause a lot of unnecessary distress and guilt to be placed upon the lives of their worshippers. I am not saying that the rules are there to be broken but a little compassion and understanding wouldn't go astray either.

If the world's religions wish to continue in keeping a large and happy audience, it is understood that you catch more flies with honey than you do with vinegar. You have to offer them hope, not only damnation. As well as this, it needs to be accepted that everyone makes mistakes, even the facilitators of these places of worship. Why is there leniency given to those in positions of power, while none is shown to those who come to worship once a week and in some instances, every day? Again, we have double standards. Is it any wonder why some followers of the faith feel abandoned by those people they look up to and who have authority to bring about change? This is one reason why people are leaving the flock in droves.

Why would they wish to stay when discrimination is at play in these hallowed halls of worship? Certainly, we all have to be held accountable to someone for any wrong doing but he who is without sin may cast the first stone. Some places of worship are worse than others, especially when they place themselves beyond the letter of the law and this includes God's law as well. Sorry, but it doesn't work like that, or at least it shouldn't. Much harm is being done on a spiritual, psychological, emotional, mental and physical level to those who seek religious instruction. This has to stop. The world's religions were created for a number of reasons but one of them was not to judge or abandon their followers altogether in their hour of need.

Personally, I believe it a better state of affairs if each individual simply sought their own religious counsel within, as there are a large variety of spiritual and religious leaders they could easily tune into, energetically speaking, for assistance and guidance. This is not to say that by doing so, these individuals have to abandon their particular faith, culture or belief. They would simply become independent, more eclectic and openly accepting of all sorts of religions and philosophies that sweep the globe today; which could be either similar or different to their own. There is so much more than just one road to Heaven. Try several and see. Experiencing a little bit of everything leads to becoming a healthy and well adjusted, spiritually evolved soul and all feelings of abandonment just don't fit into this picture at all.

We, as a group of Apostles, felt that Jesus had abandoned us upon his physical death, as we were just men after all. We couldn't live with the knowledge that he had gone. Even though we had a lot of understanding, we became scared and felt very much alone without a teacher to direct us in those uncertain times. We couldn't see or didn't wish to believe there was a much higher purpose for his sudden unexpected death, or at least it was to us. He had known in advance but this was something he chose not to share with us openly before the actual event and even if he had tried, would we have listened anyway? I don't think so.

Sometime later, we did eventually come to accept and understand all of what had happened but it was still hard going to do so. Many of us could still hear his voice inside our heads reminding us that he was still with us and that he had not abandoned us. Some wished not to believe it was actually his voice they were hearing, preferring to believe instead that it was their imagination and wishful thinking. After all, we didn't wish to disillusion ourselves with feelings of false hope. At other times, singularly, we actually saw and spoke with Jesus after his death but still there was an element of doubt.

Grief can do some strange things to the mind, even to the point where a man can go quite crazy. Yet, there were at least three separate occasions where he spoke with us as a group simultaneously, that is all at once. It was only a short message of clarification but Jesus implored us to speak of it out loud to our fellow diners seated an arm's length away. Moments later, one of us began to speak, to the astonishment and amazement of everyone else present. It was then that we had discovered that all of us had experienced the same internal and personal conversation with Jesus, so how could we doubt?

He did this at least another two times, just to make sure there were no lingering doubts or confusion and to make it clear that he was still with us and that each one of us had the ability to speak with him at will, any time that we liked. And so we began doing this as per his request and we received many answers and much guidance as a result of his invitation. We could never be alone and we came to accept that he had certainly not abandoned us. Before this understanding took place, we had previously been practising the art of clairvoyant communication with our spiritual brothers with outstanding success. This is something that Jesus taught us to do, with ourselves and other people. But to do the same with him after his death was something else.

We thought we couldn't or shouldn't do it, although we did this while he was still alive, so why should it be any different once he had died? We thought it did, because some of us felt we were not worthy to do so, while others believed they should leave him to rest in peace. After all, he doesn't want to be bothered by us. They were sure he had many other better and more interesting things to do with his free time but this is where we were wrong. He actually welcomed our continued communication with him. This made him feel less separated from us as well. It was most definitely a two way street, where we both gained from speaking with each other in this way and where we both got what we needed.

Once we were able to put aside our fears, doubts and 'should nots', we had an easier time of it. We finally packed away the pedestal we had unwittingly put Jesus upon. It is now your turn to do the same with him, with us, with the Archangels in Heaven and all the other ascended masters, because Jesus was just one of many great spiritual leaders. So please do us all a favour and bring us back down to Earth because we quite like it here, mixing and communicating with mere mortals which we too were once before and have been since, including today.

So, all of what I've said about the fear of being abandoned basically boils down to one thing. When someone leaves us unexpectedly and we, as an adult or child, don't want them to go, this is when we will feel abandoned. Even when they return later but in a different or lesser capacity to what they were before, still we feel abandoned and cheated out of their love. This then makes us angry, so angry and to such an extent, where we will direct it towards the one we love the most, which can in some cases push them so far away we can no longer see them for dust.

Your anger then multiplies and you turn it towards yourself that eats you up inside. Your heart becomes heavy, diseased, twisted and bitter. This is how people will then see you. What started off as only one abandoning you early on, it is then extended to include every living soul that you know, as well as yourself and this is the worst case scenario of them all.

Please don't take this path. It will only lead to despair, depression, desolation and destruction. It's not a pretty place to live in and because it is so bad, many people will not have the courage to stomach it and so will choose to stay for a short time only before they lose all hope and decide to take a leap from the fat right into the fire. When this stage is reached, no-one can help them and they certainly can't help themselves.

There is a small minority within this group who are known as masochists, where to live a life without pain is a life not worth living, so they seek out ways for people to hurt them and if no-one is willing to play that game, they will inflict pain upon themselves on all levels. Until one day, they may go too far. It greatly depends upon their pain threshold and most people who can be found wandering around like zombies in this dark foreboding place, do have a high pain barrier which they rarely ever have to jump. This is how they survive.

It's when they can no longer reach the unreachable, they burn themselves so badly that the pain draws the life force totally out of them and at that moment of release, they and their known associates believe they will be at peace. Sadly, this is not always the case. Are you willing to take that chance? And how big a masochist are you really? Do you think you can happily live in this self-created world of isolation? To consciously choose to freely live this type of existence is true abandonment of self. Because it is so pitch black there, you have lost all sight of yourself, along with everybody else and so it is that you have been hopelessly blinded by your own fear.

This is not our preferred way for you to live your life so please, don't let it be your choice. We cannot help or guide you back to the light if you are so far away and remember it is not us, abandoning you. We wish only to steer you in the right direction. Do not reject us and more importantly, do not give up on yourself. You have a purpose, so start living it with gay abandon.

Roses

Red roses were her favourite
Her name was also Rose
And every year her husband sent them
Tied with pretty bows.

The year he died
The roses were delivered to her door
The card said "Be my Valentine"
Like all the years before.

Each year he sent her roses
And the note would always say
I love you even more this year
Than last year on this day.

My love for you will always grow
With every passing year
She knew this would be the last time
That the roses would appear.

She thought, he ordered roses
In advance before this day
Her loving husband did not know
That he would pass away.
He always likes to do things early
Way before the time
Then if he got too busy
Everything would work out fine.

*She trimmed the stems
And placed them in a very special vase
Then, sat the vase beside the portrait
of his smiling face.*

*She would sit for hours
In her husband's favourite chair
While staring at his picture
And the roses sitting there.*

*A year went by
And it was hard to live without her mate
With loneliness and solitude
That had become her fate.*

*Then, the very hour
As on Valentine's before
The doorbell rang and there were roses
Sitting by her door.*

*She bought the roses in
And then just looked at them in shock
Then, went to the telephone
To call the florist shop.*

*The owner answered and she asked him
If he would please explain
Why someone would do this to her
Causing her such pain.*

"I know your husband passed away
More than a year ago"
The owner said "I knew you'd call
And you would want to know"

"The flowers you received today
Were paid for in advance
Your husband always planned ahead
He left nothing to chance"

"There is a standing order
That I have on file here
And he has said, well in advance,
You'll get them every year"

"There also is another thing
That I think you should know
He wrote a special little card
He did this, years ago"

"Then should ever I find out
That he's no longer there
That's the card that should be sent
To you, the following year"

She thanked him and hung up the phone
Her tears now flowing hard
Her fingers shaking
As she slowly reached to get the card.

Shontara

Inside the card she saw
That he had written her a note
Then as she stared in total silence
This is what he wrote.

"Hello my love
I know it's been a year, since I have gone
I hope it hasn't been too hard
For you to overcome"

"I know it must be lonely and the pain is very real
For if it were the other way
I know how I would feel"

"The love we shared made everything
So beautiful in life
I loved you more than words can say
You were the perfect wife"

"You were my friend and lover
You fulfilled my every need
I know it's only been a year
So please, try not to grieve"

"I want you to be happy
Even when you shed your tears
That is why the roses will be sent to you for years"

The Apostles

"When you get these roses
Think of all the happiness
We shared together
And how both of us were blessed"

"I have always loved you and I know I always will
But my love, you must go on
You have some living still"

"Please try to find some happiness
While living out your days
I know it isn't easy
But I hope you find some ways"

"The roses will come every year
And they will only stop
When your door is not answered
When the florist stops to knock"

"He will come five times that day
In case you have gone out
But after his last visit
He will know without a doubt"

"To take the roses to the place
Where I've instructed him and place the roses where we are
Together, once again"

Source: Jack Benny

Affirmations

A GUARDIAN ANGEL stands closely by my side.

I offer the hand of FRIENDSHIP to myself.

I am never alone.

PETER

Please God, give me the

Energy and enthusiasm I need to bring

Together, in your name,

Enough love and compassion to heal my past and

Release all negative emotions that are holding me back today.

I loved to sing. The louder the better, yet most of my friends and family did not appreciate it. That's because, although I love them dearly, they were all stone deaf. Who cares if you can't sing in tune? The louder and flatter, the better, I say. If it's positive and uplifting, it's like giving praise to my Lord, my Master. I am his faithful servant and my joy is expressed through my love of music. I used to play an instrument similar to the lute. My playing was more acceptable and some people actually were entertained when I played. This was a most pleasurable positive. It enabled me time to think clearly. Music became like a meditation for me.

I was to deliver a very important letter to someone in authority in Rome. A small town that I had to pass through on my way lies a few hours ahead. I had chosen to spend one night there before I moved on and took the opportunity to clean myself up a bit, put on some clean clothes and have some food. I had been walking for three days now but I had some travelling companions. They were not of my class but they were good company and they kept my spirits alive, especially when I was so tired and felt I couldn't go on; that all I wanted to do was lie down and die. This was all too hard. Why am I here? Why do I do this? The Lord my God no longer exists in a physical sense, so how will he know if I do or I don't?

Although I do feel guilty for denying that I knew him when the soldiers asked but what could I do, except lie? I didn't want to die. Surely, Jesus had not intended that I die with him. I had come close to death a few times. I had a family to think of. I wish I was with them now. Although, I know I shouldn't think like that. It's not practical. What I was about to do would help my family in the future. So, let's stop feeling sorry for myself and get on with it. So, here I am, with my trusty (to a certain extent) companions.

It was lunch time of the following day. We had all sat down beside the road to eat bread and goat cheese and drink some fresh clean water from a well. We were on rations and it was up to me to portion out what was needed. An old man pulling a cart, laden with wares, has just passed us. Beside him was his dog.

A sound like thunder could suddenly be heard, yet there were no storm clouds in sight. The earth shook and the land began to undulate of its own accord. This indeed was a strange phenomenon to behold. I had experienced it only once before. My companions started running in all directions. They were afraid and I can't say that I blame them.

I was having a rough time standing on the one spot myself but was determined not to run. How can one possibly outrun such forces of nature? I can't, so why waste my energy. It lasted for only a short time but it was indeed powerful. Now that it was over, I wondered if my companions will come back. I proceeded to repack the food and the utensils used moments before. As I bent down to pick something up, I experienced a flash of light and an agonising pain in my back. I tried to straighten up, which I did but with great difficulty. What was that strange light I had just seen? Where had it come from? I then heard a voice but could see no-one.

I yelled out for the person to show themselves to me. No reply. I shrugged my shoulders and thought 'I'm in no mood to play games. Let's get on with it and move on'. If my companions were to join me, they know to find me on the road. It was safer that way.

Why was my back killing me? The same voice I heard a short time before answered my unspoken question. Consequently, I spun around abruptly, causing another ripple of pain to run up and down my spine. What had I done?

The voice said 'Straighten up Peter. There is nothing wrong with your back, in a physical sense. What has happened is that you have become rigid in your picture. You have lost that flexibility and ease to go with the tide of events. Instead, you are fighting against it.'

I looked around everywhere, but still, I did not see.

'Why can you not see me Peter? Listen to my voice. Do you not recognise the Lord, your Master?'

'No, it can't be. You're dead and so will I be if I don't continue moving.'

'I'm not dead Peter. You are talking to me; you hear me but because of your fear and stubbornness, you do not yet see me. You are also not to be fearful of your inevitable death. It happens to the best of us, even to those that I love the most. I am powerless to stop or change the course of events that are about to happen. It is God's will. I therefore accept and so must you.'

'Why must I accept? It doesn't seem right. I have been accused unfairly.'

'This is so. Go back and face your accusers, who you once thought were your friends. They will not believe you but after your death, they will see the Truth and regret their actions.'

'So, why can't they see the Truth for themselves now? Why do I have to die to prove a point?'

'Sometimes the lessons we, and I mean in this case, your so

called enemies, are meant to learn, can be very painful. Without that pain, they cannot go through it to the other side, without it having to change them in a positive way. And remember that I too died to prove a point, did I not?'

'Yes, but I'm not you'

'I know this and you can never be me. You are you, as I am what and who I am.'

'So you want me to go back? What if I refuse?'

'You can but they will catch you. Eyes and ears can talk volumes and they will know where to find you. Have no doubt about that. What are you so afraid of Peter?'

'Death and dying for a lost cause. I also feel as though my work is not yet complete.'

'This is correct – your work is not yet complete. That is why you must go back. Have no fear as I shall remain with you always, even beyond your physical death. Feel me, I am here. Reach out your hand and touch mine. The connection is there. You are just too scared and so involved in your own problems, that you cannot see two feet in front of your face. You have been temporarily blinded, as this is what you have chosen. I therefore now give you a choice – do you wish for me to remove that veil of darkness that shields your eyes from seeing and accepting the Light?'

'I don't know. I'm afraid of what I might see or find.'

'So, does that mean your answer is "no"?'

'No, it doesn't mean that at all. I just want some reassurance.'

'Reassurance of what exactly, Peter?'

'I don't know how to put it into words. I feel inadequate to do so.'

'What you believe, it will be so. Think adequate and you

will be. Think success and you will be. Think fear and you will have fear. Look beyond the obvious things. Read between the lines and do not doubt what you hear, feel, see, know and understand. So again, I ask you – why and what sort of reassurance do you need?'

'I need to know I haven't let you down, as I sometimes feel as if I have failed in the task that you had set for me.'

'This is nonsense. Everything is as it should be. Stand tall Peter and be proud. Give yourself a pat on the back for a job well done. You have achieved a lot and you will be honoured by the people but only after you die.'

I digest these words for a moment. I am glad that I will be honoured and that I won't be forgotten. I think, is that egotistical of me? Perhaps it is. Is this a bad thing?

'It is neither good nor bad. It's being honest and that is all I can ask of anyone to be truthful to and about themselves. That is the key to truly being a success. Have no fear. Have I managed to reassure you?'

'Yes, I think you have and for this, I will always be grateful and yes, I would now ask for you to lift that veil of blindness that I wear like a thick coat that is slowly suffocating me.'

'And so it is done. Your faith has made you whole. Go in peace but always remember that I walk beside you. Let us face your destiny together with a strong and proud heart and learn to forgive those who have betrayed you, for they know not what they do but you now know better – they don't. Are you ready?'

'Yes, I'm ready and I am no longer afraid and look forward to being with you, once again, in God's Heaven. Thank you.'

'No, it is I who must thank you.'

I turn and start to walk away with an uplifted heart. He

calls me back and I turn to look. I can see him clearly now. In one hand, he is holding the cross and with the other, he waves me goodbye and I wonder why I ever doubted myself or him. God bless me, forever and ever, Amen.

First, I was stoned but not to the point of death. They then crucified me on a cross, similar to that of my Lord. With one major difference – I was hung upside down. My feet and ankles were bound by leather straps, which were first soaked in water. Under the steaming hot midday sun, they dried quickly. This made the straps shrink quite considerably which then tightened their deathlike grip upon me. It was a long and excruciatingly painful way to die. A quick death would have been so much better and easier. I ask, 'why me?'

All I hear is Jesus saying 'Why not you? These things you face are there for you to learn from. However, it can be either an easy or hard lesson – the choice is yours and depends greatly upon your attitude.'

It was sad not being able to say goodbye to my own family properly. I had a wife and two sons. I worry about them all. Will they be treated unfairly, as a result of knowing me? This I could not bear to think about. Will they forgive me?

I had the ability, by looking at a person, to diagnose the various illnesses that may be inflicting them. I would then offer a solution as to what they could do to heal themselves. Some listened, while some did not. Healer, heal thyself.

We all have this gift of healing. Many people are not aware of it and those who do know, quite often forget about themselves or, to be more blunt, won't do for themselves. This latter group of aware people will drop everything to heal another but when something crops up for themselves, they will do one of two things. They will ignore the symptoms and hope it will go away. When this fails to eventuate, they then put plan B into action, where they then pay sometimes good money after bad, seeking a consultation from a third person.

There is nothing wrong in seeking guidance from the experts but much can be done if we listen to and accept the warning signs that manifest themselves on a physical level, in the early stages of any disease. Other than those willing to do for themselves, and to be fair, there are still quite a few, there are those at the opposite end of the scale who:

1. truly believe they don't have the power to discern and interpret what their own body, heart and mind is telling them;
2. talk themselves out of their intuitive insights in regards to a solution;
3. don't want to take responsibility for their own health and well being; and
4. are keen to blame others when the treatment offered, does not work out.

Which of the above four categories do you fit into? Or does it change, depending upon the severity of the situation?

Looking directly into a person's eyes when you're talking or listening to them shows a keen interest in how they feel and many insights will be gleaned to show you where this person is at on a mental, emotional or spiritual level. Many will not be able to return your intense gaze, especially if they have something to hide. This type of person will look everywhere else but directly at you; they will get fidgety, will find a million things to do with their hands, and will appear to be jumpy and nervous.

That is why, when you are being threatened, look at your aggressor straight in the eye and stare them down. See what happens. Of course, if you have fear, they will see this too and more than likely will take advantage of it. The Twelve of us needed to know how to defend ourselves in a way that wouldn't cause too much lasting damage to either party.

Take responsibility for your own actions and then be prepared to live with the consequences of your beliefs, even if it means you may pay the ultimate price – that is, physical death. Death is a scary subject for most people to even deal with, especially when it is pertaining to themselves or their loved ones. Strangers don't matter. They're out there and I'm here in my self-created feather nest; remaining safe and protected from all harm.

It disappoints me greatly to have seen in the past and still see people today, deliberately falsifying and changing the Truth in order to meet their own personal needs. I am talking of many things here but my biggest heartache has been with the churches in general. Greed and control got in the way of both religion and politics. They were both intended to be separate but sadly, this was not to be the case. To do something for someone because you know that later down the track they will return the favour, is not giving unconditionally and without expectation. "You scratch my back and I'll scratch yours".

This is okay between two people who will mutually and equally benefit but when those same people are in a position of great power and influence and who control the fate of a nation in the palm of their hands, then those innocent and non-involved observers become pawns in a dangerous game of cat and mouse. Who do you think wins or loses in this situation? You don't need to be a genius to work that one out. Just take a look at your history books. It's all there, in black and white. Although, sometimes even then, one still needs to read between the lines, depending upon the person who wrote it, or later changed it – such as the Bible.

This is a book which has changed many times, with big chunks of the Truth being deleted and other parts being edited. A few minor word changes here and there, adds up to a large amount of lies. Some were intentional while others were not. What also needs to be taken into account here is the translation from the original language to another. It sometimes differed greatly. Overall, it still had the same outcome that has caused much confusion and disbelief.

Some people – and not all – truly held the opinion that they were doing it for the best, in order to protect the innocent. Why not allow the innocent to decide for themselves what is Truth and what is not? Don't interfere in matters relating to the Laws of Nature. Who gave you the right to play at being God? I do and must accept that we all make mistakes, as I have done in the past. That's what makes us human but things need to go back to the way that God had first intended.

Of course, many don't know what that truly is. Mankind has gotten itself so lost, is it any wonder there is so much chaos and destruction in the world today?

Thankfully, there is now coming to the fore, the many light workers who bring much hope and direction to the masses. This movement is expanding rapidly and it will spread across the land like wildfire and in such a way that no-one will be able to stop it. To be involved, to see and know this is happening on a large scale across the globe, makes me very happy.

Finally, I am not saying that all pain and suffering will be banished from the face of the Earth but it will have a less devastating effect upon the mind, heart and body of those experiencing it. Problems are merely dressed up opportunities from which to learn. There must always be an element of bad in order to understand and appreciate the beauty of all that is intrinsically good.

Each individual has so much healing energy held within the palms of their hands; enough to supply the electricity to brighten up a single lighthouse for many generations. Most people, I am sure, would strongly dispute this fact but it still is true.

There is a certain group of people who are more in tune with a whole range of their feelings and emotions. As well as this, they find great joy in the tactile pleasures, such as touching. For them, the 'laying on of hands' is easy and causes no great difficulty for them to do. There is more than one way to heal however, and some don't need to use their hands at all. Some will use their mind, eyes, mouth, voice or feet. Believe it or not, your whole body is one massive big powerhouse that uses, stores and re-energises itself, every day.

This happens when you're not aware of it. Unless you are suffering from asthma, emphysema or other similar health problems, do you have to think about and control the act of breathing? No, it comes naturally. The body, with the help from the nervous system, will do this automatically for us. Our breathing, amongst other bodily functions, is one of many things we take for granted. When was the last time you thanked your heart and lungs for helping you to breathe? It is such a simple thing to do and it only takes a mere second of your valuable time.

As I mentioned earlier, our whole body is involved in the healing process – of ourselves and other people. Some are most talented in controlling their mind in such a way that causes great change on a physiological level. Cancer has been cured in this way many times and the scientific community has no explanation as to why this has happened.

The eyes are another powerful tool – for not only healing purposes but also to establish a clear communication link between you, your higher self and the Spirit world. Look at your eyes in the mirror today. Keep them dead still; this is not easy if you haven't done it before. There are so many interesting distractions around us to look at instead but persevere. But here is an added suggestion – do it at night in the dark. The visual distractions will then be less.

Go into that relaxed, daydream, or alpha state, and then be patient. Watch and listen. A few things could happen – you could experience the existence of your own aura – some will experience colours and others will see a white light extended a few inches from the body. Other people will lose physical sight altogether but this is self-induced and is only a temporary affair, while another separate group will begin to see the whole spectrum of the Spirit world, in all its guises; both bad and good. There is no right or wrong. Because we are all unique individuals, what we perceive will be different to our partner or complete stranger.

When you feel you've had enough of this particular experience, all you have to do to break that link, is to move your eyes. It's that simple. Practice every day. In time, you will move into this heightened state of being, quickly and easily. It will become a smooth transition, like breathing and when this stage has been successfully completed, that is when you won't need to use a mirror. You will then have the ability to move in and out of this other unseen world, simply by willing it. This is controlling your mind and it is in this state where miracles are created; such as levitation and putting your body into suspended animation.

The yogis are one small group of people who can do this but it takes an enormous amount of discipline on the part of the disciple. Can you imagine that if everyone practised and released this extra build up of healing energy upon themselves and all those they came in contact with on a regular basis, how powerful the population would become overnight?

Of course, God in his wisdom (or some would say 'stupidity') has still given mankind the freedom of choice to use this gift and power to use it in a positive or negative way. One just has to look at the Atlanteans to see how much damage can be caused if the power is used incorrectly and when this knowledge falls into the hands of one whose heart is not so pure or true.

Those Atlanteans of ancient times have now been re-incarnated into this present day and who have chosen to help mankind to develop this heightened sense of awareness once again, but this time in a good way.

Too much destruction and suffering has taken place over many aeons. It's time for a radical change and uplifted shift of consciousness. Are you ready to make that change? If you are not willing to do so or you are under the illusion that you can't, you will be left behind; where even in a crowded room, you will feel ostracised and isolated.

Of course, some of you may already be feeling this. It's like no-one will be able to see you and where you become a non-entity. You will no longer be on their wavelength, where you become like, invisible. This is similar to what we, in the Spirit world, experience every day from those same non-believers.

But I am glad to say that the tide is rapidly turning. Don't get drowned in the rush. Go with the flow, rather than against it. That way, the transition and introduction to the reality of the Spirit world will become smoother for you and less scary. In ancient times, man was indeed more in tune with the Laws of Nature and with God but today, this is not the case. The good news is that we are rapidly being reawakened, where our eyes and hearts are opening and accepting the Truth.

I am truly sorry for denying I knew Jesus those three times when asked by the authorities. My Master has long forgiven me for this indiscretion but I have not completely forgiven myself. Even after all this time. I know I can never forget.

I was angry at Judas for what he did but then soon after, I turned around and did a similar – but not quite the same – thing. How can I judge another harshly when I am guilty of carrying out the same crime? Perhaps to a lesser degree but still, it is basically the same.

I felt like such a hypocrite and liar. No matter how much I try and justify my actions to others, the bottom line was and still is that I acted out of pure selfishness; which mainly related to the real possibility of me losing my life. I hear many of you say – 'I understand and if I were in your shoes, I would have acted no differently'. Thank you for your sincere support. It is appreciated, although I don't feel I deserve such support.

It's funny but each one of the Twelve possesses this real stubborn and personal streak, which makes us our own worst enemies at times. I know I can't change what has happened in the past but thankfully, I have been given another chance, today, to make things better for you and for me, in the foreseeable future. I have come to make amends for past mistakes and that is what we must all do in order to achieve complete understanding, enlightenment and wisdom. We continue to evolve – some at a slower rate than others. Whether you choose another physical existence or not, you will continue to learn and forever reach new and deeper levels of perception. That is essentially what life is meant to teach us, no matter what form of living you choose.

There really is no difference between the seen and unseen worlds. A thin veil of mist that blinds you from getting to know the Truth is the only thing that separates us from each other and our Creator. Ask for this invisible but penetrable veil to be made clear, rather than misty and for it to be lifted forever from your eyes. "Ask and ye shall receive, seek and ye shall find, knock and door shall be opened and the Kingdom of Heaven shall be yours". Please understand that each person who reads these words must do it for themselves. We can't do it for each other because if we do, this then is interfering in another person's growth. Besides which, it would not happen. It can't happen.

When each person – living or dead – has made this request with a pure heart and complete honesty, then the world will truly begin to see the great love and unbelievable beauty that surrounds them. You may think that this sounds like a simple solution to a very big existing problem but it is that simple, if you want it to be. Why do humans insist upon complicating things? Do you have nothing better to do with your time, except to worry and fret about mundane issues such as your love life and money? If only you can trust, everything and more will be provided to look after your needs and wants.

In the future, physical, mental and emotional barriers will no longer have any meaning or place in our lives. Our energies will be free to intermingle and communicate with each other on a realistic level. No lies will be possible. Our thoughts and feelings will become like clear as glass and we will have the ability to move in and out of each other's auric field without disrupting or taking from it. Some will think this is not possible but sometimes fact can be far stranger than fiction. It is your task to discern the difference between the two and make a choice as to which one in particular you wish to follow.

To go back to what I was saying previously, those living in the Spirit world are learning just the same as you and sometimes they will not have the answers that you are seeking. No-one is perfect, never can or ever will be. This is the nature of things. The getting of wisdom, like life, is eternal. There are no boundaries. It goes on forever and each time you believe you've seen and learnt it all, a new challenge will be thrown at you to test that perceived thought and knowledge. Don't be fooled into thinking that you are the "bee's knees".

You see, I have a sense of humour, like you. Some of the things I talk about are of a serious nature but that doesn't mean that we can't have 'fun' together with whichever meaning that word holds for you.

As a young boy and later as a man, I was always a bit of a playful teaser, mainly with my family and close friends. It's amazing how much they would let me get away with but I must assume they knew my heart was essentially in the right place. They accepted this as part of my character and ignored my teasing when they had had enough.

My belief is if you can't laugh at yourself, you might as well curl up in a little ball and die. Laughter is truly the best medicine of all. In order to be truly happy and contented, you need to both receive and give at least eight hugs a day, plus make someone else laugh eight times within each 24 hours, as well as accepting and expressing that same laughter yourself. You may ask, well, why eight? I am unable to answer that.

This all may sound like a pretty tall order but it can be done. Use this information and make it one of your goals. Some may think, 'I've got nothing to laugh about, so why bother? It's all too hard and not worth the trouble'. Even if your strongest emotion and desire is to scream or to cry, then do so but once released from the body, take steps to change that energy pattern immediately into a positive.

If you are truly at a loss to discover things to laugh about, turn to the ways of Mother Nature and the myriad of animal life, from the smallest to the biggest. Take time out to watch their antics. Tune into their wavelength. St Frances of Assisi had this amazing ability and so did remarkably well. Learn from what they get up to. They can teach us many things.

Lighten your heart rather than weighing it down with the pressures of everyday life. I'm not saying to ignore or suppress any problem you may be going through but look at it realistically and don't give it more importance than is needed. As some would say, stop building mountains out of molehills but now, let's go back to the animal kingdom.

Tai Chi releases, unblocks and keeps the energy flowing smoothly, which in turn, helps us to be free from disease. Its large range of movements was originally created as a result of man observing a variety of animals, their behavioural patterns and routines. The observer then made an attempt to imitate what was seen and from then on, chose to become a participant in the dance of life. Babies naturally do the same thing, by watching their parents for guidance. As a participant or teacher for another, you need to be careful as to how you portray yourself to others, as it may cause some confusion on the part of the observer. Because more often than not, our thoughts and actions may be two entirely different things.

That is when mixed messages are received and misunderstandings, as well as hurt feelings, can arise quite abruptly, like an unbroken and festering boil. Always maintain an open and enquiring mind. Begin to question why. Sadly, there are not enough people asking the right questions in order for Spirit to help them and if they do, they search outside themselves and seek the answers from the wrong person. The answers lie within.

While living that lifetime, I tended to be a little impatient and sometimes I would feel frustrated at how people would react and interact with each other. I was forever being tested in this area. I really admired Matthew, as he was more laid back and would wait for things to happen. He was in no great rush. Something not happening caused Matthew no great distress. For me though, I would become annoyed and feel as if I was wasting my time. Each one of us had certain inadequacies we needed to overcome.

My favourite pastime while growing up and as a young man, was fishing. You might think that this would not suit such a person as myself, being so impatient and all that. This is not correct because for some strange reason, I was good at it.

I never had to wait long before being successful in achieving my goal. It allowed me the opportunity to be by myself, to become introspective and meditative. Even when kept busy and physically active, I was able to turn within and ignore all of what is going on around me. Of course, I had a certain obligation to feed and provide for my family and village but the rest of the time, it was pure pleasure. I started off as being a mere fisherman but ended up as being a 'fisher of souls'.

Many people were not so willing to be caught up in the net; but the fish, although slippery and jumpy little characters they may be, had no such hesitation. They were like putty in my hands, where it was relatively simple for me to get them to do what I wanted. Perhaps that sounds a little selfish and manipulative but still, this was true for me. The slippery human variety, however, needed to be constantly coaxed and prodded – very much like a flock of sheep.

Many times, I would be found in a contemplative and silent state. I found no noise and no chatter, even if only momentarily, to be soothing and restful for my soul. I loved the late night for this reason. But wherever you may find yourself, life can never be completely silent. There still exists the sound of nature stirring and moving around you, both seen and unseen. I would grab every opportunity that came my way to be silent and the night catered to this purpose well. At that time, so many people who didn't know or understand where I was coming from would need to believe that I was being rude and ignorant of their needs.

I felt so tired sometimes and could feel this same weakness seep into every pore of my body and bone. I led such an active lifestyle – both mentally and physically. There was so much for me to learn and I sometimes felt there is not enough time for me to experience all that I need to.

My feelings and emotions ran deep and on many different levels, depending upon the perception of myself at the time. There were two different, but essentially the same, sides to my personality. In these days, some might say that I was 'schizophrenic'. Everyone placed on this planet must acknowledge and learn to deal with their dual identity.

To explain this briefly, God, to some, is seen to have not two but three faces – the Creator, the Preserver and the Destroyer – the last of which is opposite to being the Creator. The trick is not to allow one to dominate the other. In order to live fully in the light, there must also be darkness. This is where our fears and insecurities live and multiply if left uncontrolled. There needs to be a balance but how does one achieve that fine balance? The answer to that will be different for each individual, as each one has a different lesson to learn.

There is no point in scurrying around, trying desperately to hide and bury your head in the sand. This doesn't achieve a thing. All it's really doing is that it greatly delays and hinders the healing and learning process that we must all go through. It forces us to remain blind to our reality. Jesus was forced to go through this cycle as well but because of his main purpose, thrust in life and power, everything became intense and magnified. One of the reasons this was so is because he had less time in which to do it all in; one way to guide and empathise with other people is to have experienced the same hardship and suffering they are going through.

It was a tough road for Jesus to walk upon and I, plus the inner circle, had to go through it with him and to a lesser extent, with ourselves. It is through experiencing great sadness and pain, that we shall then have the ability to consciously flip the same coin over, in order to examine and develop the positive qualities of humility and compassion. Mankind indeed, is a complex creature. There are many avenues of exploration available when dealing with the inner mind and that state of super-consciousness. So much has been suppressed. Why is it that in today's society, you are so afraid to live completely in the present? Why are some of you so afraid and determined to ignore the negative aspects of your personality?

Some ignore the existence of God and the Spirit world. Do you think that denying this truth makes it any less real and makes it no longer so? Irrespective of where your mind is at and your personal beliefs, it doesn't change a thing. Because you don't believe, certainly doesn't mean it does not exist. All that is achieved is you are then forced, and this is self-imposed, to live out your days and nights with an incomplete picture in regards to the true meaning of life, death and its many other interesting inhabitants.

There is so much that people are missing out on because of their stubbornness and lack of faith in a power that is far greater than themselves. Please, for the sake of the world's future and this includes the birth of your children and grandchildren, walk together as one nation and help each other to open your heart, eyes, ears and mind to the overall reality and beauty of our complete existence.

Fear of Illness

A lot of people don't realise the potential healing power that their own two eyes have. Many 'faith or alternative healers' of today request their clients to shut their eyes; when really, both the practitioner and the person requiring a healing should keep their eyes open.

The other thing that needs to be changed is the positioning of the two people involved. Many, but not all, healers will work from behind where the person being helped cannot see the practitioner, even if they do have their eyes open. Why is that? As a healer, are you embarrassed by the actions you feel drawn to take? Is your procedure a secret or do you believe your client will relax more if they have their eyes shut?

If you hold firm to the latter belief, you would in most cases be right in saying this. To confront and accept the Truth by looking deep into the eyes of another can be quite disturbing. Jesus employed this technique numerous times with great success to the discomfort and surprise of many. It's like the person who needs a healing is baring their soul to another. Whether that is to a friend or stranger, it doesn't matter. The end result is the same, whether you know them personally or not. Many feel uncomfortable at becoming so intimate with someone so quickly in this way. By not having fear to see your Truth through the eyes of another lends itself for an enormous shift of consciousness to take place within.

If you are a healer, become a clear channel for Spirit, step outside your physical body and invite Jesus, the Archangels, the Apostles of Christ or any other and allow the Ascended Master to take control. This way, the person coming for assistance is actually communicating with a higher power, even though they may not recognise or understand this completely.

It's not necessary to speak on these occasions and yes I know silence can cause quite a large degree of discomfort and embarrassment, as there are some healers who feel the need to verbally express their power, knowledge and wisdom. This is fine to do this as well. Understand though that there is a right time and a right place for everything.

By both remaining silent while keeping eye contact with each other will, at times, stimulate certain relevant memories to float to the surface of the mind that will be painful to look at for both parties involved in this session; with Spirit acting as a silent negotiator between your thoughts, feelings, fears and emotions.

If you need a healing but wish not to do this with another, here is an alternative technique. In the privacy of your own home, use the mirror, step outside yourself, ask for the Holy Spirit to descend upon you and then give yourself permission to see what lies beyond the surface of your soul.

In this way, all illness can be gotten rid of as you open your heart more and more to the healing energies of the Universe, where you could receive insights about your past experiences, not only with this lifetime but with other ones as well. This whole process of open eye healing will have a domino effect, where wall upon wall of fears and disillusionments are finally destroyed and laid to rest in peace.

Illness doesn't always mean it's a bad thing and neither

does it mean it has to be life threatening. There are two main reasons why people get ill. The first being that the person or those people close to them are receiving a wakeup call, where certain aspects of their own life needs to be changed in order to ensure continued and healthy longevity of life, even if it means slowing down. Sometimes, because of our over the top enthusiasm, we forget to stop and smell the roses, which is an essential ingredient to living in a sick free zone. While the first one was in short a warning, the second reason deals with receiving a natural healing.

Even though you may feel as if you are dying, this is not always the case. It may not be pleasant but it is needed. It's your body's way of saying 'enough is enough. I don't accept any more the junk you are feeding me'. This junk needs to be expelled from our physical and mental bodies promptly. To avoid all types of sickness can cause grave illness within a person.

But sorry, I almost forgot, there is a third reason as to why we may feel unwell and that is to strengthen our immune system so it may fight against disease. Because who knows, we may need it later one day in the far off distant future. A deficiency in this area could kill us or it may not, if we're lucky.

The choice is ours as to how long or short any illness will last for. The more you accept your sickness or injury on a conscious thinking and feeling level, you are then making it far worse by giving this illness power over you, which then prolongs its unwelcome stay within your body. When this happens, your sickness gains the strength while you get weaker by the minute. And there we have the creation of two opposing forces; one more formidable than the other. While you become a kitten with a pathetic meow that couldn't frighten even a mouse, your dark friend called 'illness' will be transformed into a Bengal tiger with a ferocious roar. When this happens, why not consider switching roles. When you can do this, you can fight it at its own game.

You can then begin to hear, feel and see how your sickness operates. Use this knowledge as part of your strategy to control it. This information can be used as a forewarning to when you could be in real danger. So, are you going to be a ferocious winner or a pathetic loser in the health stakes? The choice is always yours to decide where you wish to stand or lie in life.

Before you take any action to change anything, take a moment out of your time to firstly accept and then discern the spiritual reason for your illness. But how can you do that? When you are next in pain, stop, sit and pose the question – 'what can I learn from this painful experience and what part of my attitude or belief system can I change to ensure I don't need to experience this again in the future?' The answers to these two questions will set you free to travel unhindered upon the road to physical, mental and spiritual recovery.

When I was young, so much younger than today (is that possible? – of course it is), I developed a chest and lung infection, similar to what you know as being pneumonia today. I nearly died but survived to grow into a healthy robust man committed to healing others. I was particularly blessed at this time because I had access to a master of the healing arts who took care of my physical needs. This man spoke few words and had originally been born in the Orient. My parents heard of his amazing abilities and so came to assist in my rescue. Keep in mind; this episode happened a long time before I came to work with Jesus and my other spiritual brothers.

While lying flat on my back, this man of great power and compassion bent over and placed his face close to my stomach.

With an open mouth, he inhaled heavily, straightened up, tilted his head backwards and forcibly exhaled the contents of the air he had just breathed in. This process, done in front of my parents, was repeated many times; at the end of which I fell into a deep and dreamless sleep. When I awoke about twelve hours later, my body temperature had returned to normal. I was now through the worst of it and three days later, I was able to leave my bed. I tried to make contact again with him but was unsuccessful. His mission had been completed, so there was no real reason to make that connection again with me to receive my personal and heartfelt thanks.

From his point of view, thanks were not necessary; so let's move on and see what can be done for the next person who needed his healing breath. As far as I was concerned, this man was an Angel sent from Heaven.

I never forgot what he did for me and as I got older, I applied this same technique, amongst many others, to those who later came to me for a healing. But before you try this yourself, there is a word of caution I must give to all who would like to do this and that is, be careful not to swallow what you have drawn into yourself. If this happens, you then leave yourself susceptible to falling foul of the same disease. You don't need their illness or negative emotions and you are certainly doing yourself no favours by accepting that which is not good for you.

So please, make sure you release it back out towards the Universe for purification purposes. Neither of you need to keep it. Let it go and let God heal you. Before you begin this healing process of another, place a ring of protection around yourself and ask an Archangel to take control of your in and out breaths. Stay detached. Let Spirit do all the hard work while you stay a relaxed and open channel. To relax and trust is the best protection of all, in everything you set out to do in life.

We sabotage our good health as a result of thinking ill of ourselves and others. For some, these uneasy thoughts may not be felt in the body until many years after having that initial thought. And because there is no immediate reaction to the physical other than perhaps an emotional one, we don't even think about how it may be adversely affecting our bodies in regards to the immune, respiratory, digestive and nervous systems.

In order to live a long and healthy lifestyle, we need to become aware of how the mind and heart are interconnected and which do affect each other. There cannot be damage in one area without doing harm to the other. It's the same when a relationship or friendship goes bust.

Both people will feel the negative effects of the fallout immediately prior, during and after in varying degrees, depending upon who initiated the separation and how they went about it. When you hurt, I hurt.

God feels your pain but will not step in unless invited to help but even then, nothing may eventuate from asking for assistance from above, because it is necessary for that person's spiritual evolvement as a soul to go through that particular illness or pain in order to learn something or to teach another a hard lesson about themselves. It may not sound fair or just because some diehard religious fanatics believe there should be no suffering but how can we learn to be truly joyful if there is no sadness? "Out of the darkness, there comes the light". This is what planet Earth is going through now.

She is emerging from the darkness that has been inherited through eons of time, towards the light of a new beginning and the Second Coming. This will happen, both in the physical sense and spiritually in regards to our state of awareness. It can't be stopped. You have no choice and the process for many, but not all, will be long and painful. Just as Mother Earth is going through her own growing and changing pains, she too will react quite violently at times that will be largely out of character. In order to give birth to a brave new world, there will inevitably be many tragic endings and with those same endings, there will come new beginnings.

Any time a volcano or fire erupts, when tidal waves sweep across the lands, when the trade winds blow and whip up a storm, all can be likened to a person having a heart attack or brain malfunction. For some, these circumstances which are beyond their control will bring much death, chaos and mayhem into their lives but certainly not for everyone. Will you be one of the lucky ones? The choice is still yours to make so don't procrastinate.

We can survive these changes if we maintain a fearless, trusting and positive attitude towards the Laws of Nature and the Universe. It will be less scary and less destructive on our body, heart and mind and that includes our immediate environment which is where we live, work and play. Try fighting the inevitable and you could be struck down in your prime.

Take precautions today and prepare your body and mind for what is yet to come. Why make this transformation from the darkness into the light more difficult than it already is? Have you not yet suffered enough? If the answer to that is 'no', well we can arrange something special. I implore you to be careful what you wish for; you might just get it with no guarantee of a refund at the end of it.

So what will you do? Trade your old body in for a new

model or will you take preventative measures now that will ensure a safe passage to a new future that you are destined to experience? The latter course of action will bring you many rich rewards in more ways than one. The hard work needs to be done now, not later.

The hard work will only become a lot harder if left undone for too long. As it is the same for people who choose to waste a lot of time and energy by worrying about a problem when they could have used that same amount of time more constructively by focusing upon solutions. But in order to find a solution that is of benefit to all, it may require us to step outside our comfort zone and do something a little bit different to what we would normally do. Think laterally and always remember that like our hand that has four fingers and a thumb, unless you are an amputee, that every existing problem has at least four solutions staring right back at you. Eenie, meenie, miney, mo, which one shall you choose? I say, why not try all four? Cover your back and take a bet each way. You would then be creating a situation where you have less chance of losing and more chance of winning.

Let's take a closer look at the words 'ill health'. The language experts would call this an oxymoron. The two words are opposite in meaning yet they stand securely side by side and for certain people within the community, they feel quite comfortable with this strange union of odd bedfellows, because it serves a purpose. 'Ill' is negative while 'health' is positive. Using the word 'ill' is merely a descriptive term that indicates a person's state of health and mind. As such, it can be changed at a moment's notice by deleting this word from our vocabulary.

Many may think this too is a simple solution for such a complex problem. But I would say, please define the meaning of the words 'simple' and 'complex', or 'solution' and 'problem'. Change the polarities and make them fit.

Our minds have a tendency to dwell on the negatives rather than the positives. While we are feeling unwell or when in pain, we focus all our attention on its negative aspects and by bringing it to the forefront of our mind, gives it the ultimate power over us, which is what we do when we speak of it to other people. It's like adding more fuel to the fire.

This fuel can take many forms, one of the most effective being oxygen. We take into our bodies this oxygen in order to survive but if with each in breath we take, is combined with a negative thought form in regards to our health, this will make matters far worse than what it has to be.

Exhale, not inhale, unhealthy thought processes. In other words, breathe in the good and on the out breath, let go of the bad. You can take this one step further by affirming on each out breath – 'I reject all anger' or whatever emotional or physical pain you might be experiencing at that time. You can then conclude by affirming on each in breath you take – 'I accept all calmness'. A second option would be to affirm – 'I reject the dark' and 'I accept the light'. Or to make it even simpler, more general and all encompassing for you, shorten it to 'I reject' and 'I accept'. Exhale and inhale; let go and receive.

Do this technique in your mind when someone makes you feel angry. Very quickly, you will calm down and find your perfect balance once again. Some suggest you count to ten before responding. This is good too. Acknowledge this is how you are feeling right now and rather than turning it inwards upon yourself or releasing it outwards to the other person, accept it momentarily but then take positive steps to transform it.

This is the art of alchemy. You can see a perfect example of this in the Bible where Jesus turned the water into wine. The alchemists of ancient days would take base metals and turn them into silver or gold using the principle of chemistry. It then stands to reason that negative energy can be transmuted into positive energy by using the mind alone.

We experience pain when we shut our heart down. In doing so, we think we are protecting ourselves from becoming hurt again but we end up doing to ourselves the very thing we were trying to avoid. Think about it. You may feel it elsewhere in the body but this can be a red herring, camouflaging the root cause. Doctors know this. We seek medical assistance from the experts only when secondary symptoms appear that then hopefully enables the doctor to pinpoint the primary and initial cause of the disease or pain. They will then prescribe the necessary course of action that will make you feel better.

But let's now take this one step further and take a look at your emotions before you hurt yourself. It may be a one off experience or it could be a habit that is lived out on a near daily basis, over a long period of time. If it's the latter, something has to give and your body will begin to react accordingly in the same way that you have treated it. Many people don't even realise the connection between the body and mind. In order to take some pressure off the heart from being bombarded by all this pain, the body decides to redistribute it accordingly, like your weight.

Doctors, including alternative or spiritual healers and other allied health professionals, can assist in the healing process most certainly, but this takes place on a temporary basis only. It is not long lasting but it can be if the patient or client also takes on board the responsibility to change themselves in regards to the old beliefs and attitudes that are holding them back and which are making them feel ill. Learn to put your foot down to yourself and other people; start saying 'no, enough is enough, I deserve better'. Self-love is the greatest healer, as is forgiveness and laughter. Without these three essential ingredients for a long and healthy life, nearly every moment that you live is indeed going to be a painful experience and for some really unfortunate ones, it may appear to be continuous and never ending.

It can be ended by remaining neutral and maintaining an accepting, tolerant and open heart and mind towards those people who have a different set of beliefs than you. The moment you try and change another, this is when you are asking for trouble. Let them change when they are ready and not when you are ready. It is best to remember that no one person is all right and neither are they all wrong. We consist of varying degrees of light and shade, black, white and grey. Believe it or not, you are the manager of your own energy and physical body and you alone can decide whether you wish to feel at ease or ill at ease with your inner and outer worlds. Do the right thing and with conviction, say 'no' to disease.

Superimpose and press down into your aura, the symbol of the cross upon your seven main chakras, including the four minor points that are located in the centre of the palm and sole of each foot.

The chakras will then add up to the master number of 11. Visualise this being done twice daily. Once as you first wake up and second when you go to bed and just before sleep weaves its magic spell around you. It doesn't take long to do this and if you are having difficulty in visualising, by all means, let the pictures go. Instead, ask assistance from one of the Ascended Masters to do it for you at the same time as you scan your body with your mind, jumping from one activation point to the other.

Then have faith that these crosses you have now embedded into your energy field will protect and bless you with continued good health. And at those odd times when something does break down on a physical level, it will be comparatively minor to what it could have been. The length of time for the healing process, from beginning to end, will be shortened quite considerably and you will shrug this complication off as not being important at all.

You don't have to wear the heavy dark cloak of sickness and despair around your shoulders forever. Take it off, let the light in and allow yourself to breathe easy. And while you're at it, step down from that other energetic Cross you made and set your heart and feet free to travel in an upwardly mobile direction. Stop punishing yourself and others for things that have happened in the past. Learn something good from it and then let it go.

The same advice applies to any ill health you may experience. Don't make it worse than what it really is by grimly holding on to it like the dog with a bone. Untie that tight noose around your neck that binds you to your sickness and which slowly but surely will strangulate and suffocate the life force out of your body. Stop this self-damaging process now. It can be done. Believe and it will be so. Do something positive and real for yourself. Meet Spirit halfway and raise your energy vibration by having pure and positive thoughts for the good majority of your time, even when you are feeling unwell.

Here in the higher realms of the Spirit world, there is no pain and suffering. And this is what we want for you too but you must first want it for yourself. Until then, we cannot step in and take your pain and suffering away.

Although I did mention at the beginning that there will be times when a person has something of value to learn from their sickness but by the same token, this doesn't have to take a whole lifetime to learn. Ask us for the answer, we can give it to you. The hard part then must be done by you, which is putting the solution into practice on a daily basis and to make the appropriate changes within if you wish to experience consistently good health and we know that deep down that this is what you really want.

Cleansing My Aura

*In the name of Jesus Christ and with your Blood,
I anoint, protect and bless myself.
With the backing of God and the Archangels above,
I now address myself to all negative energies
residing within my aura.
It is to you, that I command that you leave now, never to return.
You are not wanted here and you don't belong,
leave me in peace.
Go and be with the light and let go of the past.
Thank you for leaving now and I wish you only the very best
upon your exciting journey, so goodbye and God bless.
Therefore, in the name of Jesus Christ,
I once again anoint, protect and bless myself
against all physical, emotional, mental and spiritual harm.*

Source: Shontara

Affirmations

*My body is glowing with RADIANT GOOD HEALTH,
vitality and enthusiasm.*

*My mind remains CALM when confronted
by adversity and fear.*

*My spiritual self SEEKS THE TRUTH
by turning within.*

SIM(E)ON

Special am

I, special are you,

May we walk together

Over valleys and dunes,

Neither afraid nor feeling blue.

I loved to bake bread. Like Matthew, I loved my food and wine but was also lucky enough to keep off excess weight. I would spend much of my free time in telling stories, some true and others not. I was a real prankster. I loved to fish but I didn't only catch the fish, I prepared and cooked it as well. To eat freshly caught fish, cooked over an open camp fire is an experience that many, but not all, today, have lost. I had a little boy. I passed on to him my knowledge about fishing.

As a young boy myself and later as a man, I always had a healthy respect for the sea. I enjoyed spending time in watching the movement of the waves. I would also collect bird feathers. I would pick them off the ground; those ones that were already discarded. Other than fish, birds are my best nature friends. Like the Angels, I always believed them as being winged creatures working for God, in order to spread peace and goodwill to mankind across the land.

Growing up as a young boy, I came from a poor, farming background but I was happy and always found plenty of things to do. I was the apple of my mother's eye. The river that ran through our village was used on a daily basis for a variety of reasons. This precious water became our life's blood. That's where I first learnt how to fish.

I was most inquisitive and pestered people with so many questions that some could not answer. To understand the reason why something worked or how a particular object was put together was all important to me. Some lost patience with my endless probing and questioning. As I look back on those times,

I can't say I really blame them. As I got older, I learnt to curb my curiosity but there still always lay within, burning bright, my incredible thirst for knowledge. It wasn't enough for me to have knowledge just for the sake of it.

Each new piece of information I collected from whatever source I could, I made it a goal to then incorporate it into my daily life, in a practical and useful way if possible. I think it is for this reason that Jesus chose me to be one of the Twelve. He could clearly see that keenness and willingness to put into practise, all of what I had learnt.

I was as agile as a panther and this was a skill greatly admired. As a young boy, I loved playing in the trees. It was here, if I was really quiet, I could get right up close and personal with my finely feathered friends. I would spend many a long hour observing people go about their daily lives. It was most fascinating and I never found it boring to watch them mixing with each other.

As a man, my earlier tree climbing and watching people expeditions and explorations put me in good stead for the future role I was to play. While travelling in a group and because not everyone liked us, I became a 'watch post', keeping an eye out for approaching enemies. Quite often, I could be found perched high on top of some tree, like a bird.

After a while and as I am sure you can imagine, it became a tad uncomfortable but I never complained. I was providing a much needed service. At the start of each day or evening shift, a certain local birdcall would be agreed upon; that was to be used as a warning signal for approaching danger. I was to herald this call, three times in quick succession. I had the gift of being able to imitate the birds since a young age. I had a good ear for sounds and was able to reproduce what I had heard easily. This ability extended to the area of music and song as well.

You could say, because of my insatiable desire for learning and curiosity, I developed an excellent memory for how things ticked. I became like a moving library or human sponge that soaked up all there was that I needed to know and more. There is a modern phrase used today that says "curiosity killed the cat". Let me assure you my friends, that curiosity never killed this top cat. In fact, it became quite the opposite. It actually helped me to stay alive and assisted me to stay at least three steps ahead of those people who wished to see harm come to me and, as I was not willing to get caught up in their little control and power games, I led a relatively peaceful but active existence.

I must acknowledge and accept though that I loved to play this cat and mouse game with my foes. I enjoyed the thrill of the chase but always made sure that I remained the hunter and not the hunted. On occasion, when the roles were reversed, I then enjoyed the challenge of using my initiative and finding creative ways to get myself out of those difficult situations. Invariably, I would succeed, because the faith I had in God and myself, were great.

Even though I immensely enjoyed a challenge, I still got scared and nervous, especially where women were concerned. I learnt from a young age to acknowledge these negative feelings of being nervous and scared and then took the necessary steps, forcing them to take a back seat while I took centre stage and go about my business. I never allowed them to interfere with what I needed to do. You may note that I speak of these emotions as being like real people. That way, I find I can deal with them better on a more tangible and realistic level.

Why don't you too give that fear, anger and frustration a physical face in your imagination? Acquaint yourself with them. Hesitation can kill. Don't be afraid to know your enemy. How can you possibly think that you can win the battle, if you're fighting blind and where you don't know who you're up against? Then take positive action to turn your enemy's head around and make them your best friend. Go with the tide rather than against it.

Acknowledge Accept and Action – these are the keys, the three big A's if you like, to being successful in controlling the whole range of negative emotions.

Ignore, Deny and Procrastinate is to give in and allow your enemy to manipulate and defeat you in every sense of the word. This is self-imposed and doesn't need to happen and really, there is no-one to blame except yourself for this becoming your reality.

Try the technique mentioned above, that is, give your fears a face on a daily basis and see if it doesn't help you. I know it will, but prove it to yourself. Don't take my word for it, or anybody else's for that matter and always question everything. Quite often, it is best to think before you speak or take action. By putting a face or shape to whatever negative emotions you are experiencing, can create miracles within cancer and other terminally ill patients. It works upon the same principle being applied. If something is worth doing, isn't it worth doing well and to the best of your ability? You have nothing to lose and everything to gain by carrying out such a simple act.

Stop being so half-hearted in your attempt to resolve problems. Don't hold back from exploring the many possibilities and outcomes that can happen as a result of choosing a particular path. Live in the here and now. What the mind can perceive, we can achieve. Always maintain hope for the future, for without it, living today will quite often be a painful existence – as it is for a mother giving birth to a child. Have patience while growing and changing.

Even though we may appear to be adults on the outside, internally and on a spiritual level, we will always be like that new born baby who is constantly striving to express their needs in a way where they won't be misunderstood; to learn how to survive amidst all the noise and confusion that surrounds them and to then finally emerge and be transformed to become an independent, living, breathing, happy, human being.

An appropriate parable would be the transformation of the dull looking moth which changes into a brightly coloured butterfly or where the ugly duckling indeed turns into a beautiful swan. Ask yourself – who do I want to be? When you have the answer, don't let your enemies hold you back from creating your dream. Live life to your fullest potential, as this (other than love) is the greatest gift of all that God has given to us. Is it so much to ask?

I had a close and satisfying friendship with my uncle, that is, my father's brother. As a young child, my uncle would unselfishly listen to me prattle on about anything, nothing and everything. I think, if I had the necessary power and authority, I would have had no hesitation in giving this man the honour of bestowing upon him, the title of sainthood. He was so patient and forever smiling but never wasted his precious words upon deaf ears and before answering any questions posed to him, he would first seriously think before speaking.

Sometimes, the space between these two acts could be quite long and uncomfortable. The silence created was quite noisy. You could almost touch it with your hand and cut it sharply with a knife. It was like as if he was looking deep into your heart to extract, as you would a bad tooth, the reason or motive behind the question. Some adults who had something to hide, found this to be quite disconcerting and everyone in the village knew that if you didn't really want an honest answer, it was best left unsaid and avoided altogether. This man, other than Jesus, had a great, long lasting and beneficial influence over me.

When I was young, I tried so hard to emulate the ways of my uncle but this was not possible. We were two different people and he never asked or expected this of me, anyway. I quickly learnt that I can only be me, with all my innate strengths and inherent weaknesses. By trying so hard to be like another that you love, respect and admire, will actually hinder your spiritual growth. Most times we do this because we want others to love and accept us. We feel that if we were more like them, how could they not possibly fall upon their knees, kiss our feet and pay homage to us in the way that we expect?

Those people in positions of power, who are self-centred and selfish, will certainly have their egos bolstered by this adoring group of fans who try their hardest to imitate their chosen idol. Those so-called "movers and shakers" of today's world, see it as a great achievement on their part and will have no qualms about taking credit for all the good work that you do. Don't play this game of being a follower. Take control, be independent and be yourself. Walk together, side by side and not one behind the other.

Jesus always encouraged our individuality. He had no desire to see a large and automated mass of clones standing before him, mouthing off and repeating like a parrot, great words of wisdom; people who really had no feeling or understanding of the meaning or power behind these words they speak. It was insincere and totally uncalled for.

Be happy for whom you represent today and if you can't be happy, change yourself into whom you want to become; but do it for yourself and don't do it for another person. If you take action with expectations, you will no doubt experience great disappointment. The only one you can rely upon is yourself. If you let yourself down, you have no-one to point the finger at, except yourself. Take full responsibility for all that you do, feel, think and say.

Women deserve our utmost respect and admiration. Without them, the human race could not exist or survive. It is they who give birth to us and our children, who later grow up to become worthwhile members of our society. Some will go down the parenting path, while creating once again, the cycle of birth, death and rebirth. Some women or men will experience infertility but this also happens for a purpose. Some women or couples, for a variety of reasons, will choose not to "go forth and multiply". This is their choice and should not be looked down upon as second class citizens because they made this decision. For some, this can be seen to be a wise move. There is a time and season for every experience.

When we lose touch with the natural rhythm of our body though, things can begin to go a little haywire and off course. A lot of so-called 'enlightened' beings will focus only upon their spiritual needs but deny or forget about their physical. It's as if, that part of them does not exist. But in order to live happily and successfully in this physical world, we need to look after the flesh and not just the spirit. We get to play with only one body each lifetime. It's like a finely tuned vehicle which needs daily maintenance and nourishment. Some people will even go so far as to say it's a piece of art that should be admired and revered.

We need to give more credit to this fine piece of God's machinery and we need to take time out to thank the one who created us and by saying this, I don't mean only God. How many of you have actually verbally stated your thanks to your earthly parents for bringing you into this world? Certainly, I understand for quite a few of you, due to a lack of love, understanding and communication from those who raised you, this could be an extremely painful and insincere thing to do but if you can move through your own fear of rejection and hurt feelings, much would be healed if a word of thanks was spoken occasionally. It's a partnership and with any partnership, we need to work at it.

Many people don't know how to live in balance. Some are perfect weight, while still others are living in a state of either malnutrition or obesity. I mentioned earlier about the so-called enlightened ones who neglect their physical needs. If you have a look at the other side of this same coin, you will be amazed to find there are many in existence today who live to achieve their base desires only and give no thought whatsoever to their spiritual needs.

Both groups of people are sadly lacking and not living life to its fullest potential. Begin to look at the overall big picture. Step outside of ourselves for a moment and view the role each one of us plays, as individuals, in the Universe as a whole. You might believe that you are only a little fish in a very big pond and your contribution is not worth much. This is not true.

To give $1 instead of $100 to your favourite charity is still worth something to someone and collectively, it can amount to a lot. So, how does one take a look at the overall big picture?

One way you can do this is to view yourself as being part of God's body. God is neither male nor female. God is the energy force that keeps this planet and all others scattered throughout the galaxy, together. Open your heart, accept and visualise that each individual living today has a vital role to play in God's existence. Without this unseen energy force, we too would not and could not experience this life, as we know it. We are an integral part of this Universal energy force which keeps us alive and together bound, forever.

In order for this Universal and collective body to survive, we, as individuals, must learn how to live and work in harmony with each other. The moment we hurt ourselves and each other, whether it be on a physical, emotional, mental or spiritual level, we are doing God – as a complete but not separate entity – much harm. Each time we feel pain, God feels our pain with us and it then becomes his pain, in every sense of the word. How can he not feel any differently from us? God is a part of us and we are a part of God. They are inseparable. God relies upon us to give him, for want of a better word, what he needs.

Each time we go about destroying a piece of planet Earth, we not only destroy the physical evidence but on a spiritual level and from God's point of view, it's like experiencing an amputation of a limb or removal of a vital organ. It's distressing and if the body, like Earth, is already weak from lack of what it needs and is not being looked after properly and respected, things will begin to fall apart, where much disease and illness is experienced; the flip side to that are earthquakes, volcanoes, floods, pestilence and famine. The damage has already been done. Take steps to heal this situation today; it's never too late. If each person can accept this heavy burden of responsibility, we will feel within ourselves, much improved health, inner peace and contentment. We will then, once again, learn to live in balance and in harmony.

Well after the death of Jesus and as I got much older, I became a man of few words in regards to my personal and social relationships. I became more discerning about who I could trust with my innermost secrets and fears. Because I valued the importance of confidentiality, not everyone else did and once obtained, certain information would be used against me. My friends did not involve themselves in listening to these half truths and half lies. Sadly, others did – those people who had power, influence and authority and with whom I had to deal with and answer to on a daily basis.

I learnt that I had to be more careful with my mouth, especially when loosened a little bit with a fine wine. Using my words unwisely could land me in a lot of unexpected trouble. I became aware that there was a certain outside group of people I could not trust. I felt greatly disappointed and despondent. I became a touch cynical about the motives of others. Only my time and their actions would tell if they were worthy of my complete friendship.

The Twelve of us were not always together, as we made a commitment to travel as much breadth and width of the land as we could, while opening the eyes of those people who could not see or behold God's law.

In my 'retirement' years, I became more introverted, which was in direct contrast to what I was like as a child, teenager and young man but still I have no regrets. Life, people and places are forever changing. Don't kid yourself that they don't. Nothing can ever stay the same. The only one consistency – other than death – is the matter of energy. The Universal Energy that keeps us sane to varying degrees is constantly there.

We may have the ability to destroy some of it but we can never kill off the whole. Like the liver, it has the capacity to regenerate and rebuild itself, in the same way that after a forest fire, a burnt and blackened tree will bounce back and become even stronger and lusher than it was previously.

As an old man, I feel so tired. Soon, and once again, my time here will be over. I had a peaceful death. I was forewarned and like the humble cat, I took deliberate action to leave my home and loved ones behind. I didn't want to cause any undue distress. I wanted to go out with a minimum of fuss. The truth be told though, I didn't like or want to say goodbye.

So I chose to walk into the desert with great confidence, set up camp and waited for that dark and mysterious Angel to pay me a visit. Three days and three nights later, the deed had been done. My body was later found and taken back to the village by a friend.

I then went on to bigger and better things, as you will too – one day. Accept your fate gracefully and do not struggle against what is inevitable. It's not as bad as you think. Life is eternal, regardless of your personal religious beliefs or nationality. Death is the greatest equaliser. There is no discrimination in the Spirit world between the sexes. Everyone must experience the same destiny in order to be reborn again.

As a young boy, I loved to explore new places. When I had fulfilled my family obligations, I would take a wander in whichever direction took my fancy. I gave no thought to possible dangers. Even though I had a strong affinity with birds and to a lesser extent with fish, I had the uncanny ability to communicate with all animals – large and small, potentially dangerous or not. I could sense what they were thinking and knew what it was they were about to do. I came to respect their rights and personal space. I never got too close to an animal that did not want me to.

I knew when to keep my distance if the animal was a little bit aggressive, unfriendly and protective of their young. I heeded their warning signs – although some were almost imperceptible, where I then had to rely upon gut instincts alone. I was no masochist. Pain was definitely not my style.

Some of you believe that animals don't possess a thinking, logical brain or have no feelings. This is far from the truth. All God's creatures, including the animal kingdom, are intelligent although it may appear that in both the animal and human species, there are some breeds and individuals who are quite stupid and lack foresight. We are all travelling our own separate path and because of this, we are all at different levels of awareness and understanding. No one person is far more interesting than another. They are just different.

Those people who have language difficulties, doesn't mean they are stupid or have nothing to say. Some are only new in their journey. To give you a human example of this in today's society; take a look at the education system and the variety of different levels of learning and institutions involved in helping to teach our children. First, there is the playgroup and kindergarten. Then comes primary and high school, followed by college or university. Each one has a specific purpose or goal and is aimed at particular age groups. Some will go on to experience all levels of education offered and some will not. For those who find it difficult or choose not to continue within this man-made system of education, does not mean they are stupid. They just have different needs and attitudes.

Animals do not need such places to learn. Their learning is solely achieved through experiencing life on a daily basis in their own environment. They pick up the necessary guidelines by watching their parents and experimenting themselves. Some survive, some don't. The same can be said for humankind as well.

Life is like a game of cards. Depending upon the game you play, much skill is needed to win. However, there are other certain games which rely on chance, and that's where Lady Luck is introduced into this equation.

So what route have you taken? Do you sit on the fence and make a 50/50 bet each way? Do you rely on Spirit alone to give you what you want? Or instead of waiting for miracles to arrive on your front door step, do you use your initiative and take positive action to ensure that miracles do actually happen? You cannot rely on God or Spirit alone to provide all of what you want and need.

If everything was too easy to come by, there would be nothing to learn or strive for. There would be no purpose to our actions. The meaning of life will not be displayed and given to you on a silver platter. The meaning of life can only be understood and accepted by living each experience to the max. Don't entrap yourself by being reliant on another. By doing so, you hand over the control that is rightfully yours to keep. Remember, God gave us all, free will to choose.

By handing over control to another person, you become a breathing speaking robot; always awaiting directions and instructions from an outside source, before having the ability to move into action. This then becomes senseless. Who exactly is in charge here? You or them?

Some religious people will speak of doing God's bidding but how can you be so sure as to who you are indeed talking or listening to? Are you communicating with your God that you understand it to be, or are you merely listening to your higher self? By saying this, these two things originate from the same source. God and you are inseparable. There cannot be one without the other – like peaches and cream or Cleopatra and Mark Anthony.

There is a third possibility and that is you could be picking up on the positive or negative thoughts, impressions and expectations from those around you. Think about it. This is so easily done without realising it. We are all like radio transmitters and receivers. Some, who live out of balance, are highly gifted in either one of these two abilities but not both. Be discerning.

When in meditation, do you ever ask for the identity of that particular Spirit entity you are talking to and do you ask them if they are working for the light? What warning signs have you set in place in order to protect yourself from speaking and working with confused energy?

The line between the world of black and white or good and bad, is thin and subtle at a certain point. It's so easy to be misguided, both in the Spirit and physical worlds. Take daily precautions and don't assume that because you are aware of your Spirit Guides or Guardian Angels, that this knowledge alone will give you immunity against anything that has a bad or evil influence.

There are two important things to remember here and they are: "ask and ye shall receive" (protection) and "God helps those who help themselves" (taking action on your own behalf and accepting the consequences).

Fear of the Unknown

This same fear could be referred to as being afraid of the future and of change. It hasn't happened yet, so how can you see clearly. For some, it is quite a horrifying business to not see or know what is going to transpire next. In fact, it can be so horrifying that they can't move one way or the other. Any direction becomes scary. If your fear of the unknown is so great, to undertake anything new and this means having new relationships and jobs as well, you will choose not to get fully involved in living and life can be viewed as being a continuous game of chance and change. Do I or don't I?

Please note there is only one letter difference between the two words – chance and change. Why not turn your fear of the unknown on its head and do in spite of how you are feeling. Why is it so important to know the answer to everything in advance?

Although I can't talk because I too wanted to have all the answers to everything now, forget this 'tomorrow' business. As mentioned earlier and as a young boy, my passion for understanding how things worked or what made other people tick was all important to me. So what changed? I learnt there are no guarantees. The future can change direction at a moment's notice without our awareness or participation.

What you now perceive one second to be right may be wrong the next and this happens due to a change of actions and beliefs of those people around you, including yourself even though you may not realise it.

Some humans, you can read easily – like an open book, where every page stays relatively the same because they are so predictable in their reactions. Until one day they have a change of heart and do or say something totally out of character from what is expected; that can come as quite a shock to the system to the regular readers of this once easily understood and open book. The reactions of the one who is being read are no longer similar or familiar to what went before, as the reactions to this change on the part of the reader can also be different in either a pleasing or disturbing way. What I am trying to say is our future is not set in stone. So live your life fully expecting to experience the unexpected.

Another factor that affects our degree of fear for the unknown is how many times our trust of other people has been betrayed in the past. This erosion of trust is then replaced by doubt. When you choose to combine this fear of the unknown with doubt, it can lead you into much unnecessary trouble. But this same mistrust doesn't just relate to other people.

It relates to ourselves as well. Do we trust our intuition, our gut instincts or our inner knowing? How often have we talked ourselves out of success because of a fear for the future that is the great unknown? We need to question – can we accept the changes that will automatically take place as a result of that same success or do we reject it and embrace that which is already familiar to us, that is, failure instead?

Do the things you fear the most and the death of fear is certain. The co-writer of this book tries to live by this philosophy as much as possible. This is another reason why we have chosen her to be our biographer, because she is willing to put herself on the line, cop some flack, as well as receiving heaps of questions from different media – all looking for answers. Despite her personal fears and a small amount of doubt about the reactions of the wider population yet to come in the future, she is still courageous enough to do what is required. Because of this, she will remain protected and be richly rewarded, because the fear of the unknown does not control her actions or reactions. Are you as brave? Some are but some are not.

Let's take a closer look at those words – do the things you fear the most and the death of fear is certain. How do you think people with phobias overcome their deep seated fears? Little by little, they are guided by a professional to expose themselves to what scares them the most. This approach does work but it takes time, guts and a strong determination to not allow a particular fear or an assortment thereof to affect them in their everyday life. For those who care about that person can feel traumatised as well, at having to watch the person they love face their demons. As we love or care for someone dearly, we have a tendency to want to protect them. By doing so, this could hinder their personal and spiritual growth.

The kindest thing would be to personally remove yourself from that situation and support them in their desire to combat their fear of the unknown, every step of the way. They'll survive. You may not but they will. It's a bit like parents having to let go of their teenage or adult children and trusting them enough to make the right decisions, to assert their own authority, to fight their own battles, to pick themselves up again after being knocked down and to overcome their own fears. Don't hold them back because you care too much. We can make any fear greater than what it is due to a tendency to exaggerate and by placing too much importance on it.

It is devastatingly easy to fall into the trap of worrying excessively about the outcome of a situation. Our mind is a powerful tool and it should never be misused to create and hold on to our fear of the unknown that really should have no concern for us. How many have feared going to the dentist but when you finally get there, you discover to your delight – well that wasn't as bad as you thought it would be? This example can be applied to any other situation you may fear finding yourself in. It's like building mountains out of molehills. For a change then, train your mind into making molehills out of mountains.

It can be done and as I said before, it will take time, guts and a strong determination. I have great faith in your ability to control your fear of the unknown but do you have that same level of trust and faith about yourself. If not, why not? Can you seek help to develop that trust and faith? Are you willing and not just able to let go of that which scares you the most, forever and ever, amen?

As an Apostle, we breathed the same air and lived closely with that fear of the unknown every day, never knowing what might come next. Would it be good or would it be bad? Thankfully, keeping busy both mentally and physically helped us to forget about our fears for a while. Our energies were channelled into other more positive pursuits that we were dealing with at that point in time.

If one has too much spare time on their hands, one's thoughts will naturally and most definitely focus upon that which is negative. If your mind is occupied with more important things, that fear of the unknown will naturally subside and gravitate to taking a back seat and, being the driver of your own destiny, you know how annoying and frustrating back seat drivers can be.

If it all gets too much to handle, the solution is to stop for a moment and give it the big boot. Respect yourself enough not to travel down life's road where your constant companion is Fear, with a capital F. If you keep it closely by your side, even if it is behind you, any decision making will then be made difficult; where you end up feeling torn in two and this can be quite a painful experience. It's like the childhood game of tug-of-war. Whoever pulls the hardest and makes the other fall, wins the game. So let me ask you, are you a winner or a loser?

At the end of each night when it's comparatively quiet, take a look at what you feared the most during your day. Ask yourself – did I handle it well? If not, how could I have dealt with it better? What were my physical reactions towards this fear? How did it make me feel other than the obvious? Once you have the answer to these questions, then make a pact with yourself to try and do better next time.

When that next time comes and the same fear you looked at the night before brings you undone again, don't beat yourself up about it by thinking, 'I should have known better. Why was I unable to control my fear? Why could I not react differently?' These questions are indeed good to take a look at in the clear light of day and with hindsight but not to the extent where you begin to feel bad about yourself. Accept that you made another mistake and move on, knowing there will always be a next time in which you can prove yourself wrong and where you do react more positively and with less fear.

Negative energy is not the only force in the Universe that can cause destruction. By maintaining a positive believe in yourself, this can also destroy all of that which is negative. Or some would like to say that good always wins over evil and this would be true. It doesn't just happen in the Hollywood movies.

It happens in real life too but only if you become your own star, director, producer and scriptwriter.

So, how about it? Are you up for the task to rewrite the history books in regards to yourself? Yes, I know it's daunting but perseverance, inner strength and lots of hard work never killed anyone. Rise above your fear of the unknown, look down upon it as if you were a giant looking down at an ant and once you locate its small existence, lift your foot and stamp it right into extinction.

Also take a look at why the vast majority of women today in the Western world feel the need to see a psychic, medium or clairvoyant. Not just occasionally when they feel the need for some clarification and clear direction but we are talking about most of the time. For some, these people can't get enough or can't make a decision without first seeking the services from the oracle. To obsess about our future is not a healthy place to be. One needs to curb that high level of curiosity because it can easily get out of hand.

It is good to ask questions but ask them of your higher self and of your Angels. That's who you should be relying upon – not every other Tom, Dick, Harry or Jane. Whether you believe you are psychic or not, although being psychic has truly nothing to do with anything important, you still have the power to tap into the energy from the Universe and discover your own answers. I can assure you that once the true answer is received, the level of fulfilment, confidence, self-satisfaction and trust will go through the roof and it won't be easy to stop. It would not have risen so high if someone else told you about it first. You did it for yourself, by yourself.

The trick is to trust what you receive. Become your own oracle. Become your own captain. Stop giving your personal power away to strangers and even to friends or family members, simply because you have a fear of the unknown. How can you say you are in complete control of your life when in the next breath you admit to the fact that you go to a psychic on a regular basis? Where you may become reliant and dependent upon them to give you the answers for yourself. You might wish to defend your actions by saying – 'sure, I might do it on a regular basis but I only do it for the fun of it. I don't take it at all seriously.' I would then have to question – can you not find a better and more useful way to spend your money? After all, you said you don't take it seriously. It's merely a bit of harmless fun, right?

But the true fun begins from within. That may sound mundane and boring but it is true. Start trusting your own intuition. Certainly seek help from another if necessary but don't let it get out of hand.

For example, this is a little exercise for those who will speak with a psychic at least three or four times a week. It doesn't necessarily have to be the same one because you might enjoy doing the rounds, from which to compare and to judge. It's really a numbers game. The more times you do it, the more chance you have of receiving information that you do like and which is not too confronting.

But back to the exercise – I ask that for one month, you fight the desire to pick up the phone or travel to see a clairvoyant. If by the end of that time, you have become an emotional wreck due to not having your regular fix, you will then have received physical proof that your perceived harmless bit of fun has become an obsession. This reality cannot be ignored. When it becomes an obsession, it stops being harmless and it stops being fun. You then need to admit that you are an addict, not for alcohol, drugs, money, sex, coffee or chocolate but for constant confirmation and reassurance of who you are and where you are headed.

Some clairvoyants will call this group of dependants 'psychic junkies' or 'psychic vampires', yet some of those same clairvoyants will not lift a finger to stop it or help you combat your addiction either. It is these clairvoyants whose motives are based upon the dollar. Their inner thoughts would go something like this as they rub their hands with glee as they head towards the bank – 'yes, yes, yes, and all the more money for me. This is my business. Why would I want to turn away a paying customer?' Why indeed! It is these two groups I have just mentioned who are feeding off each other's bad habits.

Together, most certainly and in the short term, you make a great team because you are both getting what you need; but in the long term it doesn't work. If this happened in a personal relationship, the psychologists would call it 'co-dependency'.

Trouble begins when one doesn't want to follow the rules of the game anymore. They may not even want to play it at all or perhaps the rules have been changed but the other person was not made aware of these changes taking place. Confusion then nicely sets in and the open line of communication breaks down. So do yourself a favour – avoid this type of situation altogether if you possibly can and remember to curb your need to know all about your future and enjoy being surprised.

The most effective way of letting go or taking control of your fear of the unknown is to live in the present. As you lose yourself in the moment, you won't have time to dwell upon your fear of the future. By being involved 100% in any given moment, time stands still. It no longer exists or alternatively, it goes extremely quickly. How quickly is up to you. But when your mind is oscillating 100mph between the past and future, time seems to drag by. This also happens when you insist upon watching the clock. For these people, I would classify them as being 'minute watchers'.

Their natural habitats are various places of work, schools and sometimes worship. The second they are officially released, they are out of there. No need to dawdle. Let's now move on to someone or something much more interesting and enjoyable. These people may be suffering from the illusion that the person in charge was the 'baddie' in this case scenario and who kept them trapped against their own free will. This is not true. It was they who did it to themselves. These minute watchers are playing dual roles – that of prison warden and prisoner, yet they don't know it.

They are playing the role of prisoner or victim so well that they can't go beyond this perception. To acknowledge they are their own worst enemy would be far too painful for them to comprehend. So they don't; they run and bury their head in the sand in order to ignore the truth. But there is always a solution to any problem and that is, if you hold yourself back, then you also have the ability to push yourself forward. Believe it or not!

There is another group of people, similar to the minute watchers that deserve a quick mention. This broad category of people I would call the 'water boiler watchers'. They are the ones who stand around watching and waiting for the jug to boil. These people are also waiting and wishing for someone or something interesting to eventuate in their lives but the harder they watch and wait, it never seems to happen or if it does, it takes an awfully long time. So long in fact that they can end up losing all patience, give up in disgust and walk away seconds before success taps them on the shoulder.

This type of person will be the one desperately hanging out for that perfect soul mate, their dream job, to become an instant millionaire or to be the star of a show. This personality type will destroy the very thing they wish to bring into being by becoming annoyed if it doesn't transpire as quickly as they would like. They will then lose focus because they feel it is a waste of time and decide to look elsewhere for success. If only they had persevered that little bit more, because the very thing they were waiting for, was just around the next bend in the road. But as they lost patience and chose to change direction at the last moment, they denied themselves the very thing or someone they had craved for.

These people are normally unhappy, frustrated, annoyed and dissatisfied with their miserable lot in life. This can then lead to much envy and jealousy; wanting what another person has but never being able to achieve it for themselves. And even though they may race towards the future at full speed ahead, they have a tendency to give up moments before the future is ready to pleasantly surprise them but they will never know that because they didn't stay still long enough in the one spot to discover their dream. Although as we all know, the future will always remain that one step ahead of us.

You would understandably think the future is in control of our everyday affairs but it doesn't have to be if you don't let it. You are in a position of power while standing firmly in the present. It is there that you can reshape and redirect your future.

Be wary that as you advance upon your quest to turn the unknown into something known, which can sometimes be extremely difficult, you could easily forget about the vast array of knowledge and wisdom you already have. Why not let the unknown come to you in its own good time and not only when you think you are ready to deal with it? Never force a situation to explode in your face unless you are really, really sure. Let Spirit determine when it is time to confront what fears you the most. Nothing will ever be given that you can't handle.

Remember that ant you stamped into extinction, some lines back? It may feel like an impossible task when you come eyeball to eyeball with your fear but as you make that decision to rise above it and leave its personal space far behind, you take away its negative hold over you.

The other little thing you can do for yourself is to remove the 'un' out of the word 'un known', which then leaves you with only what is known. You may think this is a play on words again, similar to 'chance' and 'change' but all words have a power that weaves its magic web around us. These words can either caress or scratch. Personally, I would much prefer to be caressed than scratched any old day.

Why do you think affirmations are so important and can work so well? There are positive words that empower and encourage us while other words can, over a lengthy period of time, wear us down and leave us weak and defenceless – like a victim.

With an open heart, truly listen to how you speak to other people. Do you lift them beyond your capacity or alternatively, do you drag them down to a low level where it is easier for you to step on them? Begin to see the true impact of your words from their perspective rather than just your own. Some people may actually fear you because you remain unknown to them. By keeping yourself at a safe distance may then make it difficult for the viewer to see you clearly.

It's the same when you take away a person's pair of glasses that helps them to see. One look and you become some blurry furry object that has no meaning. How can one accept a concept, belief or someone that remains unclear or unknown to them?

So step forward and stand still in the light. Let others be attracted to you for who you truly are. They'll be drawn like a moth to a flame because they sense that inner strength, integrity and purpose coming from the light that is you. And while flitting closely in and around your personal space, they get to see what is now known. While the unknown can only live in darkness and like its country cousin the vampire, it's afraid to come out into the full light of day. Are you a little mushroom? Do you live in the dark?

When we place ourselves in this darkness, we stay unknown because we remain invisible to the many. This is when we can bump or crash into other likeminded souls who can't see us either; like a pair of old rust buckets, lost and colliding at sea. At the moment of impact with each other, you then put out a mayday call seeking help and when that help doesn't come immediately, you abandon ship but before you jump, you have to first make sure that you can swim; because if you can't swim, to sink is very much then an item on the menu for you to experience.

In this situation, you are not necessarily destroying yourself but you are taking other innocent people along with you for the ride. Is this fair? They may not wish to be locked up and trapped in a room filled with doom and gloom but there is always hope, for you and them. When next you're feeling glum, glum, glum, don't be dumb and hum, hum, hum. Aaahh, there you go, I'm a poet and didn't know it.

It is suggested that you ask yourself why you have this need to see your future today. Is it because you don't feel 100% comfortable living in the present? The answer to this must be 'yes' because if you felt contented about all of what is happening and how you are feeling now, there would no longer be a need to see what tomorrow can bring. Certainly, many people upon occasion will be curious to take a sneak peek into their future but don't let this same curiosity get out of control, where it becomes an obsession. Rather, play it cool.

Adopt a philosophical attitude about all matters of life and death. Relax and move into your negative experiences with ease and confidence rather than fighting against them or trying to avoid these learning situations altogether. By relaxing and letting go of the fear of what may transpire in the short or long term future, you will be creating a lot less stress for yourself. Less stress means living a longer life without disease and unease. And we all want that, don't we?

Certainly, make your plans and goals for the future, as this will give you purpose but remain flexible with your dream today because we may wish for you to change direction tomorrow, which is designed to be for your highest good. You may not fully understand why something is unfolding before you in an unexpected and sometimes unwanted way. True understanding and enlightenment will come later but it can't if you are constantly struggling against what is to be. The more you fight with yourself and others, the further you push us away. So far that you may then begin to suspect and complain about your inability to communicate with Spirit or you may direct your anger at your Angels or God because they have not given what you expected or wanted at that time.

While remaining in this negative state of mind, we cannot do anything for you directly. Certainly, we can use other people in your life to deliver an important message from us to you but if your heart, ears and eyes remain tightly closed, the message of hope and guidance may not be heard until sometime in the future when you are willing to break down some of that self-made protective barrier.

It is then through this newly created crack in your armour that sunlight can pour through and give nourishment to the seed that sleeps, patiently waiting for its queue to grow but it can only grow as fast as you will allow it. When you sabotage all hope through your negative thoughts and words, this action will stunt your personal and spiritual growth and as a result, all expansion will be painful, as it will be for those people around you.

There must always be one person in the equation in every negative situation who is willing to step aside in order to break the cycle of further destruction and despair. Why not let it be you? Don't let your fearful, stubborn or prideful streak stop you from making positive changes. One way to do this is let go of the anger you are feeling towards that other person, and sometimes towards yourself. Learn how to forgive. If you can do these two things on a consistent daily basis, good miracles can happen which will then cause you to ponder the question – why didn't I do this sooner? But be careful how you answer this.

Don't fall into the trap of beating yourself up because you didn't think of a better way of dealing with the situation earlier. Also accept that you have the ability to wipe the slate clean of your past, which then leaves you free to focus upon the present. The future will look after itself accordingly in the same way that you need to look after, love and respect yourself today. That is your number one goal, as well as learning how to tone down your fear to a reasonable level where it does not deter you from living your life's purpose. Many people at some stage in their colourful or dull existence, will wonder – what am I here for and where am I going? The answer will come when you relax and let go of all expectations and fear of the unknown.

Have no fear
of moving into the unknown.
Simply step out fearlessly
knowing that I am with you,
therefore no harm can befall you.
All is very very well.
Do this in complete faith and confidence.

Source: Eileen Caddy

Affirmations

I know that I know.

I let go and TRUST.

I will be guided to safely pass through the vast unknown, only to EMBRACE what is innately known.

JUDAS

Jesus, I ask that you lift

Up my soul in order for me not to

Drown in my own depression and help me to

Accept the person that I am today and to honestly

See that I am unique, gifted and blessed.

Let me begin by saying that I have much regret as to my past actions. I don't expect your sympathy but I do want to have the opportunity of explaining where I was coming from at that time. For ever since I could remember and as a young boy, I felt alone and apart from those around me, even in my own family. I became selfish and greedy. I wanted more than what other people could give me. I was never satisfied with what I had. Because of my inability to love myself, I could not love another, so completely and unconditionally.

There is no doubt that Jesus loved and accepted me as one of his flock but I could not return that same compliment. I was not only a traitor to Jesus, I betrayed myself. I so much wanted people – all people – to like me. As a disciple and follower of Jesus, not everybody did. Of course, this may still have happened whether I knew him or not, but life became a battle for survival. You constantly had to be looking over your shoulder every minute to make sure your enemies did not want to stab you in the back. The man Jesus caused a lot of controversy, as well as great religious and political unrest. The very fact of being associated with him was like having a dangerous love affair, which could end abruptly if not careful, by the authorities. I wanted to live. I didn't want to die and neither did the others but their faith and belief in themselves and in Jesus, was far stronger than mine.

Sadly to say, I was the group's weakest link and because of it, I destroyed something that was good. I was selfish and put my own needs first, second and last. There was no room for anyone else. You might well ask, with that type of attitude, why did Jesus choose me as a team player?

I have no doubt he had the ability to see clearly into the future of those around him and of himself. He knew what had to be done; so it might as well be me. And because of what I did, I have now become the man that Christians all over the world, love to hate. So be it, but I think it's rather ironic how all my life, I tried to avoid like the plague, people disliking me. You do indeed attract what you fear.

All I wanted was someone to love me but when it was offered, I felt unworthy of receiving it; therefore I rejected the one thing that I desired the most. How many of you can relate to this?

The cycle of denial and rejection is then repeated until we learn how to change it. I had a purpose to fulfil, as we all do. Even though my purpose was not pleasant, Jesus allowed me the freedom to carry it out with no bad thoughts, judgement or recriminations. And this, as far as I'm concerned, shows a remarkable ability to love unconditionally not only those that loved him but those people who disrespected him as well.

I am not saying that Jesus felt a deep sadness that this whole sorry situation had to arise but what could he do? Sure, he could have run and avoided his destiny, although I believe that fate normally catches up with you when you least expect it. But no, he stood his ground and accepted what was meant to happen.

I felt insecure in his presence, so when the opportunity arose to earn some extra money, I grabbed at the chance. I was well looked after but I wanted more. All I had to do was tell the authorities where they could find Jesus. In my naivety, I never believed for one moment they would crucify him.

Certainly, I understood he would stand trial for what they

had accused him of doing but I believed he would be found innocent and so be set free. As you know, the opposite happened. I wished him no harm but like any criminal of the past, present or future, it is rare that we ever stop to consider the consequences. When the sentence was passed down, I was truly horrified but did not have the power to change the outcome. From that fatal second on, I was riddled with such terrible guilt and fear. Jesus forgave me for my behaviour but I could never find it within my own heart to forgive myself. I no longer wanted to live. I no longer believed myself to be worthy of being a part of this truly wonderful world. To this end, I took my own life by hanging myself in a tree.

I knew I would be no great loss to society but was of the belief that many would mourn the death of Jesus. This I accepted quite happily and was not jealous of his popularity, although I easily could have been. By killing myself, I believed I was escaping and much preferred me doing the deed rather than having somebody else come after me in the middle of the night and terminate my life for good. I believed that by committing suicide and for the first time in my life, I was taking full responsibility for my past horrible actions.

I became my own Judge and Jury and carried out the appropriate steps I felt I deserved. Do you also do that to yourself, although in less harsh ways? We can indeed, become our own worst enemies and it can destroy us, if we let it. I must say here though, that suicide is not the answer either. Other than the obvious, where it is written that it is a sin to take your own life, there is still no escape. Life continues even after physical death. In fact, everything becomes magnified. There, you have no choice but to look at what you have done in the lifetime you just experienced.

I would like to say that it is a brave act indeed to end one's own life but it is also cowardly. You are taking the easy way out and where you see death as being a solution to your problems. This is not a healthy way to think and it's something I have long regretted.

I am sad to see and acknowledge there is so much depression, anger and loneliness in the world today. Yet, I understand it. I cannot judge those without first judging myself or to put it in biblical terms "let he who is without sin, cast the first stone". I am not without sin. I was always devising ways as to how I could make my life better and easier for myself. This in itself is not a bad thing but rarely did I follow through to completion upon my ideas. Basically, I ran out of steam and momentum.

I lacked the necessary discipline needed to persevere. If it took longer than expected for me to achieve my goal, I got bored and went on to something new and much more exciting. My personality didn't allow me to stay interested in any one thing – or person – for too long. My co-players in our little group understood this about me and so chose to be very patient and tolerant of my needs and idiosyncrasies. I was not as patient with them however, some of the time. Why does life have to be so difficult? I used to bemoan this fact during the majority of my waking moments. The answer was simple but I did not discover this until after my physical death.

Life is difficult because we make it so. What the mind can perceive, we can achieve. Negative, as well as positive thoughts and emotions can create either good or bad situations, people or karma around us. It is up to us to do something about changing anything we do not like. If you become dependent upon others to give you what you need, in time you will feel frustrated and disappointed. Sure, as young babies and young children we need definite guidance and direction but when we mature into adulthood, there is no excuse not to be independent.

Of course, I can hear some ladies think that men are perpetually like "Peter Pan", who are in need of pampering and babying all their life. This situation only comes about because they have not been allowed to fend or think for themselves and make life changing decisions. Like everything else, there has to be a balance. People like to feel needed, so we have to somehow strike a happy medium between giving and receiving. As I said about myself, I didn't know how to receive and if the truth be known, I had great difficulty in giving. This is how I continuously found myself in a 'Catch 22' position.

No matter how hard I tried, one action would always negate the other, where I then suffered greatly from inner turmoil and indecision. I was chasing my own tail, going in circles – neither going forward or backward. I sought an easy way out of my predicament.

In regards to my relationship with Jesus, I was hoping he could provide me with all the answers that I had been seeking. He did no such thing but this was done for my own good, as well as for the good of others. He treated no-one differently. Because of my association with this great and wise man, I did become a little bit independent. I was beginning to change for the better but not fast enough to my way of thinking. I wanted everything to happen instantly, right now, today or if I was feeling totally unreasonable, I wanted it yesterday.

I would have made a lousy corporate executive of a large company, who was forced to supervise and take charge of a group of people as well as handing out specific instructions. I would not have had the stomach or temperament for it and would have unfair expectations of my staff. Do you work with a boss like this and do you feel used and not appreciated? Does your boss treat you like a piece of machinery?

Jesus was so patient and quite often he would repeat the answer in different ways, until each one of us finally understood the meaning of what he said. The use of parables came in handy for this purpose.

When it came time for me to teach and guide another, invariably I would take control and finish the job off myself. This was wrong because I was interfering in someone else's learning process. Sure, I may have got what I wanted but what did they get out of it? Only a feeling of inadequacy and uselessness rose to the surface, no doubt. Which brings me back to my original point – the importance of not only yourself being independent but to be fair and allow others to do for themselves.

Think about the Golden Rule, which says – "Do unto others as you would have them do unto you". If you wish for another to respect your opinion, ideas and needs, you must first make an effort to do the same for them.

Some may hear my words of wisdom and believe I am a hypocrite and that I don't practise what I preach, where the information I pass on to you now, is useless. In answer to these possible thoughts of yours, if we were talking about that particular lifetime only, well then yes, I am a hypocrite and don't practise what I preach. You must realise though that as a soul, I have moved on.

I am not stuck in a time warp. I have learnt from my mistakes and if I can share some insights in regards to what I have done in the past, this may help you with what you are going through today. I hope this makes sense to you because it does to me.

We can always learn something from each other. I am not a completely bad person, as no-one is. We all have our good points, although they may be carefully camouflaged, as are our bad points. We only ever show a portion of our true selves. We keep a lot hidden, because we are afraid that others may not like what they see.

Jesus wore his heart and soul on his sleeve. He cried tears, just like you and me. He felt anger and great joy. From time to time, he too felt frustrated and hemmed in. He would laugh and show us his sense of humour. He would listen and empathise. He would also experience fear in all its guises. Regardless of whatever emotion Jesus was feeling at the time, whether it be positive or negative, he was not afraid to show it. This way, people knew exactly where they stood with him. He would, in no uncertain terms, let you know how he felt and what he was thinking.

Many people found his personality a little hard to accept at times because of this but I have to admit, he was one of a kind. I greatly admired him for his capacity for the truth, not only of God but of his own personal truth. Jesus, quite often had his head high in the sky while communicating with the great unseen but at the same time, he had his feet planted firmly on the ground. He acted as a go between and negotiator for the Spirit world and this earthly plane. Like the Angels, Jesus became a messenger for God and he was very effective in what he did. Not everyone listened to his words but the vast majority did and whether you like it or not, his memory still lives on in the hearts and minds of many men and women of today's society.

I used to enjoy making clay pottery jugs, urns and bowls, which were put to everyday practical use. It was a messy business but I enjoyed getting my hands dirty. Some enjoyed ploughing and tilling the fields, while others would indulge their stomachs with much food and wine. Each to their own, I guess. Even though my pottery pieces were rough and ready, they were mine – something that I created with my own two hands. It gave me a great feeling of satisfaction and fulfilment.

Pretty well much the same thing could be said, when a male and female who are bound together in love, feel such passion, enthusiasm and joy to have created a baby. The act of making love is not a difficult feat in itself. The real test and fulfilment comes only after the birth.

I am aware that some women today suffer great depression after this miraculous and grand entrance into the physical world. While for other women, the birth itself is such an anti-climax to the previous nine months and where the woman's vitality and energy can be found at their lowest. Everyone will be different, depending upon their own childhood conditioning about such matters and the level of fear or understanding. You might think as a man, how can I talk about things that I have never experienced? I can speak with authority because of two reasons.

I have had other lifetimes since being Judas and in some of those, I have come back as a woman who has given birth to a child. The other reason being, even as Judas, my older sister (by about ten years) had the pleasure of going through the same event. I saw and felt at first hand everything she went through. Even though she had much female support and companionship around her, we would spend large chunks of time together, talking, laughing and crying. Because she was older than me, I looked to her as a type of maternal figure.

Our own mother died when we were still relatively young. Our father was hardly ever there and even if he had been, I don't believe he really cared about us. We were a burden to his manhood. After the death of our mother, we were forced to fend for ourselves early on in our childhood. It wasn't easy but somehow we got through it together. You would have thought that by doing so, this would have made me independent but because my sister was basically in charge; she made many of the decisions, which I went along with, without argument. She was my one shining light, my only hope in an otherwise dull and colourless existence.

Her love and concern for me, wasn't enough though. I wanted more of her valuable time and was afraid to be by myself for long periods. I also became overly protective and as such, I caused a certain amount of tension and disharmony within our relationship. Until one day, I woke up realising I had no-one and that I was alone.

I apologise for sounding so sorry for myself. Jesus came into my life at this lowest point. At last, here was a man with a compassionate and caring nature, who would spend time with you. I loved this man for saving my miserable life and I repaid him, by ending his. It doesn't seem equal or fair, does it? Even though I had strong, positive feelings about him, I also felt fearful. It was difficult for me to look at him directly in the eyes. When he managed to make that contact, it felt like a knife had pierced my heart. I saw MY truth in his eyes and became afraid. I tried so hard to ignore what had been revealed. He never judged me but I judged myself, and rightly so, to be not a worthy subject or follower of his.

Throughout our friendship together and no matter what I did wrong, he consistently gave me another chance to prove myself. Jesus taught me about commitment and perseverance, regardless of the inner turmoil, fear and pain that it caused. We must all try and work through our fears – either real or imagined. We cannot advance quickly on a spiritual level, if we are held back by the heavy chains that keep us in the dark. We can only truly say we walk completely in the Light when we live without fear.

One of our biggest fears, for the vast majority, is the fear of death. Where do we go after we die? Because I passed over into the Spirit world in a state of confusion and depression, I never saw my God and felt cheated. However, before I came to that point of understanding after my own death, I never really knew what to believe. You could say I sat on the fence, hedging my bets. So when I made the decision to end my life, the thought of what would happen after, held little relevance to me. I saw death as a way to escape my problems.

How could I ever hold my head up high and look the other eleven men in the eye without feeling guilt, disgust and shame? I couldn't. I didn't have the guts or the heart to face my worst fear – being alone, abandoned and rejected. This is what I believed lay in wait for me, if I continued to live out the rest of my natural life. I wasn't prepared to go through all that. I couldn't. Of course, I could have given the other disciples more credit and in time, they may have found it in their hearts to forgive me but they were still human after all. They were not Gods. If our roles had been reversed, I would have sought some type of revenge and retribution.

If Jesus walked amongst us again today and I had the opportunity of working with him, I pray to God that history would not repeat itself in the way that it did, for both of us. Only time and future events can answer that thought provoking and relatively scary question.

I enjoyed sitting in the sea with all my garments on. The clothes would weigh me down considerably. The rougher the sea, the better I liked it. I obtained great pleasure in being knocked down and pushed around by the tumultuous and eternal waves. Water, in the palm of your hand or drunk from a cup, remains harmless, unless of course it has been poisoned. But when you have a large body of water coming at you all at once, to feel its intensity and power had a most humbling effect on my psyche.

It would intrigue me how rivers and even rain from above, could over a long period of time, change the shape of mountains. To my untrained eye, they appeared to be a solid mass of rock. Water, in whatever form it chooses to adopt, is a natural commodity that is a force to be reckoned with and respected. I never felt out of my depth and had no fear whilst immersed in water.

On the other hand, there was Matthew, who because of his own fear could never watch my watery escapades without some feeling of nervousness and agitation. Some might wonder; if I loved being in the sea so much, why wouldn't I choose death by drowning? This thought crossed my mind only briefly but I rejected it because it would have been too easy and relatively pleasant for me. I wanted and felt I needed to suffer some sort of pain, even if only momentarily.

The other extreme, which I was not too keen on, was to die crucified upon two pieces of wood held together in the form of a cross. This was an excruciatingly painful demise. Jesus was not the first or the last person to die in this way. Some died mercifully quick while others experienced prolonged agony. It all depended upon their level of physical fitness, endurance, stamina, inner strength, and willpower to live.

The key to success and achieving one's goals – other than perseverance, discipline and action – is patience. I believe patience, in today's society is sadly lacking. Everybody wants the whole world and Spirit to fall at their feet and do their bidding, instantly. They don't want to wait. When your heart cries out, begs and pleads for an answer in the name of God, Allah, Jesus Christ, Buddha, Mohammed, the Dalai Lama etc; we listen but we may not immediately act upon what we hear. This is not due to laziness or an uncaring attitude on our part. It simply means two things, the first of which is time.

Time is irrelevant in the Spirit world. It does not exist in the way that you think it does. There is no past, no present and no future. Secondly, your dreams will manifest themselves when the Universe deems it to be so. It is our own 'will' and 'ego' that gets in the way of our success. Let go and trust. I could say "Rome wasn't built in a day" and "all things come to those who wait" but you're not going to listen to that because it is irrelevant to your specific needs and wants of right now. What I will say then is this; your dreams – like the meaning of life – will not be handed to you on a silver platter inlaid with gold.

If only it was that simple, my life as Judas may have been completely different, as it would have been for everyone else but as I say that, if things had been different, you may not have been born at all and would not have had the opportunity to read the words of wisdom within this book. Everything happens for a reason. Patience is a virtue, as well as being a rare commodity. Please understand here that I am not saying that we were any better than you, 2000 years ago. People don't really differ all that much from one generation to the next but we do expand upon it. Like life and death, followed by life again. The cycle is repeated.

The more we live, the more opportunity we have in which to learn our lessons and to grow towards enlightenment and the Christ consciousness (or whoever it is that you believe in). Nothing is lost or destroyed. It still remains locked away within the mind and DNA.

Many people, with the exception of some doctors, nurses and scientists, truly do not understand and fully appreciate the miracle that is the human body. It is a masterpiece of engineering. Have you ever wondered about the certain timing of things? Such as, it takes nine months for a baby to be created from start to finish. Every seven years, the cells in our body are rejuvenated, which literally means we are reborn and become new again. The mind boggles at that thought, doesn't it? Every twenty eight days, a woman will begin her menstrual cycle. Every day, the blood is renewed and cleansed. How does this happen?

The full moon can affect the mood swings of certain susceptible and vulnerable people in a strange way. Women in particular follow the pattern of the moon's cycle closely. Let's face it and some of you may or may not have thought of this before but our bodies are mainly made up of water and it is the moon which controls the tides and currents of the world's oceans, rivers and seas.

Any good fisherman or sailor worth his salt knows this basic fact. When things begin to go wrong with our body and the timing is thrown all out of kilter, this is when we need to realise and accept that we are living out of balance and with disharmony. This can manifest itself in all areas of our life, not just on a physical level.

Planet Earth also reacts in the only way that she knows how when a part of her own anatomy has been destroyed or eaten away by mankind. The floodgates of Heaven shall open and the Devil's own breath can be seen and heard in the form of volcanoes and fires.

Violent and invisible winds will become like giant whirlpools and sweep everything up in its path, while the world shall shudder and experience great convulsions, which we relate to as being earthquakes. The night sky shall come alive filled with enough electrical discharges to light up a whole city or country.

There is no stopping the forces of nature once they have begun but like the human body, much of the world's illnesses and natural disasters can be avoided by learning patience; to be less demanding and more accepting of what God provides for us.

It is our own greed and selfishness that destroys us in the end. Learn to be happy for what you have and learn to refocus your thoughts away from what you don't have. A person born blind has no concept of what an apple looks like but by the sense of touch, taste and smell; he can still experience the reality of the apple. This blind person doesn't miss what he never had and this is good. You don't need to feel sorry for such people. They are still experiencing life to the best of their ability and who are we to judge whether something or somebody is normal or abnormal? Who decides this and what gauge is used?

If a person suffers from some other physical or mental disorder, does this mean they are any less worthy than you or me? It is to these people, we should give our heartfelt thanks. Because their specific purpose in the world is to help teach us some important lessons such as being non-judgemental, patience, acceptance, compassion and being fearless. Don't be frightened of those who are different from you and never feel powerless when in the presence of someone who cannot speak your own language. A smile and hug will suffice. Even animals understand this basic rule of thumb.

Unconditional love transcends all difficulties, whether it relates to the physical, emotional, mental, spiritual or religious aspect of a person's life. That same love is also the world's greatest healer. If you can accept that as being fact, then does it not make sense to then take it one step further and act upon that love to heal yourself of all your pain and illness? Or do you not believe you have this ability? Faith plays a large role in any form of healing, whether it be traditional Western medicine, new age alternative treatments or the ancient remedies of the East.

I look above and see an eagle in flight. This is a most wondrous sight. As hard as I might wish, I will never be able to fly with it. This causes me some distress. With today's jet propelled aeroplanes and other flying machines, you have come pretty close to this impossible dream. The advances in technology and science in just the last century have been phenomenal. But have you ever asked yourself exactly where is it all taking us? Are you moving further away or closer to your Creator?

If you are moving away, is this really important in the overall big scheme of things? Only you can decide upon these answers, in your own time and once received, you then need to discern upon which direction you want to take. Some say space travel is the final frontier in which to travel and explore. This is not entirely correct.

There is much more exploration to be done in the 4th, 5th,

6th and 7th dimensions and beyond. The knowledge to do so is not quite there yet and with good reason but when it does surface in your society, it will open a doorway or portal to a new and different world to the one you perceive today with your physical eyes alone.

Some have already seen glimpses of life beyond our range of vision and understanding. This shall continue until the day when there is a collective group of people who will come together in peace and pool their separate ideas and resources in order to fit all the missing pieces of the jigsaw puzzle together.

Many astronomers, astrophysicists, scientists and ufologists, as well as the ordinary man and woman on the street have often looked to the vastness of the Heavens above and wondered – are we alone in the Universe? Is there somebody out there? The answer is yes. Although 2000 years ago, to entertain such a radical thought process by the majority would have been near incredulous.

Times have changed since then – some for the better, while other advances are not so good. In any moment of history, whether it be three, two thousand or five million years ago, we will be shown and guided just enough for our minds to digest and understand the information given. Even today, each individual will only be confronted by those situations and people that we can handle. Although I do know that those of you who feel you cannot cope with your life problems, would understandably and vehemently disagree with me. A new cycle of a major shift in awareness has begun and it can't be stopped.

Some of you already know and accept this as being your reality. It will come upon each person like a tidal wave. You will then be given a choice; you can either sink or swim. Or put in a slightly different way, it will either make or break you. This depends upon your own personal beliefs, to what extent you are willing to let go of your fears and how willing or not willing you are to change. Taking all of the above into consideration, the decision is entirely left in your hopefully, capable hands. The acknowledgement and existence of Spirit, or God, cannot do this for you. If you are completely genuine in your desire for help and assistance, it will be given but not always in the way that you expect.

Many Christians have become disillusioned and have lost their faith, because they are of the belief that their cry for help has gone unheard and how their prayers seemed to have only magnified the original problem. Many will blame the church for its lack of support and to some extent, this is true. On the surface, your problems may appear to be a lot worse but on a much deeper spiritual level, it is what's needed to force that person to explore the very depths of their heart and soul and come to a heightened self-realisation and inner strength to move and break through all obstacles. I never achieved this while living in the skin of Judas but I have had a long time in which to ponder these things and come up with some pretty clear cut answers.

For example, learn from the mistakes of others. If you are able to put this one concept to practical use, it then becomes near impossible for us to judge another harshly, even those we may not particularly like, for whatever reason. Turn around, fall gratefully upon your knees and thank them for helping you to see the facts for yourself. This is part of what turning the other cheek is all about.

Fear of Not Having Enough Money

Many of us are never satisfied with what we have. We either stress about lack of money and bemoan or feel jealous about what others have or at the other end of the scale; we complain we have too much money, therefore who can be trusted?

Money is merely another form of energy. Money is not evil. It is the person handling it who needs to be judged, not the money itself. Look at me for example. I was not evil – misguided yes, dissatisfied yes, scared yes, ashamed yes, selfish yes but evil – no. Although others may perceive me as being so but really, what is evil? Are there varying degrees of evil? And if yes, how does one deal with or punish that same evil? How did I deal with it?

In the end, I chose to escape through physical death although in reality, the escape I was wishing for was so much different to what I found. I still had to face my fears and yes, my sins as well, like it or not. Life in the Spirit world became so much worse for me and some might say that I received my 'just deserts' or karma had finally caught up with me and my wicked ways.

I can accept this and in many ways, I too am disgusted about the way I acted towards not only Jesus but to the other Apostles as well. To speak of the following experience is extremely painful because by doing so, I have to acknowledge that I did do wrong with no ifs or buts about it and there was nothing I could do, or perhaps I should say that I was not willing to do anything, about changing it.

Since then, up to and including today, I have and am still making amends for my mistakes. I can hear many exclaim 'and so you should'. The time for avoiding the painful truth is well over. Do you do that sometimes too and if yes, does this necessarily make you a thoroughly through and through evil person? Perhaps I should allow you to answer this question for yourself and once you have the answer, then compare yourself with me.

Okay, the facts are I was given the opportunity to act like their bank manager (yes I know, in today's society, the mere mention of the word bank conjures up impressions of mistrust). The Eleven entrusted me to look after their finances. More fool them because I ripped them off something bad but they never knew it.

They didn't recognise what I was doing because I was far too subtle for that. Whatever they earned or was given, I would skim some money off the top for myself. Bank managers, publishers, talent or real estate agents, producers, solicitors, politicians, accountants and more all take their commission for looking after another person's affairs. I wouldn't feel so bad talking about this if they had known but I repeat they did not know what I was doing.

I could say well what you don't know won't hurt you but this is only a temporary illusion which can easily be shattered. It's certainly not fair what I did and it was wrong. If I had been more upfront with them at the outset and they all agreed that I should receive a little extra for my effort, this would have been okay but the truth is, it didn't happen like that.

I didn't just betray Jesus; I destroyed all semblance of trust in regards to my fellow brothers. Although as I mentioned earlier, I didn't need to deal with this issue until I passed over into the Spirit world and there I most certainly did. To admit to such dishonesty and underhandedness is quite terrible for me but I now believe that divine truth will set me free and I do deserve to be free, as you too deserve that same freedom from living a lie.

While growing up, I experienced what it was like to be truly poor – both materially and spiritually but the issue of spiritual abundance always took a back seat to the material wealth that I craved for. This attitude stayed with me almost to the day I died.

When I had a change of heart about the importance of spiritual abundance, too much damage had already been done due to my greed and purely selfish ways, which I later paid dearly for in regards to what I felt in my own heart later.

I learnt that friendship and trust is always far more important than money but by the time I realised this, I felt I had no friends because through my actions, I destroyed their trust. And because I considered I no longer had any friends after my betrayal of Jesus, to contemplate life on my own or to start again in a new place was too unbearable to even think about. I was afraid to accept the punishment I expected to receive in regards to what I did. I felt I could no longer live a lie, at the same time lacking the courage to speak my truth.

I had already hurt enough people, why hurt them more by expressing what I truly feel to those who believed they could trust me but could not? If I had come clean after the fact, I would have rejected all offers of forgiveness, pity, compassion and understanding because I believed I deserved to receive none of their goodness. All of the abovementioned factors formed a part of my decision making process to end my life in a way which I felt was appropriate.

Lots of or lack of money can easily cause a massive rift between two or more people. It's hard enough to deal with in a business sense but it's so much worse when a long standing personal relationship or friendship is destroyed because of it. In actuality, it can be quite devastating to the one who has been abandoned and betrayed, where they are left holding the bag full of worthless dirt or an empty wallet.

Sometimes these same people who have been ripped off, depending upon their personality, can either feel angry towards the person who has robbed them blind and so embark upon a personal vendetta against them. They may alternatively have enough spiritual understanding to forgive that person, "for they know not what they do". A third option is to turn around and blame themselves for the whole sad and sorry mess, where they lacked clarity of vision and foresight into the future.

This last group of people will question – why didn't I see it coming? They will make such remarks as – 'I'm such an idiot for trusting this person and because of my stupidity, I guess I got what I deserved which in this case is nothing, as well as thinking – why did I ignore all the early warning signs? Why didn't I listen to my friend who tried to tell me the truth about this person? More fool me.'

Sadly, it is this very same group of people who cannot let go of their own mistake of not seeing the truth about another much sooner, then end up hating themselves more than the person who did them wrong. That is why it is suggested to never loan money to family or friends.

It can sometimes be a disaster waiting to happen although,

out of every bad situation, there is always a life changing and valuable lesson if you care to look. At which time you have to decide where you fit in the overall big picture. Do you stay being a victim, do you give up and become a quitter or do you tremble in your boots and remain frightened and mistrusting for the rest of your life?

Or as an alternative measure, do you pick yourself up again and play the role of survivor, as well as standing up for your rights and take the necessary steps to gain justice? What role you play will determine how you feel about material wealth as opposed to spiritual abundance. I now believe one can have both, in balance, for it is those people who have the best of both worlds, at the same time as being truly blessed.

The earning, spending or investing of money can be a good thing. Let's face it; many more dreams can come into fruition if you have the right amount of money. Money can never buy you true friends or happiness but it can still be used in practical ways to help another person live a better life. For example, money is needed to build and staff more hospitals, schools, research institutes, universities, charities, farming co-ops, police stations, shops and so on, can all be brought into being to educate and care for our fellow brothers and sisters who may in some way be in need.

It is not money itself that is bad but it has everything to do with the person holding on to the purse strings instead that needs to be judged as being either wise and honest, or not. Forget about what I did for a minute when I say that I believe God did not want us to live and die struggling, so it is okay to acquire material wealth.

Now before you shoot me, I wish to add, just as long as this is balanced with the spiritual aspects that surround the issue of money today. Don't cling or hold on too tight to money. Let it flow freely through your fingers, accept your right to have it but also let it go. It needs to move easily in the two different directions. The less you give away, the less you will receive and this principle does not apply only to money. Many people worry unnecessarily about how they are going to pay their bills. This is not needed. Trust that all of what you need will be provided for.

You might think, how can I say that? It's too easy for me to say that from my perspective now and besides that, there is no possible use in the Spirit world for money and material possessions, is there? This is correct but the fact still remains that I am not totally ignorant about the financial plight of others. Remember, I've been there and done that. My mistake was that I dealt with this problem in the wrong way which led me into even deeper trouble.

Face up to your guilt if necessary. You need not become envious and jealous of another person's material wealth. You most certainly can appreciate the richness they surround themselves with but do not despair if you have less than them, as this may not be the truth. They may have a lot of material possessions and money but does this make them happy? You on the other hand may have many people in your life that you give love to and receive love from on a daily basis that enriches your life beyond anything you could ever imagine in regards to material wealth. Overall, who is better off, you or them?

Lots of money does not provide a 100% guarantee of happiness or peace of mind. In fact, it can get quite lonely at the top, where the rich man or woman is continually looking over their shoulder, wondering who they can trust today. Again, there is that word again – trust. Never put mental or emotional restraints upon how much money you can or cannot receive but while having and maintaining a certain standard of expectation, to stay flexible and release that which no longer belongs to you.

If someone has offered you a product or service, you pay the required price. This is only fair as you would expect the same if you were the one providing the service rather than receiving it. To hold on to great wads of money, or a person, that is well past their use by date, is courting with danger. Things can then happen in an instant, which is out of your control; that will then force you to give up what you desire.

It's all too easy to harshly criticise another for having too much money including what the recipient or owner chooses to do with it. As you point the finger at someone, there are four more pointing right back at you, which can do a lot of damage when you least expect it. Besides, four of anything can do a lot more harm than a mere one can.

But for now, let's take a jump back to the area of judging another. If you were totally honest about it, you would see the very thing you hate about another person's wealth is the same thing you would love to have for yourself. As humans, we naturally want and sometimes demand what the other person is having and if we are really out of balance, we steal from what other people have.

We don't want to miss out on any of the action, money and fun in the sun. We are afraid to do without, not only money but also love. These are the two biggest issues that cause the most dissention and unrest in the world today at all levels of society. Everyone is affected in some way due to lack of or too much money and love.

You would then think that if every man, woman and child

were given the same amount of money and love to keep them happy for the rest of their lives, they would at last feel satisfied with that same capped level of abundance in two, five or ten years time. But would they end up wanting more than what they had? Can a person ever truly feel contented with their lot in life? Is peace of mind a mere figment of our overactive imaginations?

How many really 'big' Gold Lotto winners never pay for another chance to dip into the same pot of gold again that made them rich in the first place and which sits at the end of the eternal rainbow that never ends? How many times do we have to receive before taking a step back and allowing another person who is less fortunate than ourselves, a better chance of winning what we have? Do we wish to block their way due to the possibility of them surpassing or outdoing us? But if we take steps to become an obstacle to another's abundance, how would we feel if the same was done to us? "Tit for tat". It's not nice is it, when you are on the receiving end of misfortune and hardship?

I know I've asked a lot of thought provoking questions but it is you who will be answering them and now there is just one more to add to the growing collection of questions. If you had all the money that you ever wanted or needed, what would you do with some or all of it, to make the world a better place to live in? Don't reply too hastily.

Give it your time and serious consideration. You may think what a waste of time because this would never come to pass anyway, so why bother dreaming of something that is not possible? In answer to that, we are doing exactly this a good majority of our time, especially when we take time out from work to daydream or fantasise what could have been or could be.

By fully participating in this exercise will give you a big clue as to what you can do on a personal level to bring about change in your own life first which will ultimately affect every other living soul upon this planet. Let's face it, if we all had a change of heart or attitude for the better and took steps to turn an impossible dream into a possible reality in our own lives, this then would have a domino or snowball effect where everyone would positively be touched by it and where everyone would receive the same amount of goodness and abundance, in more ways than one.

Arguing with another over lack of money will achieve nothing positive. Arguing over other irrelevant matters will have a nil positive return as well. Money can always be ripped up, cut or melted down at any time where it then becomes a useless pile of rubble, ash and old metal.

Money, like each of our lives (or just this life if you don't believe in reincarnation), is impermanent, so it is best not to become too attached to its existence. The moment you fear letting go of the money you desire, that is when money becomes your master and where you become its slave. You become powerless. Yet when other people look at a rich man from the outside, they think that rich man is in complete control. But what is control? What is power?

Power and control comes from within. Money, on the other hand, as an inanimate object, devoid of all feeling and conscious thought and which has no arms, legs or a mouth from which to speak, has no real power or control over what it does. This is determined by its owner until one fateful day, the person who was in control becomes obsessed and possessed by what money can do or buy for them. This is when money gets the upper hand and this is the way it will stay until the slave who used to be a master of his own destiny, lets go of their burning obsession to possess and be possessed.

Money doesn't need to be a dirty word in your vocabulary. It can either be bad or it can be good, depending upon how you wish to view it. Some spend thrifts need to realise that money doesn't grow on trees. It's also useless in believing your fairy Godmother or sugar daddy will wave their magic wand and make all your financial problems disappear, never to be seen again and even if they could, there would be other problems to replace it.

Have realistic hope for the future but don't fool yourself either. Remain positively realistic. Go ahead and have your dreams and goals to strive for but aim for self-fulfilment and self-satisfaction first and then the money will naturally follow. It's our actions and the words that we utter that make us feel good about ourselves, not money.

So what's a fair price for someone to pay for your time, energy and expertise? This will vary according to the type of position you are holding and from which country you are living or operating your business from. It is the Governments to a large extent that will determine what is paid, which employers are bound to follow, at the same time as paying the necessary taxes and superannuation for each person in their employ. Money is big business in the corporate world, as well as in private and public enterprises, whether they are large or small. Everyone is affected, not only the employer and employee but their families as well, who rely upon the money earned, as well as the one who is working for a living or managing a business.

If that all stops and the person who once worked can't get other employment immediately, or they have not enough money to start another business, it can be scary and who are both forced to receive financial hand outs or incentives given to them by the Government. Some are more than happy to allow this but some are not. It greatly depends upon your personal work ethic. Some who are having to accept welfare, or not, can develop over a period of time, low self-esteem. They begin to think they are worthless and have nothing to contribute to society. They lack self-confidence, become bitter and angry at everyone, especially to those in authority which may then force that person into a life of crime in order to feed their personal habits and expectations.

Upon entering this world of shade and light, it can be hard to escape from, because it can become quite intoxicating and thrilling. Some criminals would admit they quite enjoy living on the edge, never knowing what the next day may bring and to be in control over the lives of others who may beg them for mercy. They are snubbing their noses at authority where they feel invincible, powerful and strong. They could develop a godlike attitude where they expect that nothing or no-one can ever hurt them again from atop of the high pedestal they have created for themselves, even when the law finally does catch up with them. Because, the laws of nature dictate that what goes up must always come down.

But before this happens and sometimes in spite of it, some people will still persist in going down the track filled with inner turmoil and darkness. They have a taste for it, it's in their blood, they know how easy it can be to obtain money, drugs and other material possessions as a result of either committing or organising crime and once it's in your blood, it can become hard to shift. Rehabilitation and conversion can still happen with these rebels of society but sometimes not. Again, it all comes down to each individual's personal priorities and the standards they have set for themselves and whether or not they are happy to stay at the bottom of the food chain, which can often but not always happen, if you choose to earn your money in an honest and hard working way.

There are many who have made it to the top of their field this way and where they are truly being of service to the many and not just to themselves. Be satisfied with what you have. I know, look at what happened to me. I ended up dead; hanging from a tree because of guilt, frustration, greed and dissatisfaction. So, wherever you are on the food chain, please learn from my mistakes and do it the easy way. History does not always need to repeat itself.

If you can, lower your expectations and believe in your heart that whatever job you may do in life, you are being of service to at least one person per day. This is reality, otherwise the position, service or product you are offering would not have been created in the first place, if it wasn't so.

And if you can't find appropriate employment to match your skills, create your own job opportunity and become your own boss but if you do this, please understand that to be the boss has its own set of problems too, even when you are working for yourself and by yourself. There are always creditors and customers to deal with and even when you treat them right, some will attack you unfairly and become driven to destroy the business you have built up, simply because they don't like the colour of your eyes and skin or they may see you as a personal threat to their security or they don't want to live with the knowledge that you are now making more money than them.

In short, there are advantages and disadvantages of being an employer and employee, employed and unemployed. You must weigh up carefully the pros and cons of each situation before committing yourself to a way of life which could make you unhappy and which may have disastrous effects upon all those you come in contact with. The choice is always yours to make, believe it or not.

Manage your money wisely, whether it is a little or a lot. Don't squander it away uselessly or cling on to it for dear life. Whatever money comes your way, make it a regular practice to put aside 80% towards paying your bills and then give yourself the remainder that is stored away in a safe place which is not necessarily a bank. This 20% is your indulgence money that you can either save for something special one rainy day, immediately get and do something nice for yourself or give it away to a friend, stranger or charity organisation in need just because you want to. Be practical about your money affairs.

Any financial expert will tell you that by splitting all moneys received into these proportions mean that all those people who have provided you with a service or product, worthwhile or not, gets paid for their energy, while at the same time not forgetting about your own personal needs and wants. By doing this, the doors of abundance will be opened unto you. The more you give freely without fear or expectation, the more it will flow back to you.

This law or principle also works with love, where one day soon, you will wake up and realise you do have an excess of love and money which you won't always know what to do with. I hear you laughing in disbelief as you naturally think to yourself – and pigs might fly while hell freezes over.

Prove it to yourself by putting this exercise into practice. That is, creating an 80/20 split of your finances. Do it for three months and see how much happier and more confident you feel about yourself. If by chance it does nothing for you and your money situation has gone from bad to worse (which it won't), then you have my permission to stop and go back to your old ways of either spending everything you have immediately upon receiving it or letting it go at a slow trickle that can hardly be seen or perceived by yourself and others.

Money is not the root of all evil as many people think it is. It simply becomes an energy tool which can be used in the wrong way, as can happen with anything else. It is the person wielding this tool, high above their head like a sword, which needs to be closely monitored and scrutinised, not the money itself.

Cave of Abundance

I am standing upon a rock in the middle of a freshwater lake that is bordered by lush tropical rainforest. Birds of all shapes, sizes and vivid coloured plumage fly together as a group, just in front of me. It's like as if they are directing my eyes to see beyond their physical existence and look in a certain direction. Their plan, if it was a plan, worked.

I noticed a waterfall cascading down a sheer cliff face. It looks inviting and invigoratingly cool. I step off my secure and steady rock and swim with confidence towards the waterfall. It feels as if I am swimming through the shimmering softness of blue green silk. Within moments, I reach my destination and allow the full force of the water to cleanse my body and soul.

It's so great to be alive and to be at this magical spot today. Thanks are most definitely in order. I close my eyes and breathe in the goodness that surrounds me. I then hear a sound like a thousand silver bells, ever so tiny. This causes me to open my eyes and look around for its source. That's strange; it's coming from behind the waterfall.

That is when I spy a very small opening into the cliff face. I move closer and the bells rang out loud, whilst at the same time shattering any residual barriers or obstacles I continue to carry with me. I followed their soothing sound, not knowing where I was being taken to. All I could do was trust. I entered the cave. It is so *unnaturally light in here. I wonder why? But it feels so good, so it can't be wrong, can it?*

I walk further forward into the light and quite literally stumble over a wise old man with a head full of thick silvery grey hair, wearing a blindingly white robe complete with a stunning pair of Angel wings. We make eye contact, our souls connect and we smile as our hearts sing. I've come home again. I have finally arrived to where I need to be but what comes next?

In answer to my question, the old man replies that I have been guided here today to receive my reward. Because I have been an excellent student, he will grant me three wishes. This is even better than have your own personal genie. I knew exactly how I should answer – I wanted good health physically and mentally, to have the freedom to take from a treasure chest of material and spiritual wealth at any time and be given access to the wisdom of the Universe. These three wishes were granted in an instant.

My body, mind, heart and soul sing out in unison, as I recognise my truth. I now have everything I always wanted. Who could ask for more when you are happy, healthy, wealthy and wise? I am indeed truly blessed.

The old man then suggested I come here when needed as I begin to feel poorly about myself or worry about lack of money but after having said all that, he also invited me to return at any other time in between. This is a place of enlightenment and richness. It's not a place of greed or ego. It's about respecting my right to project and accept an abundant and successful attitude towards all aspects of my life. I give thanks once again to my personal Angel who has my own best interest at heart.

Source: Shontara

Affirmations

I open my heart and arms to RECEIVE.

I AM BLESSED and give thanks for all the wealth given to me.

*I don't just feel but know I AM RICH,
way beyond my wildest dreams.*

THOMAS

To thine own self be true.

Help me to see clearly the truth

Of all people and situations that I

May find myself involved with and help me to

Ask the right questions that will lead me to establish a very

Special and long lasting link with Spirit.

You would have to classify me as being the world's best known sceptic and many centuries after, they are now calling people like myself 'doubting Thomas'. This makes me laugh. What a thing to be remembered for. I certainly created an image and reputation that would stick in the minds of complete strangers that has continued quite successfully even to this day.

How would you like people to remember you, after you die? Write your own obituary notice and design your own epitaph; one that you wish to be seen on your own tombstone. I can guarantee if you can do such a weird and inexplicable thing, it will help give you some sort of future direction. That information can then be turned into a lifetime ambition or goal.

Even if after doing that little writing exercise and you then put it away in a drawer in order to forget it, on a higher spiritual level it is not forgotten and without any conscious effort on your part, you will be guided to move down that path you have chosen to possible notoriety and remembrance.

So please think seriously before you begin this project and for goodness sake, keep it positive and not negative. Never wish or desire for anything or anybody that you're not quite sure of wanting. If you do, you are treading into dangerous waters. But now it's back to my scepticism.

To have this 'quality' is a good thing to a certain degree. On the up side of the coin, it is used as a protective mechanism to guard against believing any falsehoods, because it's hard to save face after you've been conned and where quite often, you are left with no recourse.

On the down side of this equation, scepticism can inhibit your experiences and limit your joy and spiritual growth. If you choose to cross over that fine line, where you exist mainly in that area of darkness, you are holding yourself back from living life to your fullest potential, in every sense of the word.

I guess the bottom line is that doubt stems from a lack of trust. What happens when there is no trust in a relationship or where you doubt your abilities?

It's not hard to figure out – misunderstandings, great sadness, anxiety, worry and wrongful accusations arise and all those good things that you once had in your life will begin to naturally crumble and fall apart before your very eyes. Once this process has begun, it is awfully difficult to stop and fix. If your trust and faith in yourself or someone else has been destroyed or betrayed, it's hard to get back and because of its insidious nature, you will find it near impossible to forgive and forget. When this stage is reached and believe me it doesn't happen overnight, you will experience much disharmony in your life on a major scale and you will begin to experience a variety of illnesses and diseases in varying degrees, which when combined with that doubt and fear of failure and people in general, will bind you to the spot. It's not a very happy picture I'm painting is it?

For this I am sorry but it cannot be avoided. The truth is quite ugly sometimes. What happens when water stays still for too long? It becomes stale and stagnant. Are you at that point where you believe your life is like that stale and stagnant water? If the answer is yes, let go and believe. Change that crisis of identity into a positive.

It's good to question things and the motives of other people, although it is essential to acknowledge your own motivations and actions taken or spoken in any situation as well but not to the extent where you completely lose the purpose and meaning behind what is said. There is such a thing as analysing and intellectualising what we hear, to death. When this is achieved, that is when we cross over the boundary line and step into confusion.

It is all well and good to seek out the varying opinions, but if done too much and if you rely upon the information received from others as being your only lifeline, then once again, you will be thrown into confusion when things do not go according to your perceived plan.

At that point too, and if you are that way inclined, you will begin to blame others for your misfortunes – justified or otherwise. Whether you like it or not and when you're ready to accept it, with blame also comes forgiveness. If we cannot forgive the sins or wrong doings of those people who have hurt the ones that we love or us, we will then take some mighty large steps to stunt our spiritual growth. Or when we begin to rely upon a single person or group of people to give us daily loving sustenance and courage, there could come a time when all of that will fall apart and where we begin not to receive what we come to believe is our right.

We then experience the same feeling of Humpty Dumpty when he so rudely and unexpectedly fell off the wall. In that situation, no one, least of all Humpty Dumpty, was able to help fix the problem. Too much irreparable damage had already been done.

When you're dealing with people giving out good and helpful advice, as was Jesus, with that always comes a certain amount of responsibility and obligation to ensure the continued wellbeing of the person who has come seeking your guidance. Be firm, fair and gentle with the words that you speak. Jesus had the ability to do this with me and everyone else he came in contact with.

Jesus was different from many others because he still allowed everyone to learn their own lessons and sometimes this was done the hard way. He never stopped us from experiencing life and all of its many ups and downs. He would never try and control a situation that would benefit him exclusively. He always made time to listen and never judged.

If you should find yourself playing the same role as a teacher and guide, try not to destroy a person's self-confidence by undermining their opinions because if you do so, the table can easily be once again turned upon yourself, where you will find the respective roles that you play are reversed.

How do you feel now – unworthy, inadequate, insecure, doubtful? All of this sounds like me or should I say, it used to be. Do you feel like this? What is one to do?

Be patient. If at first you don't succeed, try, try again. Yes, I am well aware that you have heard this tired and old, much repeated cliché. In writing circles, using them must be avoided at all costs. But if it has the desired positive effect on a person's psyche, then what's the harm? With repeated and wide-spread use on a daily basis, affirmations can easily become a cliché of tomorrow. Does that then mean we are to automatically disregard them because they have outlived their purpose and usefulness?

Like old people. Many of us will turn our back upon this large part of society. If you do this, examine your heart closely and ask why this is.

There could be many reasons and to us and on the surface, they may all appear to be quite valid and justified. Perhaps, if you're young, you may ignore the elderly because you don't want to be reminded that this frail little person standing, sitting or lying opposite could one day, be you. 'No' you scream. 'Not I. I never want to be so old and crotchety.' Some may feel bored with the repetitive nature of conversations they have with the 'grey rinse' set, with their incessant memories of the good old days. You've heard it all before so why should you sit there feeling frustrated when there are many more interesting and worthwhile things to do? Why indeed?

Some are so afraid of being in the company of the elderly because there is the real possibility of them dying in front of them as a result of an unexpected heart attack or they could possibly choke on a fish bone. What is one to do when faced with such a problem? Do you stand your ground, hold their hand and make them feel comfortable and not scared in their last few moments of life? Do you run and seek professional help? Are you capable of providing first aid to a person in need? If you do know what to do, are you able to move into action when needed? Being faced with the death of another, forces us to feel vulnerable and powerless. Many cannot handle this reality.

Besides which, you have nowhere to run except to confront your own fear of death, because yes, one day you will die too. This fact greatly saddens a large portion of today's society but in the future the whole subject of death and dying will not be so overwhelmingly scary or important. It will become easier to accept, with no regrets.

There are four main reasons why people fear death. These are not listed in any priority order as every individual will think differently and they are: fear of the unknown; not wanting to say goodbye; not wanting to let go of those people and material possessions that we love and still desire; and realistically, a good majority of the world's population are not willing to experience a painful and long lingering death and I can't say that I blame them for thinking like this.

Many wish to die in their sleep or if that's not an option, to die quickly, as they don't want to feel the grief and regret engulf them. Some of you are aware that worrying about the details of our death in regards to the when, where, why and how is all irrelevant because we have already chosen for ourselves in the Spirit world how, where and when our final journey will take place. This is decided and agreed upon by yourself and God before you chose to reincarnate again into the physical body that you possess today. And so, it is written.

By demanding proof or evidence of some extra or out of the ordinary event, destroys the magic of the moment. It limits our joy and suppresses our natural childlike emotions of wonderment, ecstasy and enthusiasm towards all things that are, on the surface, unexplainable.

An explanation for why we experience these extraordinary situations does exist and is forever present, lurking in the background. Each one of us has the power to tap into that Universal pool of knowledge to find the answer.

The sad thing is though, because of our doubt, lack of awareness and fear of the unknown, when we do receive the necessary information to understand, we reject it outright and declare it's not possible.

Yet in the next breath, you declare there must be some logical explanation. Logical or illogical, what's the difference? The difference lies in the area of our perception of life and death, the way in which we communicate, how we make decisions and how we come to a specific conclusion. Because of our uniqueness and individuality, a variety of explanations can be found for any event, so who's to say that one answer is right while the other is wrong? Truth is a personal thing and if both parties involved feel strongly that they are right, who are we to try and change their minds? Even if you don't agree with someone else's viewpoint, opinion or philosophy, we do not have the authority to go miles out of our way to try and convince them otherwise. Even Jesus never did that.

I was always given the freedom to either believe or disbelieve. Of course, there is always room for a lively debate or discussion on a particular area of interest or conflict but that is where it needs to end. Insisting that someone give up their beliefs for your own is interfering with that person's right of freewill; their right to choose. In your immediate circle of family, friends and work colleagues ask yourself this question for each individual concerned – do I expect them to change in order to suit my own personal needs? Is the answer always 'yes' or is it sometimes 'no'?

Constantly evaluate your motives by looking honestly at what you do, think, feel or say to and about others. Because the only beliefs you can change are those that originate from within yourself, if you so choose.

A life without a dream is a life not worth living. It is most important to strive towards a goal, whether it be large or small and once achieved, for goodness sake, please be happy with it. Give yourself a pat on the back for a job well done. Many people go through life with their eyes half closed and cannot see or acknowledge many of their achievements. This, over a long period of time, leads to feelings of being useless but in reality, if they could take the blinkers off, even if for a brief moment, they would see that they have done many useful and practical things. Many people compare themselves to those in their immediate environment. To compare is to judge and this can do a lot more harm than not.

But the good we see in somebody else may not be seen at all by that other person. They may perceive that which is the total opposite. For example, you may think they are the perfect shape and size but they might see themselves as being fat and grossly overweight. To try and bolster another person's self-confidence and self-esteem, can be a most frustrating and thankless task. After a while, if there is no success and where your compliments are forever being rejected, the one doing the bolstering will give up and walk away. Where does that then leave the recipient?

The other case scenario is where some thoughtful and good Samaritan will appear to be making progress in helping another but what happens when it stops, for whatever reason? There might have been some disagreement or disharmony between the two people concerned and one decides to end the relationship or friendship. Perhaps they had to leave the area in which they lived and worked or, heaven forbid, the one assisting decides to just up and die. It can happen you know and sometimes, without notice. Let's look now at the receiver of all this lovely attention.

On the surface they appear to have been improving their outlook and belief about themselves but sadly, this false confidence has been built upon someone else's ideals. Once this fact has been removed from the equation, the apparently solid foundation we built up around ourselves, collapses and crumbles under the heavy weight of being responsible for our own actions and feelings.

In order to become our own person, we must first be

independent and rely upon ourselves to do the right thing. Being dependent upon another is just putting a bandaid upon a major problem in the hope it might repair itself. There are no easy, quick fix solutions.

Self-esteem, self-confidence and belief in oneself must first come from deep within. It must come from the heart. We are very much like a rose – without love, self-nourishment and nurturing, the rose, which is representative of our body, heart and soul will wither and die. It cannot hope to survive.

In order for us all to evolve as a soul, we need to work at our own pace and in our own way, irrespective of whether our loved ones, family, work colleagues and friends believe we are wrong and being totally stupid. Take a leaf out of Frank Sinatra's book. He did it 'his' way and you must do it your own way, as I have done as well.

Be aware of what your feet or legs are feeling and experiencing at all times. It is this part of our body that governs the direction we go in, not only in a physical sense but on a spiritual level as well. Although I said 'feet and legs', I include the touchy toes, our muscles and bones in this area as well. Does it ache somewhere really badly? Is it broken or merely sprained? Do we feel weighed down, tired and lethargic after walking even a short distance? How are your toenails – are they dry, brittle and cracking or are your nails so long, they look like bird talons which could easily do a lot of damage to another, if not to ourselves? Even though the knees play a part in our direction, they also relate to humility and subservience. Can you freely bend your legs? Do you suffer from arthritis?

These questions and many more, are interesting things to ponder but ponder you must. Change your direction if need be, slightly or otherwise, and when you do, take note of whether your physical problem has disappeared along with making the change.

What I'm about to say may sound completely gross for both Christians and non-Christian people alike. If you can look beyond the surface and learn to appreciate the symbology of this act, miracles will truly happen. New business ventures and personal opportunities will present themselves on a regular basis, left, right and centre. You will know in your heart what is right for you to do. Always trust your first impressions, your gut instincts, your intuition.

Now I have spoken about the benefits, let's go back to that which can make all of the above – and more – happen. *Wash your feet in the blood of Christ. Let them soak for a little while. Allow the Spirit of Christ to lead you. Let go of that control that we desire to have, over our destiny. Trust.*

Don't be like me. I was too afraid to trust completely. Sure enough, I finally got to see the light and no longer needed physical proof but I regret a lot of that particular past as I sometimes feel – even now – I have missed out on so many blessed and magical moments. Don't make the same mistake as I have done, if at all possible.

Part of the reason why this book is being written, is for the reader to see the pitfalls that The Twelve needed to go through for their own personal growth and for you to learn ways to avoid the same thing from happening to you. We put our lives in your hands, for your dissection and analysis. You are then free to do with this information as you see fit. It's your choice. I can't tell you what to do as no-one can but please, try your best to maintain a positive and trusting attitude about all your experiences and relationships.

To forgive is divine, to blame is human. Which one do you

overall, aspire to be? Any journey undertaken can sometimes be scary and quite difficult, especially when doubt and fear are your constant travelling companions. Why not take these two negative emotions out of the picture for a while. Then take a look at what you've got. As far as I can see, the journey then becomes totally free to experience all that passes by its way. Don't be concerned about the outcomes or final destination. Our destiny can change quite dramatically from moment to moment, depending upon the daily choices and reactions we make towards life's challenges or obstacles which pop up like a Jack in the Box.

Learn to expect the unexpected but don't let it worry you too much. If we knew all about our life's journey at the outset, no surprises could ever be found and who doesn't like a surprise now and again? Especially if it's a nice one – such as winning a free trip around the world, meeting the man or woman of your dreams or picking the six lucky numbers in Gold Lotto that can go a long way towards assisting in your financial security if managed properly. Doubt comes as a result of reliving those past negative situations that we cannot easily forget.

When we make decisions about what we need to do today, we largely base it upon what has happened to us in the past, in the hope that we might avoid going through the same problem again. And in our haste to avoid a particular event or person, we run so fast in the so-called opposite direction that we slam head first into the very thing we tried so hard to escape from.

On the other side of the coin, we are sometimes faced with the fear of the unknown, which belongs squarely in the 'future' box. When we worry excessively about what is yet to come, we can easily fall into the trap of thinking 'what if?' Dwelling upon those types of thoughts will make us indecisive and we find ourselves standing still, going nowhere. You may even feel that life is passing you by.

This has been your choice and because of the very nature of some perceived future fear, we are rendered inactive. If you are this type of person and if you are not careful, someone else will come along, pick up your reigns and be the one to pull your strings. In this situation, through our indecisiveness and inactivity, we have given another full control of our decision making process. We then become like a puppet; where we find we are forever dancing to the beat of another person's tune. In this situation, who do you think is in control? The puppet or its manipulator? Of course, there is a third alternative which deals with the present.

You may be able to acknowledge that you do have a certain amount of doubt and fear but you are still the one who is firmly and ultimately in control of your destiny. This is because you are aware of the pitfalls of both your past and future but at the same time, you do not allow for it to get the better of you. You deal with any possible sadness or anger when and if it arises and not a moment before. Take a close look at the first two scenarios briefly described above. Do you oscillate between these two extremes or are you more inclined towards one rather than the other?

Or perhaps you already belong to the lucky and wise group who belong in the third category. If you are, I then offer my best wishes and congratulations to you for a journey well taken, so far.

For the rest of you who are caught elsewhere, some might say being trapped between a rock and a hard place; I say take steps to change it. Ask for assistance from a higher source. We will be there, we will hear your prayer and we will help. The trick here is to listen and stay alert for the answers given. For some, this will not be easy due to the level of doubt and fear that they may possess.

I would suggest also as a first step, you are not to worry about what your friends, family, work colleagues or neighbours think about you as a person. By doing so, you are then handing over your control to them and not only that, you are wasting much precious time that you may not have.

In human terms, time is short. For those already in the Spirit world, time has no meaning and we become eternal, forever lasting beings so don't be afraid to be selfish once in a while. How can we cater to our wants and needs if we don't do for ourselves? It's not a bad thing to put yourself first for a change but maintain a balance between giving and receiving. Fear and doubt will only confuse this issue.

Fear of Being Powerless

It's not nice, is it? Especially for those people who insist on being in control of everything that happens to them. They definitely don't like it and will accordingly react with a high level of frustration and unrelenting anger.

For an outsider looking in, they will notice a combined force of bird feathers and cat fur flying in all directions; where this whole messy event can become quite devastating for both parties involved in this power struggle. The more you struggle for power, the more powerless you become. Or to put it differently, the more you hold on to the control lever with a death like grip, this same lever you won't let go of, will begin to feel stifled and suffocated.

It will be forced to fight for its own survival but because it's ten times stronger than you, it will maintain power and throw you off balance and smash you into smithereens; on into the loser's corner, leaving you weak as a kitten until you regain your strength and go back again for another 'knockout' round. But no matter how many times you fight back, you can never win but don't lose hope. You can win if you accept the inevitable. These things are happening for a reason and one of the reasons is to strengthen your faith that everything will turn out right in the end.

We then have on the other side of the coin, those people who instead of struggling, will give up and because they don't believe any other options are open to them; will sadly lie down with lions, only to be mauled and eaten to near death by their attacker because they allowed it. They then become a victim but won't let other people forget it either. Please understand here that giving up is not the same as accepting. Giving up in this situation is done so reluctantly because they can't see any other way out of their predicament.

Whereas, to calmly accept they have no control over certain events will ensure a victory rather than a loss. The difference lies in your attitude; between being reluctant and staying calm in amidst all the chaos.

Let's now look at some situations where you will feel like a fish out of water, struggling for breath. The number one 'biggie' would be to do with death that causes the most stress with the good majority of people. Although this is only partially true, as it is dependent upon what your nationality is and what your spiritual or religious beliefs are in regards to this emotionally charged subject.

When looking worldwide, there is a minority group of people, where death poses no real threat to their existence but for the purposes of writing this chapter, we will look at the majority rather than the minority.

Yet I must make it clear though, that the beliefs of the minority are of no less value than those of the majority. They are of equal importance and they should be treated with the same respect and acceptance as their larger contingency of differing faiths. The majority could easily learn heaps if they took the time to listen to the minority. So let's take a look at this deathly scenario – someone is dying and you are with them.

This person could be a loved one or a complete stranger. If you are a doctor, it could be one of your patients. Some may think that a doctor would be in control but this is not always so. Sometimes, nothing can be done except to make the dying person's last moments as comfortable as possible.

For many of us, we feel this is not enough and that we should have the ability and skills to save their life and when the person finally dies in our arms, the fear of being powerless can then be activated big time. This then gives us cause to feel guilty and blame ourselves, or the doctor, for not saving their life. We may feel anger, self-loathing and great sadness; including a sense of hopelessness. The situation can then become a heavy cross to bear because you are not only dealing with one negative but seven.

It's not easy to cope with this much pressure all at once but if you look at the situation honestly, we have created it by accepting more negatives than what we really needed to. As I mentioned before, the more you struggle against the loss of control, the worse it will get – not better. You have nothing to feel guilty about, unless of course you set out deliberately to kill them. You have no excuse to blame yourself or others, such as a doctor, for the death of a friend. God alone has the power to give and take life but this is no reason for you to then blame God either, for this death was meant to be, even though you may not understand the why.

Anger achieves nothing except more distress for yourself and if that anger is turned outwards, other people are harmed unnecessarily and this too is not fair or just. As well as that, you need to not hate yourself because you think you failed and there is another negative in itself – failure. That now makes eight in all, rather than seven. Sadness, I guess, can't be avoided. You wouldn't be human otherwise and lastly we ask, never lose hope. Life goes on for you as it does for the person who has just died a physical death. The spirit or the true essence of that person is still very much alive.

Be happy for them – they are no longer in pain. Although you might be in pain, don't hold on to it for too long. Let it go because death may pay you a visit as well; when you least expect it or want it. Move on and let go of those things you cannot control.

Some of the other times you may feel powerless are when you have been asked a question in front of a large or small audience that you are trying to impress, where you don't know the answer but feel that you should. How do you deal with that? What is your first gut reaction or instinct?

Some wish the earth would open and swallow them up but of course, it is most unlikely this will happen (but not entirely improbable) but that still doesn't stop you from wishing it to be so. There are a few reasons why we feel uncomfortable in this situation.

Firstly, we feel that we have failed all the listeners or at the very least the one person who asked the question. The other reason lies in the fact that you have unrealistically high standards and expectations of yourself where you truly believe that you should know everything there is to know about every subject.

The other problem might be, is that you have no desire to 'lose face' or be made to look like a fool in front of those people who look up to you. And heaven forbid if the questioner/s start jeering or laughing and in the worst case scenario where some idiot takes it upon themselves to throw rotten tomatoes or raw eggs at you. Then you know you really are in trouble. So what do you do – run and hide, duck for cover and hope you don't get hit or be patient and wait it out?

The smart way to get you out of this predicament without too much damage being done to your pride and self-respect is to say – 'I don't have the answer to that question and rather than giving you the wrong information, if you could give me a little time, I could check it out and get back to you as soon as I can with the correct answer.' That is one way.

The other is to turn the question back on to the audience, that is, if there is more than one listener, by saying – 'Does anyone here know the answer to this intelligent question so you may help this person find the answer they have just posed?' Your next task after putting this question out there would be to pray that there is some knowledgeable person out there willing to get you out of a potentially sticky situation. If there should be no 'takers' to your request, don't worry, go back to the first suggested reply.

If you are a teacher, doctor, minister of religion, politician or counsellor, you will be faced with many difficult and awkward questions nearly every day. It can be quite an occupational hazard to some but really, all you can do is your best and if that is not good enough for other people, this then becomes their problem.

Don't lie in order to camouflage the fact that you are obviously 'not in the know'. Don't pretend to be someone that you're not just so they will like and accept you. To live up to false pretences can be a very tiring and draining game to play for the person who wants always to be the best.

We would call this personality type a perfectionist and as you should know, perfectionists are never wrong, or at least they would like you to think so. In their mind, they can forgive others for not knowing but when it comes to themselves, all hell breaks loose within their mind; they beat themselves up with a big stick demanding they should know better and that it won't happen again because if it does, the place that we call Hell would look like a devilishly good holiday destination.

To summarise some of the solutions I have given you so far, they are – accept that you are not a failure if you admit out loud that you don't know something, because that's what learning is all about and to learn you must sometimes listen rather than talk. Lower your own standards and expectations of yourself. You are not invincible. You are not God.

You are merely an Angel in training who, upon graduation, will get your pair of wings that you fully deserve but that is no guarantee either as once you become a fully fledged Angel, mistakes can still be made because, just like their human counterparts, they too continue to learn. This is fact, not fiction.

This is how we evolve and advance to a higher level of awareness, so yes – you can teach even Spirit a thing or two as well. Besides which, we make awfully good students and we never play up because we are good little Angels. Can you see our halos shining? No!

Don't let false pride get in the way of speaking your truth. Remain honest and maintain a two way open communication line with those people you are speaking with. Be yourself, if you know what this is, although not everybody does. If you don't know who you are, take time out to discover what makes you tick rather than focusing upon the motives of everyone else except yourself.

Really like, or even better, love the person you have become and if you should uncover unwittingly a negative quality you don't like, say thank you to that quality for showing itself and then take positive steps to change it. In other words, take charge of your own identity. It may take a whole lifetime or more before you understand the person you truly are but that's alright. Time doesn't exist in the Spirit world; it matters not to us, as it should not matter to you either.

What I am about to say, may sound like a complete contradiction to what I've just said, but accept that you are already perfect and in reality, you really don't need to change a thing.

Just be and this should be enough but don't forget to forgive yourself when necessary. And lastly; if a person judges you harshly, solely on the mistakes you have made, then this person is not worth knowing. Walk away and respect yourself. You don't need another to harshly criticise you because you will do enough of that yourself. Why add to your problems because you like them or you want them to like you? Expectations can be a real 'killer'.

The other concern connected to the fear of being powerless is money or to be more specific, the lack thereof. This is another major issue or problem that worries most people and that is why a small minority of con artists and frauds are cashing in on your fear, as they seek to sell you financial security and independence. In order to ensure their own success in this dodgy business of financial freedom, they are relying upon your greed or want for lots of money and power. Take a look around you – there are many get rich quick schemes on the market today that the mind can easily become weighed down by the sound and colour of money.

You may think, now what do I try first from this seemingly endless smorgasbord of schemes that all essentially have the same theme; where the world can be yours and more, if only you had lots of money. Money talks but don't be fooled. A good many of these schemes are based on false hope and empty promises but still you fall for it. You could say the same happens in some relationships that should simply never be. Even when you know it's too good to be true, you are still tempted to try regardless. Some are lucky and will succeed despite the sometimes not so obvious scam.

This is due mainly to their own ingenuity, motivation, drive and creative abilities which are not totally reliant upon the actual program or product that has been initially sold to them. The tool has merely acted as a catalyst for the person seeking wealth and personal independence to take a risk and win but this is an exception to the general rule.

But then, as with everything and everyone in life, the genuine included, there are no guarantees that good fortune still awaits you at the end of the line. You have to question – where does the line finish, if it ends at all? If it does stop, when do you get to enjoy the many fruits of your labour? Success comes down to having perfect timing and this is something that cannot be taught. You're guided into it.

Stop flowing against the current. It is sure to bring you down and you can't enjoy your newfound prosperity if you're buried 6 feet under. You may think you can beat the odds but you can't. Every living plan has divine timing attached to it. If your ego kicks in and demands this timing be changed, you will be pushing away from you the very thing that you want for yourself and/or others. And then to top off a bad situation, you then might turn around and blame God or the dog next door for your continued misfortunes. Is this really fair? Would you be happy to accept the blame for some wrong that you did not do? I don't think so. The reality is that I think you'd be pretty annoyed and most indignant and would protest your innocence loud and clear.

The other time when we can feel utterly and hopelessly

powerless, is when other people won't believe what we say or where they mistrust our innocent motives for doing nice things for them. In the worst case scenario, you can die for their mistake. I know, this thought is too scary to contemplate but it has happened and it will happen again. So, what does one have to do to avoid these misunderstandings from arising?

Do you pack up shop, go bush and live as a hermit, having little or no verbal and physical contact with others? You can do this but by doing so, do you really think this will make your life simpler and pain free? Not likely. By being alone, can you reclaim the power that you felt was lost because of other people? What are your own thoughts and feelings about certain stressful situations? When alone and with no-one to talk to, those things your heart and mind has to deal with become intensely magnified because they want you to acknowledge them, like real people but unlike other people, you can't run away from what is within your mind and heart.

Some have tried alcohol or drugs to inhibit their senses but over a period of time, this destroys the body and truly doesn't accomplish anything. Is this what you want – to destroy yourself? I thought you wanted power and worldly wealth but if you're physically dead, how can this then become possible? The power that you crave for is then taken away as there is no real point in obtaining those things when you no longer have a body, heart and mind to enjoy it, is there? Power comes from within. If we try and run away from ourselves, we make ourselves both miserable and powerless. No-one can take on this responsibility, except you.

There's no point in pointing the finger or the bone at another because there are always two sides to everything. One is facing your direction and the other is pointed away from you. Which end do you think will cause you more damage, if you're not careful, respectful or truthful about whom you have become?

Try this technique when you have some spare time on your hands, or even when you don't. Say the word 'powerless' out loud until you get tired of listening to your own voice. Then sit and accept what comes back to you. If you're listening properly and in the way that you need to, many grand insights and revelations will show you exactly how you feel about this whole issue and whether you innately believe you are worthy of receiving it.

Your memories will be activated, where you will recall certain past events which caused you to feel powerless. Upon seeing these bad bits, pull it to pieces as you would if you wanted to fix something. Have a good poke around and see if you can discover the real problem to your feelings of being powerless. Then remove it from the equation, put what you were working upon all back together again and enjoy once more, your own personal power; that is a force which is so much stronger than any other. And I say it's stronger because it is yours. You have not borrowed or stolen it from somebody else, leaving them lacking because to be honest, we can do that sometimes and we may not always be conscious of doing so but still it has happened.

If you find yourself in the possession of holding on to another person's strength or power, and as soon as this awareness hits you, give it back unless you wish for someone to do the same to you. "Finders keepers, losers weepers", at least in this situation, is not always the best policy to adopt.

Also allow your memories to float to the surface of your mind so it may alert you to those things which made you feel powerless when a child. Once you can tune into what they were, you will then discover that you have been stuck on the same terrible treadmill, walking the same powerless walk and talk. Isn't it time to get off? Yes! Well, in that case, let's do some pinpointing together.

Here is a possible list, some of which we may have already talked about but I'm sure you could add to it if you later wished to do so because everyone will have had different experiences. Certainly, they might be similar but because a different group of people are involved, each with their own unique set of problems and blend of emotions, these problems then cannot be the same as yours – exactly.

At last, we have arrived at that place where we can begin to point some pins. Suffice to say that in order for this technique to be effective, look at your life through the eyes of a frightened and innocent three year old child and if you can't remember what that was like, then pretend.

The following is some of what you might find within:

- People who screamed louder and longer than me;
- People who had a loud and aggressive manner when angry;
- Being forced to watch people reacting violently towards each other while under the influence of alcohol or drugs;
- Men who towered over me and, like a proud old rooster or peacock, would never let me forget how good or important they were in my world;
- People who wouldn't allow me freedom of expression and who laughed when I wanted to express a personal opinion about something of great importance;

- People demanding a 'yes' answer only. I was never allowed to say no or at least not without it causing some major distress for everyone concerned;
- Becoming lost and no-one's there to help me find my way home again;
- Being left alone to get myself out of trouble;
- Being ignored and rejected from family and friends;
- Being blamed for telling the truth;
- People laughing at me for giving a wrong answer in class;
- When I discovered the existence of those people with two faces; that is, those who would say one thing but do another;
- Chronic liars;
- Those people who enjoyed shattering my fantasies and dreams of a brighter future;
- People who took perverse pleasure in telling me bad things about those special dear ones whom I cared about;
- Those people who felt happy and important only at those times when I felt sad and insignificant;
- Being physically beaten or emotionally bruised, so my attacker could feel powerful and secure in their own little world;
- Those people who stole from me and who later denied all knowledge of having done the wrong thing or where they blatantly ripped the object out of my hands and then refused to give it back; and
- Being forced to fight in order to prove that I can stand on my own two feet and that I am okay.

Aah, for the moment, we've now reached the bottom of the well. It's truly amazing what you can dig up when you go fossicking for the truth, for within the still waters can be found a certain amount of dirt and grime. This practise should be done on a regular basis because once all the muck and clutter or dirt and grime have been removed, the water then becomes more palatable to the taste while its powerful life giving energy returns. These factors will lead to you living a long, happy and fulfilling life and isn't that what we all want?

Let's now take a brief gander at the solutions to what has just been written that you can expand upon at a later time for yourself. You can try this same technique by looking at the word 'powerful' and how that made you feel and take note of the differences. It is important to do a bit of both because once the negative has been removed you need to refill yourself with the positives. If you don't, you then leave yourself open to be filled once again with the negatives and this can happen quicker than you think.

The solutions are – remain centred and calm in the face of chaos and destruction, believing in your own power that no real damage or long lasting harm will happen to you. Believe in your own importance. Say what you feel with a dash of tact and diplomacy thrown in for good measure. Say 'no' and mean it, without the sense of guilt.

Stand your ground, don't back down when others react in a negative way to the fact that you had the courage to say no. It may not always produce your desired effect but take heart from the knowledge that you remained loyal to your thoughts and feelings. When you feel you have lost your direction, seek and ask for guidance from above. Remain neutral and listen.

Accept your intuition and follow your heart accordingly.

Believe that you have the solutions to all your problems – no matter how big or small they may appear to be. Even though other people, from time to time, will turn their back on you, let them but never reject yourself in order to fit in with the crowd. The moment you give up on yourself, others will follow suit, more so then than before. Speak your truth, even if it may be painful for others to hear.

At the same time, always be firm, fair and gentle with the truth when expressing it to others. Do not use it as a weapon to destroy another person's self-respect or belief in themselves. Understand and accept that no-one is perfect and we will make mistakes but these mistakes are necessary in order to learn what is right.

Forgive those people who are insincere, for they know not who they are but you do, as they deserve your compassion, not your anger; although this may be hard to give. However, remain cautious but not to the point where you hold yourself back from enjoying all, and not just some, of your experiences. Accept that liars and cheats never prosper. Think long term consequences for those people, as well as yourself. What was rightfully yours will be again, later in the future. Do not bemoan your loss now, focus instead upon the joy you will feel when it is (or they are) returned to you. Hold on to your dreams and fantasies. Always have hope for the future; no matter how bleak and depressing today may look.

Choose not to listen to spiteful comments made by others about people you care about. Let you be the judge rather than relying upon the opinion of a third or fourth party. Those people who are saying cruel and hurtful things about another may be wrong. Accept their need to feel powerful in the face of your misfortune. You won't have to stay there for long if you hold on to your own power and belief in yourself. Stay cool and allow your antagonists to be strangled by their own greed and ego.

You know the truth, God knows the truth, your Angels know the truth and this is all that should matter. Don't try and win at all costs. Know when to walk away. All these things, if put into practice on a regular basis, will ensure that you find your own power again. You don't need to be lost in order to be found.

Doubt will make you feel powerless and that is something I know quite a lot about but it seems there are many others, like me, who have joined this not so exclusive club that was in existence long before I became a member and I understand it's still going strong today, with a whole new generation of doubters. There is no particular age group of the patrons. Management is not fussy. They'll let anyone in, the only criterion being is you have to .... I'll let you fill in the blank. I know you know. It's all well and good to know the truth with hindsight but what about when you are living it? This is when something needs to be done.

Certainly, acknowledge how you feel and once you have pinpointed its origin and when you have discovered it's not yours, give it straight back to where it came from. If you don't, it will make you feel miserable and where you will live a life half lived but what of the other half of this equation? Will you live to regret those missing moments of feeling secure, confident, knowledgeable and wise? Doubt destroys these things with a single stroke because its energy force is all powerful, leaving you to feel powerless. Remember, this store of power has to go somewhere.

If you choose not to accept this precious gift of power, then it will find another host and this is when its alter ego steps in, which is not at all a pleasant character to be living or dealing with. Most times, it's not life threatening but on occasion it can be, as it can stop you from making the right choices when confronted by an emergency situation such as becoming involved with fire, flood, hurricane or motor vehicle accidents and more. With trust you survive but with doubt you die.

If the world's greatest inventors such as Albert Einstein, Leonardo da Vinci, Madame Curie, Alexander Graham Bell and other great minds took on board the doubt placed upon their shoulders by their detractors and non-believers in general, we would have stayed locked into the cave man era and society would not have progressed to where it is today. Do you think doubt or rejection stopped any of these people for long? No, because they had a desire and purpose to fulfil. They were driven to succeed no matter what the personal cost.

They chose not to listen to that all encompassing, annoying and sometimes loud voice inside their head encouraging them to give up, stating it's just a dream and a big waste of time. Has doubt let you down in this way, where you were so close to success but it was abruptly withdrawn from you because of your doubt? But before doubt took over, you could still sense success was there and you could feel it in your bones but still you hesitated.

So take a peek at what areas of your life you self-sabotage yourself in. Is it within your work environment, your relationships, your home and family life, in social situations, finances, your sex life, discovering and accepting your spiritual self, your general direction in life, friendships, travel, food or health related issues? The list could be longer but by now, just by reading what has been written, this should have already given you a fair indication of what area you are lacking in and which is largely affected by your doubt. Are you ready to make a change? Trust leads to continued success while doubt will lead to eventual failure.

I have given many practical things which you can put into place in the physical realm but what can you do for yourself in the Spirit world to combat your fear of being powerless? There is quite a lot you can do and although I don't recommend you rely on visualisations or affirmations alone to see you through, they can still be put to some good use. What I propose to do now is to provide you with a small selection of pictures that you may wish to shorten or expand upon later, as you see fit.

I would suggest that the other person appearing in this self-created picture with you is the one that makes you feel powerless. Energetically, they will receive your message. If done on a consistent basis and this includes taking steps to changing your own mental attitude and environment if necessary, the one causing you grief will finally back down and leave you in peace. Upon their withdrawal, you will have received your power back.

Some visions I paint, you will like more than others. There are three in all. With those you dislike, feel free to delete them from your mind and send them packing into the ether, never to be seen again. This will then leave you free to explore those that you do like and when you feel really creative, sit down and make up your own. But for now, put your feet up, relax your arms and shoulders, but not too much, otherwise you'll drop this book, and just enjoy:

- *See yourself fully protected and covered by a suit of armour. No part of your body is exposed. Enter stage left, the one who makes you feel no good about yourself. They are armed with a sword, axe and lance. They proceed to attack you with all their might using in turn each of these weapons of destruction but not even a dent is made and this is because your suit is impenetrable. After some time of not making any visible difference to you, they will get bored and leave you alone. At which time, you can emerge from your suit and breathe easy, as there won't be a next time.*

- *See yourself on a raised stage. You are holding onto a cord made of rubber. In the meantime, your enemies rant and rave below you. Because they can't be with you up close and personal, they think they've devised a full proof plan to throw hard objects at you from a distance which is designed to cause you great pain if it strikes its target – which is, in this case, you. What they don't realise but you do, is you have fully surrounded yourself with an invisible laser beam. When something like a solid object passes through this beam, the cord you are holding on to is activated, and you are lifted high enough off the ground to where they can't reach you. You are then let down again to provide them with another go, but after each time they try, you are lifted a touch higher than before. At a certain point, they'll give up and go home because you have placed yourself out of harm's way and out of their particular reach. I mean, let's face it, what is the point of your enemies then continuing? They don't like having their time wasted, so they'll look for an easier target; one that is more willing and stupid to stand exposed at their level.*

- *See yourself surrounded by a circle of hungry man eating lions. They are facing away from you. The lions are your best friends, whose sole purpose is to protect you. Along come those people who are your antagonists. They see the circle of lions and they then see you in the centre. They don't know what to do. They keep their distance, except for one particular fool. He/she steps forward, believing they can outsmart and outrun the lions if they choose to attack. This would give them a brief window of opportunity to do you harm. They don't get far though before making a hasty retreat, when he/she sees all the lions step towards their direction with mouth open, fangs bared, paw held up and claws exposed combined with a hellishly loud roar which echoes continuously in their head, frightening them to near death. Seeing this display of natural power and strength, the others join their fast disappearing and foolish companion. You are once again alone and you didn't even have to lift a finger to defend yourself. You lie down and rest, feeling confident that your circle of lions will keep a protective watch over you and will move into action if and when needed.*

It's amazing isn't it how a suit of armour, a rubber cord, an invisible laser beam and a circle of lions can cause you to retrieve and hold on to your power again!

Sleep well and have fun with creating your own grand visuals and if you're smart, and I know you are, there will always be a happy ending for you. As God knows, good will always outlive evil every time.

Ask yourself – why do people have a taste and desire for war? The number one driving force that is common amongst all instigators and dictators is that they have an uncontrollable thirst to take control of something, someone or some country which doesn't belong to them and in the process, create a feeling of anarchy, chaos and destruction to the masses. And does the number of innocent deaths cause them to sleep less at night? Of course not; the end will always justify the means. So what if a few thousand or more people die helping the cause of the almighty one to succeed in overthrowing some regime or bringing about change to a particular religious or political belief.

Some people believe that war is good for the economy and if you have a good economy, the people will naturally be happy but what people are we talking about here exactly – those on the winning or losing side of the war?

Those in authority who are manipulating others to do their bidding believe that to have control is to have power. Their motto could be – 'power to me and none to you'. If more people could let go of their desire to control what happens around and to them, peace would then reign once again on Earth. It has happened before and it can happen again. Some countries have been lucky not to have experienced war on their own land but this is only partially right to say this.

War is happening every day right under our noses, yet we don't see it – or if we do, we classify it as being something entirely different. To give you a few examples – war rages in the board rooms, in the family home, on the streets, in the churches and other places of worship, in the hospital corridors and wards, in the playgrounds and classrooms of public and private schools, at train and bus stations, airports, on the road, pharmacies, race tracks and shopping complexes. Everywhere you look, war confronts you. The casualties lie at your feet everyday – some limping, some beaten and bruised till they are black and blue, some crying, screaming and kicking, all struggling to survive what has been done to them. Some will reclaim their power, while others won't. Where do you fit in this rather bleak picture?

Are you struggling to live as you see fit in your everyday life? Have you given your control away so those in power can remain happy, while you remain sad and disillusioned? All one can ever do is do what is right for them but at the same time, not force other people to join you in your own personal set of beliefs as to how you think they should lead their lives. Give yourself what you need without interfering with the freewill of others. Accept the word 'no'. Stop pushing for things to happen. Certainly go out there and give it your best shot but be patient while waiting for success to alight upon your shoulder. And when someone or a group of people wish to start a personal war with you, just smile and state your case by saying that you can truly understand what they are feeling but with great love, you don't necessarily agree or accept their truth as your own. Then walk away and allow them to digest your power.

And as you walk away, do not feel guilty that you have disagreed with your boss, a good friend, family member or some other loved one. Because there is an element of emotional attachment to that other person does not mean you have to hand over your power to them. If you do so, this could then be seen as you accepting their emotional blackmail and this happens far too often in many relationships today. This is why there is so much friction within a marriage and why the divorce rate is so high. There is already much unhappiness because a large majority of people place themselves at the bottom of the priority pile.

You may receive accolades for being selfless while caring for the needs of others, but in your heart, can you say you are truly happy? Is what you are receiving enough to keep your memories alive and you warm at night? In order for there to be power to the people, each individual must first take hold of their own personal inner strength and as such, to stand side by side with another, each equal in power and acceptance. Peace can then once again reign. May the power and the peace be with you.

Shontara

*You
who are the
Source
of all power
whose rays
illuminate the world,
illuminate also my heart
so that it too
can do
your work.*

Source: Unknown

Affirmations

I stand with an ARMY OF ANGELS around me.

I am the POWER within.

I am a powerhouse of energy which is then TRANSFORMED into something practical and positive.

JAMES

Brother of the Apostle John and son of Zebedee

Joy to the world, put down your

Alms, blessings abound, as the

Messiah walks and talks amongst us. Behold,

Enlightenment is at hand. So thankyou God for

Sending us this man, to save our wretched souls.

I would run around town literally singing up a storm. Every spare minute I got, you could hear me warbling like a nightingale. Once started, it was hard for others to stop me. I was like a dog with a bone. Especially when walking long distances. To me, it would break the monotony and boredom of the trip. Of course for those around me at the time, I'm sure I sent them all crazy praying for silence. Sometimes, I granted them their wish. No point in pushing the friendship beyond its limitations.

Whenever I had a problem that I insisted upon working out for myself, I would – believe it or not – sit quietly and allow my mind to be filled with words that would then be joined together to give me the solution. I would often read these words out loud and while doing so, I could intuitively hear the music being played in the background of my mind. Sometimes, the written word would be turned into a song, which would be expanded upon later. Looking for solutions in this way helped me to remember the answer given.

Over a period of time, I ended up with a whole collection of songs to suit all types of emotions – ranging from joyful to sad. Whenever I could, I wrote and sang songs to women on behalf of their menfolk, who had a desire to express themselves in a special way but couldn't. I was a go-between, which I didn't mind. I felt I was helping in my own small way. When the fair maiden was not impressed, I would often experience food being inelegantly thrown at me or alternatively, I would be covered in a bundle of old and dirty clothing.

Life could be difficult sometimes but I would always

dutifully report back to the man in question, with her response. Some hearts were broken and could never be mended but more often than not, the magic spell of love was woven using the medium of song. And the same thing is still happening today.

It's always better to communicate honestly, effectively, constructively and non-judgmentally with another immediately upon a conflict arising. Of course, if the other person is not interested in being a part of the solution, at least you have done your best to alleviate the problems. We cannot force another to listen to us. Stay relaxed when our cries of help go unheard by those we direct them to. Violence of any kind is also no solution. 'Alas', I hear you say – 'but what if my life or the life of my partner or child is being threatened? Do I stand and allow it to happen? Am I not entitled to use the appropriate physical force to defend myself and property? Is my attacker going to give me the same consideration that I am expected to give?'

If you fight by the sword, expect to die by the sword. We need to try and learn the art of proper conflict resolution, even when unexpected and unjustified events happen. Try and find out what it is the other person thinks they need and then provide it, if it's within your means to do so. Agree outwardly with all of what they say verbally, even if you don't feel it inside. Don't antagonise the situation by being confrontational. Forgive, forgive, forgive. Let go of all of what's important to you.

Become an empty vessel from which you can refill yourself with the power of the Spirit. Abundance, on all levels, will then be attracted to you. A full cup is of no use to anyone, because you are then unable to accept more good that is available. Release and accept that what's happening is being carried out for a higher purpose, although at times we cannot see the obvious truth. Stay strong willed even while under attack.

Stand your ground by putting your protective psychic shield or barriers up and have faith you will survive to become a much wiser and more self-assured person.

To seek revenge or to blame another is wasted energy. You can utilise the short time you are given much better by maintaining a philosophical approach to life. Don't bother trying to fight something that is beyond your control. It will only aggravate the situation and why prolong the ordeal.

Fear and anger, if held on to and internalised for a long period, are the two most dangerous negative emotions that will cause life threatening diseases such as cancer and heart attack. Some are lucky to survive while others are not. So why the difference in outcome for some and not for others?

Those who learn to live successfully through this dreadful and physically painful experience of a heart attack have completely and genuinely made the decision to dramatically change their lifestyle and negative thought patterns. If you like, you could say they made a more positive commitment to life in the same way that some administrators of the Christian faith commit their life to God.

Many good people require a major wakeup call in order to help them relocate their true direction. Hopefully, this doesn't have to be the case with you. There are ways of preventing it from happening like this. Faith in a higher force and in yourself, coupled with love, minus the expectations and desire for control, are your two best friends, especially when you are going through some distressing and agonising times on a personal level. Learn to purify the mind and detoxify the body. Other than drinking heaps of cold water on a regular basis (which I will expand upon in a moment), try this next time you are angry, fearful or doubtful. All that we ask is that you listen to your breathing.

On each intake of breath, say mentally 'I release'. On the next out breath, add to these words by forcefully saying 'all anger, fear, pain and desire for revenge'. When you have run out of air, hold for a short time and give thanks. Then start the same process again by taking another breath in and then out, while affirming what it is that you want. Decide how long you wish to do it for and at what time of the day or night you will carry this task out. Once a decision has been made, then try and stick to it. Find your own natural rhythm. Do the breathing at your own pace. Adapt the words to fit your personal needs.

This is merely a guideline which may inspire you to do something extra positive for yourself. When you feel you're ready, then take it one step further by doing the opposite; on each out breath, you mentally affirm 'I accept'. Then breathe in slowly and deeply while sincerely affirming to yourself the words 'all love, truth, faith and good health'. Then hold your breath and believe it is so.

Always replace a negative concept with a positive. Once you become an empty vessel, in order not to be refilled again with a variety of poisons that will deteriorate the mind and body, quickly replace it with all that is pure. Once you have taken enough for yourself, then let go of the rest by channelling that remaining goodness to others in need.

There is more than enough to go around everyone but never leave yourself out of the picture. When emptied again, ask for some more to be given. Become like the ocean tides that move in and out in a rhythm that never changes. Accept and release. Accept and release.

Before I continue much further, here is one word about water. By drinking this precious liquid, although I understand that it is no longer as pure as what it was, you will cool the body temperature down enough that helps open the doorway in which your Spirit Guides can maintain clear communication with you. Water is used in this way, as a means of connection with our higher selves.

If you are in the business of psychic, spiritual or physical healing, it is advised that before you work on a client/patient, drink some water and again immediately after they leave. Do this consistently throughout your day or night when working with others.

Water is a cleansing agent that works on all levels of our consciousness and subconscious. Staring into a mirror while your eyes go out of focus is another energetic connection tool. Nostradamus used one to foretell the future and we all know how accurate he was.

Learn not to be afraid to try new things in all areas of your life. You will never know if you don't give it a go. Try and have no expectations about something before you get involved. If you do have expectations, this is then setting yourself up for possible failure and disappointment. Clear all thoughts of failure completely from your mind. Believe you will succeed and then let the thought go. Don't hold on to it. By doing so, you are strangling the thought of its light force, which then makes it impossible to manifest itself. This is why many relationships fall apart.

Some people try so desperately hard and expect to succeed where they then manifest within themselves, impossible standards and expectations for them and their partner to live up to. It doesn't work like that. Let each other be. Be together but separate. If from the first day you continuously undermine the relationship, even if it's only in your head, you are setting yourself up, and them, for a fall. What you think, you are. If you don't like who you are, quit complaining and change it. Positive change will not and cannot come about until you make that sincere commitment and desire to do exactly that.

Attempting change in a half-hearted manner is not good enough. You may make some advancement but it's like taking three steps forward and two steps back. Universal energy is very obedient. We can mould this energy or light force into any shape we want it. You could liken it to a computer, where you input certain information and as a result of this, you get back what you put in. If you make a mistake, it's not the computer/energy that is at fault here. It is only providing you with what you asked for. It's as simple as that.

I hear many of you say – 'I never asked for this to happen to me.' You may not have asked for the specifics but deep down, there is a weakness there in your psyche which attracts bad events and people into your life. What happens outside of ourselves is a mirror image of how we feel about ourselves inside and there is no escaping this fact. Unlock the doors of your mind and discover what exactly it is that you are afraid of.

There are many fears to choose from – abandonment, rejection, success, failure, money, poverty, LOVE, death, abuse, neglect, hatred, God, emotions, abundance, recognition and loneliness – just to name a small handful. If you sat quietly for a moment, I am convinced you could honestly add to this list. Once you know exactly what it is that you fear, and more than likely, it's more than just one, do it's opposite. Find a solution. Perhaps you no longer trust because in the past you have always been let down and hurt by another.

Turn that upon yourself and ask 'Do I trust myself?' You might be surprised and shocked to receive the answer. 'Why does love always seem to go wrong?' Change that to 'Am I worthy of being loved? And what about when I have a lot of extra money in the bank, what compels me to overspend and waste it until it's all gone? Is it because, I'm afraid of money, where I want to get rid of it as quickly as humanly possible?'

Be honest when answering these questions and more. Once the truth behind the reason is revealed, you can then move forwards with renewed confidence and inner happiness. This is when change will take place. If you have self-loathing, how else do you expect other people to react to you? Again, they are just a mirror image of yourself. Think about that, next time you mentally beat yourself up and then expect the same back from others.

On our many travels through the different lands, we hid certain important written documents deep inside mountain caves. We knew this would be a safe place for these documents to wait out the years till later generations would find them again and hopefully translate them correctly. Some have come to light and some have not. Some are still being kept secret, even after discovery. This fact does not overly bother us because we know the Truth, in little bits and pieces, will be revealed to the wider populace when they need it the most. This time is coming soon and it will turn religion largely on its head.

The forces of nature live within us all. This was understood by us and we had the ability to use this to our advantage. The clearer your mind is, major miracles you can create. This is an inherit gift that we (meaning you) all have, even today. This has never changed, even since ancient times. Some races of people know how to use and develop this power well, while some do not because of their mental conditioning and suppression of this power.

Times have negatively changed and as such, we have lost touch with our spirit and heart, although this is now being brought to the fore, in all its many forms, to see the light of day again and this can only be for the good of all mankind, woman and child.

If we as adults could see life through the eyes of our children and then take the appropriate action upon what we perceive, the world would become a far better, safer and peaceful place in which to live. As an adult, we distort the Truth a lot of the time to suit our personal needs and ego.

Between the ages of 0 and 7, children have no ego. They, if treated carefully with love and respect, have no fear of what might hurt them. They see life only in terms of innocence. Children possess such great inner strength, flexibility, drive, motivation and enthusiasm for everything they experience. They welcome it all with open arms. They don't hold back. Everything is sacred in their world – other people, places and the forces of nature that includes the world of Spirit. Children like to explore every different possibility of a situation. They are accepting, loving, tolerant and forgiving. Would you like to be all these things that I have just described?

As adults, some are and sadly, some are not. Those first seven years are so crucial but can pass by so rapidly like the blinking of an eye. Some parents are taken by surprise. One minute, they remember their children as little babies and then the next, they are all grown up; making their own decisions, getting married, having children of their own and the cycle begins again.

Some adults believe it is their duty and responsibility to teach the children and this is correct to a certain extent but in reality, our children are there to teach us some valuable lessons about ourselves as well. If parents could only take one step back from this need to control everything and everyone around them, they would then gain much insight and pleasure as to what life and their children can really offer them.

Some adults are not destined to become parents and to those people I say, practise learning with the children of your friends, neighbours and relatives. There is an abundance of children in this world to go around everyone concerned. No childless adult has to miss out. If to have a child is vitally important and it is not physically possible, there are always alternatives – some of which are better than others. Don't be rigid in your way of thinking.

There are more ways to skin a cat than just one and so it is with finding a variety of ways to fulfil your basic nurturing needs. Sometimes, we need to think outside the square. This represents progress. Open your mind and heart to receive new ideas.

Your Angels, the ascended Masters and the whole range of other beings you know nothing about, are all here to inspire you to great heights. Never be afraid to fly and let loose your wings. Begin living your dream with passion and don't just think about it, do it. But at the same time, try and maintain a balance between receiving good for yourself and giving freely to others what they might need.

Become like the ebb and flow of the tide. Always empty and replenish, give and receive in equal amounts. Don't be thrown off balance because we forget about ourselves or we do everything in our lives because we have a burning desire for others to love us. Learn to give without expectations and to receive with gratitude.

I felt strongly for those people who were being unfairly

treated or persecuted because they were different from the large majority of the community. They were not criminals. They had done nothing wrong. Quite often, I felt it was so unjust and unfair but to a large extent, I was powerless to change their destiny, when it came to the law. Jesus taught me and all the rest of us, to understand and accept that we can only assist and guide but no more than this sometimes and that these people have chosen this particular experience to be down trodden, spat at and condemned in order for them to learn a valuable spiritual lesson.

Because of this, I find myself inextricably linked to their lives and that I too have a powerful spiritual lesson to learn from their experiences as well. Life and all its personal ups and downs can and do affect the lives of many; some of which are positive while others are negative. There is no escaping this sometimes horrible fact.

We, being the Apostles, were different but in order for us to do our work properly and long term, we had to blend in more and play the game set down by the law of the land and to live by the rules set by the governing body of the day. Even if we didn't like it, we found a way to live and work within some extremely confined boundaries yet still maintained a certain amount of personal inner freedom to express our beliefs.

It comes down to discernment as to how you say something; when to say it and to whom. There were certain signs that indicated that it would be safe to do so. We became experts in the art of reading a person's face, hands and heart. Most people but not all, when pushed and who wish to cause you harm, will not be able to look you directly in the eye for too long. Even though society in general has progressed in leaps and bounds in regards to technology and science, human nature has not.

The rules, even those set by the person in control of a particular country or province, are still essentially the same.

There is an old saying "history repeats itself". Sadly this is true in most instances but it doesn't have to be like this for all time. What the world needs now are those people who are not afraid to step outside their comfort zone, including those people who are not afraid to speak up for their own individual rights, as well as the rights of those who are being badly treated. In short, we need good and honest communicators as well as those who can implement the ideas of others and move into positive and constructive action with it that will bring about radical change.

Life is about learning how to share knowledge, abundance, good health and wisdom equally between all of mankind and when I say 'mankind', I am not only talking of men but our womenfolk as well, including the children of our future, while not forgetting the whole of the animal kingdom.

This last category, in some countries, is largely overlooked and where the human variety cannot see or overlook the true value of our animal brothers and sisters. We can learn so much from studying animals living in nature, whose lifestyle and lessons learnt can then be transferred into our existence to help us advance.

I know there are many groups in today's society who have dedicated much love, money and time to doing what I suggested but what about the individual who are not involved in such organisations or groups that study animal behaviour? Some may think that by focusing upon animals and nature, we are taking a backward step in evolution. This is not true. They can teach us many valuable things, as can our women and children. *Look and see beyond the square. Go deeper beyond* the surface, as within that square you may come across a circle and within that circle you may then see a small white dot. Now what could that small white dot represent?

Focus upon its true meaning and purpose, allow it to expand and grow brighter until it encompasses your spirit and soul. Absorb its all empowering and healing energy. Become one with this light of the Universe. No darkness or evil can dwell here. Not even death, for life is eternal. It never truly ends. It simply changes shape and form and this takes place across the board within the human, alien, plant and animal kingdoms.

As a young boy, I enjoyed hiding in between the branches and leaves of an old fig tree and picking a handful of fruit that I could use to throw at any people who went by. Most were good sports about it. Others reacted quite angrily, while some remained stunned and confused. Some spotted me before I could get my act together and they laughed at my slowness, but good naturedly of course. Some tried to catch me and drag me away by the ear or any other useful appendage they could grab hold of in order to take me back home to my waiting family. Most times, I never allowed myself to get caught.

Later, I knew who to avoid and who I could have some innocent fun with. It was during this period of my life that I began to learn the most valuable art of discernment. From my young point of view, I knew it as just understanding people. Don't you think it's funny how different people come in all shapes, sizes and colours as well as the clothes that they wear but essentially they all desire to have love in their lives? Love is the greatest common denominator and equaliser of them all.

The word 'love' has a variety of meanings or at least the expression of it and this may differ greatly from one person to the next. And yes, we can love more than one person at a time.

If this wasn't the case, can you imagine what a limiting world this would be? God loves all his children, so why shouldn't we? Let us be God's living example.

Because most of us are only human and where we experience many other human emotions that are directly opposed to love, life then becomes more complicated. Some of these emotions deal with:

- Wanting to **control** the thoughts and feelings of another
- Wanting to make other people feel **guilty**
- The **inability to forgive** or forget past hurts and injustices
- Passing **blame**, holding **grudges** and seeking **revenge**
- Feeling **jealous** and **insecure**
- Feeling **unworthy** to receive the type of unconditional love that we deserve
- Feeling compelled and **driven to prove** to the world that we are okay

It is highly advisable that we do not dwell upon these negatives for too long. These emotions will cause your heart to:

- become hardened
- become blocked
- fill up with foreign bodies that will attack the heart muscle
- enlarge or shrink in size
- become sluggish and so slow that it may stop altogether prematurely

Are you recovering or suffering from any of the following and how do you feel about it?

- heart attack
- stroke
- angina
- cardiomyopathy
- tachycardia
- bradycardia
- hardening of the arteries
- blocked heart valves
- cardiomegaly

And it doesn't stop there. Perhaps you can relate to such illnesses as:

- Lung cancer
- Pneumonia
- Asthma
- Pleurisy
- Emphysema

I could go on but check it out for yourself instead. Consult your heart specialist or GP to give you a more expanded picture on the harsh realities of life and death. Is this the type of health you wish to look forward to? Next time you undermine or doubt yourself, as well as being harshly critical of others, take a step back and ask yourself these two essentially important questions:

1. How will it affect me physically, if I tightly hold on to my anger and hatred towards myself or others?

2. Are those perceived negative experiences, really worth getting all upset about?

The answer to the second question is most vital as to the length and quality of your life because both will be greatly reduced if you can't let go of the vast majority of those 'not so good' emotions previously talked about. Think about it.

Fear of Spirit

Have you been frightened about what you have read so far in this book? You shouldn't be. Where do you think all these words came from – under the cabbage patch or possibly even from the author's imagination? Wrong but the right answer would be to say it came direct from Spirit. It states this clearly on the cover by saying 'channelled to'. Of course, you could question who is she really talking to? As far as you know, the spirit entities could merely be earthbound souls posing as the Apostles and the author has not recognised this fact.

This is a fair enough statement to make but you wouldn't be correct in believing this. Certainly there are earthbound and low energy Spirits we recommend you stay well clear of but how can one do this? Create your own protection, that's how. This is where the use of visualisations, affirmations and prayers can come in handy and if possible, you can sometimes recreate in the physical world what you see in your mind's eye. Everyone creates or visualises different symbols or objects for this purpose and there is no-one item better than the rest but to give you a slightly bigger picture, here is a suggested list. They are in no priority order of effectiveness but don't limit yourself by using only one.

The more you use, the more you will stay protected. Switch and change what you are doing from time to time until you find the perfect combination. I'll give you an example later.

Everyone will be different, keeping in mind the more you deal with people on a daily basis, the stronger the protection techniques will be needed in order to stop you from absorbing the sick or weakened energy of those people you help. Here's a brief list:

Amulets; Archangels; Ascended Masters; the Blood, Body and Cross of Christ; Candles; Chakras; Charms; Circles; Coloured or White Light; Crystals; Fire; Flowers; Herbs; Holy Spirit; Incense; Mirrors; Music; Numbers; Potions/Spells; Prayer; Pyramid; Sword and Water.

Now to give you that example I promised earlier. Nine items from the above list have been used and as a side note, the number nine indicates change:

> *Visualise yourself sitting in a **circle** that has been created by placing **crystals** an equal distance apart from each other. All of a sudden, you realise the inner circle where you are sitting is on **fire** and you are in the middle of it, remaining calm, unharmed and purified. You then reach out with your mind to create a solid wall of **mirrors** around the outside of the circle that encapsulates the crystals, yourself and the fire. The mirrors must be reflected towards the outside.*
>
> *This wall of mirrors will then act as a protective shield to ward off any approaching negative energy. While in this protected circle of fire, crystals and mirrors, invite one of the **Ascended Masters** to join you who then proceeds to mark you with the sign of the **Cross** upon the seven main **chakras** using the **Blood of Christ**. You then offer a **prayer**, chant, toning, affirmation or invocation that you repeat out loud*

or silently in your head for at least 15 minutes if you can, at the end of which will indicate the end of your particular protection technique.

As I said, this is an example only. You can make it a lot simpler or more complex. That choice, we leave up to you. Create your own ritual or ceremony and make it a habit in the same way as you do now when brushing your teeth in the morning, picking up the paper, eating your breakfast, getting dressed and so on. A habit becomes a routine after three months of regular practice, as it takes the same amount of time to break a bad habit that you no longer wish to be a part of your life.

Make it your personal goal to open up the communication lines between yourself and Spirit, at the very least, once a day but more would be preferable. Here are some ways that you can do this. Chanting, toning, drumming or any other repetitive soothing sound, is a good place to start. The other thing you can do is to visualise your crown chakra being opened up wide to allow free access for Spirit to enter your aura. Another suggestion would be to build a rainbow reaching to the other side that you use to travel upon; at the end of which Spirit is waiting for you. The umbilical cord can also be used to connect you to whomever you wish to communicate with.

You may visualise this cord originating from one chakra or all seven, joining you to Spirit. While calling upon the Archangel Michael, he too can help with both protection and communication. The secret to having effective communication with your Spirit Guides, Guardian Angels, Archangels or Ascended Masters is not to impose your will upon the session. In other words, if you ask a question, still your mind completely by stopping all thought, then wait for a reply. Be patient while waiting and if nothing comes in a reasonable period, don't feel you have failed.

It may not have been the right time for you to know the answer or alternatively, it was not your business to know. If your reply does come, don't reject it simply because it was not your preferred answer or because you didn't understand its full meaning. Ask more probing and in depth questions if you are unsure of what Spirit means. You have the ability to find the truth and sometimes your Angels merely wish for you to practice this ability in order to develop your intuitive abilities more but most importantly, trust what you receive. Have no doubt, as this will interfere greatly with your communication.

Remember, Spirit has the big picture, where you can only see a small portion of it at any given moment in time.

Other than doubt, what else is stopping you from exploring the inner workings of Spirit? Are you afraid of becoming possessed by some evil entity that then runs amuck with your body, wreaking death and destruction upon everyone and everything it comes in contact with? Are you afraid your negative thoughts will attract only negative Spirits to you? Are you afraid of losing control over your level of consciousness and free will? Are you unable to relax and remain tense throughout the meditation process forever wondering what should be happening or questioning the validity of what you see or hear? Are you afraid of what other people think of you? Here are some possible solutions to what has been mentioned above. The first problem deals with your fear of possession.

Well yes, there is always that possibility but this can easily be remedied by you controlling your own negative thought patterns. "Like attracts like" but when dealing with the Spirit realm, everything is magnified and becomes so much more intense than what humans feel but the underlying emotion remains the same. The responsible thing then would be to stay away from trying to consciously communicate with the other side until you have mastered the art of positive thinking and looking for solutions, as well as putting psychic protection techniques into place on a daily basis. A mentally unstable mind needs to first find balance and harmony through the use of inner strength, patience, discipline and determination to live the opposite.

Until this can be achieved, all communication with the world of Spirit should not happen. The use of drugs and alcohol will only cause more problems rather than solve them. To communicate effectively with Spirit, it is most important to have a clear head and an essentially pure heart. You need to understand that you don't need a pack of Tarot cards, a crystal ball or any other physical item to help you make contact.

The next problem deals with lack of control over your level of consciousness and free will. You still have both of these things, unless of course you are gifted to enter a full trance where there is no conscious memory of what was said or done, as in the case of Edgar Cayce. The majority of the time for most people, a full trance is not needed in order to receive your answers. You are aware of what is happening immediately around you, including any Spirit messages you may receive. You could say you have one foot in either world, where you can slip in and out of each different dimension quickly and easily, just like breathing. And don't believe it when some say you have no free will. If you don't wish to receive what we can give, you have the right to say no and we will respect this decision and not push you to enter where you have no desire to go.

The other issue deals with not being able to relax and

remaining tense. All I can say is enjoy the process and go into each meditation session with an open heart and uncluttered mind. Have no expectations or preconceived notions of what you will experience and once there in that sacred quiet space, put all questioning doubts aside because this in itself will help create a feeling of tension. This then defeats the whole purpose of meditation, although it is not designed specifically just for relaxation. It is mainly a technique that helps you to tune into your higher self and receive the answers to those questions uppermost in your mind.

Perhaps you may not always receive a reply at that time but later, when not thinking about the problem or question at hand, the answer will pop into your head without willing it to be there.

We now need to address the problem of you worrying about what other people will think if they knew you liked to meditate or communicate with the world of Spirit, in whichever form that may take. If this issue is causing you great distress, meditate or communicate while alone and share this knowledge with no-one.

What you do in your spare time behind closed doors or in the open country is really no-one's business to know. This is an experience that is between you and your God or Goddess. No-one else's point of view should enter into the equation.

I hope this has helped you move a little way towards your desire to willingly embrace the world of Spirit with both hands and to immensely enjoy living in the two different worlds at the one time. Remember, nothing can hurt you except fear itself.

The more importance you place upon a particular fear, the more power it will have over you. You may not be able to eradicate your fear completely but you can – like a radio

– turn it down to a low enough level so the voice of fear may not be clearly heard above all your other thoughts running rampant inside your head. You are the master of the control knob. Which way will you turn it – less or more?

Most average people believe their spirituality is a serious business and as such, there is no room for poking fun at your own frailties or laughing with your Angels. There is a general consensus doing the rounds at the moment that deals with the belief that those of us who reside on the other side of the fence to the physical realm, all lack a sense of humour and that we never laugh, sing or kick up our heels to dance. What's closer to the truth is that you have put us all (God, Jesus Christ, the Holy Spirit, The Archangels, The Ascended Masters, The Twelve, Spirit Guides, Guardian Angels, Mermaids, Fairies and other heavenly beings) on such a high pedestal of respect, that you stand in rigid awe of our perceived power and brilliant countenance that we shine upon you.

For the poor misguided souls who truly believe that, the only movement allowable to them is to look continuously upwards. From our point of view, we wish for this not to be the case and from your point of view, this stance of staring up at someone or something must generate an enormous pain in the neck and who really wants that? It would then become all too hard and would be something to avoid at all costs. Even a giraffe, who has the world's longest neck, would find it a strain after a while.

When it comes to Spirit, some of you have become so confused in thinking that to be respectful of our presence; one must maintain a deadly silent composure, where that same respect does not include having a good time with us, thereby kicking us out, unintentionally of course, into the cold. Which then leaves the only time you get in touch with us is when you have a problem or when you have something serious to say about the people or environment in which you live.

We accept your fears and tales of woe but it can be somewhat tiresome, not to mention lonely. We desire human companionship just as much as you do. But unlike yourselves, we don't need or crave that friendship to make us feel worthwhile and useful but occasionally we like to be reminded of what it's like to be human again. To put it in a better perspective for you – take a look at your friends or acquaintances. Do you respect them so much that this stops you from going out and having fun together? Hopefully the answer would be no. Learn to be friends with us as well.

Because you can't physically touch us does not mean we can't feel what you are feeling. By keeping us on a pedestal built so high that reaches the sky, we no longer have any room to move sideways and at the same time it makes it extremely difficult, but not impossible, for us to make contact with you, because you have placed yourself in a position that is so far away. Move us closer, embrace us fully into your lives at all times, speak with us, accept and listen. Be brave and take us to the back row of the movie show.

Does this sound musically familiar to some of you? Invite us along on your next picnic in the park, when you walk the dog or dance the night away. By including Spirit in your extra-curricular physical activities and not only your spiritual ones, you will discover you are filled with a never ending supply of energy, much like your Eveready batteries that last and last. The more you accept us into all aspects of your life, the more we can teach, inspire, guide, warn and protect you.

Don't put limitations upon us as to what we can't or should

not do. You don't like it when others do the same to yourself, so why should you treat us any differently? "Live and let live". Put into practice the Golden Rule – "do unto others as you would have them do unto you". When you read this rule, keep in mind they were not only talking about other humans. It should encompass Spirit dwellers as well. So take our hand and have a pint, and a laugh or two or three on us. We are more than willing to join in the fun and share your joy while carrying out the special and sacred act of laughing.

You should know that love and laughter is what makes the world go round and around. If more and more people do it while including their newfound Spirit friends, the Universe can turn so fast it will make your head spin to the point where we all fall down in one screaming heap of laughter, only to pick ourselves up, dust ourselves off and do it all over again and again and again.

We have talked about health and healing many times already elsewhere in this book but I'm about to add my little bit by claiming 'you can lose or gain weight with Spirit'. What a wickedly delicious idea that is! Or perhaps you might be thinking it's more preposterous and slanderous than wickedly delicious but if nothing is working and all else fails, who will you call? Why, 'The Body Busters' of course. Good name for a business don't you think? Just joking or perhaps you'd prefer 'The Shape Shifters'? Aahh, yes, that is so much more suitable. By the way, this idea is not copyrighted so if anyone wants to pick it up and run with it by turning it into a business reality, you have my blessing. Now I wonder how this idea could be successfully marketed and who would make all the money from my idea?

But here's the crunch – you can't capture and bottle the

pure essence of Spirit, then expect to sell it to the gullible general public which will make you a fortune, although some entrepreneurs are doing exactly that and doing a roaring trade. While some unlucky mugs have been caught in the act red faced and red handed and have slipped down the slide, thankfully never to be seen again. When you truly think about it, there is a plethora of visual and verbal advertising that bombards us whichever way we turn, nearly every minute of each new day and it's coming from all different directions and destinations.

Ask yourself – what or who can you believe? I say, believe in yourself first and foremost, then believe in us. What's more exciting is that we come free of charge and we don't need any fancy packaging. We are on call 25 hours a day (I'm part Irish, didn't you know? I can't count but who's throwing stones? Certainly not me.) What's that I hear you grumpily say? – 'let's get to the point of the matter and stop waffling on' because you're here to learn and not be entertained by some irrelevant nonsense.

In order for any good book to be successful, it must have an element of both. It then caters to everyone's taste, not only to your own and you may find that at a later time, you too will come to need the opposite to what you are receiving now in the days, weeks or months ahead.

So, here's the nitty gritty business of how you can lose or gain weight. Of course, these same principles can be applied to any other health matter. Other than using visualisations and affirmations which have been talked about before and I will give you one more to work with later, why don't you give us permission to completely enter not only your auric field but your physical body as well, so we may then make the necessary changes on a DNA, molecular, cellular level?

Up until this point in time, those people unhappy about their overall weight and shape are slogging it out the hard way by insisting on doing it all themselves. In conjunction with this, they have sought help from all the wrong places and people. Some would even go so far as to say this is a problem that ultimately, they alone should have the ability and willpower to work out, so why pester the Spirit world for a solution. It is time for you to acknowledge that you can't do this alone; otherwise you wouldn't presently be glued to the pages of this book.

By accepting our help and energy force does not mean you have failed but it does mean you have at last planted your feet firmly upon the path that leads to great success. All we ask, is for you to invite us to take sole control and then give yourself the time needed to silently sit, perfectly still in both mind and body, for at least 15 minutes a day but it can be longer if you wish. See, hear and affirm nothing for this time. For some, this will seem to be an impossible task but your perseverance, dedication and belief that all is well, will pay off handsomely in the end and people will begin to compliment you as a result.

When a thought form enters your head, acknowledge its presence, then gently ask for it to go away and to come back some other day. If you feel pain arise anywhere in your physical form, again acknowledge it but this time; don't push it out and away from your body. Simply feel this pain with a detached mind and heart, knowing you are being healed from the inside out. The more you give in to and accept this pain, the quicker it will let you go; this frees us up then to work with your weight or lack thereof and other important issues. You need to approach these 'silent and staying still' sessions with no expectations or time frames in mind. Let things happen in their own natural timing and not when you demand it to be so.

You need to also accept that because there are no visible results immediately, it doesn't mean that nothing is happening. If you can trust, it will make you feel better about yourself. Put all feelings of doubt out of your mind and move on. We understand what your goal is, as you have already made it clear to us but you don't have to keep on reminding us every second of the day and night. If you wish to try and maintain control over this energy's preferred direction, we could be battling against each other, where nothing can then be gained.

While out of sessions, take a look at why you eat too much or too little. You could be surprised to find the answer and if both groups of people sat down together and compared notes on the insights received, then you would both learn you have lots of things in common. Try it and see if I'm not right. There is one other little thing you can do for yourself and that is – be happy about the way you look and who you are. Focus always upon your best assets and if they remain stubbornly hidden from your sight, ask a friend to help you look. Find the silver lining.

And here is the visualisation I promised you earlier – *you might like to picture yourself looking like a sumo wrestler who is standing on your left and on your right there stands a skeleton of your former self covered only in a thin layer of flesh. This is another aspect of yourself looking back at you. Place your spirit body in the middle and believe that you can achieve the 'in between' of these two extremes. Then blend all three shapes to become one and thank them for teaching you a valuable lesson about yourself and life. There will then be no more fat or thin once this connection is made on a heart to heart level. You'll become perfect* like the blossoming of a new rose and Spirit would have helped you do it.

Are you still afraid of Spirit? Do you still need some extra cajoling and convincing? What extra benefits are there? Have you heard of the "Fountain of Youth" and do you know where to look for it? If you tap into the Spirit within yourself, this is where it can be found, believe it or not. You will discover whilst there, that life is eternal; never ending. The more you partake of Spirit, the more your physical body will change for the better, where older people will begin to look and feel years younger than their biological age.

This is when your hair will have more shine, body and bounce, your eyes will sparkle, your spine will straighten, you can walk for longer distances before getting tired, your arms will be stronger to carry those heavy loads, your heart will maintain an even beat and you will think more clearly, while the actual brain remains fully alert and aware of all possible dangers. You will discover that you'll want to imitate the ways of nature and to protect the land. You will come to respect and work more effectively with the four elements of earth, fire, air and water. All these things I guarantee can happen when you fully immerse yourself in the energy of Spirit on a daily basis.

Not to mention all the creative ideas and inspirations you receive from us which you can then use in a practical way to ensure your success on a physical and spiritual level. And we do want you to be successful in every sense of the word. We have been where you are today. We can relate to your needs and fears, and we will endeavour to do our best to help you receive what you need while helping you to let go of your fears.

Trust, patience, love and a good sense of humour will take you far in life. Who can say they live these four qualities consistently? Successful people do, that's who. And irrespective of how you measure success, whether it is based upon material or spiritual wealth, underlying everything will still remain the ability to laugh, to love, to be patient and to trust.

Sometimes, the world's happiest and most successful people are often the poorest in material wealth. Why is this? The answer is because it doesn't cost a cent to purchase these qualities that are scattered like jewels in abundance within, waiting for you to pick them up and accept their true worth. When you live and express these qualities every day of your life, everything you touch will then be turned into gold and you will be given the honour of manifesting miracles, both large and small and you'll naturally have Spirit cheering you on to greater heights. So how high do you want to go in life? They say the sky is the limit but why stop there? You can break through that society imposed barrier and reach beyond eternity. It can be done.

All you have to do is believe in yourself and believe in us. Together, we can make a great and unstoppable team. Why not grab hold of this golden opportunity and really show the world what you are made of. Move out of your comfort zone. Don't always stick to the tried and true. Do something out of the ordinary. You may, on occasion, find that you can't do something but I am sure you'll be quite delighted to discover there are many other great things you can achieve when you put your whole being and energy behind whatever you choose to get involved with.

Include us in your madcap escapades and wild adventures. We are more than happy to tag along for the ride of your lifetime and while travelling the Milky Way, we can richly reward you for all your courage and effort. Understand you don't have to do it all alone. That is the hard way.

Be smart, let us be on your team, so you may achieve your dreams and goals quicker and easier. And please don't think for one moment that to do it easily, is a cop out and where you might question as to how can anything be learnt?

The lessons can still be learnt, my friend. It just means you won't feel as much pain and the length of time in which you feel that pain will be a lot less than those who choose to take the hard route. Those poor misguided souls have taken the bumpy road and believe in the concept of "no pain, no gain". If they want to believe that, so be it but I would prefer to stick to my philosophy which is, no pain and everything to gain.

So what else can you gain? Correct revelations and insights for your future if tapped into the right source but fear will keep you tied to earthbound, low energy, vibrational beings. If you have an unhealthy fear of Spirit, you will attract this unhealthy horde of horribles to you and believe me, these earthbound souls have the ability to use anyone in your life to cause major disruption, even a stranger. Guard against this from happening and I have already given you some clues as to how you can go about doing this. Be brave while sifting through the many veils of darkness (darkness refers to ignorance) and really look at what lies beyond. I can assure you it's not more darkness but light.

This state of darkness and fear does not have to go on forever. There is a way out. Shirley McLaine has a book called **'Dancing in the Light'** and her life has been one long dance. Her feet may now be tired but her heart is strong, vibrant and every inch alive with the sights and sounds of Spirit. When you relax and then do nothing except be guided, you will begin to meet the most amazing people who not only can do miraculous feats but who can also teach you some of what they know. This way, a little part of them will stay with you forever and it is then your responsibility to leave some of your magic behind when dealing with others.

This process of giving, receiving and giving is what makes the world jump up and down with joy. When was the last time you were truly joyful? You know what I mean – those times when you wanted to jump out of your skin, where the overwhelming depths of happiness could simply not all be stored within one small container that you call the body and if you couldn't share it with others, you would explode or if you managed to inhibit and constrict this light, you knew it would fizzle out eventually and die of suffocation. If you suppress your natural enthusiasm for life on a regular basis for too long, you will destroy yourself through the creation of natural diseases or making the unnatural decision to suicide. Spirit sees this happening all too often.

If you really believe you are alone and you know of no-one who would appreciate receiving some of your boundless Spirit force, take yourself off to the mountains or the beach and give this energy back to nature. You are then being of service if not to the people direct but to Mother Earth. She too has feelings, just like humans, so never believe that the act of giving away some of your love and joy to something other than people, is ever wasted. It's not. This is so much better than leaving this overabundance of light and life to stagnate and disintegrate. Why do you think Jesus had to separate himself upon occasion from those who were not always so helpful, forthright or accommodating?

Often his words of wisdom and healing touch were not truly accepted or wanted, so Jesus chose to release some of this positive ball of light and energy back into the ground and consequently out into the Universe. The direct approach is sometimes difficult and painful for some people to accept but by taking this indirect approach, no-one ever missed out. Everyone gained, although they may not have been aware of it.

So next time someone blocks you and creates a barrier to keep you out because of their fears and limitations, forget about the front door, go around the back and surprise them. They won't shoot you. Of course, they may try but they won't succeed.

The light can always penetrate the shield of darkness quicker and more effectively than the other way round. See your own body as a vessel of pure light. Cancer and other life threatening diseases of the heart and mind cannot live for long in such a cleansed environment. And because it's all too painful for them, the 'baddies' will then insist upon doing a runner and in the process, destroy themselves before you have to consciously step in and lend a helping hand. What a smart thing to do. The diseased cells do not survive while you stay very much alive.

Prepare to die if you live a lie, but if you stay true, you'll never be blue and you'll be renewed.

Even Jesus had a team of Angels that worked closely with him. Jesus was very much in tune at all times with these Spirit helpers who enabled him to create miracles the world had not seen for a while. Miracles have existed since before mere mortals were born.

Later along the time line, came some ancient races like the Atlanteans, the Lemurians, the Incas, the Egyptians, the Aztecs, the Australian Aboriginals, the Native American Indians, the South Pacific Islanders and the African Negro all have witnessed and produced these same miracles that Jesus did, and better, on a daily basis. Jesus was not the first to have had this ability and he will certainly not be the last. Miracles were a part of ancient culture. It wasn't something unusual or to be kept at arm's length but these miracles and more will come to the surface again and be accepted for what they are.

A miracle is happening around and to you right now yet you don't recognise it as such. This is because you have shut yourself down due to your earlier childhood conditioning, your past personal experiences and your present living or working situation. You are afraid and for as long as you remain afraid of what is not obvious, you will continue to live partially in the dark.

No piece of scientific equipment, whether it be big or small, can ever be able to prove the existence of those beings who live in the etheric realm. They are immeasurable yet they show themselves to you in so many different ways, but still it doesn't register on your Richter scale.

They can work through other people quite effectively as well; such as those who they have chosen to be their public voice, like the author of this book. You either listen and take note, or you don't.

The other reason you may choose not to believe is that you feel you're not truly worthy of receiving such Divine assistance. This help is available to all, no matter what your social or financial standing in society is. These facts are irrelevant to us. You could appear to be a bad and evil person but we are still there for you because we know you haven't always been like that in other previous incarnations. There is always a spiritual lesson for them as well and for others, which has to be learnt; a lesson that can actually benefit mankind rather than hinder it.

Reread the chapter on Judas if you want to be reminded of an actual example. Because you live in the one dimension of space and time, it is difficult to grasp the big picture of what has gone on before, about yourself and other people. You can only see and judge what is immediately presented to you now. But if you ask Spirit to remove the veil of fear and ignorance from your eyes, you will begin to see what Jesus saw – the soul's true essence that is based on love. Others may think you are ugly and mean spirited and you may justifiably think the same of them but please, never judge on deeds or words alone. Go deep within the heart.

Sure, you may find a few grey or black patches here and there that can't be mended but the majority of the heart still remains untouched and pure. This part of the heart can sometimes remain elusive to our sight and remains well hidden from view, in the same way the world of Spirit does to some of you now. We implore you to take us out of the closet and off the pedestal. Be proud to bring us into the open, where everyone has the opportunity to be embraced by our glory.

Introduction to Your Spirit Guide

I close my eyes and allow my mind to drift back to the time when I was young, with no fears or concerns. I once again become that seven year old child.

I now see myself standing before an altar and kneel down in front of it. Suddenly, there appears before me in a straight line, a group of twelve men. I carefully look at their faces and commit them to memory. Later, I can call upon them again and get to know them properly, as I would when meeting any new friend.

Four men step forward – Matthew, Peter, Mark and Paul. Each one is holding a gift they wish to give. Matthew holds a pink rose, Peter has within his hands the golden chalice, while Mark carries a snow white lamb and a bowl full of crystal clear water is held by Paul. They invite me to advance a step and accept each of their gifts. Each time I reach out to receive these special offerings, Matthew, Peter, Mark and Paul share with me a message explaining the significance of each item they give. I will now give myself a few moments of silence, in which to listen. I have no doubt of my ability to hear.

(Pause for 4 mins)

I am then directed to place all the gifts at my feet. The twelve men then move aside and standing behind them is one of my

Spirit Guides; who is my protector and best friend. They wish to introduce themselves. They could appear as a man or a woman, human or alien, someone I know or someone I don't. I do not try and control what I see as a result of my expectations and preconceived ideas. I allow their existence to naturally unfold before my eyes.

(Pause for 4 mins)

No matter what form my Spirit Guide adopts, they love me with all their heart. I move closer and as I do, I see myself as I am now, as an adult in this present day but minus any ill health, fear or anger.

I ask for a name. If I can't hear it, I will ask them to write it down for me or perhaps I'll get a feeling or inner knowing for what it is without actually having been told. I shall remember it well. My Spirit Guide then moves closer to me.

With authority from God above, he or she reaches out their hand and with one finger, they mark my forehead with the sign of the cross. In times of great stress, it is suggested that I re-visualise this cross and draw strength from its existence. It is now soon time for me to leave but before I go, my Spirit Guide would like to give me some of their energy and love to take back with me to the real world.

I understand that what I see or experience in the Spirit world can manifest itself in the physical world. This is where miracles are created and which then becomes my reality.

Now that I have introduced myself to my Spirit Guide, I will pay them regular visits at a later time; I will talk with them, I will ask questions and then listen to what I receive. When I'm ready, I come gently back to the room I am now in.

When I open my eyes, I will feel revitalised, refreshed, and full of enthusiasm and great love. I give myself a big hug and a pat on the back for doing so well. I go in peace. I am my own best friend.

Source: Shontara

Affirmations

*I have come direct from Spirit, I AM SPIRIT
and will return to the world of Spirit.*

*I breathe and ACCEPT THE LIGHT OF SPIRIT
into my soul.*

May the Spirit be with me!

JOHN

Join hands dear sisters and brothers. Let us unite

Our once more happy

Hearts. Then step back and embrace the dawn of a

New 'Golden' Age of peace and prosperity.

I am sitting braiding my sister's hair. I patiently thread wild flowers through her crowning glory with much love and a tinge of sadness in my heart. Today is her wedding day. I love her dearly. Not that my love will stop from this day forth but it will change. How can it not? We have a strong soul connection with each other. I tenderly kiss her on the cheek and bid her a fond but temporary farewell. She looks so radiant, happy, alive, enthusiastic and very much in love. I shall protect her always to the best of my ability but now I must let her go. After today, she will be moving away from my physical environment.

I have grown quite accustomed to her pretty and fresh young face but I know it won't always be like that. Look at me or perhaps that is not a fair comparison. I'm a man and she's a woman and women are divine creatures who are born to be protected, nurtured, honoured and cherished, like a fragile rose but this does not mean to say that women are fragile because this is not true. The extent of their inner strength to persevere regardless is quite miraculous. If they are handled correctly, then you can expect a lifetime friendship but if abused, beware the wrath of God will fall upon you and strike you down when you least expect it. So beware and be aware my brothers of today.

You may take advantage, control and manipulate but always remember there is a high price that one day you must pay and when that day comes – as it surely will – it won't be to your liking or desire. Let go now of that need to win at everything. The more freedom you give to someone, the more they will return, much in the same way that a boomerang does but with additional and copious amounts of love, respect, passion and thanks. Try it and see. It's not going to be easy, especially for some of you. Focus upon the big picture rather than holding on to a selfish and limited point of view.

If you can do this one thing, you will be richly rewarded beyond your wildest imaginings and I'm not talking only about those rewards when you finally get to Heaven. No, divine abundance – in the truest and every sense of the word – can be yours while alive here on planet Earth. Besides, Heaven or Hell is just a state of mind.

Each one of you – both male and female – are experiencing it every day and every moment of your waking and sleeping existence. Your lives react in much the same way as your computers. You download a truck full of junk and that is exactly what you'll get back but it will return in a magnified manner and this is most painful to have to deal with on a daily basis. When I speak of 'junk', I mean those negative emotions that manifest in the qualities that we possess such as greed, control, jealousy, blame, guilt, regret, manipulation, anger, fear and doubt.

Apostle James, the one who came before me within the pages of this book, spoke of these things to you and I'm repeating it here again, in case you missed it the first time round. Many can learn only through repetition. This does not mean you are dumb. It simply means two things and they are firstly, you need more time to digest the information you are receiving and secondly, you are not always listening to your Truth. Some would prefer to 'sweep it under the carpet' and to ignore it but once seen and acknowledged, it is not easily forgotten, at least on a subconscious level and these fears are then filtered through to appear again in our dream state. There is no escape from our Truth.

Have you sometimes wondered why some people suffer from insomnia? This is a sleep disorder for those of you who didn't know. Ask yourself or perhaps those insomniacs need to ask themselves – 'What is it that I'm so afraid of looking at?' Once our fears are brought to the surface and controlled on a conscious thinking level, restful and dreamless sleep will come to those who are struggling against receiving what they desire the most, that is worry free shut eye.

In short, sleep has been designed in such a way to help us let go of that control, because this is exactly what we do in the dream state. If you feel vulnerable and frightened of possible attack of whatever kind, or you simply don't like not being in control, even for a few minutes at a time, then of course you're going to remain guarded, alert and wide awake.

For many, sleep is a most pleasant experience while for others, this time can become a regular and reoccurring nightmare and when it reaches this stage, we will do everything in our power to avoid facing our reality.

The mind, like any other useful tool for creation or destruction purposes, can be sharpened and polished to a high level of precision and exactness. The choice as individuals is always ours to make freely but once that decision is made in regards to which direction we wish to go in and where later on down the track, we discover it is not to our liking, we can always change it. Why put up with something that is only harmful and distasteful to you? We were not put on this Earth to live as a martyr. Accept or reject, create or destroy.

What a magnificent force you are, yet you don't realise it. Some think they need to use dangerous weapons and great armies of men in order to control the masses and indeed, they do control but they use fear as their basis of command. When a person's free will to choose is taken away from them, one day the worm will turn and they will lash out, in order to obtain freedom, liberty and independence. This is nature. This is the law of the Universe being put into action.

If you kick a dog in the guts while it's eating, expect to get bitten. If you don't wish to get hurt, leave well enough alone. Some people think they are helping when really they are interfering. Always share from the heart, like Jesus did, then let it go; the positive and negative emotions expressed and then have no expectations. Accept rather than struggle. Just because you don't like someone's reaction to your Truth, this does not mean they are wrong. They are merely looking at the same situation from a different perspective. It's like speaking to a bunch of witnesses at the scene of a murder.

You could be standing side by side one another and both people will notice different things while the crime is played out before their eyes. Some people will give the facts with no exaggeration or deletions.

When you share an important piece of information, do you add to it in order to make it more interesting for the listener or do you take away from the story because you make a judgement that they don't need to know that because of your shame, guilt or fear? Of course, the bit you choose to leave out may be a vital piece of the puzzle that's missing, and this is where the term, 'missing link' comes from.

It is this latter painted scenario that has sadly happened since time began and which is still perpetuated today. In order to bypass this minefield of lies and half truths, people have learnt to erect protective barriers and have chosen not to trust what they perceive, even themselves. People make judgements and decide what one should or should not know, read or see. This doesn't only happen in the corridors of power.

The individual passing by on the street is also guilty of this crime at least once if not more times in his or her life. This book has been written in order to right some of those wrongs, as well as to give you a bigger picture into who we really were and to behold the face behind the mythical mask that was created for us.

Will you come and break some bread with me? Always, at some time during the night, we would sit down together to eat bread and drink wine. Sounds like a great life, doesn't it? These were happy and sometimes thought provoking times but on the odd occasion, as in any good family, when we had a problem with each other, we used this opportunity to air our differences and find solutions to the perceived problems.

As Jesus always listened to us and many others without judgement, we tried our best to emulate this same quality of the Master, not only within our own ranks but we would listen to complete strangers as well with an air of detached compassion, wisdom and understanding.

We didn't care about the colour of their skin, how old or young they were. We never gave a moment's thought to their religious or spiritual persuasions, healthy or sick, male or female. Because of this and later on, many did become followers of Jesus. We also allowed them to talk. By doing this, they slowly came to trust us until one day they came to listen as well and that is when the energy shifted. Words are a mighty powerful tool.

Some will use words as a weapon to make people feel inadequate or fearful and so cut them down to a more manageable size. Once reduced to someone less significant than they were before, these people then become more compliant and susceptible to control and manipulation by the person wielding the sword and who continually threatens to bring it down hard upon their head at some unexpected time.

Did you notice that the sword contains within it, the name 'word' and if you place the letter 's' at the end rather than at the beginning, you would then have created 'words'. Perhaps you have never noticed this before.

Some may be fearful of the sword when threatened with it, as they can feel just as frightened when swamped with a barrage of cruel and hurtful words. But there is a particular nursery rhyme within your English language that you teach to your young children today and which you need to keep in mind next time someone is 'blowing off some steam', which can indeed burn, and that is – 'sticks and stones will break my bones but names (or words) will never hurt me', unless you allow them to, of course. You have the ability to accept or reject their power. You have the right to make personal choices.

Give yourself permission to make your own decisions and once made, trust and then let go of all preconceived ideas as to the possible outcomes. Allow Spirit to guide your direction in life and as I speak these words, this doesn't automatically mean you are then destined to live in poverty and despair. It is, in actuality, quite the opposite.

When you let go of that self-control and place your trust, but not blind faith, in a 'being' who is so much more powerful than yourself (whoever you believe that 'being' to be), then an abundance of all good things physical and spiritual will be given and shower you with blessings.

It will lift you out of the doldrums and place you high above the rest where you can experience real freedom in every sense of the word. There's that word again – word. In other words (oops) there are no self-imposed limitations tying you down. Other people don't limit us although on the surface of things, this looks to be the case. You can't blame or convict a person upon circumstantial evidence alone, or at least not here in the world of Spirit.

The higher your vibration becomes, the words blame and convict no longer becomes a part of your state of consciousness, along with a myriad of other words that hold a negative meaning. To your ears, these words will become foreign in meaning to you. As such, they will lose their power due to you not being able to understand their true meaning.

To give one fine example of this, you go and visit a foreign country where you can't speak the language. While shopping, browsing or cruising the many market places, someone angrily approaches and yells in your face an abusive and cruel torrent of apparently 'unintelligible jumble of sounds' that appear to be words of some sort and which is spoken in a dialogue that you don't understand. How are you going to react? Certainly you may flinch with surprise but what is being directed at you will be like water running off a duck's back.

It will have little effect because you are not attuned to that level of energy or understanding. More than likely, you'll walk away scratching your head wondering, 'what on earth was that all about?' This exact same situation I have just described has certainly been experienced by the author.

Fear of any sort and this includes negative thought patterns, hold within its boundaries, a great deal of force and power but so does love. Laughter too has much the same effect as love does. So which one shall you use to cut your perceived enemy or foe down to size – fear, love or laughter? What's that? I feel a build up of love and laughter from within, which is about to explode any moment now.

For those not way that inclined towards the two 'l' words, you'd better duck for cover and not get burnt because here it comes, like a volcanic lava flow and it's heading your way. It can't be stopped and it will crush you like an ant and a crushed ant has no power.

I took my responsibilities seriously but beneath all of this, I had a lighter side to my nature. I loved to make people smile and would do this in many ways. One way was to burst into song quite unexpectedly combined with some exaggerated facial and hand moves which made them roar with laughter and if you had seen me, you'd be laughing too. Life, religion and spirituality is a serious business but it all needs to remain grounded and a perfect way to ground yourself is to smile, laugh, sing and dance, believe it or not.

There are some religious orders and philosophies which frown upon the practice of enjoying oneself to the fullest. Some may consider it, a sin. For this joyless group of people, I feel greatly saddened when I watch them. Sometimes and for some of them who are caught up in this particular pattern of belief, you can see they want to have a giggle or to burst into song but they then force themselves to stop by swallowing down hard or suffocating their natural instinct to live and express their feelings with an abundance of joyful exuberance.

Is it any wonder why so many people suffer from throat and heart problems? Jesus had quite a wicked and fun sense of humour. He could laugh with the best of them and not feel guilty or self-conscious by doing so. Believe me when I say that laughter is the best medicine. It aids the recovery of those sick in heart, mind, body or soul. That is why many of the young people are turning their back on the more traditional and conventional type churches and dogma, as there is not enough light or laughter being expressed within these four walls. Lack of light and laughter is hard enough to cope with on the 'outside', let alone experiencing it on the 'inside' as well. Why would anyone want to subject themselves to this form of punishment in both places? Many people believe it is a sign of respect to remain silent within the 'church'. To laugh out loud in God's house, even briefly, is considered to be a sin.

I would have to question this and say – in whose eyes is it a sin? You could say that about me; that I was commissioned to be the comedian or 'light relief' for the masses. Great public speakers and motivators travelling world-wide on the lecture circuit today know that to capture the immediate interest of an audience, it is best to open with a joke or if you're game and insane, you would begin with an apparently impromptu song and dance routine before getting down to the real nitty gritty serious stuff.

It is also a well known fact that if the speaker is unable to hold his captive audience's attention, they then counteract that by doing something totally different. In this way, you are bringing your listeners back into focus, where they will once again want to pay attention to your particular words of wisdom. And so it is with Jesus.

He could read the reactions and needs of the crowds and so acted accordingly, with a few unexpected outbursts and surprises thrown in for good measure. Give the people what they want and if you can do this on a consistent basis throughout the entire talk, then they'll be more receptive into listening and accepting any additional information that may not be to their liking or taste. Inspire people, do not preach.

We all communicate differently so if you have to repeat yourself in several different ways, then let it be. You may have noticed this already happening within the pages of this book. It may take longer but it would have been worth it, as you would have reached the hearts of many rather than one or possibly none. Jesus used this technique many times in any one session by using parables and analogies.

For example, if you should find yourself speaking with a bunch of footballers one day and a group of doctors the next, the content and delivery of both talks will be entirely different to each other, or at least it is if you're smart. Let them empathise with your words on a personal level. To listen and understand may not be enough to propel people into taking action.

To brow beat a person into believing what you have to say, will always end in disaster, if not immediately, then eventually, where they will realign their ears and 'tune out' to the words being spoken, valuable or not.

Children 'tune out' from their parents a lot of the time. Husbands do it when their wives batter them with a war of words that may sometimes be quite confusing or meaningless to the man. So why do the men do this? It's a form of protection and self-preservation. Brothers and sisters turn off from listening to each other and that can end in a whole large series of temper tantrums.

I could go on but I think you've got the picture. "You can catch more flies with honey than you can with vinegar". I am sure you have heard of this saying before. Capture your prospective listener with kindness and then offer them something they can't refuse. If you are unsuccessful in your attempt to persuade them to your particular way of thinking or belief, then give them the freedom to say 'no' without you making them feel guilty.

When you manage to push someone into taking the wrong course of action because they feel guilty or are fearful of your rejection and anger if they dare say no, this may work for a time but mark my words, one day they will rebel and find their own voice and what you began will explode in your face, causing great pain and agony for you. There is no escaping this reality.

For those who have short term memory loss, fear not. This happens because you have successfully let go of the past on a deep spiritual, psychic and subconscious level. It's like starting each new day with a clean slate. Rest assured though that when you need to remember something important, you will. It's all still there.

Learn to unclutter your mind and one way this can be achieved, other than the process of letting go of the past, is to live completely in the moment. I know this is not always easy to do. At this stage of human development, the brain, like a car, can move in only one direction at a time; such as drive, reverse or neutral. To put it another way, we can move either forwards or backwards or a third option would be to remain still and hear His voice.

Another good technique for grounding oneself to the present is to focus upon listening to your breathing or alternatively, your heartbeat. When you clear the mind of all superfluous noise and memories, it's amazing what other wondrous things you can hear coming from within and without.

Believe it or not but your body, and all that it encompasses, has a voice of its own. How many people truly listen to what their body is saying? Initially, you may not know what you are hearing and why, but all you then need to do is ask for clarification.

When completely in balance and harmony, we live in three different dimensions at the one time and those dimensions relate to our physical, mental and spiritual states; body, mind and soul; God, Jesus and the Holy Spirit; flesh, blood and bone. We work to the power of three. You need to learn how to move in and out of all these three aspects of your persona or psyche with ease rather than with unease.

Separation from God is really a separation from ourselves. Let us mend and strengthen this link that we have together. To work with each aspect separately will eventually cause you to feel that something is missing in your life and that things are not quite right. You may not always be able to pinpoint the problem but at other times, you will.

When I was a young man and even before then as a babe, I was taught to share my treasured possessions freely including my knowledge and to have faith that I will be blessed and protected from ever going without. Did Jesus worry about not having enough bread and fish to feed the masses? Some neat trick you might think or it can't be taken literally but what's literal and what's not? Your belief or non-belief still doesn't change the overall facts.

A good example is that mankind, at one point in history, believed the world was flat and if you went too far, one would abruptly fall off the edge into some great dark abyss of nothingness. Until one day, someone came along who thought differently. Persistence in his belief that the world was round eventually paid off and the masses came to see and accept the Truth.

There were many who didn't believe in the words spoken by Jesus but do you think this stopped him dead in his tracks? No, of course not and the same can be said for you, if you are willing to try.

Because you personally have not seen, touched, heard, tasted or felt something, doesn't necessarily mean it isn't so. To think this, is to have a limited view on life. Do not judge another person's experiences, if you wish for them to accept your own. Some disbelieve the existence of aliens inhabiting other planets and galaxies far removed from this one. Where on the opposite side of the coin, there are many who do believe; while yet a third group are sitting on the fence waiting for the verdict to come in – guilty or not guilty, for or against.

Some believe that planet Earth is particularly blessed and is the shining jewel in God's crown. This statement is true but you also need to realise that it is not the only jewel in the crown. There are many other shining beauties that make up the whole or complete picture.

When humans and aliens alike are both reduced down to size; where they are taken off that pedestal of greatness or awe and placed under a scientific microscope to be prodded and probed, we learn that we are both of the same energy force which can be quite a formidable power if you know how to use it properly. Remember here, that energy can never be destroyed. It can only change its shape and form.

When you have the ability, one day, to tap into the secret of how you can make this energy truly work for you on all levels, then indeed major miracles will occur in your everyday life because you gave birth to its creation, no-one else. Our thought forms are only one type of energy. You could include money as well, along with the desire to either love or hate ourselves and mankind. What you believe, you will create, even if you know or don't know how to utilise this power source of energy that is you.

Many lost civilizations have been given a brief glimpse of this knowledge but have sadly used it to self-destruct. That is why many of them became 'lost' but not completely. Their existence is still locked in to our own memory cells and DNA. As I said previously, there is no separation. Whatever level of understanding you are working from, this still does not alter the reality that we are all connected, whether we like it or not.

If you like it not, then you will struggle, that in turn creates an environment of great hardship and sadness. If this goes on for too long and is left unchecked, this will then explode into a full scale war, both internally with ourselves and externally to those people we communicate with. That can then have a snowball effect, where great nations and empires of the world will collapse and crumble into a thousand shattered pieces under the strain, but it doesn't always have to be like this.

All countries, both big and small, are made up of people and it's these same people who possess the power to harm or protect their own piece of paradise here on Earth through destructive or creative means. The choice is always ours to make. What is happening here on the surface of the planet is a mirror image of how we truly feel about our inner selves on a worldwide scale. Unconditional love, acceptance, trust and belief in ourselves and all other alien and Spirit beings that make up the whole, will turn the tide for the better and never for the worst.

To sit quietly and unjumble your brain is not a waste of time. I am sure you could find at least another 1001 things that are more productive and better to do, for example sleeping. I mean, why not take stillness of the mind that one step further? But the Truth is that even when asleep in the Land of Nod, our brains are still active and much good work is being done on a psychic, spiritual level when we are sleeping.

In cases of extremely deep trance, relaxation and meditation, time becomes non-existent and your physical form is no longer your main focus. You are so detached and connected at the same time, that all sensation of thoughts and feelings are stored in limbo and eventually cease to exist altogether, at least on a conscious thinking level, in much the same way as time. The other thing you will notice, if you could, is your heart-beat is slowed down to such an extent where it's barely discernible.

Some would say, you are balancing precariously on a knife's edge between life and death but don't let this belief frighten you off too much, although it has for many. It is here that you can experience total freedom of expression and being. There is no longer any need or desire to struggle or control. It's the ultimate act of letting go.

If we have a naturally possessive nature and are stubborn about holding on to those beliefs and things that are an illusion, what I suggest you next do will be difficult if not impossible. Rest assured that our brain and heart don't need our conscious thinking mind to breathe life into this body. They do it automatically because that is how God created us. It is also in this state of suspended animation that the following things can and do happen instantaneously. Your Spirit can split into a thousand different directions at once and travel wherever and in whatever dimension it chooses.

It is then you become omnipresent; you become one with the Universe, where you become a master transmitter and receiver. With this magical state of being, you then become omniscient – that is, having infinite or extensive and expansive knowledge. This will then flow naturally to a sense of being omnipotent, that means having infinite power that we can use in a practical way upon our return to this physical third dimension. While all of this is going on, without any input from ourselves and on a completely different level, the physical body is given a much better chance to destroy, regenerate and purify any disease and unease that lies within.

I know this sounds all heady and heavy and quite unbelievable except for those highly enlightened souls such as Jesus, Buddha, the Dalai Lama, yogis or medicine men. You may think it would take a long time to reach this level of un-consciousness and for all of the above to take place, we need to stay in that state for a long time. This is not the case. Jesus had the ability to visit this sacred space and took full advantage of all its many benefits. Every man, woman and child has this ability. It is a gift that only a small number of people have embraced and accepted totally.

For some lucky ones, they do this naturally without even realising their own power or what they are doing. Even if you can achieve this only once in your lifetime, the deed has been done. There is no going back to the way you were and you won't want to anyway. A desire to be of service to all humanity will be activated and remain strong within; where you will create your own miracles – in the same way that Jesus did. Yet at the same time, we need to still remain grounded and to stay humble. If you try and use this power and knowledge in a negative way, it will destroy you.

Fear of Being Judged

The fear of being judged will stop you from being who you are. The fear of being judged will cause you to remain silent when really you should be doing the opposite. The fear of being judged means you are always protecting your back from a possible stabbing attack. The fear of being judged causes you to stand still in life. The fear of being judged will have an adverse effect upon your relationships because they are based on your fear and not on honesty or acceptance.

Two thousand years ago, I chose to live a life where certain people, including some of my immediate family members, continuously judged my choice of destiny. They questioned – 'why put my life in possible danger just because I was willing to follow and believe another man's principals and not only that, what about my own?' They need not have worried because I still had my own separate identity but I was able to expand upon that by accepting the thoughts and feelings of a person I greatly admired. I was then able to become two rather than one.

Nothing I could do or say would convince some people who lived in fear of my choices, that I had made the right decision but regardless of their judgement based on their fear and not mine, I stood strong in my resolve. I personally chose not to accept their fear. I could understand it but I was not about to let it stand in the way of me following my true path or calling in life. Sure, there were moments that I could have lived without but when all these hardships and obstacles are put into context, it was the best thing I could ever have done for myself. I have no regrets. I am satisfied and how many people can truly say that?

If other people decide to feel sorry for me or judge my every decision as being wrong, well I cannot do a thing to change their attitude or belief and I certainly don't bother wasting my energy and valuable time in trying to do just that, because I know it won't change a thing. My choices are my own affair and other people who disagree with those choices will need to learn to live with it and to hopefully one day accept my decisions. The longer I continued in my chosen direction, the more the fear of being judged became less and less; one day their judgements could no longer hurt or make me doubt myself. That was the day I freed myself from being bound to my environment and expectations of others. There was no looking back.

I was only interested in moving forwards and this is largely what I achieved. Certainly my life could have been made less complicated but what's the point in dwelling or wondering about what my life could have been like if I had chosen to say no to the offer of becoming one of Christ's Apostles? By reflecting upon the 'what could have been' serves no useful purpose, except to cause regret and doubt. So please, stay away from falling into this trap.

No-one likes to be judged harshly by others but what about when we judge ourselves? This can give rise to us then becoming our own worst enemy which then creates much inner turmoil, indecision, doubt and self-punishment. So try this – listen carefully to your thoughts for a day, at the end of which calculate the time spent in judging others, including yourself and separate the two. What percentage of time was left over where you lived in a judgement free zone? Which particular internal space did you prefer to occupy and why? Which was worse and why?

By discerning the truth, this exercise will give you many valuable insights about yourself. I think the worse place to be, would be where I judge myself because I fear the rejection from others. Each time we judge ourselves and doubt our decisions, causes us to split and separate from our true self. If this split or crack then becomes large enough, our true self or soul may become buried alive under a tonne of rubble, never to be seen again and where our physical/emotional part of our nature surrounds itself in the darkness of despair and hopelessness. What value does this sort of a life have then? None, as far as I can see, which brings me to the question of how much value do you place on your own decision making processes?

If it has little or no value, you will then persistently and consistently seek guidance from other people you consider to be in authority or who you feel are better qualified than yourself. The trouble with this way of thinking is that no-one is more qualified than yourself when it comes to your own life. You may not think so and other people may not think so but this is reality regardless. Besides, other people may not always have your own best interests at heart and there's the catch, which should cause you to question – who can I trust?

The answer is that you can trust yourself. You'll never, never know until you give it a go. The secret is not being afraid to make an occasional mistake. Really, these minor mistakes, although you may believe them to be major, are of no important consequence. Learn from them, move on, then try and do things differently next time because believe me, there will always be a next time.

Let's now look at the question – why do you feel the need to judge yourself? Some possible answers could be because you lack faith in yourself; you don't like yourself very much as an individual; you see everyone as being superior to you and where you feel guilty for voicing your own opinions.

If you can relate to what I've just said, then this is most certainly a sad way to live your life. The solutions would then be to believe in yourself, to love yourself, to see yourself as everyone's equal and to remain guilt free.

So what situations are you in when you succumb to beating yourself up? Are you at work whilst communicating with your boss and colleagues; are you at home whilst getting cranky with your partner or kids; is it at school, in front of your friends, when you can't come up with the correct answer and you feel like a right young fool; is it in social situations where because of your insecurity, you become tongue tied and your stomach reacts in nervous knots; or are you in church where you're so afraid to put a foot wrong? Is it one, all or none of the above?

Once you can pinpoint what area of your life gives you the most trouble, you can then work towards changing it that will then leave you no plausible excuse to judge yourself. It all boils down to having the ability to forgive ourselves.

God can forgive your many mistakes and indiscretions, so why can't you accept this and leave it at that? Why try to force blood out of a stone? Why continue to punish yourself when it's not necessary? Begin to value every facet of your personality – the good, the bad, the beautiful and the ugly.

Accept yourself, warts and all because if you can't or won't, how can you expect others to value you? We only receive what we give. Knowing all this, how would you then answer the following – if you were put up for auction and taking into consideration how you truly feel about yourself, what monetary value would you place upon your being? What would a fair price be for someone to bid for you?

If by chance you were bidding for yourself, would you match the previous buyer's offer, would you go higher or would you go lower? If you were offered more than you felt you were worth, how would you then react to this situation? Would you feel guilty about accepting another person's obvious belief in you and so reject their generous offer or would you feel honoured and take steps to believing that perhaps you are worthy of a lot more than what you had first anticipated.

Let's now look at the other side of the coin. Please take steps not to trample over and devalue another person's feelings by making a quick and harsh judgement about them. It is best to work with the facts of the situation rather than your emotions which cannot always be trusted when feeling stressed or anxious. To make a judgment call then will be incorrect. But of course, you are never wrong, are you? It takes great courage to admit we have made a mistake, especially to the one we have judged unfairly or wrongly.

It's like losing face and heaven forbid if you present yourself to the world without a face of some value. If you judge others, expect to be judged back. Before being critical of another person's situation, try and place yourself in their shoes, if only for a moment and then evaluate your feelings. Can you see more clearly now? Not many of us will take the time to do this. It all seems too hard and besides that and as you would say to yourself, 'I don't want to be like them, not even for a moment'.

My suggestion would then be to stay for more than a mere

moment, put your feet up and stay a bit longer than what you think is necessary. The more you slip into another person's shoes or energy force, the greater your understanding will be. You may shake your head in disbelief and disgust but there it is – in black and white – the other person's truth staring at you in the face. You may not accept it as being your own and this would be right but you do need to accept that it is theirs and there is nothing you can do to change it.

Although, if the other person is still listening, you can perhaps guide them gently to go in a different direction but if they decide not to, allow them the right to choose as hopefully they would give you that same right. But even if they don't accept your right to choose and allow you to make decisions for yourself, that doesn't mean you must become like them. Some people have a "tit for tat" or "an eye for an eye" mentality. This can work upon occasion but if both people involved cannot stop, it can then quickly get out of hand and become an all out, no holds barred battle to the death.

Where does one draw the line between continuing and withdrawing? If you make a judgement to withdraw, please don't see this as being a cowardly act. In fact, it is quite smart, not stupid, so thank yourself for making that decision. You won't regret it if you do. Certainly you may wonder if you have done the right thing and all I can say to that, because it can't be proven to you, is to have faith. Base your decisions on today and not on the future. In other words, don't fall into the trap of thinking 'what if … ' or 'if only … ' You can't predict the future accurately as it changes all of the time from one minute to the next, so please don't fill your head with futuristic concerns that may never happen.

You can only deal with the now and, depending upon your

immediate response to the wrongdoings of another; this will determine the course of your future. So before you judge and react aggressively towards a perceived unfairness to yourself, take a momentary step back from the situation to discern the real truth about the other person rather than to judge them harshly.

Let's now take a closer look at why people make judgements based upon their own fears? Is it because they have nothing better to do? It is always easier to sit in judgement of another than it is to be a judge of your own behaviour, attitude and belief. To do the latter can be difficult and requires great conviction, courage, discipline and detachment. We can all go within and bring these qualities to the surface, because it will be needed at that time you choose to face yourself, as well as facing the truth about others.

To stand boldly in this space filled with confidence can be scary but it can be quite inspiring and life changing as well. And once the truth is seen, you can never completely forget or go back to your old habit pattern of deluding yourself. Trust me when I say this. You may suppress the truth, as you do with a whole range of your negative emotions, but they are still there present in your heart which will react accordingly. Have you ever stopped to wonder about the cause of that sudden sharp stabbing pain the chest or in any of your other body parts? The answer, my friend, is simple.

Each time you shut yourself off from the truth's sometimes harsh reality, you cause a minor blockage which over time builds up to create a major pressure and if you don't give this pressure any escape route to follow, your body will begin to bitterly complain and if you choose to ignore on a consistent basis what your body is saying, it will shut itself down in the same way that you have done some time before, when you chose to ignore your truth.

So now you know – the fear of being judged and to judge another cruelly, with or without just cause, is damaging to your health.

There are many zombie-like people walking around today carrying out their day to day duties under half mast. The other half of their energy is spent trying to deal with the pain they are feeling as a result of other people judging them. And more often than not, these poison arrows of judgement come from many sources which are scattered but come together from separate directions to form a collective whole. This combination of sources or poisonous arrows that I speak of can and often do come in the form of your boss at work, your partner or child at home, your best friend, your parents, your teacher, your psychiatrist or doctor, local council member, neighbours, the church or police. The list goes on.

After being thoroughly bombarded, attacked and ambushed nearly every minute of your waking day, is it any wonder why you would want to escape from it all, to go on a holiday and leave everyone behind to achieve some temporary relief?

Having your actions being constantly criticised and undermined, can wear you down and can be a real drain on your energy and when your protective barrier is low, your immune system becomes weakened and initially you will begin to experience little mishaps that will in time escalate to major accidents or illness. These could require medical treatment in the form of drugs and possible hospitalisation and can lead to probable death if not attended to quickly enough. In this situation, an imbalance of justice has been created in this person's life.

In order to correct this problem before it kills us, the

judged then becomes a judge and jury for someone weaker than themselves, who lacks the power to fight back. Playing this new and foreign role as a judge of others, leads us to believe that we are still in control. This is not right. You then become no better than those people judging you; this then becomes a self-perpetuating cycle of destruction, great sadness and heartbreak. Some people will even go so far as thinking 'if I have to put up with being hurt by others, I will hurt them or someone else back'. Again, we return to the "tit for tat" or "an eye for an eye" mentality. And you know what I've already said about that.

To fear someone judging your actions and words should not be your main basis in making choices or decisions. Put this unhealthy fear well and truly out of your mind, or perhaps it already is. Just because you do not consciously agree to having this fear of being judged, it is still there. Your decisions need to be based upon what you feel and believe and not on what other people believe, even if those others, including the rest of the world, disagree quite strongly with your heart felt belief. You have to do what you feel is right at that time. If the same situation cropped up in six months time, you may react differently or maybe you won't.

But if you should do something that you know is wrong and you go against your better judgement, don't act surprised when you receive a negative response and knowing that it was the wrong thing to do, don't then turn around and judge the judges for judging you.

Jesus never made snap harsh judgements of another. He took the time to look deep into that persons' heart and examined closely, every nerve ending. It is so important to look beyond the immediately obvious. If you rush headlong into the act of judging, you are then more inclined to miss the finer and more subtle details which are of as much value, as those details that supposedly leave you with no doubt in your mind as to what happened.

As mentioned elsewhere in this book, the mind can play tricks and confuse us. So how often can we really trust our thoughts that spring forth, sometimes unannounced, from this receptacle that we call the brain or the mind?

Think before you act and attack. Not lashing out is the best way to avoid an awful condition which is known in this business as having "foot in mouth disease". If you persist in sabotaging yourself despite all the warnings not to, the only solution then left open is to forcibly remove your foot from mouth and ensure that future steps are taken not to put this part of your body in a place where it naturally doesn't belong.

I mean, can you imagine that when you have one less foot to play with, you will feel less secure but what's so much worse is that two less feet will most definitely cause you to fall down in a screaming heap; where you end up in a bigger mess than when you first started this ridiculous campaign. Save yourself from this particular embarrassment, please.

When we die and our soul is taken to where it needs to be, initially, we will find we are in a space that is similar to a blank void which is later filled with the sights and sounds of your life. Your job is to watch and listen to those major events that have shaped your existence, including those experiences that threw you off track. Your purpose is to judge yourself, although I would much prefer to use the word 'assess'. Not only will you see, hear and feel what happened from your perspective but you will also be made aware of how other people saw and felt that same event and that is where and when things can get really interesting or painful, as the case may be.

Other than watching, listening and assessing your life with detachment, it is hoped that you might come to an understanding about what the specific lesson was that you and they needed to learn from this whole ugly or beautiful episode. Even if you kept on repeating the same habit pattern throughout your entire life, this is when you can re-tip the scales in your favour and start afresh by accepting the truth revealed about everyone's perspective, not only your own.

You need to remember that while you are still living in your physical body, everything you do, think, feel or say will have some impact, whether that be good or bad, upon those people who come in contact with you. This impact may make a little ripple in the pond, while other events you set out to create could result in a tidal wave of emotional upheaval. You might have survived this dramatic ordeal but others around you may not have been so lucky. You may believe that the thoughts, feelings and welfare of others is not your responsibility, so why should you waste a moment of your time before taking action to look at the possible consequences and effects it will have on other people? Some will travel with you in the same direction, while others will be washed away down-stream, struggling to stay afloat.

So beware, dear one, understand that when you finally rejoin the Spirit world, you must expect this level of confrontation. It is not designed to punish and upset you or make you fearful. It's just another valuable lesson that needs to acknowledged and evaluated before moving on to your next, hopefully better, life. Also understand that the time you spend in your earthly years judging yourself and others, needs to be multiplied by ten; this will give you some indication of how long you will be required to work upon yourself. This is something you cannot avoid.

For example, if you spend a total of say 10 years out of your entire life sitting in judgement, another 100 of those same Earth years will then be needed in the Spirit world to become at least a little bit enlightened. Sounds like a frightening prospect doesn't it, when you look at it from that angle? But I can assure you that because the matter of time does not exist in the Spirit realm, this apparently long time in human terms will pass as quickly as the blinking of an eye.

In other words, how long you spend in this assessment period is hardly noticeable. In fact, when you start to refocus upon another earthly life and you look at how time has passed on this planet, you could be truly amazed as to how quickly it flies when you are busy having fun and learning can be fun; it doesn't always have to be a painful bore and a chore.

But the time of assessment and re-evaluation I have been talking about doesn't have to happen only when you finally reach the other side. This same process can be done right now. Why wait? If you can go through this constant evaluation of your thoughts, feelings and actions, say at the end of each day, then a whole lot less time will be needed on your personal Judgement Day that will make the transition between one life to the next so much smoother and simpler. Don't make everything so hard for yourself. Take the easy route for a change.

You may believe you don't possess the ability to evaluate how another person feels in regards to your actions but if you combine your energy with theirs, this then becomes possible. One way to do this is to visualise in your mind yourself and the other person. Can you see them now? They are standing right in front of you while you stand three steps behind. When you have them firmly fixed in your mind's eye, take three steps forward and become one with that person. You will only be shown what you need to see and hear for your own spiritual growth. The rest of it will remain hidden because this is not your business to know, as it has nothing to do with you.

This way, you are not invading their sense of privacy or personal space. Sometimes when you do this technique, another person you hadn't thought of could appear. If this happens, understand that Spirit has sent them to you because due to your negative or positive actions, they too have been affected by your actions but which are not consciously known by you. Sometimes, we are not aware of the full amount of damage we have caused to not only one but to the many.

For example, you may have stepped on someone's toes, unintentionally or not and because of that one single act, this other person then offloads about how they feel to a third, fourth, fifth party or more. Some of these indirect participants could react negatively and that leads them to take certain action/s that could have a detrimental effect upon yourself or some other involved or unrelated person.

Our actions can have far reaching consequences beyond our conscious comprehension, until we make an effort to move beyond our own boundaries and to truly start taking into consideration the needs of other people who we may or may not know very well in life. Once you can see everyone's truth in any given situation, you can then learn from it and vow not to make the same mistake again later down the track, if necessary. A mistake, like the past, can never be undone or unspoken but you can ensure that a similar disastrous situation doesn't have to happen again.

When you truly understand and accept this, you will come to know that you have the power to control your own future. Keeping in mind that as you maintain that control, the future of those people who come in contact with you as a result of your actions could be changed perhaps in a direction they were not meant to go in, which then forces them into a position where they have to counteract your moves in order to avoid further calamity in their lives. This is when karma steps in and this is where it can all get a bit hazy and messy. We are all one and we all live together in a fine and complex web of interconnecting invisible threads of energy that binds us all together, forever.

All in all, life is like a giant game of chess but remember that there will always be certain partners who won't know how to or don't wish to play the same game as you. And to complicate matters even further, there is more than one game being played at the same time, consecutively with the same or different people.

In short, the only thing I wish to now point out is that to constantly judge yourself or others will keep you walking in a never ending loop of sameness, ill health and despair. Stop now or forever find yourself searching for peace that can never be found, for as long as you stay judgemental.

As I faced my maker at the Last Judgement, I knelt before the Lord with all the other souls ...

Before each of us lay our lives like the squares of a quilt in many piles. An Angel sat before each of us sewing our quilt squares together into a tapestry that is our life. But as my Angel took each piece of cloth off the pile, I noticed how ragged and empty each of my squares was. They were filled with giant holes. Each square was labelled with a part of my life that had been difficult, the challenges and temptations I was faced with in everyday life.

I saw hardships that I endured, which were the largest holes of all. I glanced around me. Nobody else had such squares. Other than a tiny hole here and there, the other tapestries were filled with rich colour and the bright hues of worldly fortune. I gazed upon my own life and was disheartened.

My Angel was sewing the ragged pieces of cloth together, threadbare and empty, like binding air. Finally, the time came when each life was to be displayed, held up to the light, the scrutiny of truth. The others rose, each in turn holding up their tapestries. So filled their lives had been. My Angel looked upon me and nodded for me to rise. My gaze dropped to the ground in shame. I hadn't had all the earthly fortunes; I had love in my life and laughter. But there had also been trials of illness and death and false accusations that took from me, my world as I knew it. I had to start over many times.

I often struggled with the temptation to quit, only to somehow muster the strength to pick up and begin again. I spent many nights on my knees in prayer, asking for help and guidance in my life. I had often been held up to ridicule, which I endured painfully, each time offering it up to the Father in hopes that I would not melt within my skin beneath the judgmental gaze of those who unfairly judged me.

And now, I had to face the truth. My life was what it was and I had to accept it for what it was. I rose slowly, lifted the combined squares of my life to the light. An awe filled gasp filled the air. I gazed around at the others who stared at me with wide eyes. Then I looked upon the tapestry before me.

Light flooded the many holes, creating an image, the face of Christ. Then our Lord stood before me with warmth and love in His eyes. He said 'Every time you gave over your life to Me, it became My life, My hardships and My struggles. Each point of light in your life is when you stepped aside and let Me shine through, until there was more of Me than there was of you.'

Source: Unknown

Affirmations

> *GOD DOES NOT JUDGE with envy in his heart, so why should I?*
>
> *No one person or being is BETTER OR LESSER THAN me.*
>
> *I stand before you on an EQUAL FOOTING.*

BARTHOLOMEW

Beauty that's pure is found within the heart.

Acceptance of oneself brings with it a sense of peace and understanding.

Responsible acts will bear responsible outcomes.

Tools of success, like ourselves, needs constant reshaping and sharpening.

Happiness will always create even more happiness.

Opposite hate, stands love.

Laughter is the best medicine and will keep you forever young.

Outstanding actions cause outstanding results.

Magnificence can be found, everywhere you look.

Enthusiasm is your best driving force to keep you moving forward.

Walk your talk.

I loved to laugh a lot. I had two sons and a daughter, plus a fourth child who quickly passed back into the Spirit world soon after being born. My son Mark was sickly as a 9 year old and was healed by Jesus. You might ask why Jesus did not save the life of my fourth and youngest child. It wasn't meant to be. I certainly do not bare any grudges or hold Jesus responsible for my child's death.

Mark looked up to and admired the many qualities and abilities of the Apostle Peter, while I taught all my children as much as I could about their native flora and fauna. I taught Mark in particular, the principles of Jesuit law and he used this knowledge later in life to help the weak and oppressed. Mark, while growing up, developed a close bond with Shontara, where he became like Mark's other dad. This annoyed me greatly sometimes but I guess to have two dads is far better than having no male role models at all. There was much professional rivalry and competition between myself and Shontara.

This largely stemmed from the fact that we were both involved in a similar trade. I was a silversmith, while he was a goldsmith. We were both similar in nature and we were both as stubborn as old mules; forever wanting to prove to anyone that would stop long enough to look and listen, that we were so much better than the other. To be brutally honest, I always breathed a sigh of relief when Shontara put down his tools to travel with Matthew. This caused us to spend a lot of wasted time while in each other's presence trying to compete and outdo each other in order to gain respect.

The funny thing was though, we already had the respect that we both craved. We couldn't see this until much later but by then it no longer mattered. Jesus, on the other hand, always saw us as being complimentary to each other's skills and as being equal. Jesus never compared but we did.

Shontara made a gold cup that was originally given to his great friend the Apostle Matthew, who later passed it on to Jesus as a gift (with Shontara's approval); it was used at the Last Supper and later caught the blood at the crucifixion of Christ. It was of a simple design and a few days and nights before Jesus sat down for the last time to have supper with the Twelve, Jesus requested that something be added.

That something was a square cut blood red ruby that Shontara set at an angle which created the illusion that it was indeed cut into the shape of a diamond. Later, when Shontara married the man of her dreams (that is, in this lifetime today), she went shopping for a chalice she could use as part of their wedding vows; at which time would be filled with a blood red port. Again, Shontara didn't know why she felt drawn to do this but this she did.

In the meantime and back to the past, I too received a request from Jesus to make twelve silver medallions for each of the Apostles to wear beneath their clothing. Basically, it showed the Star of David enclosed within a circle. In this outer circle were set twelve stones, upon which different Hebrew characters were inscribed. Six were located at each point of the Star, while the other six were positioned in between. When translated, these characters listed the twelve virtues of Man. The twelve stones also symbolically represented the Twelve Tribes of Israel and the Twelve Apostles.

Shontara today, without being consciously aware of what I

had done then, was later guided by Spirit to create a pendant similar to what I've just described. Once the design work was put down on paper, Shontara then sought out the expertise of a professional jeweller to turn her dream into a reality that could be touched and admired by many. There were three main differences from the original design that I had created approximately 2000 years before.

The pendant that Shontara wears today has seven stones rather than twelve that symbolically represents the seven Archangels and the seven main spiritual centres (or chakras) of the body. Six stones are positioned at each point of the Star (as per the original), plus an extra stone being in the centre. The original I created was made of silver but the piece Shontara designed today, is gold. The third major difference was there were no inscriptions etched on to each of the stones.

To give you another example of how our past can impact greatly upon our present without realising it, is that seven years and one life cycle later, Shontara was guided to learn the craft of silver jewellery making. She knew nothing of me at that time. Shontara was first taught the basic principles of how to cut, shape and polish rocks and precious stones. If you are an expert in the field of lapidary, you would say she learnt the art of cabochoning. This gave her the taste of what would come next. Jewellery making was a natural progression from what she had just learnt.

This new craft came easy to her, where she fell into it like a duck does to water. It then suddenly dawned on Shontara that she had done all this before but didn't know any of the details. Several original pieces of jewellery were designed and made by her own two hands, under the close supervision of a professional teacher who allowed her the freedom to learn from her mistakes. Sometimes Shontara found the theory of designing a perfect piece of jewellery was so much easier than the practical application of that same theory. But there eventually came a time when she would make a piece of jewellery that Jesus was waiting for and wanted her to make. This was the real reason as to why she was there.

She was requested to make an equilateral cross. That is, the four arms of the cross are of equal length. In mathematics, it is the same shape as the plus (+) sign. Shontara was also guided as to what size she should make it. The cross turned out to be big and I mean in your face big. You couldn't miss it easily and she wears it with great pride. Set into the middle of this cross and where all the four arms meet, is a deep red garnet. She so much wanted a ruby but couldn't afford to buy one. She was remembering the golden chalice. The red signified the healing power that was the Blood of Christ.

To go with this cross, Shontara created a most unique and special chain to hang it off that contained a complete set of twelve links. She carefully placed at the end of each arm of the cross, three additional silver bars, which when added together came to twelve. Both the silver bars and the links in the chain represented the Twelve Apostles (which of course she is now writing about).

As an added note of interest, some years after finishing this piece of jewellery, an accident happened, where one silver bar positioned on the cross fell off, never to be seen again. It has never been replaced. Could that have been representative of when Judas left the group?

Upon completion of this cross, Shontara moved away from jewellery making and was then free to explore new avenues of study. Shontara uses this cross today in a practical way but that's another story for another time.

Ever since being a young child, Shontara, as you know her today, has always had a strong yearning and leaning towards both the Star of David and the cross without ever really knowing why. Now she understands. But back to Mark, my son.

I hope all this flitting backwards and forwards in my narrative, from the past to the present and back again, is not too confusing for you and if it is, I do apologise.

As I mentioned near to the beginning of my story, Mark had developed a close bond with Shontara. As fate would have it, Mark was later forced to play a part in his death as well.

At the time of writing these same words that you are now reading, Shontara had no idea or desire to look too closely at how she/he had died. What came next is something she did not expect would ever be channelled. It needs to be said though and it's a part of her life that needs to be known.

It is important for her own self-healing to understand and accept what happened and I, as Bartholomew, shall share later with you dear reader, how the manner in which Shontara died then, bares a direct impact to what she fears and dislikes today.

My son was forced to do what he had to do because his own life was gravely at risk if he dared to disobey the orders of the authorities. He was being tested and punished at the same time. It was a most distressing moment for all three of us, as I watched my son brutalise Shontara, which was the very last thing he ever wanted to do but he had no choice. I felt their collective pain, both physical and emotional.

In the open air and in the heat of the afternoon sun, Shontara was required to lay face down semi-naked on a burning hot circular metal slab. Attached to the outside perimeter of this circle were four metal clasps or manacles, made of iron.

Shontara was then forcibly placed into a spreadeagled position, where each arm and leg was stretched and held in place by the metal clasps. Once closed, these clasps could not be opened again without the key. To struggle was useless. Mark was then ordered to stone and whip Shontara until the blood flowed freely. This was done in front of the whole community.

This was the ultimate in humiliation and was another form of torture. In amongst this crowd of onlookers were a mixture of both supporters and detractors of Shontara. The whipping and stoning finally stopped and Shontara was forced to die slowly. To give comfort in any form, along with food or drink, was not allowed. It was unbearable to watch but watch I did. Finally, Shontara's pain and misery ended but the suffering my son felt from that moment on would haunt him for the rest of his days. He blamed himself for Shontara's death. It haunted me as well but for a different reason.

Let us now jump back to the present, where Shontara hates being tied up. You might ask, as a woman wouldn't this be a natural thing for her not to want? Yes, you are indeed correct but sadly in today's reality, there are certain people, both men and women, who have fantasies of being gagged and bound; where the 'victim' willingly hands over complete control to another and where they are forced into a position of powerlessness, which they consequently enjoy.

I don't quite understand and accept this way of thinking myself but it still exists, whether I like it or not. Are you a victim of circumstance, where to resolve the situation is out of your control? How does it feel? Most people would say it's not a nice place to be. Keeping this in mind, do not do the same to other people. An individual's freedom of choice is always all important.

When two people are very much alike, combined with when one wishes to be in control of the other, sit back and watch the sparks fly. You would think that because of their similarities, they would get on well together and this can be true. But some of these similarities may be of a negative nature, such as our fears and weaknesses, and for some people, to confront this can be quite distressing. Each and every person we are involved with is put there for a special purpose, even those we dislike the most. We are mere mirrors, reflecting and bouncing off each other what we see, or don't see, in ourselves.

It's all well and good to accept those good qualities about a person but what about the not so good? How do we deal with that? Do we reject them? Do we get angry at them? Do we bad mouth them to a sympathetic third party? Do we fight with them by endlessly and hopelessly trying to point out the error of their ways, which only leads to a sore head because of the constant bashing up against a brick wall? There is a Biblical saying, although I don't know it exactly word for word and that is – "let he who is without sin, cast the first stone".

Other people in our personal, business or social life are there to remind us of what good we have forgotten about ourselves, as well as reminding us in a sometimes not so subtle way, that there are certain issues and bad habits within us that need to be resolved. Don't ever be afraid to look at the bad and good together, in equal amounts, and then learn to tip the scale more towards the positive. No-one is completely all bad.

For example, you may have one hundred people gathered together around one person stuck in the middle. Those one hundred people can all see the same bad qualities, because that is what they want to see.

Each individual that makes up that group may not be able

to accept the other person's spiteful and nasty attitude but if you are a part of that one hundred, take time out to look beyond the surface of that person's angry actions and you will then begin to see behind the mask, a scared little boy or girl, crying out for some attention. They don't care about the quality of attention, just so long as they receive it. They are confused. They don't know a better way of going about getting what they want or need, so they become aggressive and go about taking certain steps to possess what may not be theirs to take, which automatically puts everyone else off side.

Learn to understand their motives and never assume you know everything there is to know about the one that pushes your emotional buttons so well. Ask direct questions of them. Attempt to find a crack in their armour and take a walk inside their mind and heart before you pass a harsh judgement.

If you can break down the walls that stand between you and them, you can then reach out to each other in mutual trust and support and there begins a developing and possible deep friendship. You've seen them at their worst; now see them at their best. Remember, loud and aggressive people are too scared to see the good in themselves.

When they act badly and we react accordingly in a negative way, all that manages to do is send back a message of confirmation to that person standing all alone. They think, although sometimes not consciously, that all of these people think I'm bad and mean, so they must be right. I don't even like myself. The majority rule. I must be a bad person; so I shall be what they expect.

Then we have a second more difficult situation where the hundred previously mentioned are all negative, while surrounding one strong positive light.

How is that one supposed to react to all this heavy dark energy? Do they walk away? Do they stay and be themselves? Or alternatively, do they cave in under the pressure and join the negative crowd? "When in Rome, do as the Romans do", whether you like it or not.

If they do become like the majority, is there any guarantee that this one person will be accepted? In the second situation mentioned, the real problem lies with the hundred and not with the one. The boot is now firmly on the other foot. It is the group now who feels scared, vulnerable, insecure and threatened by someone they see is far better than themselves.

But is that any reason to blame or judge the one who is different? Does that one positive person try and change the opinion of the majority? Or do they merely accept that the majority don't know a better way of dealing with their own fears?

Because, once there is a full understanding of the individual standing or sitting opposite us, and we are looking at this from both sides of the fence now, tolerance, respect and patience will always follow. A potentially volatile and dangerous liaison can then easily be avoided.

I loved playing and communicating with young children. They were always so refreshingly honest and you always knew where you stood with them. There was one boy I was particularly fond of. When he walked into my life, he was only ten. He was of a small build, with big dark brown soulful eyes and a thick mop of short and tight jet black curls. He didn't have a loving and supportive family around him, so he would seek me out as I too would naturally gravitate towards him. I felt strongly that I wanted to take him gently and keep him safe under my protective wing. Not that he really needed my protection or assistance in this way, because he was – what you would term today – 'street wise'.

He was as agile as a deer and always knew how to get himself in and out of trouble. From a young age, he learnt how to quickly defend and look after his own needs, as a matter of survival. In the meantime, all I could give was my moral and emotional support, whenever he needed it. His name was Matthew but please don't confuse this child with the Apostle of the same name.

He was most keen to learn the craft of silver smithing. He would spend hours, patiently watching and absorbing everything I did. Matthew never got in my way; he made sure of that but I was always aware of his eager beaver presence. I watched him grow up into a young man and when he became fifteen, I started to give him some responsibility in order to further educate his young mind. It was around this same time that he became my helper, or apprentice.

Mark, my son, and Matthew stayed out of each other's way a lot of the time. I sensed a certain amount of reserve between the two of them when together; for whatever reason, I'm not sure of. They made an unspoken and unwritten pact to leave each other alone as much as possible. This saddened me a little because even though Mark was a couple of years older than Matthew, I felt my son could have learnt a useful trick and tip or two from Matthew but alas, it was not meant to be. You can't force someone to interact with you, let alone get them to like you. It has to be a decision that both people make as separate individuals and these two boys were not interested in developing a friendship with each other. But they did have one thing in common and that was me.

Perhaps because of my friendship and the length of time I

The Apostles

spent with this young vagabond boy, I may have unwittingly pushed Mark into Shontara's direction, although Mark never needed to feel rejected but perhaps he did, just a little. This situation later taught me a lot about the danger of favouritism towards certain children and believe me, it happens in all different environments – in church, hospital, school and at home.

As adults, we don't mean to do this but we still do. And we don't only play this game with children but we play it with other adults as well. From this union of two or more people, certain cliques or groups are formed and sometimes, it is extremely hard for someone different to break into such a group.

Can you imagine quite a different world where the whole human race was welcome to join in and be a part of the Universal circle of friendship? This could become a yearly event, like when you celebrate on New Year's Eve, Christmas or Easter Day. On this special day and taking into consideration the different time zones the world over, all the residents of each separate continent, country or island would line up shoulder to shoulder at the same moment, with joined hands to make a perfect link around the outside perimeter of the land in which they live.

Once joined, each individual would then call upon the Holy Spirit and the Angels to fill up the surrounding space with a powerful cleansing and healing energy, while they themselves would send love in whichever way they knew how, to all those they were linked to, even if they couldn't see them. Each participant would then give themselves permission to receive the same magnified wave of peace and harmony to flow over and through them. It would certainly take some time to organise and international co-operation from governments and other authorities to do this. It could be recorded live by satellite as well, which would then be played back on the TV airwaves later.

I feel that doing such a thing would bring major change to this world for the better and really, it doesn't take much effort or strength to hold a person's hand in friendship. Young or old, healthy or sick, rich or poor, stranger or friend, you can all do it.

And if no-one on this great planet of ours feels they are capable of organising such a grand event on a worldwide scale, for those who wish to see this happen I say don't lose heart, because you can always bring it to reality by visualising it all happening in your mind. It will still have the same effect, if enough people are doing it at the same time. Seeing clearly an event in our mind can be even more powerful than seeing it eventuate in reality. It is within our imagination where miracles are first created which can then later manifest themselves in the physical. This is the truth, not make believe.

I used to love watching my wife make bread for the family. Sara would put her whole heart and body into it. I was especially fascinated to look how well she kneaded, punched and manipulated the freshly made dough. It was rather sensuous and hypnotic to watch her work. She had a strong pair of hands. They had to be, with all the lifting she was required to do. And even though there was forever a swarm of young children playing at her feet, they never seemed to disrupt her flow. Sara expertly navigated her way around them. The children knew better than to get in her way too much but they didn't need to be concerned because even if they did unwittingly stop her from doing her chosen task, she would never raise her voice in frustration. She would take it all in her stride and continue on regardless.

Sara was my opposite. My level of patience and tolerance

was far less than hers. I admired and loved Sara greatly for this quality and more. She taught me a lot, just by observing her speech and movement. Can there ever be another like her?

How do you react when someone is annoying you? Do you become like a raging bull, where you completely lose your cool, make all sorts of charges, stamp your feet, rant and rave? What a frightening sight this could be, especially for those so young and tender in age. Or perhaps your targeted audience would merely stand and laugh out loud at your rather silly antics. How does that then make you feel – even more frustrated and angry perhaps?

No-one likes to be laughed at, especially when we are trying to make a point. It can be a cruel blow to the one on the receiving end of that laugh or it could possibly turn the situation into something more positive rather than negative.

To win an argument, it is best never to fight fire with fire. Do the opposite to what they are doing. Throw some cool soothing water over the fire by saying something nice rather than being nasty. The trick is though that when you are saying something nice, make sure you are sincere. Otherwise it could fall upon deaf ears and your voice will not be heard.

The voice of Jesus has been heard across the centuries and it is still being heard today, as are a blend of many other voices but in the end, they all merge into one large voice that can change the shape of a nation for the better. Each country has its own particular lesson to learn.

Some do well in learning it, while others struggle against it. The more outer strife there is within a nation, this merely reflects the inner torment of those who have chosen to live and work there. Doubt and fear are what holds us back. These same emotions can then spread like some infectious cancer, jumping from one person to the next. One day, when you least expect it and if not stopped, they will destroy us all.

Let's now talk about the vibration and specific lessons that each nation is required to learn. Before I go into too much detail, some countries are doing better than others at this time; but that doesn't mean those countries that are struggling to learn the appropriate lessons are lesser than them. A country is only as good as its people. Without people, there would be no lessons to learn.

So let's blast off with Australia, as this is where the book you are now reading was first written.

Australia

This is a country of way showers, light workers, inspiring motivators and inventive personalities. The people of this great nation need to learn about acceptance and tolerance of those who are different to themselves. For those fortunate enough to have been born here, they have to be careful not to bury their head in the sand (like their native ostrich) and ignore the plight of people in other parts of the world. Don't become too complacent with your lot in life. Most certainly, enjoy your good fortune and protection but never take it for granted. Always take time out to give thanks to the higher force you choose to believe in. Remain independent in your leadership while helping to empower and guide other nations.

Summary – Acceptance, Tolerance, Thankfulness, Independence, Leadership

The United States of America

This is a nation of rebels, hard hitters, movers and shakers. Don't be ruled by your emotions alone. Don't shoot first and ask questions later. It could be too late by then. Receive and work with the facts. There is a lot of power playing going on behind closed doors. Everyone wants to be in control of the masses. There are too many chiefs and not enough Indians. There is another saying similar to this and that is "too many cooks can spoil the broth". They like to seek attention from the rest of the world and when they don't receive what they expect, they'll push hard until they do and will sometimes pay large amounts of money to ensure their success. They will create certain situations, both positive and negative, to bring about recognition.

Summary – Factual, Introspection, Acceptance, Humility

Europe

The good majority of the people are expressive and creative in the area of music and the arts. Their culture is steeped heavily in tradition. As a result of this, they may find it difficult to let go of the past. They are patriotic and passionate. They may lean towards having a fixed picture. Some may find it difficult to accept change. They would much prefer to stick with the 'old ways' and will only follow the tried and true method. New and progressive ideas can take quite a long time to be accepted and assimilated within their community. They have clearly defined boundaries.

Summary – Release, Flexibility, Change, Acceptance

Russia

This is a strong willed race of people. Many perfectionists can be found here. This means they can have a fixed picture, become rigid, inflexible and rebellious towards any change that takes them away from their perceived ideal. Each individual needs to learn about independence and not feel threatened to voice their opinion, even if it is different to the government of the day. The people need to be given more choices, as well as being given the freedom to say 'NO'. They need to focus upon finding beneficial solutions rather than dwelling only upon the problems at hand.

Summary – Flexibility, Acceptance, Change, Independence, Communication, Solutions

The United Kingdom

These people are patriotic. They find it difficult to forgive those in the past who have stepped upon their sensitive toes. They may hold grudges and steadfastly refuse to speak about what is bothering them. They can be secretive and keep a lot to themselves. They must always be seen, on the surface to be in control, even though all they may really want to do is scream and hurl abuse or cry buckets of blood, sweat and tears. There is a feeling of being trapped within their traditions and expectations passed down from others. They will tend to follow rather than lead. They will place themselves last a lot of the time. They are good listeners, polite, compassionate and caring to a fault and because of this, they can easily be used and manipulated.

Summary – Forgiveness, Communication, Honesty, Freedom, Choices, Leadership, Boundaries

India

This is a nation of great spirituality, including much internal and external conflict. The people are creative with their hands and love to give pleasure and wisdom to others. They are to learn not to demand that there is only one way of doing things. Flexibility is the key for them as a nation. They must learn not

to give all the help or assistance on a silver platter but allow other people to reach their own conclusions.
Summary – Flexibility, Freedom, Choices

Africa

They have great balance and rhythm. Music and dance is very much in their blood. There is too much expectation on the world governments to come to their aid. They need to be more self-reliant. They need to be better educated in how they can best utilise their many natural resources. They need to harness the forces of nature in a practical way. They need to find balance between the rich and poor, healthy and sick. The vibration leans more towards the negative rather than the positive. This has been caused because of their personal circumstances, over which they feel they have no control.
Summary – Acceptance, Self-reliance, Education, Practicality, Balance, Empowerment

South America

Their willingness to learn is potentially great. They have a strong faith in their religious beliefs. They will look for guidance from above or through their ancestors of ancient times. But they are stuck in a time warp. They have a need to move forward but don't know how. They need to find a balance between the old and the new.
Summary – Faith, Change, Balance

Canada

Have a need for independence. They would prefer to think of themselves as being separate from their closest neighbours and in any neighbourhood, there is always the need to live in harmony alongside each other. You don't want to create any undue waves, do you?

Summary – Independence, Harmony

Asia

Money orientated, they look largely to the future and many great electrical and technical inventions have come from here. They are artistic, when they allow themselves the time to stop work and relax. They are forever on the move. Some are workaholics, whilst those not so fortunate to earn good money have turned to a life of crime. But then again, crime exists wherever you go in the world. It's certainly not an exclusive problem limited to Asia. They have difficulty in accepting people of different nationalities. They are cautious and judgemental.

Summary – Focus, Direction, Relaxation, Acceptance

South Pacific

These people are friendly, warm and generous. They give a lot with low expectations and receive little for themselves. They are a significant and spiritual race of people. Nature plays a major part of their lives. They express their emotions through their music, dance and song. But they need to work more with the facts. Their heart often rules their head. The sense of touch is important to many of them and this has produced many great spiritual healers who can be found in small villages dotted throughout the islands, going quietly about their work.

Summary – Acceptance, Communication, Factual

New Zealand

They need to loosen the control and desire for the people to carry out the strict guidelines that have been put into place.

They need to accept their spiritual awareness more and give doubt the big boot. They are competitive and price conscious. They think twice before they spend their money and when they do dip into their wallet, they will try and get the best possible deal. This is not necessarily a bad trait though to have. Any one item will be used in lots of different ways, where it becomes multi-purpose and truly practical. Who needs a lot of 'things' when what you do have can double up as something else?

Summary – Freedom, Flexibility, Acceptance, Practicality

Middle East

They are stubborn and will tend to have one fixed picture. They are fearful, angry and rebellious. They will follow a particular cause or religion without question. They suffer from blind faith. They need not to be so possessive of what they have. There is plenty to go around for everyone who needs their goods and services. They are highly motivated individuals and cannot easily be swayed away from their convictions. The good majority are not afraid to speak their mind but at the same time, are afraid of change and losing control.

Summary – Flexibility, Peaceful, Acceptance, Introspection, Giving, Change, Self-reliance

In a nutshell, the two most important and valuable lessons that need to be learnt right across the globe, are acceptance and flexibility and as I mentioned at the beginning, some countries are doing better than others in these two areas.

You need to be aware that the Spirit of the Twelve plus One has each been allocated a particular country or continent to look after, but before you go blaming Spirit for your misfortunes, they can only guide and advise but will never interfere in your own free will to make choices. A country is only as great as its people.

We create our own good fortune and/or misery here on Earth as well as in Heaven. We need to sincerely, and not just pretend to, accept responsibility for our own actions that leads to either a positive or negative outcome. If the negative outcomes far outweigh the positive experiences, this means you are definitely in the wrong place at the wrong time while associating with the wrong people.

The time is then ripe to make a change, preferably in the opposite direction. Some people don't like change and even though they wish for a better life, they lack the necessary motivation and energy to take practical steps to ensure their wish for a better life becomes a reality.

Any sane and rational person would think that ill health, poverty, abuse and depression, coupled with a deep sense of unease and unhappiness, would be incentive enough to move away from what they no longer want in their life and move forward towards achieving what they do want.

You will hear these types of people loudly complaining but you will also note that no action is ever forthcoming. Ultimately, this means they are not sincere in their desire for positive change. Because, buried deep within their psyche, there is a part of them that truly believes they deserve nothing better for themselves.

At the merest hint of something great happening, they naturally think it's too good to be true and so become cynical and mistrustful. Because of these negative thought patterns, and sometimes they are not even consciously aware of this, these people create what they fear or dislike the most.

As I said before, we create our own good fortune or misery.

It all comes down to belief and attitude, coupled with your level of acceptance or non-acceptance, as the case may be. To not accept something or someone can be good in regards to rejecting those things or people that can be harmful or damaging to your personal development and spiritual evolvement.

The Tree of Life presents many choices to us and if you stand back some distance, you will see that this Tree has many branches which one can follow, but the trick is discerning where that particular branch will lead you. Not all of us have crystal balls to rely upon; and as we are Angels having a human experience, we have to take certain risks and chances to get to where we want to be. If you don't like where you are being led to, turn tail and run hard and fast in the opposite direction, then start again afresh. Don't hold grudges against those people who have hurt you in the past. Let them and your hurt go.

By constantly remembering only the bad times, you still drag them along upon your journey through life; even if they are not physically present, their Spirit will join you. When one chapter has finished, like any bad book, it needs to remain closed. Leave it behind.

Why weigh yourself down with unnecessary emotional baggage? By having regrets and not forgiving, you become the victim. Even though that person or group of people may no longer be in your physical surroundings, their energy still has control over you from a close or faraway place and in some instances, this could mean from the other side of the grave; where they still have the power to manipulate your thoughts and feelings because you allow it to be so.

And you allow it because of constantly dredging up old experiences that cause you pain when thinking about them. Many people of this planet today have grand masochistic tendencies. Otherwise, why would many people spend so much of their precious time remembering the past in a negative context rather than in a positive way?

Change your focus and attention upon those things or people which give you a feeling of satisfaction and upliftment. If, by chance, you feel you have no-one you can trust or rely upon, then turn to the animals and nature for comfort.

There is an abundance of this all around you, if you care to look. Even in the big, crowded and sometimes scary streets that make up the cities of New York, Hong Kong, Calcutta and Bangkok and where in order to go places, 'push and shove' is the name of the game, there can still be found a natural sanctuary that exists within. Don't be afraid to look and never feel isolated in this sometimes unfriendly world in which you live. Turn back to nature, go within, ask for help and give thanks.

From that moment on, I can guarantee that your sincerity, openness and acceptance will pay off and you will be richly rewarded beyond your fondest dreams. Besides, the only way to go from down is up and this is where you can find us. Always remember this important fact – you are all Angels in training while having a human experience.

We are but awful creatures of habit. When someone comes along and disrupts our routine, ritual or habit, many can be thrown into a state of chaos due to unexpected change – and it doesn't have to be about major important issues either. We blurt out like a cracked record to other people, comments such as – 'don't sit there, that's my chair'; 'leave the toilet seat down when you've finished with it'; 'that's what I always have for lunch or dinner'; 'I always like to catch the 5.15pm train home from work'; 'I must always ring my husband or wife to let them know of my movements'; or 'I always go for a jog with the dog in the mornings' and so on.

So how do you react when someone unwittingly takes over your precious space; who is inconsiderate of your personal needs; when the shop you frequent no longer offers that particular service or product you crave for; when the train runs late; when your mobile doesn't work or where a public phone cannot be seen for miles around or when the weather turns ugly and it's not practical or smart to go for a walk or jog in the park?

Again, how do you react in these situations that are beyond your control? Do you let everyone around you know of your displeasure and frustration, even if they had nothing to do with it, or do you quietly fume away to yourself until all these little things one day add up to something really big and then you let your anger loose in all directions?

Pity those poor victims who may innocently get caught up in your crossfire. Either way, your anger and resentment released over a short or long period of time, quickly or slowly, can cause much damage.

Ask yourself; are these minor issues really worthy getting your knickers in a knot over? All of the above case scenarios indicate a certain degree of inflexibility, non-acceptance and judgemental attitude on your part. Is this how you want to be remembered by others, as being bad tempered and complaining?

Here's a little fun technique for when you get angry at someone specifically or at the world in general. At the next earliest opportunity and while in the relative sanctuary and peace of your own home, find some dirt that you can dig up, with either your bare hands or a spade, which will be big enough to stick part of your head in. Once the hole has been dug, bend down and scream all the anger, frustration, depression and verbal abuse picked up during the day into it. Once released, then quickly cover it up, leave and don't look back. You'll be so glad you did.

You may feel like a complete idiot by putting this into practice. It may even make you laugh and any eye witnesses to this event that you may or may not be aware of, could think you have a few screws loose.

But the point is, you've gotten rid of the pain in a most physical, positive and practical way. It may be different and radical but what the heck? If it works for you, then that is all you need to be concerned about. Don't get trapped into holding on to any negative feelings for too long and always look at the end result. In other words, always look forward and not back. The past is behind you, the future lies in front of you and all the best you can hope for is to be fully present in the present.

Fear of Persecution

In the bad old days, although it is still happening today in a few small pockets of the world, the word persecution was synonymous with execution. The merest hint or threat of persecution in the right ear would send people running for the hills, their dug outs or caves. And this is how those who valued their earthly life, or had a fear of dying for no good reason, were kept on the straight and narrow. This is how the powerful minority in authority would control the masses and who implored their faithful subjects not to rebel and go against the law of their land.

On occasion, a handful of stubborn souls chose to ignore this threat by going ahead with what they believed was right to do, in the same way political activists and other lobby groups do today. History has shown us some of these souls got away with it by not getting caught, while others paid dearly with their lives so they could bring about justice, awareness and change.

Mainly, it was those people who possessed a passion and a purpose in life who would more often than not lose their life prematurely. As far as the authorities were concerned, it was the one sure way of silencing them forever, although this doesn't always solve the initial problem as one single person may have many followers ready to walk in their footsteps and so it continues – the cycle of persecution and execution.

This is how war can sometimes break out. The good portion

of those who died in the process of revolution and evolution, are proud to have given their life to uphold the truth but there are many versions of the truth, so which one do you subscribe to and do you stick with it till the end, sit on the fence and play it safe or swap and change sides according to who is winning or losing at the time?

All three ways can be fatal but not always. It's a chance one must take if you want to see something different happen. Some causes have been quite damaging and destructive but there are others which are most definitely worth fighting for, but not to the point where oceans of blood are spilt.

Some persecution techniques are akin to torture, where the strong or determined have a better chance of surviving compared to those consumed with a large amount of fear running through their veins. There is no strength in fear. It will have the opposite effect on the body by making you weak. And when you are weak, you become exposed and vulnerable to attack and your chances of survival are decreased quite dramatically. A small amount of fear can be most beneficial by keeping us on our toes; forever being alert to possible dangers looming up ahead but a lot of fear will blind us to the truth from all perspectives.

Persecution and execution can be a terrible thing for the individuals or groups involved who wish to bring about positive change within their society and who can sometimes be quite innocent. Their only crime was to be born in an era way beyond their time; where they have tried to introduce new ideas, beliefs or concepts well before the majority were ready to accept a massive shift in consciousness. Many of the world's greatest and worst spiritual, religious and political leaders, past and present, have died in tragic ways. Some you may think were justified but this would greatly depend upon your personal set of beliefs and ethnic origin; while you may regard other deaths as being unjust.

On both sides, there will always be people who shall disagree with your point of view and this is where compromise and acceptance really needs to come into play. Sadly, this has not always transpired. Think about the various ancient tribes still in existence, such as the Australian Aboriginals, the Native American Indian, the New Zealand Maoris and the African American Negro to name a few. They are still being persecuted to a large extent for their culture today, all because the masses demand they be bought into line with modern day thinking but is this such a good thing really and who does it benefit in the long term – you or them?

Look at the Spanish Inquisition along with the witches of Salem. There is the death of Jesus, Ghandi, John Lennon and Princess Diana, along with Hitler, Mussolini, Napoleon Bonaparte, Rasputin and Joan of Arc, not to mention the curse of the Kennedy clan as well. Speaking personally of the last one mentioned, if I possessed the family name of Kennedy and lived in America, I certainly wouldn't want to enter the political arena in any way, let alone aspire to be President, as they have a shocking history of being assassinated and who needs that?

There are many more movers and shakers of this world, good and bad, who could be mentioned but there is no need. You know who they are. Perhaps you are or will be one. Time will tell whether you'll change the face of the world as we know it today but will it be for the better or for the worse? Maybe the negative needs to be in existence before the positives can come into being; to enable the phoenix to rise from the ashes of destruction.

Persecution is taking the act of judgement too far. To judge something or someone, whether sensibly or unfairly, will be with us forever and a day because this is a part of our personality but persecution is a deeper and more insidious form of harassment and steps should be taken to eradicate this ugly part of human nature.

To persecute one or a group based solely upon their religion, race, age, financial status, sexual preferences, social standing or disabilities is quite abhorrent. For the one who is being persecuted, their existence can represent a living hell or if you would prefer, a waking nightmare.

No one should ever be forced to live a life under these circumstances simply because a group of narrow minded and bigoted people got together and decided they couldn't accept who others wanted to be. In their humble opinion, the rest of the world should fall into the same step and be like them and those seen to be different should lay down their alms while passively and peacefully submitting to a change of beliefs and lifestyles, regardless of whether they want to or not.

There are many discriminatory groups who demand this 'sameness' but who cannot be mentioned here on paper, as certain personal and legal ramifications could arise which will affect the author in a detrimental way and we do not wish this particular fate to befall her. We need Shontara for bigger and better things in the future, as we have chosen her to work on our behalf. If anything bad should happen to our chosen public voice as a consequence of me spelling certain things out too clearly, I would feel personally responsible and I don't wish to have this on my conscience.

If you want to know more yourself about what groups I'm alluding to, I suggest you watch, listen or read the current news stories. It won't always give you a complete and honest depiction of what's happening where and who's doing what to whom, by any means, yet it is still a good starting point from which to understand and draw the right conclusions. This way, no one can get into trouble for discovering and uncovering their own sometimes ugly truth.

Much persecution is also happening behind closed doors and which goes largely unreported. It can take place at school, in the work environment, at home, in church, on the streets, in nursing homes, youth hostels, pubs, mental institutions and more.

So, if you are unfortunate enough to be either young or old, unemployed, homeless or chronically sick in some way, you can quite safely assume that one day you could become a victim of persecution and abuse; most of which will be uncalled for but in the same breath I say, you don't have to accept it. You can end it all. Perhaps you don't believe me when I say this now. You may think I'm talking absolute nonsense along with the fact it is utterly foolish to think these things can ever change for the better. Yet they are already changing; it's just you can't see it happening. This is because you have one small portion of a thousand piece jigsaw puzzle and if you're really lucky, you might even own two or three. This is why you can't see. You have a limited small picture but this is through no fault of yours, while we can see and absorb the big picture at a glance.

Read on, as later I'll tell you how this change can be real for you, although it will take a fair amount of faith on your part for it to become a fact; and where everyone has the pleasure of experiencing this change for the better. The sad fact is that an earth shattering negative must come first before a life changing positive can come into play. The positive will then be greatly appreciated and which can never be forgotten or taken for granted.

Let's now turn the spotlight closer on you for the moment. I wish to begin by asking – are you a refugee, legal or otherwise? Are you seeking asylum from another country's government or do you already have this protection? Have you arrived in the country of your choice or are you still trapped, where you are experiencing great difficulty in finding an escape route? Are people helping you or are you battling to organise everything yourself? Do you have other family members travelling with you or do you have to leave them behind? Do you feel excited or anxious of the new life awaiting you? Do you live in fear of being killed for your beliefs? What motivates you?

Talking from a refugee's perspective, allow me to fill in some of the gaps, keeping in mind some will have slightly different ideas to mine of what it's like to be a refugee. If you've never been one, it could be difficult to understand and empathise with a refugee's plight.

Some will do it the legal way, while others can't afford to wait to wade through all the bureaucratic red tape; although the politicians will argue there are many good reasons why these rules need to be adhered to by any incoming visitor seeking refugee status. Some fear for their life or are concerned about the continued welfare of their children and elderly parents, so seek a better way.

Some potential refugees are now living in great poverty where little or no adequate food, water and shelter are available. These are things most of us take for granted. While others can't get enough work to care and provide for their families basic needs. How do you think this makes them feel – inadequate and worthless perhaps? Their country may place education as a low priority in a child's life but all knowledge is empowering. Knowledge provides a level of independence. Knowledge is the basis upon which all good decisions are made.

Education could be important but not where only the rich can afford it for their children. In this situation there is no equality and much discrimination occurs between the two class distinctions of being rich or poor. There is the fear of getting caught by the authorities of the country you are leaving, including the possibility of the same happening at the other end in the land you plan to live and work in, especially if you gained access by shady means. And even if everything was organised above board and completely legitimately, there is still a chance the accepting government may all of a sudden change their policy and renege on their original deal.

Either way, the refugee can never truly relax in their new environment and this makes it extremely difficult for them to trust. Because of this, there is always an element of uncertainty. This can lead to the refugee being too frightened to express how they truly feel in case they are dobbed into the powers that be; who consequently deport and ship them off to where they originally came from. What awaits them is a future filled with starvation, deprivation of liberties, torture and death. But hey, who cares? Do you? Can you imagine what it must be like?

On top of all this, the refugee must deal with those who wish to persecute them for who they are, in this new and unfamiliar territory they find themselves in. Who needs it both ends? These refugees have left their homeland to escape persecution. They don't seek it in the place where they choose to settle for the rest of their lives as well . Be mindful of their needs and fears, for they will then be mindful of yours. Try and find some common ground. When all is said and done, they are only human – like you and me.

Who knows, one day, you too may come to experience a fear and uncertainty so great it propels you to seek a safe haven for yourself and your loved ones in another country, even if it means you may have to break the law to achieve this goal. How will you feel then?

Would you like someone to help you, to give you a bed with warm woollen blankets on a cold winter's night, paper and pen to write with, a car to travel around in, expert medical care when necessary and a phone which can be used to communicate with your loved ones you had to leave behind? Remember, life can sometimes change quite dramatically overnight, and for the worse. How are you going to cope with this unexpected misfortune? More than likely, you will seek guidance from a family member or friend but what if they were all killed in one massive big explosion? Who do you call upon then?

All I'm trying to say is this – the person who has been doing the persecuting, could one day become those they despise – the persecuted. Don't attempt to tempt fate, because fate has a nasty habit of fighting back in ways which you could not or ever want to imagine.

What I'm about to say may offend some readers, especially those who are already persecuting this minority group I wish to talk about next, while the diehard Christians would proclaim it's a sin against God and what's more, the Bible confirms it.

The Bible does not necessarily reflect the whole truth about the teachings of Jesus. A lot of varied personalities and different points of view have gone into this book which has been rightly or wrongly added to its original form. Much has been changed, where a small word here and a little word there have been altered slightly to give it a whole new meaning to what it was before.

Yet many people who rely upon the Bible, rather than themselves, for all their answers to life's problems will prefer to see me burn in Hell for who I'm about to defend. I think that is an un-Christian thought or desire to have. I mean no harm to those who have a different opinion to mine, so I expect the same respect I give to you. So, who is this group of people who has needed such a lengthy preamble?

They are the homosexuals (both male and female) of today's society and this is quite funny and absurd in itself because during ancient times and in various cultural backgrounds, homosexuality was widely accepted. Even today, there are still some pockets of the world where this group of people are not judged harshly or persecuted and neither should they be. A person, regardless of what gender they are and there's only two to choose from, should not be persecuted due to their sexual preferences. Nothing in life is so black and white. Certainly, it may not be your way and it may not be mine but they still deserve our respect and compassion.

If the sex is consensual between two people looking for love, regardless of whether they are of the same gender or not, it means they are giving pleasure to each other and how can this be a bad thing, where there is an equal partnership of giving and receiving.

Do you think Jesus persecuted others for their beliefs? This would be a highly unlikely scenario. Did Jesus ever turn a homosexual away if they came seeking his counsel for some other totally unrelated matter? Of course not, in the same way he never turned his back on Mary Magdalene who many said was a lady of the night, a jezebel, a harlot and a whore.

Through the eyes of many, she was seen to be someone who preyed upon the needs of men and provided this service quite happily and willingly. What she did for a living was not important to Jesus or to us. Jesus was keener to see what lay in her heart and her heart was good. This is why he spent time with her.

Homosexuals and prostitutes are not bad people. They still have human feelings. These feelings only become distorted when alcohol or drugs are added to the equation which can cause some problems for themselves and other people but essentially, when you take away the substance abuse, they still require what everybody else is asking for, which is to have someone love them completely for who they are and not what they appear to be.

Humans are such complex creatures really and who have so many varied layers to their personality, which makes it hard to know what's real and what's not. Men say women are complicated and no male on Earth could ever truly understand them but all one really has to do is sit and truly listen – not to their spoken words but their unspoken thoughts and feelings. How difficult can that be?

Sadly, many 'straight' men don't bother taking the extra time out to read between the lines of their women folk, where the homosexual is more than happy to do so. This can cause much unfounded and unprovoked jealousy and insecurity to arise within her chosen male partner in life. So please, don't blame the homosexual friend of your wife or girlfriend. This is not their problem.

The real problem lies within the man who feels jealous and insecure. These are his feelings, no-one else's. In general, many more women accept homosexuals than do men; where other men, who are opposed to the whole subject, will feel their masculinity is being threatened (whatever that means), which can cause an explosion of testosterone and violence erupts. Most male homosexuals are lovers not fighters but due to the constant persecution and abuse from those men who will not accept or understand their needs, they are forced to retaliate in a physical sense so they can defend themselves and survive.

Is it any wonder why 'gays' are so often afraid to come out of the closet if this is all they have to look forward to – other men picking fights with them. It's much more straight forward and uncomplicated if they keep quiet about it. Who needs this extra aggravation? Just go away and let me live in peace.

Everyone should be given the basic freedom to be themselves. Otherwise, they are forced to live a lie and this, over a long period, will create some devastating health problems for the homosexual in hiding, including their similar friends such as transsexuals, transvestites and others like them.

They are children of the dark where secrets are more easily kept. Sometimes in this same dark space, they may be lucky to connect with their soul mate but can it really work, long term, if both are trying so hard to keep it a secret because of the real threat of persecution? It's highly unlikely, as the pressure would be so intense and this must go somewhere and more often than not, their partner will cop it.

Let's now look at the above slightly differently, so you may get a real feel for what I am saying here. Imagine if you will, the society in which you live, think it's a crime against humanity to be a heterosexual. You know this and try and accept it in the best way you can until one day you wake up and meet the woman or man of your dreams. What do you do? Not pursue it and do a runner, deny yourself what it is you need or do you stay and work at the new relationship?

If you choose to give it a go, do you make sure your relationship is conducted behind closed doors; where you never take the chance to invite your friends around while the two of you are together and to lead totally separate lives during daylight hours, coming together secretly at night with the lights out?

This may work up to a point but what happens when the woman falls pregnant. Don't laugh as this is a real possibility. What then? The problem has suddenly got bigger, not smaller. How can you possibly keep this a secret, especially after the child's birth? Do you walk away from your partner when things get too rough? You may rightfully question – what will society think of me? I'll be persecuted, ex-communicated and run out of town. Is this what I want for my soul-mate and our child?

No doubt, the pressure would be immense and when it reached a certain level, the relationship could end and it could do so quite violently, where people can get hurt or even killed.

How do you feel while reading this, as a heterosexual, taking this little trip I have described? Do you think it so unlikely it's not believable and for this reason why should you take it seriously? You may even laugh at its sheer absurdity but don't laugh too loud because your children of both genders may one day surprise you as an adult by saying – 'hey mum and dad, I'm gay and I'm proud of who I am'. What, as a parent, are you going to do then? Have you got enough guts to reject and persecute the kin of your own flesh and blood?

If the answer is yes, you won't have much to look forward to in your old age, yet you have no-one to blame for this except yourself, for the horribly sad moment when you turned your back on someone who loved you and who you once loved before you knew anything. And this all took place, simply because you were unable to accept the existence and lifestyle of homosexuals in the little corner of your personal world. As a result of this judgement, you may die alone, especially if they were your only child and your partner has already left this Earthly plane before you. Who will be there to support you in your hour of need? We will but your homosexual child may not. I must ask one last question – was all that hate you wouldn't let go of, worth it in the end?

A little while back, I said there is a way to stop from becoming a victim of persecution, yet it would take a fair amount of faith on your part for it to become reality. Please, feel free to adapt this following visualisation to your personal situation.

What follows is a true story – but before I speak about this technique or visualisation, here is some background information which will help you appreciate what can be done. It all began at the height of the war against terrorism between America and Iraq, within the first six months of 2004.

The two leaders involved were President George Bush and Saddam Hussein. Shontara was dreadfully concerned and felt scared with the threats going backwards and forwards between the two great men in power, both being as stubborn as the other and both believing they were right and their opposing force or enemy was in the wrong. But who was going to do what when, which would lead to the eventual annihilation of the whole world? How many other countries had to be dragged into this war that someone else started for the good of mankind? What was worst – nuclear, chemical or biological warfare?

These questions and more filled the heart and mind of Shontara on a daily basis. It became so distressing for her that at one stage she walked out of the room whenever updated reports were spoken of on the TV news, broadcast each evening into her home at 6pm.

During one particular meditation session which took place when these world events were unfolding and while allowing her body and mind to remain completely still, we planted a seed and the seed grew. We could have done this ourselves but we wanted Shontara to be involved in facing her fears and conquering it.

The visualisation worked so beautifully, she now employs this same technique when necessary with people who are being difficult (which has not been many but there have been some). Shontara has done this freely because she has seen what can be achieved, not only on an individual basis but on a world wide scale, if you believe. And the great thing is, it was all done in her home, while quietly going about her daily life. You can't get much more practical than that. She was causing no disruption to others and it was so much more effective than organising and participating in some 'in your face' protest.

Not that these street rallies for peace are a bad thing, as they do send a definite message to those in power but they do require a lot of time, energy, money, organisation and emotion which can be better channelled elsewhere to do the same thing quicker and easier. There ends the background information I wanted to give you. On a regular basis and whenever she thought about this dangerous situation happening around her, she visualised in her mind the following:

Shontara saw a large swimming pool filled with the Blood of Christ. There was no shallow end to this pool. It was 7ft deep all over. In this pool of blood, Shontara placed Jesus in a position of power which was smack dead in the middle. Behind him in the diagonal corner to his right, was placed President Bush from America. Next, she positioned Saddam Hussein from Iraq in the front diagonal left hand corner. A line of energy between the three was created.

As the pool was so deep, all three men were completely covered in this Blood. Shontara next visualised Saddam Hussein shrink down to the size of an ant. When she had this picture firmly in her mind, she turned her attention towards President Bush and did the same to him.

Up until this stage, Shontara had not entered the pool, yet after reducing both Saddam Hussein and President Bush to a more workable size; she jumped in feet first and swam across first to Iraq's corner and jumped upon Saddam's head to make sure he was well and truly squashed.

She invoked the following prayer which was "In the name of Jesus Christ and with this Blood, Saddam Hussein invokes the light of Christ within. Saddam is a clear and perfect channel, for God he is and Divine Light is Saddam's Guide". This was repeated three times before moving on to America's corner, where President Bush awaited the same fate.

Such violence is deplorable you might think in such a spiritual setting as this but don't stress, they weren't dead – just momentarily stunned into submission. Shontara returned to face Jesus. She stepped forward to melt into and be one with his energy.

We suggested she use the Blood of Christ because it has many healing and miraculous qualities unknown to much of mankind. She has used this same pool of blood to heal people of physical injury or sickness with quite dramatic and startling effect, minus the jumping on the head bit.

If you can't stomach such a thing as moving about in the Blood of Christ, by all means replace this with something you can relate to such as white or gold light, clear quartz crystal clusters, water or fire would all be as useful. Its success relies more upon the intent rather than on the tools you use to bring about your desired objective, which was for a relatively peaceful end before it got too much out of hand.

As mentioned earlier, Shontara acted out this scenario on a daily basis. Three weeks later, Saddam Hussein was found hiding in a bunker, half starved, cowering in a corner like a frightened, old and broken man; a mere shell of his former self, barely recognisable to his family, friends and the authorities who found him. Ex-President Bush is now retired and a new era in American politics, and for the rest of the world, has begun.

The whole purpose for me sharing this important event is we wish for you to do the same – but do it for yourself first, see how it works and then focus your attention upon the needs of the whole planet rather than only upon yourself. The mere act of seeing and invoking in this way will create miracles and we are there helping you to help us, create a safer and happier environment for all in which to live.

We cannot interfere in your evolution directly without first being asked but once the invitation is out there and if it is in the best interest of all concerned, we are then allowed to move mountains to ensure your continued spiritual advancement. God bless Shontara and everyone who comes after, who wish to follow in her footsteps and do other great things.

In days long ago, I have seen many wonderful people come and go in my life, including those more distant living abroad, who have had persecution thrust upon them, quite often through no fault of their own. And quite often I remained ignorant to this fact until it came to light much later, although by then it was quite often too late to help.

As an aware bystander, what can you do for the persecuted? There will be those occasions when you will feel powerless but this is not entirely true. You only think you are. There is always something which can be done. What you do may not stop the abuse from continuing but this doesn't mean what you are doing, is worthless either.

Normally the person being persecuted will be most thankful for what little you think you can give although in their mind, it will be a lot and which is regarded as being most valuable. Remember, how they perceive what is given may be different to yours.

Sometimes, your mere presence will often give the persecuted a feeling of confidence to persevere and where their will to survive is strengthened. To hold their hand will heal many internal wounds. You may be convinced this person you know of and care for can choose to walk away from this devastating experience but to them, they can't make that move and they can't make that move because they are under the illusion they are being punished and they deserve it for what they have or have not done. This happens quite a lot for women who find themselves in a domestic violence situation.

They feel they are not worthy of receiving the same rights and freedom which is given to everyone else, everyday. They may or may not be conscious of these thoughts but they are there, at the back of their mind and this is where they get stuck.

Taking into consideration what has been mentioned, it is with these people you need to show large amounts of compassion, if not acceptance or understanding while listening to their truth. You may see an easy way out but no matter how often you express this, the more they can't see what you are saying. Not that they don't want to see but it's because they are afraid to in case it all goes wrong and blows up in their face. This is something they have to live with and not you and so they feel they have to reject your advice.

This is where things may get tough for you and it would be easy to lose all patience with the person you are trying desperately to help. A build up of frustration could lead to quick or protracted bouts of anger from you towards them, where you will begin to accuse them of stupidity and even worse, which makes the person recoil in horror and withdraw from all offers of help, may they be genuine or not.

Stay silent and bite your tongue if you have to. Tread softly. Look at why you are getting angry in the situation where a person you care about won't listen to reason. There are two possible explanations, the first of which you may not like.

Do you explode with venom because you became angry with yourself for not getting your message across and by them not doing what you say? Or is it due to you genuinely feeling saddened by this other person's plight and where your personal feelings don't enter into this picture at all?

It could be a combination of both reasons but please take a close look at the first suggestion when you can.

Persevere in your offers of help and support, no matter how painful it is for you personally and remember, what they are feeling is a thousand times worse than what you might be going through. Keep everything in perspective when under great stress. Stay balanced and calm. This will flow over to the one you are trying to help. You are doing a lot rather than a little. Be at peace with what you can or cannot give to another in need.

Be alert to the fact when you persecute one, you persecute all and this includes yourself. You may think this person is of no real consequence and no-one else is affected. Yet this is not always the case. It can create the most catastrophic blow to the whole of mankind. Because the individual or minority group being persecuted today doesn't mean they won't rise up, find their voice tomorrow and retaliate in a big way towards their persecutor and all who follow him or her. This is when things can turn quite ugly and quickly get out of hand, which has already happened but to ensure it gets no worse, it is hoped by reading the pages in this book, followed by word of mouth, a blanket of heightened awareness will cover the lands and a resultant shift of consciousness can indeed bring change for the better; where every soul – living and dead – will benefit.

Many religious and cultural beliefs and attitudes need to be revised and accepted or alternatively, those that are inhibiting and strangling a person's spiritual growth needs to be banished from ever being used or looked at again. Have respect for the rights and freedom of others while still maintaining and fulfilling your personal needs. This cannot be accomplished for as long as we remain the persecutor or persecuted, abuser or victim. None of these positions need apply in a future brave new world of peace and glory.

If you truly wish to experience a sense of peace within and for this same feeling to encompass the rest of humanity, you as an individual must take matters into your own two hands, because as we change ourselves from the inside out, this can have an effect that will expand and spiral outwards into an amazingly intricate web, making up a complex pattern of networking which connects each of us together in some way.

There are those who are aware of the big picture while

others are struggling to cope with everyday problems, let alone having enough energy, enthusiasm or compassion to be concerned about the plight of everyone else.

It is this latter group of people who live a half filled life of opportunity and pleasure, as they insist upon holding on to a limited point of view. Embrace the whole rather than just a small part. A jigsaw puzzle is built one piece at a time. Why not rebuild and reshape planet Earth by beginning with one important person, ourselves, and as a consequence, reach out and invite others to join you, even those you don't like? And so it will go, until everyone is included and our plan will be complete; which is for mankind to live in harmonious unity, to walk hand in hand together, side by side and lend their support to the one standing next to them. Sounds like a big job I know but it is possible. Many pieces of the overall puzzle have been steadily increasing day by day but there still remains some missing links. Are you one of those missing pieces? If yes, help us to help you find what you are missing.

And if by chance you are not lost and you know exactly where you fit in the overall big scheme of things, please can you help by finding those still missing and place them in a position of power rather than in a position of weakness, which will enable them the freedom to once again shine their individual light for all the world to see?

Here's one last visualisation from me which I hope you will practise on a fairly consistent basis or whenever you feel all is lost. Let us begin:

> *Rise above and look down upon Earth. The Universe can offer many great views, which includes such grand sites as the pyramids in Egypt, the Sydney Opera House, the Eiffel*

Tower in Paris, the Colosseum in Rome, the Statue of Liberty in New York, Jesus in Rio de Janeiro and many other great feats of architecture and inspiration. Alone they stand but together they hold the key to a new beginning, meaning and purpose.

Next, visualise seven rows of people holding hands which creates a human chain embracing Mother Earth and protecting it from all harm that completely covers it from pole to pole. In fact, you can't see the world for all the people. Then at the top of their lungs and at the same moment, every soul is to repeatedly chant the tone of 'Om', which in the English language translates to the two most powerful words in creation, which is 'I Am'. Blessed be and behold a glorious sight.

I shall leave you to discover this particular surprise for yourself but ask one last thing, which is for you to later encourage your friends and family do the same visualisation with you, remembering what each person may see or share is right for them, as this is their unique experience as yours will rightfully belong to you. There are no wrong outcomes in this instance. I am who I am. I am the Word. I am the Alpha and the Omega. I am. Om Keryahti, Yahweh Om, Bagdivah.

Shontara

> *When there is light in the soul,*
> *there is beauty in the person.*
>
> *When there is beauty in the person,*
> *there is harmony in the home.*
>
> *When there is harmony in the home,*
> *there is order in the nation.*
>
> *When there is order in the nation,*
> *there is peace in the world.*
>
> **Source: Ancient Chinese Proverb**

Affirmations

The TRUTH will always set me FREE to be me.

No real harm can come to me here.

I REJECT the twin roles of being a persecutor or persecuted.

PHILIP

Peace be with you, dear children of God. My

Heart I give to you, with eternal love.

I am the Way, the Truth and the

Light. Allow me to guide and let me

Inspire. May

Peace be with you, dear children of God.

I am walking through the village markets, minding my own business and enjoying the sights, when from behind, another man pushes me. I lose balance which caused me to loosen my grip on a piece of jewellery I had bought moments before for my wife and that I was holding in my right hand. It was this gift that this man was after, because it was extremely valuable and expensive. I should have been more alert and careful but I wasn't. It was then that I decided in my wisdom not to let him have it. When I found my two feet properly again, I gave chase and soon caught up with him and tried to take it back. I had it within my grasp but so did he. He wouldn't let it go and neither would I. Someone had to give. Would it be him or would it be me?

He pulled a knife and cut deeply and quickly into the wrist and palm of my hand. This caused me to flinch, open my fingers and lose my brief hold upon the piece of jewellery that I wanted back so badly. As a consequence of my actions, I lost some blood, as well as the gift. The knife attack was so unexpected and he left with what belonged to me.

I chose not to pursue it a second time but felt deeply saddened that I would not be able to give my wife something special. She had to put up with a lot from me but she never once complained. She was a gentle and compassionate woman with much inner strength and courage. I stood there and watched my assailant quickly disappear into the crowd.

I fixed my hand up in the best way that I could before resuming my travels but I had lost my enthusiasm. I thought it best to return home but on this particular occasion, I decided to go a different route. A short distance out of the main town area and with head hanging down with regret, I spied upon the ground what was taken from me a little less than an hour ago. I looked around cautiously to see if anyone was watching and realised that the man who robbed me came this way. He couldn't have realised that he dropped it. I then gave thanks to God that I found it again without really trying and felt truly blessed. I picked it up to check to see if it wasn't broken. It was fine and all in one piece. A bit dirty but no real harm was done as a result of the ownership struggle that broke out over it. I then found some water to wash the dust and grime off.

My wife was never told the whole story. She didn't need to know. Why upset her unnecessarily. Now, I am not normally so possessive but it was not intended for me to keep. I was going to give it away with love and I wanted it to go to the person it was intended for. As you can see, my wish was eventually granted.

I learnt quite a number of important lessons from this one encounter and they were – the more I struggle and fight against losing something that is important to me, the worse I'm going to feel. As well as this, I learnt that when I willingly let go of the desire to control the outcomes of all my experiences, then miracles can and do happen naturally.

I realised too that by wanting to hold on tight to either people or material possessions, that more often than not, this same possessiveness can have some adverse and unhealthy consequences. I realised the importance of change. Relax, stay flexible, be guided, trust, do not doubt and never lose hope.

Other than having a wonderful wife whom I worshipped and adored, I had a son who grew up to become a strapping strong man, full of inventive ideas that were way ahead of his time. I would sometimes feel concern for him because being too different from the crowd caused those people around him to act and react with suspicion and would draw to him the type of attention he did not want or crave for. He so greatly wanted to bring about change and in this way, he was like a 'chip off the old block' but we just went about it in different ways.

I had to learn that even though he was my son, this didn't necessarily mean we had to have the same ideas, philosophy or beliefs. To presume otherwise would have been wrong and even when I could see he was headed for a fall, I needed to maintain a caring but neutral stance and let him learn from his own mistakes.

Although, I knew that everything happens for a reason and who was I to argue the point with my Lord, my God? So, when does a parent need to step in or step out of the life of their adult children? This can be tricky.

A balance needs to be found, including a willingness to accept and compromise where both people are concerned. Why cause unnecessary waves within the family unit when it isn't necessary? Enough trouble and chaos is caused outside family life that we often have no control over, so don't take it home with you as well. Take steps to leave any disruptions and negativity behind.

Our home is our castle, whether it be big or small, a mansion on a hill or a tent beside a river and whether it be made of brick, wood, glass or mud, makes no difference – or at least it shouldn't. Be happy with the lot or little of what you've got, make improvements if necessary but don't complain.

Make it your own but always leave room to share it with those you live with and love, including your friends. Your piece of land needs to become your paradise, your quiet sanctuary that you go to and where you can recharge your batteries. And when you leave again for whatever reason and for however long or short, try and store some of those good memories and energy that you can draw upon, when your heart is aching and when things get tough.

There is a saying that successful people like to use today and that is – "when the going gets tough, the tough get going". Even negative experiences, no matter how apparently bad they are, have a specific purpose in our lives in order to make us stronger, more resilient to the knocks and blows we will receive from time to time and more determined to achieve the goals we have set, and lessons to be learnt for ourselves.

Patience is a virtue and yes, I know you have heard that spoken many times before but you don't necessarily need to put your whole life on hold while being patient. Whatever area of life you need to learn patience in, continue to take your mind off it, if it becomes too difficult and find something else to do while waiting for something else to happen.

Not many people like to wait. Some tolerate this waiting or transition game better than others. But there is always a breaking point where all we want to do is throw up our hands in disgust, pull out our hair (if we have any) and scream out our frustrations at others. Some people will experience this turning point sooner rather than later. It depends greatly upon the personality and what level of importance we have placed upon the overall situation. If it doesn't matter too much, you are then going to be able to hold out for a lot longer.

It's the same when dealing with pain, either in a physical or emotional sense. It greatly depends upon how many times before you have been forcefully exposed to pain or need for patience. 'Practice makes perfect' they say and it does, little by little, and hopefully the length of time before one breaks down in a bundle of exasperation and lost hope again, is lengthened.

It's a lot like learning how to crawl before you can walk, to walk before you can run, to skip, to jump, to ride a bike or to fall in love for the very first time. At what point do you give in while going through these development stages? Do you stop short, when running in the race to success? By seeing the finishing line, do you panic, slow down and allow another to overtake and let them take possession of what is, or could have been, rightfully yours? You worked hard for it, so why not go further and claim it as your own? Why give it away?

Some people think it's selfish to achieve or outdo another in the area of success, so they hold back and forget about their own wants and needs. The mentality of the one who leaves themselves out of their own picture goes something like this – 'the other person's success is so much more important than my own'. And are you so close to your destination that you have the end in sight, like that little white light seen at the end of a long and dark tunnel, but soon realise that your eyes are only playing tricks with you because even though you are moving towards your goal, it never seems to get any closer? It could even appear that the end is moving away from you but how can this be if you are still moving straight ahead?

Let me ask you this – can you really tell in what direction you are headed? Forwards, backwards or around and around like the merry-go-round? Speaking of which, did you know that by the simple act of closing your eyes while your body is being pushed around and from side to side at very high speeds, as you would when you are on a roller coaster ride, your perception of what is really happening then becomes distorted and confused, where you have no idea of what's up and what's down, what's hot and what's not? Ask the astronaut next door whether this is fact or fantasy and it's the same with our mind. Shut it down and it will take a holiday from thinking straight and can get quite silly.

Your mind has the power to spin the owner right out of control and will then go that one step further by kicking them over the edge of a cliff and into a never ending abyss of frustration, anger, annoyance, harmful thoughts and actions. Is this what you really want for yourself on a permanent basis? If no, then take the appropriate action to experience life with your eyes, mind and heart wide open. Never be afraid to see what's coming from behind or what lies immediately ahead. Stop walking around half blinded to your reality and don't experience a life half lived as a result of having your eyes wide shut.

When I was younger (so much younger than today), I was a rather gangly and gawky looking kid. In case you don't have a dictionary or a friend who's handy to ask immediately, the word gangly means tall and skinny, where the word gawky means someone who is awkward, ungainly and bashful, or so it says in the Concise Oxford Dictionary.

In order for me to overcome these pitfalls then, I made it a point in front of other people, to always laugh at what little assets and talents I had. By doing so, this then encouraged and promoted great inner strength and courage. Try it and see. Don't worry if they find your humour to be in bad taste or don't get the joke. Besides, who are you doing it for – yourself or them?

If you do it exclusively for their entertainment and benefit and if they don't react in the way that you want them to, this can then lead you to experience feelings of great disappointment and sometimes bitterness. And the same goes for anything else that you do in life.

For example, do you have a job that you hate because that is what your parents or teachers expected you to do but you always dreamed of doing something entirely different but didn't, because you were afraid to stand your ground and stay true to your convictions?

Perhaps you married someone because you felt pity for them, you were afraid to be left on the shelf or it could be, because you couldn't say 'NO'. You may think it's not nice to hurt someone else's feelings on purpose, especially if they have been exceptionally kind and you would be right in thinking this but neither is it nice to give someone false hope and aspirations for the future.

Now there's an unfunny word if ever I've heard one. It's only two letters long in your English language, so you may be forgiven for placing little importance or value on the word 'no' but sometimes, to say no for your own protection and sanity is vital and should be voiced properly and firmly. Saying maybe is not good enough. It's too indecisive and again could infer that something could happen but maybe not. And when you say yes to something, try and ensure that you live up to that promise.

I know the latter is not always possible, as situations do arise from time to time that are completely out of your control and where it forces you to move in an entirely different direction that you had never reckoned upon. But please be careful when you make an offer of help, especially if you don't mean it, because how are you going to feel if they say yes to you. Or more to the point, what are you then going to do? Let them down by finding endless excuses as to why you can't fulfil your promise of help. Be clear in what you speak, whether you say yes or no. Be honest, not only with yourself but with others as well. Don't force them to listen between the lines of what you are truly saying or thinking.

Some people don't have that ability or if they do, they choose not to utilise it. This type of person is the easiest to con because they will accept everything they hear, see or read as being gospel. I would question here – the gospel according to whom? Someone they can't believe in or trust. When a person's trust and faith has been betrayed, it's awfully hard to retrieve it again.

To live in fear is like living in a big black hole. It can sometimes feel like as though you are forever falling into a bottomless pit of despair and where you pray for the day when it will all end. Some will take steps to bring that blessed last day sooner rather than later, while others will sit out the sometimes long wait in agony, with fear being their constant companion.

Nothing, absolutely nothing, can be achieved while in this state of mind and it can be quite dangerous and damaging. This is where fear is compounded, where one fear can become two, two fears can breed like rabbits and then become four.

Those four fears can then be blown out of all proportion which merely adds more fuel to the fire and where four has now become eight and the cycle of continuous perpetuation has been put in place.

For those poor souls who live in this space, you need to find a positive way out of the darkness and back into the light. One of the things you can do is sit and write down a list of all your fears on paper. Divide it into four columns. In the first column, you state the particular fear you wish to work on. In the second column, you write down all the negative emotions attached to that fear. The third column is filled with a variety of solutions and finally, you are to imagine what benefits you would receive if you could put these solutions into practice. Once written, it is the benefits you need to focus upon.

By doing so will give you the necessary inner strength, drive and motivation to kick your fear in the butt once and for all. You can then take pride of place at the head of the table, feeling secure and confident that no-one can ever hurt you again, especially yourself. Take back that power you gave away to these self-created fears.

Sure, another person may have triggered the initial response and reaction that gave birth to the fear in the first place, but we then have a choice of either catching and running with the ball full speed ahead or we forcefully throw the ball back to the bowler, wishing to have no part in playing these stupid, controlling and manipulative mind games.

For those who need a bit more detail, what follows is a brief example of what I have asked you to do. These four columns are by no means complete. I am sure you can add to it. If you have nothing else better to do, take time out and make it your next project. Now, I could have chosen from a long list of fears but one of the most common that the vast majority of people will suffer from, in some degree or another and from time to time, is the fear of rejection. So let's make that our starting point. Fear of not being accepted is the same thing.

FEAR	NEG. EMOTION	SOLUTIONS	BENEFITS
Rejection	Angry	Stop expecting recognition from others.	Independence
	Guilt	Give people the freedom to say NO.	Confidence
	Blame	Reward yourself for a job well done.	Secure
	Depressed	Participate in social or other activities regardless of how you might be feeling.	Proud
	Lonely	Don't argue the point.	Determined
	Introverted	Understand the fear you are feeling may not be yours.	Self-acceptance
	Perfectionist	Believe and accept that you are already the best.	Positive thinking
	Unworthy	Stop forever trying to prove to yourself and others that you are OK.	Inner knowing
	Dislike for self	Stop trying so hard to seek approval and attention.	Calmness within
	Lack of personal priorities/ boundaries	Walk away from those people in your life who are constantly under-mining you – even if they are family.	Respectful of your own needs
	Procrastination	Take a stand and just do.	Decisiveness

The negative emotions, solutions and benefits have been listed in no particular priority order. If you put some of these ideas into practice, even if it's only one, soon you will begin once again to see the light and you'll be so glad you did.

Follow your heart. Do what is your passion. If you have a fire in the belly, satisfy it. The only time I would advise differently is if, by following and fulfilling your heart's desire, a lot of physical or psychological harm is done to others as a consequence of your actions, then it's best to let it go.

You may ask – why should I? All I can say is use the Ten Commandments as a practical guide. Whether you believe in God or Jesus Christ the man or not, is irrelevant. Even an atheist cannot argue with common sense rules that have been put into place so mankind has some sure and right direction to follow. If you have to break even one of the guidelines, and I prefer to use the word guidelines rather than rules, because there are some who think that rules are made to be broken, chaos can quickly catch up with you and bite you on the bum when you least expect it. And if you don't take note the first time you receive such a warning, it will happen again and again until you do.

If you choose not to listen, things will go from bad to worse, while you passively sit there stewing in your own deep pool of despair, complaining about how everyone hates you, that everyone owes you a living or how you always seem to attract the wrong type of person continuously into your life.

At which point, you then throw your hands up in the air and cry 'Why me? What have I done to deserve this?' The answer to these two questions can always be found deep within, my friend. Responsibility always begins and ends with you. Please note I haven't used the word blame. No-one, including you, is to blame, no matter how black it looks. If you truly have done nothing wrong, then why should these seemingly endless disasters keep falling upon your head? Look for the answer beyond this lifetime. Yes, I am talking about past lives or as some would say reincarnation.

You may be thinking that this last comment is a most surprising thing for me to say or believe in, as a Christian. This may come as a surprise to some and not all of you, but from where I sit now, I have seen my truth and I haven't always been a Christian by faith. Over many lifetimes, I have been many different people who experienced a variety of belief systems. Christianity is a relatively young religion when you look at how long mankind has walked upon this planet called Earth. I have had many colourful and varied lives before I was Philip, a disciple and Apostle of Jesus and we, meaning my fellow eleven spiritual brothers, have been back since. God has given us all eternal and everlasting life, regardless of our religious or spiritual persuasions. No one religion or philosophy is better than another.

What needs to be achieved today in order to create a peaceful future for ourselves is a high level of tolerance, flexibility, compromise and acceptance of each other's belief system, including our dislikes and fears.

Do you really think that if you are Chinese, your feelings will differ greatly from that of a black American Negro? It's not the nationality, the colour of our skin, the deities we worship that matters. What lies deep within our hearts still basically remains the same. There is a song and one of the lines says – "What the world needs now is love, sweet love". Don't ever underestimate the power of love. Like the diamond, it can withstand a lot of punishment but it does continue to survive.

Even if we do from time to time, for our own protection, suppress and bury this grand love for ourselves and others. The flame still flickers, even in those people we hate the most.

The fire can never completely go out, it can never be extinguished. Let me end by saying some words that have been given to the world by St Germaine and they are – "I am a being of violet fire, I am the purity God desires". Immerse yourself in the fire of your love. Let it destroy all fear, hatred, doubt and for those who can't do it for themselves, you do it for them.

Upon my father's death bed, he gave me a special ring. I was only twelve at the time and it was far too big for my little hand. I still had a lot of growing up and filling out to do before I could wear it with pride. My mother kept his ring for me until I could wear it with any real confidence and until she felt secure in the knowledge that it wouldn't fall off my finger when I least expected it. Before his death, my father didn't have many assets to his name but he always managed to give me, my mother and two brothers, good shelter and regular food. At the time of his death, I assumed more responsibility and when the going got tough, I sought comfort from throwing myself into the pounding waves of the ocean.

Being buffeted and pushed around was oddly soothing to my physical and emotional self. I found that the rougher the waves, the more I liked it. Although, I was smart enough not to go above my head or beyond what I was capable of and even though I mourned my father's death, I had no desire to join him so quickly as a result of me drowning.

My mother was concerned about my welfare of course while frolicking in the sea but she had to learn trust and to let go of me when the time was right. She knew this and endeavoured to do her best, to trust that is, but it was still hard for her, as it is still for mothers today. Our children are not children for long and they are on loan to us, as children, for only a short time.

It is within the first seven impressionable years that much good can be done, that will pave the way to your child's successful transition into adulthood but even then, sadly to say, there are still no guarantees. Remember, we have all been given freedom of choice, as an adult and to a lesser extent, when we are a child.

Those people involved in that particular child's life, create certain boundaries for themselves that the child will insist upon playing with, in order to explore and determine how far those same boundaries can be pushed. The main objective of the game, in the child's mind at least, is to break through to upset the apple cart, while parents need to remain detached and non-reactive to the constant testing of the boundaries by our children.

Be firm in your resolve but not be so rigid where you don't allow for flexibility. If you don't learn to bend a little when under pressure, you will surely break in two. This is where compromise comes into play.

As well as this, be careful not to fall into the trap of being overly protective or never giving the child a certain amount of freedom to express their feelings or opinions and not allowing them the right to make their own decisions. What this can then produce are overly anxious, rebellious, insecure, angry and withdrawn adults. These qualities are then transferred to their children and on again to their own children's children.

Little by little, generation by generation, a relatively minor defect in one's personality can then be blown out of all proportion and become a major catastrophe, which can cause much chaos and disruption within the family unit, no matter how old or young you are.

This is largely what we are seeing today and the only way to reverse the cycle is to give our children and parents, sincere thanks and forgiveness for their sins they carry out against us. Learn, talk, listen and respect each other. Most importantly, love one another with all your heart, mind and soul. Children and parents, parents and children must go hand in hand together. They cannot be separated. They are one and if this union is torn asunder, trouble will ensue. Strive for that togetherness but in that togetherness, our individuality still needs to shine through. The same can be said for two adults in a long term relationship.

Fear of Being Alone

You need to have no fear of being alone. Look at the advantages for a change, instead of the disadvantages and there are some really good ones (advantages that is). Firstly, if alone, you have no-one to talk back at you who is being belligerent, impatient, rude and possibly violent. You have no-one to answer to except yourself which enables you to then come and go as you please. As well as this, you don't need to ask anyone for permission to see Tom, Dick or Harry, Jane, Mary or Scarlett. You can see them all without judgement or fear from another who may wish to try and save you from making a terrible mistake.

The other advantage of being alone is that you can have silence whenever you want it, as well as taking up the whole and not just some of your double, queen or king size bed. Do I need to carry on (alone)? Have I not convinced you yet? All of this is good or perhaps not.

Perhaps you're not ready to take advantage of your aloneness. Perhaps the real truth is that when you are alone, you continually and internally do battle with yourself, to-ing and fro-ing, this way and that, saying yes no yes no yes no, coupled with grand statements such as 'what if …' or 'if only …' If only you would keep quiet and still your mind.

Don't kid yourself into thinking that by having someone in your life, they will be the answer to all your prayers and who can magically, with a mere wave of their hand, stop the internal bickering and indecisiveness that goes on inside your head and heart.

Indeed, for those in a relationship now, how many of you communicate these conflicting emotions to your partners? Certainly, you may discuss it with those people you are not so attached to in order to get a sometimes impartial and unbiased opinion but what about speaking of your feelings to those that are directly involved? Do you stay silent because you are afraid of being rejected? Are you unselfishly thinking of their state of mind where you have no wish to confuse 'the poor old dear'? I mean, why add to their already large set of existing problems?

How noble it is of you to think this but it's not allowing the other person to get close enough to really understand you and when these misunderstandings are made apparent, you judge them harshly with no forgiveness in your heart. But who do you think initiated this problem?

Until you can learn to communicate honestly and effectively with yourself, you cannot hope to maintain a long term friendship or relationship with another. To ensure successful future liaisons, you need to feel good about being in your own space. In other words, you get great enjoyment about being in your own company. As it stands to reason that if you can't stand a bar of yourself, even in the good times, why then should you expect another to put up with you, especially if you can't or are not willing to do the same for yourself?

What you give out, you get back but be aware that you can't give something you don't already have. So make good use of those times when you are alone, as this is when you can learn many of your most valuable lessons. This can then become a time for great personal and spiritual healing that must work from the inside out. If you are laden down with obligations put upon you by other people while in a relationship, this healing process will take longer.

If you should have no fear of being alone, this sacred quite space and time can be the very thing the doctor ordered – lots of bed and rest, as well as lots of tender loving care and you don't always need to have someone else give this loving to you. In order to gain what you want from another, it must become a need and where you give it to yourself first. Only then can it expand outwards from there.

So why do you fear being alone? Is it because you don't like yourself as much as you like all others or are you looking for someone to do things for you, to protect and save you? Are you looking for a companion to do social things with? Do you wish for someone to be on call 24hrs a day so they may carry out your requests or demands, with the major difference between the two extremes resting in the eyes of the doer? Or perhaps you want what your neighbour or best friend is having? Is it all these things and more?

If yes, take a look at how you personally react when you can't get what you think you need, for whatever reason. Do you throw a temper tantrum in order to force people to take notice of you or do you become like the tortoise, where you retreat further into your shell in order to protect yourself from becoming fatally wounded?

Do you become like the water rat and jump ship by slashing your wrists, taking an overdose, shooting yourself or drowning? Do I need to continue? There are many creative and quite innovative ways you can end your misery here on Earth on a permanent basis. You are merely limited by your imagination.

I am not here to judge one way or another as to your

reactions and decisions. If you knew a better way of dealing with your problems, you probably would have done it a long time ago or at least I would like to think that you would have.

There will come a time in everyone's life where they will be faced with being alone, with no-one to hold their hand. The more you have to learn about your dependency upon others will determine how often you are placed in this unwanted position of being alone. The less dependent you become on others for your internal happiness and physical welfare, is when the floodgates will open unto you and in will walk all sorts of interesting, helpful and influential people. And this is because your want has not become a need.

A need implies that you can't live without something or someone, where a want indicates a more relaxed and philosophical attitude of – 'oh well, if it happens that's great but if it doesn't, I won't lose any sleep over those things or people that I'm lacking in my life'.

When your needs become like an obsession, this is when you have cause for worry. At this point I must ask are you a love addict? Where, if you don't get your daily dose that only another can give, do you get all upset and weepy, where you tear through your day upsetting other people, because you believe you don't have what you need and because of that, they too can suffer right along with you? If this type of behaviour persists, you may begin to act out the belief that well, if no-one loves me, I will withhold my love from them or if I do allow myself to love others and they don't reciprocate within a reasonable time frame, I'll walk away and not look back.

But don't kid yourself, you will always look back by living in the past and remembering what could have been but sadly wasn't. In both scenarios I have just described, the end result is that you will withdraw your love and by doing so, this then becomes a form of punishment but the bottom line is you are really punishing yourself.

Believe it or not, the solution is simple. Give without all the grand and unrealistic expectations, both to yourself and other people.

There is another reason though as to why you might be alone. Everything I have talked about so far has been concerned with superficial symptoms only. The real endemic cause lies deep within, where you have an ingrained belief that you don't deserve to be loved properly.

Read these last few words carefully – you don't deserve to be loved properly. How does that make you feel – uncomfortable, angry, defensive? This belief may be so inherently strong, you have become blinded because it is so well entrenched and hidden in your aura, attitude, energy vibration and genetic code but this karmic imprint can be changed and renewed, as can the cells within the body and neuron pathways within your brain be repaired and multiplied.

Until you can let go and move on, you will continually crash into that proverbial brick wall with which you have grown so fond of and which you will use to bash your head in. This would be fine if in the process it made you see some sense but in most cases, many people have chosen to learn this particular lesson about relationships the hard way.

Climb off the karmic wheel of destructive love, because you deserve better, believe it or not! Once you can accept this basic truth, you will then free yourself to receive and give love in equal amounts. Balance, balance, balance. To maintain a sense of balance is so important. When you neither crave nor fear love, then love will come. Let's now take a look at your past and present day relationships.

Hands up those of you who have believed it's all too good to be true and where you spend a lot of your quiet time worrying about how it all might end? What a terrible waste of energy this is. Not only that, it is thoroughly damaging because what we think, we create. If this negative thought of the future becomes habitual and it plays itself over and over again in your head like a cracked record, it will come to pass. At which time you will blame the other person and walk around feeling sorry for yourself, feeding off the sympathy from others before the cycle begins again and it will start again.

You may say no to future devastating relationships but this could be different to what you might say tomorrow or the next day, where you do an about face and scream out at the top of your lungs – yes, yes, yes.

Yes, I can hear you denying this truth but one day, you will forget all about your resolve to say no to a harmful future relationship because some relationship, any relationship, is what you really want. Whether it is any good for you or not apparently doesn't always seem to matter. Some people's irrational fear of being alone is so strong that it overrides all common sense, good judgement and discernment about the other person whom they wish to connect with. They think – at least someone is better than no-one.

It's like women who stay with their violent husbands, boyfriends or lovers where they suffer great physical, verbal, emotional, spiritual and psychological abuse. This is a sad fact of life but it's only because they don't believe they are worthy of receiving what is best for them.

They live under a cloud of illusion, a fantasy world, where

they believe that their partner will change and all they need to do is be there for their partner when their life falls to pieces but what about their own life? Who will be there for them? If you expect some maiden with a sword or knight in shining armour to come and rescue you from further abuse, you may be disappointed, which only leads to stronger feelings of being alone, rejection and abandonment.

The solution here is to pick your own self up again, although it would be better not to put yourself in such a harmful situation in the first place but where love is concerned, sometimes we don't think of the consequences of our actions that can lead us into future troubled waters. Because, once you begin to drown in your own despair, it is mighty hard to try and begin building bridges, with which you can use to escape.

You are not alone as you have a whole large team of spirit helpers guiding your hands and feet. Just because you can't see them clearly or touch them in a physical sense, doesn't mean they are not there. But soon you too shall advance, where the scales of fear and injustice will be lifted from your eyes, including those who already know they are not alone. Then you will all see what we now perceive to be true and this is not a day in the far off distant future. It is indeed, a lot closer to happening than what you think, on a world wide scale. And speaking of thinking, they say that "Love is a many splendoured thing" where thinking can be downright dangerous, especially if you don't think in the right direction.

If you think you are alone, then in your mind this is so, even though this may not be the truth. There could be or are many people in your life standing by, ready, willing and able to lend you their heart for free, with no strings attached. Thinking we are alone shuts us down from accepting this reality and where we separate ourselves from the truth. That is why many bemoan the fact that they are alone and have lost their way, like little Bo Peep who lost her sheep. They have lost their way because they have stepped outside themselves and have chosen a different path to follow from that which was originally intended.

When this happens, we then have the situation where people will question – what's my life purpose and what am I here for? Your soul has the answer to both these questions. All you have to do is ask and then stop long enough for the answer to catch up with your conscious thinking and analytical mind. If your mind is racing ahead into the future at a thousand miles per hour, it is awfully hard to hear what Spirit is trying to share with you. Once you can slow down, the next trick is to trust whatever insights you may receive to the extent that you begin running with it, in order to give it substance and life.

Granted, you may not be given the whole picture all at once as there will always be certain things about your future that cannot be revealed. As this is the case, why not develop the gift of patience and acceptance. Be happy with what you have rather than being unhappy about those things we have not yet shown to you.

Sometimes knowing too much can interfere with the future direction you decide to take in life and perhaps that different path you as a person chose, and not as a soul, was destined not to be, which is often weighed down with one obstacle after another. This is when we hit, sometimes at full speed ahead, the bumpy and lumpy bits of life.

Hand over your ego, that is the 'I, me and my' to a higher force and allow them to lead, as they can protect the way ahead, if you let it be. More pleasant surprises, riches and rewards will come by following the path of Divine Will rather than your own.

So next time you feel compelled to go somewhere or if you are invited to attend some event, business or social, that you don't really want to go to, say yes. Because it may just be our way of letting you know we have set you up to meet your soul mate, so don't blow it. If you don't go, we will then perhaps much later than you would like, try our hand in matchmaking again but why should you wait till later, when you are given the opportunity to enjoy it right now?

In other words, there is always a reason why certain events take place in our lives and the answer may not always be apparent until much further down the track of time. Trust and enjoy the company of those people we have put immediately in front of you.

Even those people you intensely dislike are there to teach you a valuable lesson, one of which could be for you to discover what it is that you don't want for yourself. Once learnt, and we hope this doesn't take forever, give thanks, push them aside gently and move on.

Don't let them force you to go off the beaten track. Your way is straight ahead and as Jesus said – 'I am the way, the truth and the light'. Allow Him to light your way with Divine Truth. Or better still, let your own inner light shine and show you the way to discover your own Truth.

When my wife died while giving birth to our second child, I felt thoroughly devastated and alone. The fact that she died during childbirth was not an unusual occurrence 2000 years ago. It happened to many women and not to an isolated one or two.

Just to remind you, I first had a son but the second child

was a girl, so beautiful like her mother was, and whose soul I never knew, at least not in that lifetime anyway. My whole world came tumbling down upon my shoulders and I could barely stand or breathe because of it being so heavy. To have the support from my son, other family members and friends were great but that is not what I really needed at the time. I needed to be alone and that is exactly what I set out to do.

I placed my son into the care of another that I could trust and sought to be alone in 'no man's land'. This is merely a figure of speech and not the name of an actual place. I took enough supplies of food and water and other essentials to last me for three weeks. I found an isolated spot in the country and prayed that any wandering nomads would not stumble across my path. I set up base and this is where I stayed for the duration of that time. Certainly I did some walking but I always made sure to return to my base by nightfall. It was time to explore my heart more than the new terrain, although I did both. Walking, eating and sleeping with nature certainly cleared my head. I was ready to face my emotional feelings and my fear of being alone.

This was my personal space now and here is where I was going to stay, even though I did not greatly relish the thought of leaving behind my support group that included my young son. They didn't want me to leave either because they were fearful of my physical welfare and fragile state of mind but they need not have worried.

I knew I would be fine but I needed to be alone for my own self-healing. This event happened before Jesus entered my life. To remove yourself from everything that could distract you while going through this necessary process of healing can be quite overwhelming and scary. What might you uncover and unleash while studying those bits and pieces of your heart you were too afraid to poke and probe at before? If you dig too deep, will more pain come to the surface? Can you handle that level of pain without falling into a screaming heap?

These are some of the issues I had to face then and yes, I was fearful of what I might find and yes, I didn't want to be alone but I knew I was not to place too much importance or emphasis on these things. My job lay elsewhere. I couldn't afford to allow my earthly fears and family obligations to distract me at such an important time, as it could adversely affect my future if I did. Innately I knew everything would be okay and by trusting my inner knowing, I went ahead and did what I needed to do in my own space and in my own time without the help, or well meaning interference, of other people.

The first nine days were the hardest but then after this, everything in my life took on a whole new meaning for me, my soul was enlightened and because of this, my heart also came to be healed.

It's not a good feeling or a good look, to walk around with a gaping big hole in your heart, profusely bleeding over everyone that you meet. If there's a problem today, take time out, right then and there, to fix it properly. Don't suppress it or put a bandaid on it and besides, you don't always have to walk away like I did then. But there is one other little thing I would recommend everyone do at least once in their life and that is to attend a spiritual or religious retreat.

It is here where you will be forced to stay in a protected environment, where you can let go of all those things or people that are most important to you, which then leaves you to deal with what is left, that is you. It is advisable no matter how or where you do it, to practise letting go now rather than later and if that means being 'alone' for a short time, then let it be.

This shouldn't be too difficult a task for you and let's face it, when you die, you can't take anything or anyone with you except your energy, that can never be destroyed, and your memories which extend over more than one lifetime.

While looking at our fear of being alone, are we so scared of facing our true selves? Is this the real reason for our fear? By putting ourselves in this state of 'aloneness', we no longer have the excuse to use other people as a distraction from seeing our truth and this can only be for the good.

In order to not fear being alone, one needs to accept the concept that we are all souls with a physical body, that we are all electromagnetic energy, both living and dead and these two basic facts when combined means we are all connected energetically, if not physically, to each other.

This means that when we hurt ourselves, this is automatically mirrored in other people to varying degrees. When we accept responsibility for our own thoughts, feelings and actions, we are then being responsible for all souls. Because we are all joined at the hip so to speak on an energetic and psychic level, we can never truly feel or be alone. We would easily be tapping into the thoughts and feelings of others. This is happening now quite naturally as it has since the beginning of time, yet some don't realise it yet.

What affects one, affects the whole. If you wish for no harm to come to you, then wish no harm on somebody else. Our thoughts alone are more powerful than you think. Because you may not carry out your antagonism you feel towards another or to a specific group of people, this thought is immediately transferred to the person or organisation you feel angry at or are fearful of. They may not know where this is coming from and so accept this anger and fear as their own and react accordingly to those they make physical contact with.

When you expand that scenario on a worldwide scale, you are then left with humanity running scared, anxious, angry and sick, where chaos and disharmony rule at every turn in the bend that you take in life. Just open and read the front page headlines or turn on the TV and listen to the 6 o'clock news. They'll fill you in on these facts. That's their job or at least that is what they would have you believe.

If you should change your negative thought patterns today, by cleaning up the personal rubbish that is cluttering your mind, this then unblocks the heart charka to emit tidal waves of great love and compassion, peace and security.

It's not an impossible dream but in order for this grand plan to work, it must first begin from within each and every individual upon this planet and once this healing process has begun, which it already has, the darkness will eventually be eaten up by the light. This is when all of mankind, and this term incorporates all women and children as well, will become true messengers of God and this is exactly the role of the Angels and Archangels. Don't worry. You won't be doing Spirit (which is the breath of God) out of a job if you combine forces and energy with your fellow human travellers in a harmonious way.

In fact, by joining forces on all levels and this includes your perceived enemies, you become one with Spirit rather than apart, thereby eliminating that fear of being alone. Because when you can reach this high level of awareness, you will know that no such fear exists. How can it be when you all become united as one body, one mind, one heartbeat? You will then truly experience what it's like to be that pure energy force that for want of a better word, we call God. I am God therefore I am. This is not blasphemous; this is the whole truth, so help me God.

Change your focus from thinking you are alone to knowing that you are together. Once your mind has been sufficiently retrained to believe the latter, it will then come to pass.

The other Apostles and I would spend many long periods of time travelling apart but never did we feel we were ever alone. Our soul's purpose was the same, which meant that we were forever linked together, to make one strong chain. The moment when one begins to think they are alone within any group, that is when a weak link has been added to the equation. This is when cracks and breaks can occur within society. Is your closet crammed full of black sheep and skeletons? Who do you propose is the weakest link in your family unit? Is it the parent/s or is it the child/ren that is to blame?

If you are a parent, you might say it's the children and you have come to this conclusion because of what you see being acted out on the streets today. Then I would have to ask – who are the children's role models? What or who have they based their ideals on? Are you, as parents, willing to be there when their world comes crashing in on them or would you rather wash your hands clean and have nothing more to do with those same difficult children you have agreed on a soul level to bring into this world? If you choose the latter route as being a solution, then who shall look after them as they certainly can't? Who then takes over the role of parental responsibility – the law enforcement agencies, the medical profession, the Education Department, the clergy, the military or other distant family members? Is it one specific group or is it a combination?

The reality is that before you became a parent, you were first a child. If you are a teenager while reading this and you were asked the question as to who do you believe is the weakest link in your family, you may wish to point the finger of blame towards your parent/s and if you are really mixed up and confused about your identity and where you fit in your world, you could extend the finger even further to include all law enforcement agencies, the medical profession, the Education Department, the clergy, the military and other family members for letting you down.

So who is right and who is wrong – the parent or the child? Are both to blame equally or just one? Who can really tell?

We can't, because we are so closely bound and linked together, yet we stubbornly persist in our belief that we are alone and separate from each other. I have news for you – we need each other to survive. Besides which, without the chicken, there cannot be the egg and without the egg, there cannot be a chicken. Or some might pose the question that if God created the world, then who created God?

The parents of today have been given the opportunity to create a wonderful world through their children. The children then ideally need to continue living their parent's vision and dream of a bright new future and at the right time, these same children will one day become parents themselves who will then pass on their expanded knowledge to their own flesh and blood, where the cycle of life, death and life again forever perpetuates itself.

The limiting attitudes and severity of fears passed down from parent to the child within their first seven years will determine what our future generations can or cannot look forward to.

When two people marry, they make certain vows to stay together for better or for worse, for richer or poorer and in sickness or in health. We make this commitment in the sight of God and some of us try to do our best, while others may not.

If there is a ceremony such as this that binds us to our partner in love, should there not be another such sacred event created where the parents and children (but only when old enough to understand) come together and pledge themselves to love, respect, accept and protect everyone that is blessed enough to be part of that family unit.

Then, like the wedding, great feasting and laughter can take place after to celebrate the togetherness of parent and child, where each has agreed by Law to work and live together in harmony. You may think this is a pipe dream – that this is all well and good in theory but definitely not practical. You could be right but you could be wrong. You will never know for sure until you put this idea into practice, along with the many others already outlined in this book. If it does work in the way that I envisage, then it's all the better for you and your young children.

This will then have a snowball effect and touch the whole of humanity. Over time, values, beliefs and attitudes will change – all for the better and most certainly not for the worst; that will bring much richness and good health into your life. The added bonus is feeling a deep sense of inner peace and contentment in knowing that you are never alone.

I Am the Rose of Love

I have come from beyond the door
that when opened reveals a
grand palace, overflowing with love.

I happily accept the love and respect
my Angels have for me.
I receive and feel love all around me.

I let go and give perfect unconditional love
to myself and those around me.

My life, my body, my heart, my soul
is filled with joyous and endless love.

And with God's blessing from above,
I am the Rose of Love

Source: Shontara

Affirmations

> **YOU AND I remain one.**
>
> *A spiritual split away from myself is far worse than any physical parting.*
>
> **I AM INTERCONNECTED** *with all people and all things.*

ANDREW

Acceptance of myself and my many gifts, is absolutely vital and

Necessary to give me the required motivation and

Drive to be successful in all areas of my life.

Rejoice, for change is just a heartbeat away. Greet it as an old friend, with

Enthusiastic open arms and turn this newfound knowledge into

Wise and right action.

I was always laughing, even when bad things happened to me. You could say I was the eternal optimist, where poor Thomas, bless his soul, was your eternal doubtist. Yes, I know there's no such word as 'doubtist'; I just made it up because I felt it best suited this particular comparison.

At certain times, my joviality could annoy some people and others would accuse me of not caring but I bear these people no grudges. I knew myself better than they and what a lot of people tend to forget when dealing with others is that we all dance to a different tune. I understand and accept this as being fact rather than fiction. I'm not one for trying to change people. My own desire is to merely educate, inspire and motivate.

If as a result of that education, you make certain changes, well this is good but if you choose to stay the same, this is okay too. In order for successful and permanent change to take place, you must first desire it for yourself. If you force change to come about as a result of wanting someone else's attention, approval and acceptance (the big three A's), you could either become extremely elated or bitterly disappointed, depending upon the reaction of those you are trying or not trying to impress. Make your own independent decisions. Certainly, take into account the opinion and experience of others but go back to your first impression because 99% of the time, it will be right. And don't, under any circumstances allow the negative feedback of another to deter you or sway you from your truth. Don't lose sight of your own purpose and direction.

You may not consciously know what that is but if you can

stay relaxed and trusting, you will be gently guided by unseen friendly Spirit forces which you may or may not be aware of. Always turn within and there you will find your own personal and individualised gold key that was created especially with you in mind.

If you borrow, steal or reproduce a key that belongs to a different source of knowledge and wisdom, you will no doubt soon become frustrated and exasperated that then may leave you thinking – 'what am I doing so wrong, why am I being punished for doing something right, why me, what's the point of it all?' Certainly, we can learn a lot from the experiences and mistakes of others but instead of remaining a voyeur in your own life, jump in with both feet, get thoroughly wet and revel happily in your own clear or muddy situations.

You created these situations, so take time out to enjoy all of what you are experiencing. And if you can't enjoy, take responsibility for your creation and change it, if it depresses you too much but do it for yourself first. And if you do take that step towards changing a wrong into a right, give yourself a pat on the back. Don't wait for recognition or thanks to come from others. It may not. Because even though that same change may be obvious to you, it may not be so clear to them. Plod along regardless.

What do you do when you are surrounded by a group of people who are hostile to you, with the majority of them being bigger than you? Run and head for the hills, stay and take whatever they dish out to you without putting up too much of a struggle, scream blue murder in the hope it may attract some unwanted attention to the group's activities, do some quick talking and have them turn against each other, create a diversion, make them laugh or use your feet and fists to defend yourself and try and take everyone down? There are many different options to choose from. Perhaps you've tried them all at the same time or changed tactic over several episodes.

Life is full of choices. It doesn't matter what the situation is – there is always more than one solution. Or as some have said before me – there are more ways to kill a cat than just one. That may sound like a fairly violent analogy for me to use but I can't think of another one that is more appropriate.

Too many people have such a fixed picture of how things should be; they can't see another better way around a particular problem. My philosophy is to broaden your range of vision and try everything at least once and settle upon one that works. Although even then, you will still need to remain flexible and change at a moment's notice. Because when dealing with different people at different times in different situations, that person may react differently to the one you encountered before. That's because we are all different, we are all unique.

Sure, we may have similar desires and fears, along with our likes and dislikes but we are still not the same. And to judge a group of people harshly and unfairly based solely upon the colour of their skin, the God they do or do not worship, whether they are young or old, male or female, heterosexual or homosexual, Angel or witch, criminal or victim can lead to all sorts of problems for everyone concerned. Every group or class of people will have a mixture of both good and bad apples within their bunch. Is it really fair to compare all men or women to the one or two who might have hurt you? You could say the world and the people in it, is like one giant bag of mixed lollies.

Some will melt in your mouth and are sweet to the taste, while others are quite bitter and hard to swallow. Spit out what you don't like and try again, until you do find what, or who suits you best. It costs little to be a part of this lucky dip.

Certainly it can lead to disappointment and heartbreak one minute but that doesn't mean it has to always be like that. The moment that follows may bring a pleasant surprise, where your eyes sparkle with excitement while your once downcast mouth will lift into an upwards position that then causes you to have a smile that's wider than the widest ocean and bigger than the Cheshire cat that ate the cream or should that be the cat who ate the canary?

Again, you can choose what scenario you wish to accept. In this case, I guess it largely depends upon whether you have a sweet tooth or not. My dietary needs could be different to yours but does that then mean that one of us is wrong? Why can't we both be right?

A new day is always greeted by the rising sun in the east, which leaves after dusk and where it creeps below our line of vision to make way for the moon and stars. The sun and moon must always go together. There cannot be one without the other. Can you imagine what chaos and destruction would be caused if the two were torn apart from each other's orbit? I don't really think you can.

It is the same with men and women. We cannot have one without the other. We may like to think we can do without them but this is not possible and even if it was, it would create a whole new set of problems that we haven't yet imagined.

We need to learn how to get along better than how we are today; in a society that desires individual power, control, independence and freedom from each other. While one person strives to get the upper hand and break away from feeling confined and hemmed in, the other person's sense of worthiness and self-respect is squashed firmly into the ground. Occasionally, each person will trade places with the other but this is only a temporary measure.

So who's the boss in your family? Does there have to be a boss? Is there no boss at all? Do you each have an equal say as to what does or does not happen? Is there complete fairness and compromise in your relationship? Who does most of the listening, talking, demanding or screaming?

Men and women I know are different (men are from Mars and women I believe are from Venus), their approaches to life are not the same, as well as how they go about solving certain problems. The real problem here is that there is no acceptance or true freedom of expression. The vast majority of people will insist upon wanting to change those same differences we find in the other and turn them into a clone of ourselves.

Certainly, we may come close to achieving this goal but again, it is only a temporary measure. It cannot last. There will always come a point when the worm decides to turn and eat its antagonist. And especially, we need to understand that if our partner or friends were exactly like us, what could we possibly learn from each other?

To have a difference of opinion does not need to cause chaos or World War III, but it often does when the other person disagrees with our beliefs and we don't like it. What do we do then? We then get on the offensive of course, and feel compelled to attack back in order to defend our good name, honour and integrity. We expect that if they know what's good for them, they will agree and submit to our way of thinking and doing. I say, let go of all expectations, accept and not try to change each other's personal weaknesses, to not feel jealous of their strengths, especially if we do not perceive it within ourselves and we would like to have what they are having and above all, be happy while agreeing to disagree.

Do we sit and wonder why the moon can't be more like the sun and vice versa? What would be the point? Each has a vital role to play in the welfare of all mankind, as do all women and men, boys and girls.

And to those women who wish to act and be more like a man and to those men who wish to act and be more like a woman, to both of you I say – strive for balance, for there you will find the equality and happiness that you have been so long in looking for. Blend together rather than divide and in your togetherness, it is still possible to maintain your own individuality and by so doing, each person can then fulfil their purpose and meet their final destiny with peace rather than anger in their hearts.

Stop struggling to be someone that you are not. Relax and allow others to see the true you. Be proud of all your achievements and never regret a moment of those mistakes you may have made along the way. Mistakes are greatly needed because if we were already so perfect, again nothing new could ever be learnt and we would never advance and expand into a higher state of awareness. That's a major part of everyone's purpose. If you separate a fish from its water, it will die. If you remove man from wo-man, both will die a slow and agonisingly painful death. So stop punishing each other for our differences.

There is nothing better than to have some freshly baked bread, roughly broken off from the main loaf and dipped into a generous helping of soup. The Twelve of us were all good eaters. We needed it in order to give us strength and stamina, as did everyone else around us. Many other people went hungry though. We tried our best to share our good fortune with others but we couldn't reach and help everyone we would have liked to, all of the time. It was not humanly possible. Remember, we were only human after all but it was also not necessary. Some people needed to fend for themselves and be independent. Not all our wants and needs are to be hand delivered personally to us on a silver platter. We sometimes have to work for what we have.

If everything was too easy, we would quickly take for granted the person that come bearing gifts. But I say – what happens when that person no longer delivers the goods? Do we feel angry, cheated and rejected? More than likely, and not so long after the gifts have stopped coming, we will seek out another more willing gift giver without ever really trying to obtain things for ourselves.

That is why Jesus was wise enough to realise it was not in his best interest or theirs to offer assistance all of the time. People had to experience the feeling of accomplishment in doing something for themselves, for at least some of the time. And that sense of accomplishment, achievement and fulfilment cannot be established if we have someone constantly at our beck and call 24hrs a day, to cater to our every want, need and ego.

This is taking for granted another person. It's also taking advantage of their giving and generous nature. It stops the giver from spending quality time to achieve great things for themselves. By taking this action, you become responsible for blocking their progress. Just because they are too polite to complain verbally, this does not always mean they are happy about the situation that has arisen.

When dealing with others and ourselves, a balance needs to be struck between giving and receiving. If it's weighted more one way than the other, problems are created. Put yourself and them on the scales of justice. Who weighs the most and who is the tallest? Whose heart is heavy and whose is filled with light? In order to find that balance, both parties concerned needs to be the same.

In other words, let go of the belief that you are better than. Certainly, you may be better educated than the person standing or sitting opposite but that doesn't necessarily mean that you are smarter.

The well of knowledge is full and you cannot know how deep it is simply by taking a quick cursory glance at the surface. Dig deep, strive to find the bottom and along the way, freely share this knowledge you have with others but always keep half. Don't ever completely empty yourself. Once depleted of everything you have to offer, to retrieve it again is going to be that much harder. Be wise – work smarter and not harder. You get no extra brownie points as you reach the Pearly Gates for working harder but you do if you're smart.

Bedding, while travelling on the road, was exceptionally basic; it really would amount to only being a thin piece of material thrown on the ground. Not all that comfortable but your body got used to it. They bred us tough those days to withstand all types of conditions. In the morning, you would simply roll it up and carry it on your back. I loved sleeping under the stars. It made me feel connected, that I was a part of the whole that was the Universe. Some people, when looking at the countless stars above, would feel real tiny and insignificant but not me. I felt the opposite.

Instead of weakening my position in the overall big scheme of things, it strengthened me. I drew upon the stabilising power from the Earth beneath my feet and the potent energy from high above my head. The Earth represents the metal silver, while the Heaven above symbolises the precious metal of gold. Female Goddess, Mother Earth and Male God, Father Sky. We need the two polarities in order to achieve and maintain balance. Some will feel an affinity for one rather than both but it is not wise to give too much influence and power to one while rejecting and neglecting the other. They are to share equal importance.

At this stage, we are doing much damage to the Earth and this in turn affects the quality of air that we breathe. It has become tainted and impure, along with our thoughts and actions. But we can still take positive steps to clean up our act and it begins from within.

As we become once again balanced and connected to every other living thing or person, our desire to destroy what is naturally good will no longer be a priority. We may think that by our thoughts and actions alone, we are not hurting anything or anyone but we are and the main party being hurt is ourselves; while like the ripples in a pond will spread outwards until it affects everyone in its path.

What we see around us is an indication of how we feel and treat ourselves. Take a look at your home from the inside out. What sort of an impression do you give to those visiting for the first time? Are they keen to come back or are they too scared to return? And it's the same with your car, even your pets. A cluttered car and untidy house translates into a cluttered and scattered mind.

Perhaps you may think that what I say is too harsh. That sometimes, to change our personal environment is out of our control due to lack of finances, time, motivation and discipline. These are all mere excuses in order for us to accept more easily, our non-action and non-productivity. You couldn't hope to get away with it at work, so why do so at home? Are we such rebels at heart? Is it because that in our own homes, behind closed doors and gates, that we expect to do what we like and that no-one is going to tell us what we can or cannot do? No sireee, no way.

But think about this for a moment – rubbish in, rubbish out. Start with a cleansed and pure heart, work your way out from there, turn around and retrace your steps back to the centre. The cycle of regeneration and rejuvenation can then begin again.

You can also not hope to put an old head upon young shoulders. Certainly, the contents within may stick for a little while but when it becomes too full with information, it will weigh too much and combined with a young child's lack of physical neck strength, the head will eventually topple over and fall off its temporary perch. The child can then easily run around in circles, like a chook with its head chopped off.

Older children may learn to listen properly and absorb the information received but young children lack the necessary concentration which then causes them to forget easily. Of course, this can equally apply to adults as well. Don't try and force feed a young child with your opinions and beliefs. They are already assimilating much information that will shape their adult life automatically and unconsciously but there is only so much that one can take in.

If the head is filled up with too many facts and figures, what will finally happen is that your well intentioned words may fall upon deaf ears, or if the child does hear it, they will let it enter through one ear and allow it to trickle out the other.

What I would like to see happen in your primary schools, are compulsory meditation classes, along with English, History and Maths. Teach them how to focus properly, to turn within and receive the answers they need for themselves, which then brings a deep feeling of contentment and inner peace.

More and more young children are turning to crime as a way to release their anger. You may wonder why such a person of a tender young age should be angry. They have been conditioned this way from birth by the older people around them. They may not understand completely where their anger is coming from but they will act out the behaviour patterns that they see or sense. Don't fool yourself that children don't feel pressure. This is not the exclusive domain of adults only. A young child will rely largely upon visual or oral stimuli to learn. They are like human sponges and because of this, they have the ability to soak up any unspoken positive or negative emotions and accept them as their own.

In a child's world everything becomes magnified, until one day it gets so big that they can't handle it anymore. That will lead on to an emotional or physical release or explosion of some kind, where other children and adults, can get badly hurt. And once the damage has been caused, you can't go back and change it.

We, as adults, also can't shut our eyes to what just transpired and pretend it didn't happen, when it did. The ideal would be to work on a solution before the problem arises. And that is where the hard part comes in to it.

Some parents, teachers and other adult role models in a child's life just don't know how to. Some will make a concerted and long term effort to do something good for the child, in the hope that they can bring about positive change, while others don't want to know and lack the energy or motivation to change a potentially volatile and negative situation into a positive. From day one, they give in. This is because those same adults don't know any other way.

If you look really close, you will see that they cave in when dealing with the constant pressure of their own problems. It stands to reason then that if the adults can't handle in a positive way what haunts and worries them the most, why should we expect them to do the same for the very real or imagined concerns their children might have? "A leopard cannot change its spots". And the cycle of self-destruction continues, from generation to generation and as time passes, it will get worse.

In order to avoid all this future chaos and confusion, teach the young how to be independent, detached and confident individuals in their own right, so they can make a conscious effort to be more discerning in regards to what and how they learn. Consistent meditation is a good start.

Keeping in mind the very young have wandering minds, ten or fifteen minutes is all that is needed to begin with and as they progress through the school system and as they get older, extend the time to half an hour, finally stopping at hour long classes in meditation. If this becomes a regular part of a child's learning practice at school, they will get a taste for it and will be reluctant to stop, even when at home and especially when they begin to feel and see the benefits for themselves.

Another idea would be to have the teachers give their students homework. Get them involved in a practical way. Have them write their own guided meditations/visualisations and let the teacher share it out loud in class. That way, they receive recognition for the effort they have put into writing it and they get to experience a variety of different ways they can meditate.

Perhaps a competition could be run for the best meditation piece that would bring about world peace and for the winning entry to then spread to all children across the globe. Perhaps I'm being too idealistic or unrealistic for some but it's something to think about.

I invite you to come up with your own ideas and then make some attempt to put them into action. If the schools are not interested, then do it at home. Take the pressure off the children. If this can be accomplished, those same children will then grow up to become well adjusted, solution orientated and positive thinking adults.

What sort of a future would you like for your children and grandchildren? Or don't you care? Perhaps it's all too difficult; "Woe is me". Children learn mainly from adults. Let us be better role models. Responsibility for world peace must lie within each individual. It's too big a task for one or even a small handful to take on. Each and every individual's help is gravely needed. So, are you ready, willing and able to help?

Fear of Failure

The fear of failure will stop you, even before you have begun, from trying anything new. And when I say anything new, this relates to all aspects of your life that includes relationships, career and parenting choices.

People who have a fear of failure are certainly not the risk takers of today's world who would never dream of becoming involved in the fluctuating and sometimes unstable arena of the stock market, the politicising of politics, the complexities of finance, long term palliative care for the terminally ill, the sometimes unjust justice system, air traffic controllers, nursing and lots more.

All of these areas of business need a lot of courage to take the appropriate course of action, where each step must be taken without fear or hesitation. He who hesitates can wind up dead. Whether you approve or not about the often unconventional methods and tactics used to achieve their business goals, along with the objectives of their clients, is not important. At least they are there on the front line, so to speak, trying to do the best they can for all concerned. Where are you?

If this group of people suffered greatly from the fear of failure, nothing would get done. While the day to day services we take for granted and which they provide, will come to a crashing and dramatic halt. Where would you be then? Perhaps madly scurrying around like rats deserting a sinking ship, where chaos and anarchy would rule; there would be no leaders to organise, teach or guide us and we would begin to fear for our future. But let's look closer to home now.

When it comes to the subject of personal failure, we can often be our own worst judge, jury and executioner. Let's shoot first and ask questions later, keeping in mind no excuses will be accepted. That's how hard we can be on ourselves.

For example, there you are standing in the role of a parent. Single or married makes no real difference. You have done everything in your power to teach your children right from wrong. You come from a variety of socio-economic backgrounds which encompass both the rich and poor, including all those who fit neatly in between these two extremes.

Then one day you receive a knock on the door from the police informing you that your son or daughter has been taken in for questioning and charged with unlawful breaking and entering, shoplifting, drunk driving, taking drugs, armed robbery as well as rape and murder. And the worst case scenario for any parent who loves their child is to receive the news that their own flesh and blood has committed suicide. Some people will not blame themselves for the actions their children take, but others definitely will.

It is the latter group who will cry out in pain, shame and sheer agony about how they failed at being a good parent and question, 'where did I go wrong? If only I had paid more attention to their needs. If only I had read between the lines? If only I had listened properly when they were speaking? If only I could have seen it coming, I may have been able to stop it from happening? If only they could have trusted me? If only I could have helped them?'

The 'if only' dialogue that fills your brain and makes you

cry, can go on ad infinitum. But what good does it truly do? Do you believe that by thinking yourself a failure, you must then seek to punish and destroy yourself and any semblance of happiness you might have in the future?

Why commit self-sabotage in this way? No-one else does or at least if they do, they shouldn't. Do you think that by punishing yourself, it can change the past? The answer of course is no.

Let's look at another scenario that you may relate to. There you are, the 'bread winner' of the household. You believe that you are totally responsible for earning lots of money to keep your family happy and safe. Anything less won't do. If you can't provide what your partner or child asks of you, you will inwardly spin out of control and feel enormously guilty for having to say no to their requests. This then drives you to work harder; where you become a workaholic because you can't bear to see the ones you love, go without.

It also upsets you terribly to watch them try and cope with any type of stress and because of this, you take on board all their worries and emotional pain that is then absorbed into every living cell of your being, with all sorts of negative emotions attached but still you push yourself to perform well beyond your, dare I say it, limitations. Yes, we all have them, like it or not. Then what do you think happens? Your health is compromised where you could have a heart attack which is not enough to kill you but which will give you a scare and a quick swift kick up the backside; but some people choose to ignore both the scare and the kick.

A heart attack is an obvious warning sign to slow down, take it easy and become less responsible for the welfare of everybody else, because if you don't, it will be to the detriment of your own health. Those who choose not to listen to this warning are those who feel they have failed and you can bet your bottom dollar that a week after being released from hospital, they can be found back at work, being driven by some unconscious force to continue, no matter what.

For them to be sick, even for a small amount of time, is admitting failure. 'If I get sick, who will look after my family and who will do my job as well as I can?' The answer in their mind is no-one of course. I can't afford to be sick. I'd be letting everybody else down. They rely upon me to help them get through life.

But stop and ask yourself here – who do I rely upon for help? Again the answer would be no-one, because by claiming you needed any help whatsoever that came from another person, you would be admitting that once again you failed.

But what good really are you to anyone, least of all yourself, if you don't wake up one morning and where your loved ones are then forced to farewell you for good in a pine wooden box that's tailor made to fit your overworked and under nourished body shape? Fear of failure can be the end of us if taken to these extremes.

Certainly, you must take some degree of responsibility of those you care about or live with but please be realistic by not leaving yourself out either of your own picture. You too deserve to have what you want and need from life. Expending all your energy, time and money on others will leave you with nothing for yourself and then you really would have failed yourself. It all comes down to deciding who is more important – you or everybody else? That will determine how you live the rest of your life and what level of fulfilment and happiness can be achieved.

The Apostles

We, as Apostles of Jesus, all felt we had failed because we were unable to save his life and for this, after his death, we had to learn to forgive ourselves for this perceived failure on our part. Jesus never blamed us for what we could not do; so forgiveness was not needed, at least not from his point of view anyway. He knew the unwritten contract he made with each of us was temporarily finished; that he had to leave and allow us to move forward and grow into our own Guiding Light but this could never have truly happened completely while he was still with us in the flesh. At different points in time and even while he was alive, each one of us came to experience that horrible feeling of failure.

It was with constant reassurance from Jesus that we were able to work and push through it to the other side, largely unscathed. Each one of us had a separate purpose to fulfil after his death. We knew what this was and we did the best that we could, under sometimes extremely difficult circumstances. To do our best was all that Jesus ever wanted from us. He knew we needed to remain independent and to stand strong with our head held high.

You can't do this easily if around every bend, you feel you are a failure, so step outside yourself for a moment and look within. After removing all the surface dirt, there exists a being that is clean, pure and perfect. This true essence is who we really are and not many get a chance to see it for themselves but when this vision of holiness and completeness touches your heart, you will see that you have not failed.

The trick then is to believe in the gift you have been given and not put it down to mere wishful thinking on your part in order to soothe a guilty conscience. You have truly nothing to be fearful or ashamed of. To feel one has failed can become quite a depressing affair where no-one can win. I say pick yourself up, dust yourself off and start all over again. We had to do this many times throughout the term of our natural life. That assisted us in remaining flexible while achieving our personal goals, which was sometimes different to what God had planned for us.

Occasionally, we would rebel against God's will as well but with his never ending patience, we had divine help in placing our feet firmly, once again, on the right path. We were largely left alone to make our own mistakes, like you are today. No-one can protect us forever. We need to learn to live with the bad while at the same time, embracing all that is good. Seek and find your centre of balance. Once found, stay there for as long as possible but when you begin to veer off course, stop, be still and travel inwards to your core, your heart, your all.

Failure does not exist except within our own mind and as such, it can easily be destroyed by our thoughts alone. Don't let the fear of failure overwhelm you to the extent where it can capture and hold you prisoner. That, at times, can feel impossible to escape from.

Have you ever received an 'F' on your primary school report card? Have you ever shivered in your shoes with dread as you walked home with it in your school bag, along with the half eaten lunch your Mum had prepared for you earlier that day? You would have been requested by the teacher that they needed your parent's signature on a duplicate copy confirming they had sighted it. This was to be returned as soon as possible, while your parents kept the original for safekeeping and comparison with the following year's report card, hoping for some visible signs of improvement.

So there you are, at the age of six or seven; this is now your second year at school and again it's that time of the year where still you are given an 'F' for certain subjects that indicate for the world to see that you have failed.

Of course, it doesn't help any if your parents then turn into thorough and quite frightening monsters who, upon sighting your dismal results, proceed to take great pleasure in reading the riot act to you; which of course you try and forget about the next day but they won't let you. Did you ever, as a child at these times, get the feeling that you're never going to amount to much, that you're never going to be good or smart enough, that to fail was to bring automatic shame on the family, as if you're going to say anything? Yeah right! No way.

The trouble is that your parents were not so inclined to hold their tongues and complained loud and long to their friends and strangers about how you failed them, where they had paid a decent amount of money to provide you with a good education and what do they get in return for their trouble? A big fat 'F' on your end of year report card. And sometimes, they'll go on to explain that they are to blame, that they failed you as a parent. Does this all sound strangely familiar to you? For Shontara it does.

She lived with that fear for her entire school life until her parents did the smart thing by removing her from the public school environment at the age of sixteen and placed her in a business college instead, where she passed all her subjects with flying colours. No more symbols of failure were ever seen again.

So, is it any wonder why children believe they're no good, as their teachers certainly thought they were, while their parents readily agreed and supported the teacher's opinion? Exam time is quite nerve racking and hard enough in itself without being degraded in this inhumane way at the end of it. These children will one day grow up with real beliefs of insecurity, doubt and indecisiveness; always afraid of making a move in case they were wrong and heaven forbid if everyone in their own little Universe found out about it. How could they ever live it down?

To look like a fool, an idiot, an imbecile in front of your friends caused quite a devastating blow to your ego and where your self-esteem took a battering. These same 'failures' of society will forever seek confirmation or sympathy from others unless they do something positive and constructive about it and to bring about a change for the better. It won't be easy to let go of the childhood conditioning that is holding you back from being successful today but you can do it, if you want change badly enough. For Shontara, it took ten long and painful years of much honest soul-searching but finally, she did it.

At the end of which time, she met the man of her dreams, her knight in shining armour, her soul mate, at the age of 30. At the time of publishing this book, 22 years have passed by since they first met and they are still running on honeymoon mode. So it's not only fairytales that have happy endings. Real life relationships can last long term, if you'll let them.

And there is another thing – people who have been divorced will often feel they failed their partner somehow. That is why they are no longer together. But why must blame, guilt or the tag of failure be added to the two parties involved in this unfortunate breakdown of their relationship?

Those same people who believe they are left with nothing, especially if the decision to end it all was not theirs to make, will become ultra cautious and perhaps turn their anger and mistrust towards the opposite sex in general, to get back at the person who hurt them. This is a complete waste of time, not to mention it being totally unfair to everybody else. Why cut off your nose to spite your face? Why destroy any future happiness you might have with another because of one wretched person upsetting your apple cart in the past?

To compare all others with just one is quite an unrealistic approach to adopt in life. Set out to repair bridges, not burn them for good. Trust and have faith that you have not, and will not, fail. Life's too short to be stuck in the past. The time to move on is now.

Even leaders of great or small nations being invaded by their enemies can feel that they are a failure because they should have done a better job of protecting their borders, airspace and people, so no advancing army could enter. Sometimes, especially with today's modern warfare, this is not always possible.

What then one needs to do is accept what has happened and find a solution to change it back to the way it was. If you adopt a 'victim' mentality, then failure will closely follow you around like a bad shadow and a shadow, like your aura, can never be destroyed. Just because you can't always see it, doesn't mean it no longer exists. Be confident about your decisions.

Don't look for blame or place unnecessary guilt upon your shoulders for the accidents or death of everyone under your care. While under your care, these individuals still need to be responsible for their own actions or non-involvement in the direction they are to travel.

Say for example, you are a doctor in the Emergency Ward of a large public or private hospital. This is where you must wrestle with the possibility of death visiting your patients every minute you stay there and the longer the time you spend in such a place, the greater the likelihood of death showing its true face. Not everything can be in your control.

There are certain (but not all) events that are preordained and no matter who you are or what your occupation is, they will still happen, regardless of what you try and do to stop them from eventuating. It is at these times to make sure you keep uppermost in your mind that you are not a failure. Shontara had such a devastating experience in her early twenties where she felt a complete and utter failure by not being able to help a person who was choking on a fish bone.

This elderly lady was quietly lunching with friends. Minutes before, Shontara went up to the table and asked this small group of women to borrow their container of sugar, which she promptly returned to their table after using. Shontara then went back to her own food and drink and thought nothing more about them. No more than five minutes had passed before sounds of choking came from that same location. From what Shontara heard a few feet away, you could tell the person was in great trouble and struggling to save her own life.

This is when Shontara went into physical shock and became paralysed with fear. She did not turn to look at what was happening because she already knew. The feelings were scary enough to try and deal with but in her defence, she could not have moved even if her own life depended upon it.

What she did do, was to repeatedly pray to God for the welfare of this woman. She was then guided to visualise getting up from her seat, walk towards the lady in trouble, offer her a gold cup filled with the Blood of Christ and invite her to drink from this cup, which this woman gratefully received.

While this was all vividly happening in Shontara's mind, a man nearby who was knowledgeable about what to do in this situation physically came to this lady's aid. Another bystander had already called for an ambulance but Shontara had no mobile phone to do such a thing. Within minutes, this elderly lady coughed up the fish bone lodged in her windpipe and promptly collapsed, crying into the arms of the man who saved her life.

Not once did Shontara turn to look around but she sensed that everything would be okay. Soon after, Shontara discreetly left the coffee house and returned to work where she couldn't stop shaking and who had turned a whiter shade of pale.

Upon arrival at her office, she collapsed into a puddle of tears, at which time Shontara's boss found her and after receiving the facts, ordered her home for the rest of the day.

As the shock took hold and in this particular instance, Shontara believed she had failed this woman terribly by not physically moving to help and consequently, Shontara for a long time after hated herself for not assisting where she felt she should. She had great trouble sleeping that night, as she felt guilty, although the woman survived her ordeal. This was small comfort in Shontara's mind.

She allowed this most recent memory to overload her, which stopped her from ever going back to that same coffee house where she had happily been a regular lunch goer in the past because, according to Shontara, they offered good food at reasonable prices and where the staff were always extra nice to her.

Since the fish bone episode, this had not changed but Shontara had and because of this, she could never go back without that fear of failure springing to mind. She tried to forget and the only way she knew how to do this was to avoid the place that held only bad memories for her.

How many of you have done that or have gone out of your way to avoid those people who have hurt you in the past because it is too painful to remember?

It would take another year before Shontara became strong enough within herself to reface her fears and to stop believing she was a failure. Shontara, at the beginning of this channelling session had no idea what was going to come through (as she never does except perhaps for the first couple of sentences) and we gave no prior warning because even today, she still has twinges of great sadness when thinking about this woman's plight and disgust about her own inability to help.

But here is a gentle reminder for you, as well as for Shontara, that she did help in her own way by energetically offering the Blood of Christ to this unknown woman struggling to hold on to life. In Shontara's heart, she never quite believed that this was ever enough but we say to you and all concerned, never underestimate the power of prayer and visualisations. God answered her prayer immediately by sending this woman in need, a man who knew exactly what to do; so Shontara's contribution to this situation amounted to something rather than nothing.

What she did not realise at that time but does now, is that there were many other people present like her, who were all too fearful to make matters worse by becoming involved but who prayed to God with strong intent. Their call for help was heard and answered. Much was to be learnt from that one experience for everyone and each may have come to a different conclusion or truth.

The moral of this story is never judge a person for having failed their duty of care to another because some facts will always remain hidden, safely locked away in the mind and heart of man, never to see the light of day again, because they feel ashamed. That is until one day, they are brave enough to reopen their heart and share their painful truth with others, although it may not be as bad as what it may first appear.

And as an end note to this particular channelling session, Shontara has never eaten any type of fish with bones again, so shark, also known as flake, has become her personal favourite. May God continue to bless you my dear, dear friend Shontara.

If you believe you can't, you can't. If you believe you can, you can. What you believe, it will be. Our negative and angry thoughts will do us in every time, which in turn will make us sick if we hold on to those black thoughts for too long. Which is it to be, black or white magic? Quite often, there is not much difference between the procedures, words and implements used. The main defining line that separates the two is the power of intent that lies behind what you do. Besides which, you can't be angry or envious when you practice white magic. It won't work.

If a casual outsider was watching both being performed on the same stage at the same time, the intent may not be so openly obvious, as intent lies within the heart and mind of the practitioner, which many people cannot see or hear.

But Jesus, and we as his students, could perceive the real truth of the matter and often it was painful to gaze upon the face of darkness that appeared to the average uninitiated eye to be coming from the light. As a result, we witnessed many people becoming more and more confused on a daily basis as they chose to follow the dark.

Although to be fair to them, they truly believed they had chosen the opposite path. Now any intelligent person could argue that their heart should have alerted them to the reality of the situation and you would be right in saying this but who ever truly listens to their heart, then or now? Who trusts their true feelings implicitly and without question? What are your true feelings anyway? How does one discern fact from fiction? When we don't listen, when we doubt what we first feel, to ignore those first warning signs received (and believe me, we do give them to you. It's just that you haven't picked them up as such), all will lead us down the path to failure.

Let's backtrack for a minute here to the point where I said we witnessed many people becoming more and more confused on a daily basis as a result of choosing to follow the dark that suspiciously looked like the light. You might ask us – 'you had a responsibility to save these people, so why did you not step in and educate them to their Truth?'

We did, although perhaps not always because upon occasion, depending upon who we were watching, we were requested not to interfere with that person's chosen path, as they had certain karmic lessons to learn by going through that particular experience. Know when to help, as well as accepting those times when you must take a step back and allow them the freedom to make their own mistakes.

You may consider us as having failed to enlighten and save every soul we came across and you would be right in believing this. In our defence, we were not in the business of 'saving souls' as such. Our job was merely to enlighten, to educate and to encourage but it was not necessary to save them. The reason for this is that every soul, both living and dead, are already saved, regardless of all the bad or sinful things they may have got involved with during each incarnation. Although, this doesn't mean that you have an open licence to create fear in the hearts of mankind and get away with it either, without some form of retribution or punishment coming your way, in this lifetime or the next. Remember, with your self-imposed limited vision, you are looking at only one brief existence out of a possible thousand.

I ask, how can you stand in judgement and tag them as being evil by accepting only 1% of the overall facts that you consciously know about but what about the other 999 lives that you are not yet aware of? What happens to this information? Does it remain hidden and lost? Not to Jesus it doesn't. He looks beyond the present, sees clearly what has gone before and what is yet to come in the future. Before he passes judgement on any soul, he sets out to ensure the scales are first equal in balance and quite literally, everything is then taken into account.

You may think that you don't have this same ability to scan another person's past or future lives but you do. Ask your heart to take you there and when you sincerely are ready to behold the whole Truth and not just that which you want to believe, you will then be shown all. Trust what you are given. For to judge another person's actions upon a half truth is being unfair to them, as it is equally unfair when others wrongly judge you without first having all the evidence before them. Wouldn't you expect a fair trial?

Of course you would, so it would then stand to reason that if your roles were to be reversed, you would do the same for them. By not making any effort whatsoever to go beyond what is obvious is a form of failure in itself – to yourself and others.

Many people have barely scratched below the surface of their heart and mind, being too fearful of what they might find. Certainly, there may be instances where the negative comes strongly to the fore but there is much beauty to behold, once you can get past this initial blackness. In order to become an Ascended Master, you must first pass through the darkness before you can get to the light.

Once you have learnt to master all that is bad or evil, you can then live fully in the opposite arena, for without one, perfect understanding cannot be achieved about the other. This is the yin and yang principle. It applies to all and not just some of us.

So never think in terms of failure, think in terms of success. Don't believe that because you have returned to planet Earth at this time, you are not already a highly evolved being. Certainly some are not but some most definitely are. That is why you are here. These are the light workers of the world who come in all shapes, sizes and colours. They may be young, they may be old. They may be Buddhist, Christian, Hindu or Moslem. You cannot tell. They can be found in all types of full or part time employment.

There is another separate group of people whom we classify as being 'white Angels'. You could be living with one. They have chosen to come back again and accept a physical body. The white Angel's specific purpose is to help others move through their darkness quickly and assist them in accomplishing their life's purpose. They are a joy to behold and to work with. They still experience pain and fear and often they initially go about their life totally unaware of their true identity until the light dawns and when that light of awareness is switched on, nothing can stop them from moving all perceived insurmountable problems out of the way. So how many are there on planet Earth at this time?

This is not important for you to know, except to believe in

their existence. Also, what is not important is whether you are advanced or just beginning to experience your life on the spiritual path. We will all work at different paces and this is how it needs to be for now, while giving each other the space to breathe and grow. Don't demand they speak or do everything, exactly like you. This is respect. Lack of respect will lead to failure. So wherever you fit in God's plan at this moment, it is right for you, so don't waste large amounts of your time and energy by struggling against those things you can't control.

Please, turn a blind ear to those voices that accuse you of being a failure, because deep in your heart, you know you are not. If you are still not convinced, please read these words again and again, until you do accept.

Who has known the parent, sibling, teacher, partner, boss, doctor, psychiatrist and priest from Hell? Did they all (or just some of them) make you feel you were a failure? How many of these people still exist in your life? How many of those can you walk away from? If you feel you can't leave any of them for whatever reason, why do you inwardly accept and outwardly subject yourself to these constant daily reminders about how you have failed miserably in life and that you are no good? Perhaps you are unaware of why you feel drawn to stay and so do nothing positive to change your situation. It's funny peculiar how failure can appear around every corner (if you let it) in both large and small doses.

But being continually exposed to its virus like properties can erode away and destroy all feelings of self-esteem and self-confidence; where one day you are left only with tears of bitterness and regrets about your past.

It is these same feelings that you will take into the Spirit world upon leaving your physical body behind; where contact will be made with similar type souls – bitter and regretful. You will then have no choice in the matter, as like attracts like and fear attracts fear. Is this the type of afterlife you wish for yourself? If no, start doing something about it today before it's too late. If you think you are trapped now by surrounding yourself with people who think nothing or little of you, wait until you have arrived in the etheric realm. Then it really will be Hell.

You could start changing things by affirming that 'I am successful now'. You may not initially believe it but this is not the point. Sometimes you have to first practise acting out the role before you can become one with it. That is why affirmations can be so effective but now try and take them to the next level of success, by creating for yourself little bite size goals you can chew off and achieve easily throughout your day. This will give you a sense of achievement.

The third step could be that when you have accomplished these daily goals (it could be three or four or more), immediately write them down in black and white and later refer to them at night before you go to sleep; at the same time as giving yourself a well deserved pat on the back for a job or jobs well done. Do this on a day to day basis and on the seventh instance, tally up the figures. Whatever the grand total comes to, go out and reward yourself properly in style because you can now see clearly (because it's all there on the piece of paper in front of you) which indicates you have indeed accomplished what you originally set out to achieve. Of course, you have always been doing this but you weren't looking in all the right places and where you allowed other people to distract you from seeing or believing in your target; that is success.

This exercise may appear to be an oversimplified solution to a very big problem but it can and does work. A little bit of effort on your part can bring great results. Enjoy and accept the changes that this success can bring. Make the fear of failure work for you. Use it as your own personal diving board, starting point and driving force to carry out the perceived impossible. Nothing is impossible to those who believe. Do you now believe or are you still wavering in the wind?

There was one particular instance where I felt I let my brother down badly. I was unable to protect him from getting hurt because I was too self-absorbed in following my own interests to take much notice of the imminent danger Peter was in. There was just the two of us, as young men. He was more gentle and reserved in nature and dialogue, while I could be the opposite the good majority of the time. We were walking together but became separated, as Peter went off to inspect some medicinal plants, while I left him to his own devices and wandered about with my head in the clouds, not bothering to watch where I was going.

I certainly wasn't tuned into what was going on around me either. Although out of sight, I knew he was not far behind, but I didn't worry until I heard his urgent plea for help, the rustling of leaves and the angry growling sounds originating from some, as yet, unidentified animal.

In a blind panic, I rushed through the trees to his aid, not knowing what I would find when I got there. As I approached closer, the animal stopped mauling him. I yelled and it fled in the opposite direction. Peter lay deathly still while collecting his thoughts; his clothing was partially torn and bloodied from this encounter.

I thought he was dead but Peter never entertained any such idea. I cleaned him up as best I could and later, when Peter regained some semblance of strength, I assisted him to return to the community for some extra professional attention to be given to his wounds. Thankfully, there were no deeply penetrating cuts, as he could have lost quite a lot of blood if there had been. Instead, they were mainly surface wounds that would quickly heal. Other than being young and relatively healthy, Peter knew what steps were needed to be taken in order to quicken the healing process and which he had no hesitation in applying.

While cleaning himself up, I chose to stick by him like glue and watched him like a hawk, as I was so fearful that something else bad was going to happen to him. I stayed with him throughout the night. In the process, he sensed my guilt and fear of failure and tried to reassure me that it wasn't necessary for me to feel that way. He wasn't dead, so what was the big deal?

To me though, it was a big deal. He came good again after a few days but from that day on, when we were travelling together, which didn't always happen, I would insist upon walking behind him, so at least his back was protected from possible future attack.

Whatever or whomever next tried to mess with my brother had to get pass me first. I never wanted to feel I failed Peter ever again, by not being there when he was in trouble. He never asked for a sentinel to guard his every move but I had to put my own mind at rest by at least being there, by his side, as much as possible, while still giving him his personal space.

I was often told that I was being foolish to blame myself but I wouldn't listen to these wise words until much later. Then, but only when I was ready, was I able to let go of all the guilt I harboured from this one incident and move on with the rest of my life without looking back over my shoulder with any regrets or sense of failure. This is also what you need to do.

Two seeds lay side by side in the fertile spring soil.

The first seed said "I want to grow! I want to send my roots deep into the soil beneath me, and thrust my sprouts through the earth's crust above me ... I want to unfurl my tender buds like banners to announce the arrival of spring ... I want to feel the warmth of the sun on my face and the glistening of the morning dew on my petals!"

And so she grew.

The second seed said "I am afraid. If I send my roots into the ground below, I don't know what I will encounter in the dark. If I push my way through the hard soil above me I may damage my delicate sprouts ... what if I let my buds open and a snail tries to eat them? And if I were to open my blossoms, a small child may pull me from the ground. No, it is much better for me to wait until it is safe."

And so she waited.

A yard hen scratching around in the early spring ground for food found the waiting seed and promptly ate it.

Moral of the Story

Those of us who refuse to risk and grow get swallowed up by life.

Source: Patty Hansen

Affirmations

The seeds of success relies upon me to HAVE NO FEAR.

I MEASURE SUCCESS in terms of how I feel.

I look to the stars and CLEARLY SEE THE PATHWAY to success unfold before me.

LEBBAEUS

Let no

Evil dwell

Between God,

Beast or Man.

Action, when coupled with an

Enthusiastic belief in the outcome will bring

Unlimited

Success and surprises.

Other than a smattering of religious scholars and theologians, few people in general have known me as being one of the chosen Twelve. I have written no great books, am poorly educated, had a large family to support and because I had two major roles in my life to fulfil, I needed to rely upon others to help when necessary. I found I didn't like being put in that position where I needed to ask for assistance and felt that to ask for help was a weakness but a weakness only within myself. I encouraged other people to ask and accept help for themselves but not for me. I should be man enough to do it all by myself.

Certainly, I would bend over backwards to help another but to receive the same assistance for myself was somehow a bitter pill for me to swallow, which may have had more to do with my manly pride rather than being due to anything else.

By maintaining this tough line attitude, I made my life a lot harder than what it needed to be. I was like an old mule but underneath that stubborn streak beat a heart of gold. If Shontara, being a goldsmith, had his wicked way with me, he would have refashioned my heart and turned it into something more aesthetically pleasing to the eye yet practical. Although a heart in my book is a most practical thing to have on your side because without it, life would be extremely short indeed.

I also had a short temper but most people in my life came to know quickly that my bark was always worse than my bite. With strangers though, I was strangely more tolerant and patient. Perhaps I placed fewer expectations on them than I did on my family members and friends. That's the trouble with knowing someone well. You can always see that they have great potential but are not truly utilising the untapped source of wisdom that lies within. What a waste of good resources but of course, I can't judge. I am sure that when my family and friends looked at me, they too could see what I see in others but which I can't see in myself. I think to see oneself truly, one must maintain some distance.

It's similar to the poor person who can't see the wood for the trees. They are standing too close to the problem where they can't see the solution. If they are able to take a few steps back or rise above the trees, then everything and everyone around them would become so much clearer rather than murky.

Within your mind, look deep into the eyes of Jesus and maintain perfect stillness while doing it. Do not allow your eyes to wander and believe me, this is not an easy thing to do. If you try doing it while looking into the mirror at your own two eyes, you will soon find out what I mean. When a strong connection has been made, you will gradually notice a laser beam of white gold light being created and which emanates from his eyes and piercing your own. Do not attempt to close or move your eyes at this point and throughout this whole process of connection. If you do, you will find the connection will be broken easily and you'll have to start all over again from the beginning.

After a small amount of time has passed, you will begin to feel or sense the heat of his energy being bored into you like a drill. What this is doing is burning through the varying layers and degrees of blindness that keep you in a limited state of awareness that separates you from fully experiencing the reality of the Spirit world. As well as this, it is destroying all manner of blockages and fears created earlier and which have been steadily growing over the centuries and which stand in the way of your success. Maintain eye contact with Jesus for as long as necessary and do this on a regular daily basis. To do so at the end of your day would be most beneficial.

It is during this evening period when you need to let go of a possible build-up of toxins collected throughout the day, such as stress and anxiety. The laser beam of light that pours forth from the eyes of Jesus will absorb and remove all negative debris and will leave your physical and spiritual bodies thoroughly cleansed, which then leaves you free to explore the past, present and future in your dream state. This is where lucid dreaming will become a very real part of your everyday life, where answers to your many questions can be found.

The meditative state of perfect stillness will also become a time for you to receive solutions to any problems you may be going through. Listen with your heart and not your ears. Even though you may not consciously receive what you need during the meditative or dream state, just believe that the answer will be revealed later when you least expect it. And trust that once action has been taken upon what has been received, it will produce a beneficial result for all concerned. By maintaining eye contact with Him in your mind while connected together by the laser beam of pure light, will greatly increase your level of psychic and spiritual awareness; where clear two way communications are reached.

If by chance, someone is attempting to emotionally break your heart or mind in two, use this technique with them as well, while using the same laser beam of white gold light, while connecting with their higher self in the Spirit world. Ask questions. Look below the surface of their anger and discover perhaps for the first time, the real cause of the pain that is making them react to you in a nasty and hurtful way. The insights you receive could be quite enlightening and surprising.

Once you know what you're truly up against, you can then help to destroy their pain by maintaining eye contact with them in your mind, which could be a difficult and uncomfortable thing to do in your physical reality. Another thing you can do is to step into the body of Jesus and begin to look at other people through his eyes. He will allow you to do this in order to learn their truth rather than being caught up in your own little world of woe.

I used to love kicking up my heels and dancing. I didn't care who I danced with because my partner in life wasn't always around to grab and sweep them off their feet. So I would merrily dance with anyone and everyone who would have me – men, women and children. My life was not work alone. If it had been, I and the others surely could not have survived. In order to protect us from burning out as a result of constantly helping and healing others, we each had our own interests that we used as a natural release of tension and tiredness.

Some who have come before me in this book have spoken already of what they found to be relaxing. As you have read before, or at least I hope you did, Shontara worked with gold and even though this was his occupation initially, he loved working with this precious metal even in his spare time. Although the tools were primitive compared to what are being used today, Shontara created many beautiful pieces; where with myself, I needed no such tools when it came to dancing. All I needed was my two left feet, although I suppose you could say they were tools of a sort. Does that mean to say I was a clumsy dancer? Yes, you bet ya but that didn't deter me from doing what I loved.

Of course, I apologised profusely when I unintentionally hurt someone. So you now must ask yourself – do you withdraw from being truly successful because you doubt your abilities? Do you have to be perfect in your field of expertise before doing anything about it publicly? Are you afraid of making mistakes as you learn? Are you afraid of people laughing at you?

Was that a yes to all those questions? Yes, in this case, is the wrong answer, therefore you'll get no brownie points to get you through the pearly gates of Heaven. Sorry, just kidding, that's not entirely true either.

The only way to know if you're good enough at what you have chosen to do is to get out there and strut your stuff, like a peacock if necessary. How else are you ever going to know? You need the feedback and this can be made apparent in many different ways from other people. Without it, we are left floundering in the future and wondering about what could have been. We are not always our own best judge of character. Who has never undermined themselves or been too self-critical? Who has never once said they were stupid?

This is okay if done in moderation only but when it becomes a daily whipping session within your mind, then it becomes a real problem; where you begin to live closely side by side with your unseen but not unfelt companions aptly named doubt, fear and self-loathing. If this is happening to you now, then try and break the habit. Because to continue upon this track keeps you limited and frightened from experiencing all of what life has to give. And like a cracked record, it keeps you stuck in the groove of failure until you or someone else lifts you out of that particular rut and puts you in a place where you are free to blossom.

But even then, if this happens, there are still no guarantees that once your feet have been set free, you will again gravitate towards that overwhelming belief that you are destined to fail and believing this, you have then created your own self-fulfilling prophecy; "Thy will be done, amen". And each time failure happens, two things will eventuate and they are – what little confidence you had left before you began will further be eroded away and secondly, it gives you confirmation of how right you are. That consequently gives you a perfect excuse to later, not do anything. As I am sure you are aware, everyone hates a 'know it all'. How often do these situations happen in your life?

One area that it is most prevalent is in the area of relationships. Outwardly, you hope that this will be Mr or Mrs Right, but inwardly you're waiting around in anticipation for the axe to fall and when it does, you draw comfort from knowing the truth of failure from the beginning. So, who bought this situation to a head – the one who had doubt and fear of course? Who might that have been? Think about it.

Don't forget to reward yourself sometimes for all the good you have done. You know you deserve something nice in return, so why deny yourself this small pleasure? Is it easier for you to accept if someone else did the giving rather than you giving something worthwhile to yourself? What if you were abandoned on a desert island or that you were the only man in the moon? Who are you going to rely upon then to give you what you need or want? The answer should be you.

To give to oneself is considered to be selfish while giving to others is selfless. Maybe this is true to a certain extent but maybe it's not. Besides, is it such a bad thing to be a little bit selfish some of the time? My opinion is we need a balance between giving to and receiving from others and giving to and receiving from ourselves. Without that balance, you would become lopsided and eventually become run down, as well as feeling bitter, resentful and regretful about what you have or haven't done with your life. Rather than going down that self-destructive track, why not stand tall, straight and proud like the majestic and quite awe inspiring giraffe?

Of course, if they had still been alive today, which they are not, I would have said a dinosaur rather than a giraffe because they were so much bigger and never made a habit of hiding themselves behind a tree.

Be fearless like a warrior of God, don't cower in the corner, feeling defeated even before the good fight has begun. Believe in your own inner strength and practical abilities to overcome all obstacles, no matter how big – real or imagined. It might do well to think about the story of David and Goliath. Who do you think won that little battle and why? When you come up with the answer to that, apply the same principle to your life today. Size doesn't count (although many men think it does). What does count is how smart you are in utilising the knowledge that you do have that will be of benefit to yourself and others.

I have seen much bloodshed and horror cross my path. This made me appreciate so much more what I had, rather than stressing out about those material goods I did not possess or suffer from anxiety, depression or panic attacks about people and situations that are out of my control. When you've seen the worst, anything must be better. You react differently and in a calmer manner than if you never saw or felt the carnage and chaos that, in the past, has happened to or around you, to other people. I guess real grief and tragedy can work for you. It all boils down to perspective, regardless of whether you are an observer or participant. Some would say that to be a participant in some unforeseen tragedy makes you a victim.

This negative term does not sit well with my limited vocabulary but I use it here so you may relate to what I am saying better. You can either stay a victim all your life or you fight back; stand up for your legal or moral rights and become a survivor.

Some say Jesus survived the ordeal on the cross and lived for another so many years continuing his ministry. Which camp of belief do you fall into? Did he die or did he live? Is it really important to know the answer to this question? Whichever way you look at it, each separate group of individuals is getting some benefit from their respective beliefs. The same doubt surrounds Elvis Presley. Did he or didn't he die? Why do people wish to believe in someone's death, while others don't and won't accept that it did happen?

Some people live with denial every day of their life. How much evidence and proof is needed before we accept our truth? How many times do you want things confirmed before you can trust your gut feelings, inner knowing or women's intuition, which incidentally, men can also possess?

It's a mighty fine thing that our Angels are forever patient and tolerant with our consistent, repetitive questions. Any normal, sane, rational human being could quite quickly, go round the twist and pull their hair out by the roots in sheer madness, anger and frustration. Mere mortals are fickle beings. They can change their mind and attitude in an instant and sometimes without warning, which could be seen as being for the better or it could be for the worst. Take your pick – eenie, meenie, miney, mo, what or who shall we believe in today, next week or three months?

Our beliefs can change over the years that are shaped accordingly to our past personal experiences but essentially, the instinctive nature that we were born with and the basic foundations upon which we have based our life will essentially stay the same. Can a zebra hand in his stripes for dots? Can a fish breathe without water? Can pigs, or man, fly? And if by chance you believe that any of the above is at all possible and you have no doubt about it, I then would demand proof and even when you do give me the evidence, I will more than likely still doubt what I see; which reminds me of the story of a man who believed that God would come to rescue him in the impending flood.

This man of great and unflappable faith, whose name was Fred prayed for help and believed that God would deliver. Earlier that morning, the SES personnel went around the streets with a loud speaker attached to the car, indicating to people they should evacuate the area. The man said he would be fine, he wasn't going anywhere. In fact, God would save him. The floods rose level to his front door. Fred lived in a double storey house.

This time, a group of men concerned for Fred's safety rowed past him in a boat and implored him to hop on board. Fred stood firm in his convictions and told them he had nothing to fear. God would save him. Soon after, Fred thought it best to grab a ladder and climbed carefully on to the roof, as the flood waters began to rise even further.

The next day, the waters had reached the top of the roof and there this man sat, calmly waiting for the waters to subside any minute now, while eating a Vegemite sandwich. This is when they sent an emergency chopper in. Fred waved all help aside and told them he didn't need their assistance. God would save him.

They reluctantly left Fred to his own resources. During the night, the flood waters continued to rise and early the next day, there was no sign of the man. Three days would pass before they found him; face down in a pile of mud. Poor old Fred was dead. The Coroner's report said – death by drowning.

Soon after Fred's death, his spirit gravitated to the big Pearly Gates in the sky, where St Peter greeted him with open arms. Understandably, Fred was a bit upset that he was dead and demanded to know why God didn't come to save him, his faithful servant who never complained. In the same vein as the Mona Lisa, St Peter smiled with empathy for poor old Fred but tried to explain that God had indeed appeared three times to help him but three times, Fred had rejected God. So remember that, three strikes and you're out. Those people who suffer from blind faith can be a danger to themselves, as in the case of Fred.

Sceptics can also be a real nuisance to deal with but they still serve as a useful tool to weed out the charlatans from the genuine article. Can you discern the difference between what's real and what's not? For that matter, would you be able to recognise an Angel when you see one? Maybe or maybe not! Would you run a mile or stand your ground and say hullo? For that matter, do all Angels have wings?

Mary, the mother of Jesus, loved the little children especially. They needed to be cherished, nurtured and protected properly. And believe it or not, babies are super intelligent, as are young children, and depending upon how they have been raised and in what type of environment, will determine whether they can later cope with the pressures of the rebellious teenage years and supposedly responsible adulthood. Don't ever fool yourself into believing that these babies and children are not smart because they are. They are focused and clear in their direction; they know what appeals to them and normally they will stop at nothing to get what they want – good or bad. Their determination is fierce.

They can see so much clearer than what we can, because life for them is not yet made so complicated by experiencing the whole array of negative emotions, overanalysing, doubt and fear which as adults, we tend to develop and cultivate exceptionally well. Decent doses of affection are essential for a baby and young child's spiritual and personal growth as well. If taught young, they will learn to create a balance between giving and receiving in all areas of their life. Balance, equality and equanimity are the keys to leading a satisfactory, happy, successful, uplifting, meaningful, fulfilling, contented, harmonious and joyful life experience. Have I used enough adjectives yet? Does adjective mean descriptive, I wonder? My English does not rest at a professorial level.

But sorry, I digress. You see, that's what happens when too many words are used which can confuse the issue or get in the way of expressing a truth. Sometimes less is best, although the author has a little trouble coming to terms with this concept. But she doesn't have to worry about that at the moment because a book is being written here and what use is a book with few words? Who would want to buy it?

Perhaps if you bought a book full of blank white pages, you could add your own words of wisdom which would be symbolic of filling your life up with many worthwhile experiences. Oops, I did it again. I got sidetracked but even when that happens in our life, there is always a good reason why it had to happen that way.

If we were never to explore new avenues that branch off the straight and narrow road, we could become too single minded and inflexible to new ideas and new people that may cross our path from time to time.

All change is healthy, even if that change feels terrible, shocking and devastating. From all bad there comes something good. It may take a little while to find it but when you do discover its buried treasure; hold on to it because it is worth the value of pure gold. Or should that be silver? As some people would lead you to believe that every cloud has a silver lining, while the road to the Kingdom of Heaven is paved with gold, which consequently finishes outside the Pearly Gates and that's only the beginning.

As you can see, the Spirit world is filled with much material abundance, as it can be the same in your physical world. It's all about perception, attitude and belief. Is your belief in yourself strong or are you floundering like a fish out of water, gasping for air? Help is a mere breath away. Ask and ye shall receive. Don't forget to be specific though.

Water is precious. So please, don't abuse this precious commodity by polluting it and the same goes for our body. It is a well known and scientific fact that our physical body is largely made up of water (albeit salty) including such third dimensional matter as blood, flesh, muscle, sinew and bone. We release a certain percentage of this same water as a result of going to the toilet, becoming overheated where our sweat glands are activated or the release of water through our tear ducts due to extreme laughter or crying. On a day to day basis, we are not normally aware of how much of this fluid we lose.

As a result of that ignorance, we don't bother too much to replenish the supply by taking in more water.

Many researchers of all types have sought out that fabled ingredient called 'the fountain of youth' but they were looking in all the wrong places. It's not something to be found outside of ourselves. It can easily be procured, stored and utilised within. Much like a camel, really.

Water is all around us from the time of conception. For example, the foetus is protected by the amniotic fluid. When we get sick and are admitted to hospital for surgery or treatment by drugs, they may provide us with a saline drip which is a combination of salt and water. The brain is another vital organ that requires constant watering (like any plant), in order to keep it in tip top prime condition. If your brain dries up, you're dead but before it gets to that critical stage, you will experience much memory loss, lack of concentration, sleepiness and scattered or unclear thoughts.

Your kidneys too need a good supply of water to function properly, as do the liver, bowel and intestines. These four organs work together to eliminate a build up of toxins created throughout the day and night. Lack of water slows this process down where if left unaided, clogs up our system where constipation is the name of the game. This is when you need assistance, in the same way that when our drains become blocked at home we call in a plumber who will flush them out with, you guessed it, water. Our body works in much the same way, as we have an elaborate plumbing system as well.

Our skin needs water in order for it not to shrivel up and dry out. I am continuously astounded by the phenomenal amounts of lotions and potions that mainly Western women of today apply to their face and other parts of their body to ward off the dreaded wrinkles. If you're going to use a cream of one type or another, please find something that is based on water, as water keeps the skin soft, silky, supple and smooth, much like a baby's bare bottom. By the simple act of washing your face in cold water will help the natural cleansing process of the skin greatly. To swish and gargle with warm salty water will kill any nasty bacteria lurking that may cause mouth ulcers or sore throats.

I could go on but I think you now get the picture about how a steady and ever ready supply of water is needed for our continued good health and good fortune. Before I speak of the symbolic aspects of water, there is one thing I must say about the subject of saunas. A sauna certainly helps us release a poisonous concoction of chemicals no longer needed in the body, by sweating them out, but we also lose an excessive amount of body fluid (salty water). In order for a sauna to be truly beneficial, we must take in soon after, at least twice the amount of water that we lost. Some overweight people think that they'll lose excess kilos in a sauna.

Well yes, this is correct but it's only a temporary quick fix measure that doesn't last for long. Saunas should not be recommended as a long term solution to weight loss and there ends this short biology lesson in regards to water. Let's move on to its spiritual nature.

Water is symbolic of Spirit. We are born and live in Spirit, yet many of us are not aware of this or if we are aware, we take this fact for granted or don't really understand its special significance. If you dream of water while sleeping, the type of water you find yourself in or are looking at, will give you an enormously big clue as to how you presently communicate with Spirit or your higher self.

Put briefly, clear water indicates clear communication with both your higher self and the etheric world. Murky or muddy waters signify unclear thoughts. Rough water represents turmoil of the mind and yes, water can also represent our emotions.

Moving away now from dreams, we have holy water which is used to baptise and protect a young baby. Any body of water really, big or small, is all symbolic of Spirit. Baptising Jesus the man in the river by John the Baptist, was highly representative of his pure connection to Spirit.

There are many people who believe and who have been cured by the healing waters that flow at Lourdes in France, as well as many other places scattered throughout the globe. To immerse a cut and bleeding body in the ocean of salty water has great healing potential as well. To stand in the rain can be quite refreshing, rejuvenating and invigorating. So, the next time it rains, don't rush inside to complain. Disregard for the moment what you may be physically or emotionally feeling, which could be cold and annoyed. Look beyond the surface to see the bigger picture and receive a blessing from Heaven.

And as most of you will know, to splash cold water on the face will instantly wake you up. To drink a glass of warm water with a dash of lemon juice from between fifteen minutes to half an hour before breakfast, aids digestion.

It is recommended that anyone who is a healer, psychic or spiritual consultant to take in some amount of water before and after seeing or speaking with a client, as well as before and after meditation. This is a form of protection, as well as the water being used as a link between yourself and Spirit. Aahh, what else can I say about the elixir of life, this fountain of youth? Perhaps the Water Board might commission me to be their representative.

So, as you can see from what little I have said, there is much significance and importance that should be placed upon water. Start protecting and utilising this divinely precious substance better than what you are today and even though the water you may take in will not always be pure, some water is better than none at all.

Fear of Rejection

If you don't like the word 'no' being spoken to you after making a request or demand from another, then you will have problems with rejection. I would suggest then to be particular about the type of career you choose. Anything to do with sales would be exceptionally difficult for you to survive happily in such an environment, where the answer 'no' is a real possibility that happens on a consistently regular basis.

The other area of hardship, especially if you're passionate about what you do – is in the area of writing, whether that be journalism, freelance in particular, writing a book (such as this one), copywriting, advertising and so on. Shontara knows all too well about rejection in this field and more often than not, she takes it like a man and perseveres regardless, while at other times, she will completely lose the plot because she has taken the word 'no' to be a personal attack against her. Now this can happen to the best of us occasionally. The secret is to let go of that feeling of rejection and the quicker you can do this, the better.

If people are continually saying no in your daily life and where you choose to hold on to those negative emotions associated with that word for too long, can create quite a big collection of rejections, that as a consequence, could lead to very real problems and where much damage can be done to your self-esteem, confidence and trust.

You then become a person who sits hunched over and who cannot stand up straight as a result of your spine being broken in several places and has never been healed properly; your spine in this instance, being symbolic of your strength.

Rejection is not such a bad thing to experience now and again. Especially for those people who are getting too big for their boots, who like to throw their weight around, who are pushy and presumptuous to the point where they like to tell people what to do and how to feel.

To pull them into line and to ensure they come back down to Earth, an event will cause them to come crashing back down to reality and this is okay. We all need to be disciplined now and again but because you've had the wind knocked out of your sails and where you can no longer fly so high does not mean it has to remain a permanent thing in your life. Grab on to the invisible cord floating before your very nose and ask to be lifted out of the doldrums you created. Your request will be heard and when we feel you have learnt a valuable lesson, we will then try and soothe your ruffled feathers by sending you people who are warmly receptive to your ideas and who are willing to say yes rather than the already all too familiar word 'no'.

Having someone say this doesn't have to be the end of the world. It can be a beginning where you will learn about acceptance of another person's right to not do as you want. Acceptance and letting go are two mighty big keys that will help you survive a fall from grace or losing face.

Then we have another group of people who cannot possibly bring themselves ever to say the word 'no'. This presents a most painful experience and impossible dilemma for them. And when they are brave enough to state what they need to, they then feel obliged to go into a lengthy explanation as to why they are saying no. Even when the listener is accepting of what has been said, the speaker will soon after try and take it all back or if they don't withdraw what has been spoken, they will feel guilty and can sometimes beat themselves up for being put into a position where they were forced to protect themselves unnecessarily.

They can then stew in their own juices for days or weeks at a time, worrying excessively about what others thought or will think of them and all of its possible ramifications and outcomes by taking a stand.

The listener on the other hand, can sometimes recoil in shock, especially if the person saying no has never said it before. As far as the speaker of the word is concerned, let go of the guilt and allow other people the right to respond accordingly to how they feel but never take the blame or feel overly responsible if the other person doesn't like what they hear.

Then we have another outstanding collection of people who wish to keep everybody happy and one way they can do this is to use the word 'maybe' instead. It sounds less cold and harsh than the word no.

It offers the other person a glimmer of false hope for the future because maybe, just maybe, there is a possibility of the person changing their mind, where the only thing to say is 'yes please'. 'Maybe' is fine under some circumstances if you wish not to step on too many toes all at once but there is a very real danger that can easily be attached to this word.

In particular, for a woman who repeatedly says 'maybe' to a man's unwanted advances or demands in order to soothe the savage beast and to keep them at bay or to keep the peace, rather than being forthright with their feelings and by saying a simple and straight forward 'no'. After a while of being thoroughly frustrated of being fed the same old line, the man may then take matters into his own hands and take what he thinks is rightfully his.

This brings me to another class of people who don't believe what they are hearing; where 'no' really means 'yes' and with 'maybe' meaning the same thing. This can cause confusion at its best and violence at its worst. In some cases and with these types of people, you can't win, no matter what comes out of your mouth and where the only word they will accept is 'yes'.

There are also those people (again mainly women), who feel compelled to say yes to everything where they really want to say no and this is done mainly for two reasons, both of which relate to putting the needs of other people first. The two main reasons are – to keep the peace and where the person has a craving or obsession to be liked, if not loved, by everyone.

But saying 'yes' to all who ask something of you will tear you in two, where your loyalties will become confused, where you could suffer from 'burn out' or mental breakdown and where you become a mere nervous blob of jelly, easily manipulated while allowing another person or people to push and pull you in a mish-mash of different directions at once, all because you were afraid to be rejected. Is it really worth all this hassle? What price should you pay for peace? Is it costing you your life? Why do you really fear rejection? Can you not live with yourself knowing that someone out there doesn't like you?

By accepting these self-imposed fears, you will never feel truly comfortable enough to show people who you really are. Accordingly, you will then wear several layers or more, of masks which can be altered to suit the occasion and person you are with. But this in itself can create a whole new set of unique problems because what are you going to do when you find yourself in a group of people who all expect different things from you? Can you possibly please all of them at the one time? This is not reality and cannot ever be achieved. Our valued suggestion would be for you not to even bother trying.

But if you choose to try, who do you pick to be of service to first? And what about those who come second, third or fourth in line? Are they expected to wait patiently until you turn your attention to them? What if they don't want to wait? The solution is, be aware of how much you can or cannot do for another and accept those situations that you cannot change.

The only time when rejection from another will not bother you, is when you feel 100% secure and confident about who you are; where you can completely trust your abilities to perform well, including a sense of being able to make a real contribution to your family and society as a whole.

But if you are plagued by feelings of insecurity, believe you are no good for anything and have doubt about the majority of decisions you make, this will lead to a feeling of vulnerability, at which time to receive a 'no' answer, will come as a severe blow to the ego. Depending upon your attitude and in which two categories you fall into, this will determine whether you can pick yourself up quickly or not. And here we have another possible problem.

If you rely too much upon friends, family, work colleagues or professionals and as a last straw, you turn to even strangers to pick you up after being rejected, who will pat you on the back and say 'There, there dear, it's going to be alright' whilst offering you large portions of tea and sympathy, you could be headed for a further fall.

What happens in the situation when no-one is available at the time you need them? Do you sit back and wait while wallowing in self-pity, do you overeat to pass the time of day until someone finds your emotionally battered and scarred body cowering in a corner, do you drink to drown your sorrows, do you partake of legal or illegal drugs to numb the mind or as a last resort, do you blow your brains out?

None of these actions serve any real useful purpose, especially not to yourself. The only person who is being harmed by carrying on so stupidly is you. No-one else is adversely affected. How can they be when they are not made aware of your inner agony, because they are not present and who remain unreachable throughout your ordeal? And when caught in this negative state of mind, you could become quite unreasonable by verbally or mentally abusing and accusing those people who you think should have been there for you. But isn't this a tad unfair? Turn that around and ask – 'have I always made myself available to someone asking for my assistance, help and time?'

The answer is more than likely no but if it's okay for you to say 'no', why is it then that when other people say the same thing to you, it all of a sudden becomes radically wrong? Again, what you have here is double standards. And if you choose to take being unreasonable to the next level, you then step into the area of revenge and where you think – 'how dare they reject me. I'll teach them. They're going to pay for that'. They say revenge is sweet to the taste but this is an illusion. Besides which, would you enjoy having someone taking revenge out on you over some little misunderstanding that could have easily been resolved but which was blown out of all proportion? What was that I hear you say – 'no?' I didn't think so. Acceptance of another person's right to say 'no' will banish all feelings of rejection forever.

Personally, I think the hardest time to be rejected is when

you ask the great love of your life to marry you. Once the question is out in the open, it appears that time is put into a state of suspended animation and nothing happens as quickly as you would like. You begin to pray, even if you are not religious and ask God, or any other deity you believe in, to help the person responding to say 'yes' because you know that sometimes the course of true love doesn't always go the way you planned; while at other times, it does. But here now is a multiple choice question. Who do you think is in a position of power – is it:

(A), the person who asked the question;
or is it
(B), the person giving the answer?

If you chose (B), you are correct. Person (A) is normally quaking in his boots, waiting for a positive reply and who believe that if their chosen one says 'no', that his life will abruptly and violently end there and then. Please note that I say 'his' twice because in most cases (but not all), the one asking is the male. It's funny how that should be. And this situation is made far worse if you are the type of person who can't bear to receive a definite no.

It will serve a most crushing blow to your man or womanhood, along with your ego, because there you are, wearing your heart on your sleeve – hoping, praying, wishing, cajoling and begging – the other person to say 'yes'. And if it can't be a 'yes', anything else will do but please never a 'no'. It's too heartbreaking, too final but as the judge would say, the case is closed, court's adjourned, dismissed. In reality, if you have asked the question and received the reply you didn't wish to hear, you can do either one of two things – stand and argue your case for the affirmative or you slink off into the darkness with your head pounding and heavy with shame.

Take heart because things could be a whole lot worse, especially if your proposal was made in front of other witnesses (because you have been so sure of yourself and of the person you wish to marry), where the tables are turned and you end up with egg all over your face and looking like a right old fool. This is most definitely one instance where you don't want to look foolish in front of your loved one, strangers or friends. For some poor souls, they can't move on from this moment and will lack the necessary courage to ever ask the same question again. Yes, you know the one I mean 'will you marry me?' Even if their love, the second time round, is pure and strong, they won't take a chance.

This is sometimes where the tender ministrations of a woman's hands and lips can come in handy and which would be most beneficial for both parties involved. At times like these, the woman then becomes his strength and courage to face the possibility of rejection.

Whether you are male or female reading this, can you relate to this particular scenario and the feelings portrayed? And what of the poor person receiving this proposal of marriage who wishes that it had never happened. In their head, they might be screaming 'no' but because they don't wish to hurt the other person's feelings or if they believe this is the last chance they'll get of someone else popping the big question to them, they will blurt out the word 'yes', even if they don't sincerely mean it.

They might be clinging on to the belief that if today I don't love this person; I might grow to love them tomorrow. This is always possible but as most of us who live in the real world know, tomorrow never comes, as it lies just beyond our reach, so close and yet so far. Alternatively, what happens if the woman is expecting a child? She may further feel obligated to accept or suggest marriage because she wants a man who can provide them with financial security and stability within the family home. Again, this may work but more often it won't or at least not in the long term. There are many more reasons why one will say yes to marriage and some of them will most definitely be wrong. Especially where you are not marrying out of love; but are marrying only out of fear.

Let's take a look at the mail order bride racket as a first example. This is big business. For the organisers, it means making lots of money but the women do it because they think they'll be looked after, they believe that with the extra money they earn, this can then be sent back to their families at home or these women simply fear for their life in the country they were born in.

Again, if these are the only reasons why you are accepting a proposal of marriage, you could quite quickly and easily become disappointed, devastated, depressed and disillusioned. What a sad fact this would be. To sum it up, in regards to love or no love, be happy to receive or give a 'no' answer, no matter how much pain or sorrow is attached to it.

At one time or another in our life, we will all have experienced a sense of rejection. There is no escaping this but we can change our reactions to it when it does occur. Take a look at the number of times when you were a young child, when all the 'grown ups' seemed to do is reply to your requests with 'no' and if you were really lucky, you may upon occasion hear the magical sounds of 'yes' coming your way; that was music to your ears and filled you with a pulsating warm glow that came from within.

But as I am talking about rejection here rather than acceptance, look at what the circumstances were. How old were you when it happened, where did it take place, why did it happen (from their point of view at least), who said the offending word and how did you react to it?

When you have answered the hard questions as to the what, when, where, why, who and how, decide whether or not you still react in the same way when placed in similar situations today, as an adult.

Meanwhile, as a child, there are many reactions you might have had to choose from upon receiving a negative answer from the one who is in a position of authority. For example:

- Did you throw a temper tantrum that involved much screaming and stamping of feet?
- Did you turn the waterworks on, where the tears flowed freely in the hope this would make the other person feel guilty for upsetting you?
- Did you become petulant and withdrawn, choosing not to speak to that person for days?
- Did you stand and argue your point?
- Did you hold grudges?
- Did you withhold your help and assistance from them until they backed down and gave in to your demands?
- Did you spread nasty rumours about this person to your friends, their enemies and anyone else who was willing to listen?
- Did you seek something out that belonged to them and consequently stole or destroyed it, knowing full well this would upset them?
- Did you become rebellious and ignored what you were told; where you did, said or took what you felt was your right?

- Did you plot and scheme up some diabolical plan that would get you what you want?
- Did you end up hating yourself for being such a fool?
- Did you accept gracefully?

There's quite a lot to ponder upon, isn't there? Perhaps you have gone down all of these avenues with a variety of success and failure. Did you take mental notes as to what worked best for you and which ones did not? Those reactions you put on display as a child that were successful- do you as an adult today, still employ these same techniques as a means to achieving your goal? Have you found that if you have a wide variety of tricks up your sleeve, the better the outcome, because you have realised that what works for one may not necessarily work the same way for another?

For example, some people are a pushover for tears, while others will remain quite unaffected by your sadness but will lose all resolve and back right down when confronted by someone screaming and hurling verbal abuse in their face.

How easy is it to give in to the demands of others and how long does this transformation take? If it takes only a short amount of time, this would indicate that you wish so much for people to like you and where you crave for their acceptance and attention, even if you know you are being used and taken advantage of. So what if you lose all credibility and dignity in their eyes. They're happy, so you're happy but are you really and how long can you expect this unreal sense of happiness to last?

Long term, these outward displays of false acceptance can turn quite sour one day, because if you continue saying 'yes' without meaning it, something will eventually have to break.

Will it be your marriage? Will you be bypassed for promotion even after all those long years of saying 'yes' to your boss? You would feel outraged and you would think to yourself – 'can they not see my true worth?' The answer to this is 'yes' and that is why your boss cannot trust you to be honest and would rightfully question where your loyalties lay. They would be concerned about how you would react if someone else came along and who dangled a larger carrot in front of your nose as an extra reward. Will you lose all sense of self-respect and peace of mind? Will the pressure become so much after running around for everybody else, that chronic ill health will attack your body and leave you in all sorts of pain?

How would you truly feel if you experienced all these things at the one time? Devastated and most distressed no doubt. You would become bitter and twisted in your way of thinking and where you would adopt a more cynical approach to life that then leads to no longer having the ability to trust your fellow man or woman.

And even when you reach this darkest point in your life, will you still say 'yes' rather than 'no', all because of your fear of rejection is so great. But what you don't yet realise is that if you continue down that track of keeping everyone happy except yourself; you begin living that rejection full time.

Where this particular fear has become such a large and normal part of your life that you can't or won't see your truth and this then makes it near impossible to divorce yourself from what ails you. Think about it and give it some serious consideration. We do not wish to see you suffer this horrible fate but many people are. You deserve so much more than that. Believe and it will be.

The next time someone says 'no' to you, don't argue, let

them go and move on to the next one. It's their loss, not yours, even though you may not feel this in your heart right now but because you don't feel it, doesn't mean it's not true. Go forward, not back, after receiving a knock-back. Persevere. You can never reach the pinnacle of success if you cave in at the first or second sign of a 'no' coming your way. Because remember, it doesn't always have to be like that. Look at it from a sales point of view instead. As every good sales rep will know, it's a numbers game. The more people you talk to, the bigger the likelihood that eventually you will get a 'yes' response to what you are trying to promote or sell.

Where, if you give in after only the second or third attempt of having the door slammed in your face or having someone hang up the phone abruptly in your ear, you will sink. Rather, choose to swim.

Look closely at those famous men and women in history who have changed the face of a nation. There was not a shrinking violet to be found amongst this esteemed crowd of achievers. They had substance, they had strength, they had courage, they had faith but not always did they have the support. Many a time, they would be shot down, laughed at and ridiculed for a particular belief and thought pattern. But do you think this lack of support deterred them?

Of course not, they had an important purpose to fulfil and they knew it. So they got on with the job, irrespective of whatever obstacles were thrown in their path. They took it all in their stride and steadfastly stepped over the offending block in the form of other people's fear of the unknown and moved on.

For these great achievers, it became a game, where each obstacle they encountered, they saw as a new but not impossible challenge to overcome. Who doesn't like a good old fashioned challenge now and again? It keeps you dancing on your toes. Sometimes, they were given no rest or breathing space between obstacles, as they were hit fast and furious by forces opposing them.

A lesser man or woman would have given up a long time ago but for them, to give up was to admit failure and where they would lose all self-respect and trust. They would have begun to doubt the sincerity of their convictions and consequently, lose the true meaning behind their divine purpose. This would have been a shame if this happened, especially for us but this was not meant to be and so with an army of Angels pushing them forward, they had no choice but to win. 'No' did not compute with their way of thinking and doing.

You may not be destined to change the world in a big way but you can still achieve great feats of excellence and where you can help change the lives of those you personally come in contact with for the better, at the same time as getting what you want and need, out of life as well. And along the way, to lend a supporting hand to those that have lost the way. This cannot come to pass if you fall to pieces each time you hear the word 'no'.

If you feel that it's all so unfair, dissect the questions you are posing to others. Why are people responding in the negative? Perhaps you need to be more subtle in your approach. Plant the thought, dream or objective firmly but gently in someone's mind and water it daily, until it is ripe for the picking. Sometimes, you may not even have to lift a finger to achieve what it is that you want because at the right time and in the right place, the temporary host for this new idea will fall over backwards to become your benefactor, as they become a beneficiary of yours. When success works both ways, you are more inclined to receive a 'yes' answer.

Don't try and hard sell the product or idea, sell them on the dream behind the idea that can come true for them. This way, both can benefit and not just one. It pays sometimes to be subtle in your approach but not to the extent where it passes right over the recipient's head, where they just don't get it at all. If at first you don't succeed, try a different tactic.

You are a winner, not a loser, so go out there and make us proud and show us what you're made of. Although, that is not to say we aren't proud of you already, because we are but so much more can still be accomplished. Remember, losers never win while winners never lose and even when you do receive a 'no' response, this does not automatically make you a loser.

Another thing you can do, before you put any plan into action, is to take time out to visualise the person or people you are proposing to approach; state your message clearly, then listen to them shout a resounding 'yes' loudly in your ear. Believe and it will be. Miracles are first created within the minds and hearts of mankind. Move forward into action with the power of intent and if by chance they say 'no thanks', clear the decks and start again from scratch, although you can never really go back to step one. You will always advance just that little bit further. Don't let a little bit of hot air, rumours and negative gossip stop you from taking the next step. And please, for your own sake, never say, 'it can't be done'.

It's bad enough listening to the gloomy predictions of the doubters but don't become one of them. Because the majority says it can't be done, doesn't necessarily have to ring true for you too. Who would have believed that at the beginning of the last century, man would fly and land on the moon successfully?

They said it couldn't be done but a band of dedicated people set out to prove the majority wrong. So stop taking to heart the sometimes well meaning intentions of your friends, family and workmates when they say 'no, don't do it, you're wasting your time'. Perhaps you are wasting your time but you have been given the freedom to choose for yourself. Don't allow others to dictate to you what must be done.

Listen to their advice with half an open heart and make your own decision based upon what you feel and not upon what they fear. Often those people who strongly oppose what you want to achieve, secretly have the same desire themselves but know they lack the necessary courage and strength to do anything practical about turning their dream into reality. In the meantime, and because they believe it is impossible for them to implement it, they will think – 'why let another beat me to the punch, where they accept all the power and the glory of bringing to fruition my own dream?' Sometimes this kind of attitude can kick start these types of people into action but sometimes not.

Perhaps they feel they lack certain resources, contacts, time or money to be able to do it properly, which makes them give up before they even begin. And if any type of asking for help is involved, coupled with an unhealthy dose that deals with the fear of rejection, will stop this same group of non-movers and couch potatoes. Get involved in life, don't avoid it. Don't make excuses, created in your own mind, to problems before they exist. Because the more thought you give to these imaginary obstacles, the more the energy force you put out there will come back at you a thousand times stronger; where your once imagined problem becomes a living nightmare that's been blown out of all proportion and it's only gotten so large because it's been feeding happily on your fear, on a daily basis.

But even then, you still have the power to reduce it to a more practical size, where you can work with it rather than fighting it. Giving up on yourself will achieve nothing but believing in yourself and in the essential goodness of others will produce miracles beyond your wildest dreams and one final word about that – have the courage and commitment to dream BIG.

Dreaming small keeps you limited. Don't be afraid to broaden your picture and try something new, despite any fears you might have. And if you make all the right moves while advancing upon your goal, you will one day be given the honour to shout 'checkmate', 'bingo', 'eureka', 'jackpot' or 'hallelujah' on top of your lungs because you have finally made it to your chosen destination.

But before you get to that point, you must ask yourself – where do I want to be and what do I want to be doing in one, five or ten years time? When you have a clear answer to these two important questions, your progress will be made a lot easier. I can't guarantee it will all be smooth flying but at the same time, you won't be held back either when you hear that small two letter word that means rejection.

Of course, after reading this particular section of the book, you have had a change of heart and the word 'no', no longer has the power to upset you. It's not the end of the world but a new beginning. Believe and it will be.

The Plum

You should learn that you cannot be loved by all people;
You can be the finest PLUM in the world;
Ripe, Juicy and Succulent and offer yourself to all;
But you must remember there will be people who do not like plums.

You must understand that if you are the world's finest plum;
And someone you like does not like plums;
You have a choice of becoming A BANANA;
But you must be warned that if you choose to become a banana;
You will be a second rate banana;
But you can always be the best plum.

You must realise that if you choose to be a second rate banana;
You must remember that there will be people who do not like bananas;
Furthermore, you can spend your life trying to become the best banana;
(which is impossible if you are a plum) or you can seek again
to be THE BEST PLUM

Source: Anonymous

Affirmations

I reject all of that which is no longer BENEFICIAL to my heart and soul.

I am MY OWN BEST FRIEND.

Rejection from other people no longer bothers me.

JAMES

Son of Alphaeus

Jesus

And the belief in

Miracles

Equals an overabundance of

Success

In the latter days of my life, I became what you know of today as being a Minister of Religion in the Christian faith. I had my flock, as Jesus did when he was alive. This gave me much fulfilment and joy; although I still had to be careful of whom I ministered to. We had our enemies, before and after the death of our Lord and Master. I was living on the edge, never knowing what or who might appear around the next bend and I would think – 'could this be a trap that would end my life or is it someone in genuine need of my assistance?'

Life was a gamble then in regards to religious freedom and some died because of it, which is a terrible thing for me to say but it still is true. Quite often, my level of faith and trust would be badly beaten and tested but each time I survived to become a stronger, more secure person for the experience. These sometimes scary situations made me stronger rather than destroy me.

Are you, bit by little bit, being created or destroyed as a result of the physical and/or emotional pain that is thrust upon your already tired and worn down shoulders? If you begin to feel it's all too much for you to bare, think of the personal load Jesus had to wear and carry around with him, as he was responsible for the welfare of many – not only one – although this was his choice, as it is with your doctors and spiritual healers, including the clergy or anyone else in the business of caring for today's society as a whole.

They too have taken an oath to be of service but as a possible recipient of their abilities, you must remember that when consulting with any type of physician, they are still just one person who can only do so much to help your body, mind or soul. They can take the first few steps with you but after that, you are on your own and this is the way it should be. Never be totally reliant upon one, two or even three others for your physical survival, emotional protection and peace of mind.

Jesus taught us to stand on our own two feet because he knew that one day, he would not walk amongst us anymore and in preparation for that day, he warned us that from time to time we would find ourselves alone, cut off from all support, family and friends. It was suggested, for our own future survival, it was necessary for us to remain independent.

In other words, don't shift your responsibility on to another person's shoulders so they may carry this burden for you, as well as their own. This is not playing fair. Besides, if it came to the crunch, would you be so accommodating? More than likely not, so why expect others to drop everything to help you out of a difficult pickle or jam?

Are you hungry yet? No! Then let's move on then. If the boot was on the other foot, you would then not be too keen to accept on board the many fears and failings of those around you. "Do unto others as you would have them do unto you". This is the Golden Rule.

By putting this principal into practice on a daily basis, you can't go far wrong but do it without expectation or recognition. This way, you won't ever be disappointed in your fellow man because you will have peace that is absorbed into every living cell of your body. You could, if you're smart, tack a little bit on to the end of the Golden Rule which in today's terms would read – 'be kinder, more gentle and loving with yourself in the same amount that you would naturally extend to a friend'. Remember, to look after your own needs is not a sin against God or humanity. It's simply called self-preservation and only the strong and most resourceful will survive but not necessarily the richest.

Don't let the passing of time control you. Instead, you control it by taking charge of what you need to do for yourself and when you need to do it. This is not to say or give you permission to be irresponsible in your life, where you disregard completely the needs and timing of others. Just be respectful.

When you are not working for example and you have no other appointments to keep, leave your watch off your wrist. The watch or clock hasn't been around that long and in those days when timepieces were non-existent, life didn't stop turning. People continued to get on with things as per normal. The Heavens above didn't all of a sudden open up and fall upon their head.

Life went on regardless of whether you understood the passing of time or not. Enjoy not knowing for a while. One thing that will happen, amongst others, is it will force you to live in the present; you will begin to listen and trust what your body is saying. You will know, because your body will tell you in no uncertain terms, when it's time to eat or when it's time for you to lay your head down and get some sleep. Too many people ignore what their body is saying to them. They brush away the signs, both subtle and blunt, often to the detriment of their body, as well as their mind, if not immediately then shortly after.

It isn't until things get pretty bad (and each individual's perception of this will be different) that we make appropriate changes to our lifestyle. I sometimes wonder why it takes so much before people are willing to at least listen, even if not yet ready or willing to take action.

To listen is certainly a dying art form. There is also selective listening or hearing, where your ego or personality chooses what to listen to or not. So many valuable insights are passing us by without our knowledge. This is why it is so important to be still. Don't be afraid to stand in the one spot. This way, things can come to you and you will be aware of them all.

But if you keep rushing about from one person to another while talking all the time, the information wanting to seep through can't keep up with the mind and some, if not all, of the brilliant ideas and insights will get left behind; which in the long term is exactly what will happen. You too will get left behind – like the old spinster left on the shelf. Sorry ladies, I know that hurt. I could feel you cringing inwardly at that last picture I gave to you but it was necessary.

You may think how I, being a mere male, can speak of such delicate matters. I can because I have been a woman many lifetimes, so I know something of what I'm talking about. Besides, in the upper levels of the Spirit realm, there is no 'him' or 'her'. While there, it's no longer important to acknowledge the differences between the two sexes. Highly evolved spiritual beings are no longer trapped by the existence of their physical bodies, mind or time. We have complete freedom to explore both the male and female aspects of ourselves in relative peace; where these two different sides to our nature are no longer separate from each other.

In this Spirit reality, we have been able to blend the two together to make a perfect and complete whole. This then creates perfect harmony and balance, where our aura glows and believe it or not, you can find this blessed state of being on Earth, if you care to look and the place to look is within your heart. And when you are taking a peek at your other half, go deeper still, way beyond the obvious differences that annoy you. Take time out to be still and be brave of heart while peeling back the outer layers that blind you to your true outer glow and inner beauty.

The brain is an incredibly sharp and powerful tool if used correctly but in the large majority of cases, our brains are under-utilised; where they have become sluggish and weak. To wake them up fully can be incomprehensible to some. The brain is a most fascinating place to explore, especially if you know where to start.

So let us start with our imagination. Without imagination, progress would never have existed. Can you imagine what a deathly dull and colourless place planet Earth would be if ancient man chose never to develop their intuition or imagination? "What the mind of man can perceive, we can achieve".

These are certainly not my words, as I am sure you have heard and read of them before, but their meaning and sentiment still remains true. All miracles initially exist from our desire to see something out of the ordinary happen. Then there is intent. Our goals or wishes must have some purpose, otherwise why would you wish it into being in the first place? It would then become a waste, enjoyed for one brief moment in time and then forgotten the next.

What's your attitude about miracles? Do you think – 'well that was interesting. Now let's move on to the next thing' and because of your expectations, the next thing must always be better than the last. But what if it's not? Do you dismiss altogether, the miracle that then comes after the last one, because it lacks impact?

Do you sometimes do the same thing when you receive golden glimpses and flashes of insights, where momentarily you become inspired to follow your truth and heart but then you quickly get sidetracked into thinking and doing other things that you consider to be more important but are not really? You need to take a look at the belief you have in yourself. Do you feel powerless and not able to create what you wish for? If you believe you can't do this for yourself, then what do you do about it? Do you kiss your dream goodbye or do you give this job to someone you feel is more capable of bringing this miracle into reality?

This may work but that other person will never feel as enthusiastic about the dream as you do, mainly because it is not theirs to begin with. Stay in control and take charge of creating your own miracles. If you give someone else the power to create what you desire, the outcome may not entirely eventuate exactly according to your plan. This is because you have all the specifics or blueprint of what you want to see happen but they don't. And when things don't go as perfectly as you would have wished, don't then turn around and blame the person you sought out for help in the beginning. It's not their fault. In short, my message is this – trust your own abilities, have faith and take action upon the insights received.

By shutting the gate, what are you keeping out? By opening the gate and walking through, what are you moving towards? The answer will depend upon the experiences of each individual.

Symbolically for many, it would signify not receiving, or receiving, all manner of things. For example, when you shut the door to your heart or the window to your soul, you have made a conscious decision to isolate yourself from accepting all that is good, yet everything that is good is not necessarily pain free either and there lies the crunch. It hurts to feel pain and disappointment and many of us will go out of our way to avoid it, even if it means not learning a valuable lesson about life.

As much as I would like to protect you or where you wish to protect yourself, there are some instances where to learn anything worthwhile at all, it needs to have some impact. If these life lessons are too subtle, too 'airy fairy' or lack the desired amount of 'punch', you will not remember. It will easily bypass the memory cells and float through one ear and out the other side. How can you capture the feeling or its message if it flitters across your mind for a mere nanosecond (that is smaller than a second by the way) and disappears the next, like the illusive butterfly?

You might acknowledge there was something important you just learnt or had to remember about that person or situation but because the pain didn't stick around long enough, like a bowl full of thick and gluggy porridge, there is no real feeling attached to that particular lesson. The heart is quicker to learn and accept, while the mind takes a little longer. Besides, we can train our mind to forget the pain but we have no such ability over our heart. You may think you have but there's no fooling it. The only way to stay safe and feel secure, albeit falsely, is to build a massive big wall around us that even the owner of this same heart cannot ever hope to penetrate.

I say falsely because the wall is not impenetrable. Those painful emotions do filter through, little by little, slowly but surely until one day, there is no more room to accept any more, so the heart ultimately gets squeezed out and squashed. This is when the heart has a desire stronger than your own to break free and this is, quite literally, what it tries to do and anyone (and in this case, we are talking about you) who is dumb enough to stand in its way, gets all trampled on in the process.

The score then becomes – heart one, person none. But this should never need to happen, especially if you're smart.

The solution is not to erect a fortress around your heart. You would be actually doing it a favour by leaving it to do its work naturally. It doesn't need your assistance. Let the heart deal with the pain when it arises and don't underestimate your abilities to deal with a crisis. The heart, like the mind, is a powerful piece of equipment. If you don't struggle, it then has the ability to release and dispose of the pain naturally, rather than unnaturally, which happens when we tend to interfere and demand our own way. So, give your heart a better chance of life today and remember that in moments of great stress, breathe deeply. It helps, believe me.

Both the brain and heart need a good steady supply of oxygen to survive, so give these two vital organs what they need. They will thank you for it and you, in the end, will also thank your heart and mind for getting you through a difficult transition. Don't suppress, fight and ignore any painful facts of life. It's an essential part of living, as is experiencing all the good that comes along with it.

When you are carrying out God's work, this is when the action really starts hotting up. And this can unexpectedly happen at the oddest moments throughout the day or night, so be prepared to make a move or change your level of acceptance and awareness to carry out what is required at that time. God's work doesn't only mean preaching to the non-believers and already converted faithfuls, or healing those people who are sick in heart, mind, body or soul.

It could simply mean cooking a meal for someone who doesn't have the means, ability or income to do this for themselves. It could be doing the shopping for a friend who is unwell or immobilised. You might also wish to assist an elderly lady cross a busy city street. It could be anonymously paying for a complete stranger's lunch or dinner in a restaurant without their knowledge and where there is no chance of them thanking you for your good deed. It could be helping out a person who has no savvy about business or financial matters, where they need some smart, down to earth and practical accounting advice for free.

In short, what I'm trying to say is that God's work can take on many shapes and guises. Choose those deeds that suit you best and do them well. All these extra bonuses and blessings you bestow upon your fellow brethren, will return to you one thousand fold. And when they start coming back to you, thick and fast, be smart and don't reject them. Why should everyone else be happy and successful? Don't be a martyr by leaving yourself out of the picture.

We want you to receive as well as give, and the returned blessings will come in many shapes and sizes. For example, it could come in the form of money; material objects both large and small, people, good health, new situations and opportunities. Grab it all, make good use of it while you can but never take it for granted and always give thanks. Balance, that's the name of the game. Harmony, that's your objective.

Angry people fear love. Lack of love provides them with a perfect excuse to stay angry. If you can love an angry man, woman or child today, then they will always thank you tomorrow. And rest assured they will be drawn to come back for more. Love transforms anger extremely well. If you try to make a stand against anger with even more anger, this negative energy force splits and multiplies, as a fertilised egg does in the woman's womb. The anger takes on a power all of its own.

It then expands like a giant balloon suffocating those people who get caught up in it.

Once caught, there is no escaping from this balloon of madness that is headed straight for Hell, until someone decides to prick it with a pin. The anger is then allowed to go free and away from its original creator. And the further away it gets, the less power it has over anyone. It becomes weak in its velocity. Like a cyclone, it eventually blows itself out. Or to put it a different way, it runs out of puff, like an old steam-engine, which is an apt description of myself sometimes. If you don't give the body its daily requirement of nourishment, and I'm not only talking about food here, your energy levels are going to become pretty low.

Good nutrition to the human body is worth the same as coke is to the steam train. If you don't give enough of what it needs, it slows right down, begins to miss deadlines, doesn't care, lacks direction and when all the reserves dry up, it finally stops and stagnates where it stands. No amount of cajoling, pleading and begging could get it started again but with heaps of TLC (tender loving care) applied to this lost cause or angry adult or child, there is hope. Hope and love is really all you need, to keep your engine running smoothly and your heart pumping strongly.

In what little spare time I had, I would enjoy focusing upon the antics and behavioural patterns of animals. Anything that had four legs or wings would do. It is truly amazing how much you can absorb and understand when you are switched on to seeing the truth that lies ahead of you. The thing is to watch and observe with a feeling of detachment, coupled with a desire not to interfere with the laws of nature. When you get too close to somewhere you are not wanted, you lay yourself open to possible attack or withdrawal. Depending upon your mindset at the time, you will prefer one over the other.

To sit and observe, to wonder and question as to why this is happening to you or around you can be quite a fascinating journey into one-self that includes an awareness of the one you are trying to figure out. In order to comprehend another person's intentions, you must first fully understand and accept their motivations and reasoning first.

In the animal kingdom, firm boundaries and unwritten laws are laid down between family members and those groups that are of a different makeup and nature to themselves. Looking on, as an outsider, we may think it all seems a little harsh, cruel and unfair. But this is the law of the jungle and it needs to be adhered to and not interfered with.

I'm not saying that everything should always stay the same. There would be no progress otherwise and besides, change above and below the surface takes place naturally, even when we do nothing about it. But the species of beings that make up the animal, human, alien and spiritual kingdoms need to live separately and alongside each other in harmony. This is respect. Know when not to cross the line when dealing with family, friends, strangers or foes. They may each need a different approach.

Don't ruffle their feathers or rattle their cage, just to annoy them, on purpose. Besides, can you really trust the smile of a crocodile? That is why I suggest that in order to learn what is needed in your own life, the domestic and wild animals can teach us a thing or two or three about boundaries, respect, communication and acceptance. So take action, adopt an animal mate or mates today.

Depending upon your living environment, this could mean

watching, listening and learning from your pet dog, fish, cat, bird, turtle, rabbit, chook, ant, rat or snake. Or if you live on the beach, seek counsel from your ever so friendly neighbourhood dolphin, whale, crab or jellyfish too.

Start asking the animals direct questions about themselves and listen to what is received within your mind. This way, you can possibly help them get what they need and sometimes all that they need is a friendly ear that they can talk to, just like humans need the same thing.

You may think you can't talk to the animals like Dr Doolittle or St Francis of Assisi but you can. Have you ever tried? Have you never said to family or friend how your dog or cat knows exactly how you are feeling the minute you walk through that door and will react accordingly to your feelings?

Animals may not be able to communicate by using words but they show us by their actions alone and some actions can be made more obvious than others. If we allow ourselves to relax and be in tune with the wildlife that we live with and sometimes take for granted each and every day, we will grow in understanding and respect their needs, as they too will then go out of their way to help protect us.

For only one day a month, see if you can communicate your wants and needs to other people without the use of words – verbal or written. Pretend you've lost your voice and see how effective you are. You may not have raging success the first time you try but persevere.

You can choose to speak till your blue in the face but does it really make an impact, especially when communicating with those who are spiritually death, dumb and blind? Our actions are what matters and they are a true reflection, most times, of what we think and feel inside. What do your actions reveal about you? Are you being a hindrance or a help to society? Hopefully, it would be the latter, keeping in mind there is a fine line that separates the two and it is so easy to fall into the hindrance trap without realising you are in it. It can be that subtle sometimes. It could be that one man's help is another man's hindrance. It's all a matter of perception and how you wish to use the information given to you.

Fear of Death

For the Western Christian world in particular, as opposed to the Eastern or Mid Eastern countries that practice other religions such as Buddhism, Hinduism, Shintoism and Moslem just to name a few, the word 'death' can quite literally scare people to death. Sorry, I couldn't resist.

Some choose to ignore it altogether and hope it will go away. People certainly accept the reality that one day they will die but until then, let's not think about it. Because, if you become too preoccupied with your own death or people dying in general, you could somehow attract this to your doorstep by unknowingly inviting it into your environment and once it has its deadly toehold in the door, like an unwelcome visitor or a bad smell, it can be mighty hard to get rid of.

Death is seen as being our number one enemy rather than being a welcome friend. So much mystery and myth surrounds this one subject, that it is extremely difficult to sort out the facts from all the fiction and believe me when I say there is much more fiction than fact.

Some worry about the process of dying, while others focus upon what happens to their physical body once pronounced dead. If you fall into these two categories, I implore you to visit your family doctor or friendly funeral director to have the grim facts of life explained to you in a practical, down to earth, uncomplicated and matter of fact way. This particular truth will then set you free.

Explore the basis of your fear and once you can understand it, acceptance will come easier. Some who don't believe in reincarnation have difficulty in accepting that their life is over and it's time to say goodbye. Many, but not all, are often filled with much anger, regret or guilt about their past. And in the case of those people still in love with themselves and other people, it is then so much harder to walk or drift away from a life well lived. And lastly, we have another group of individuals who have no doubt about the existence of a Spirit world but who believe wholeheartedly they are not good enough in God's eyes to be given this opportunity of everlasting life.

Some may admit their fear openly while others will strongly deny (if asked) that they see themselves as not being worthy of receiving God's most precious gift to mankind. And when I speak of 'God', this being or energy force encompasses all deities of all religious and spiritual groups. God is not confined to only the Christian faith. It would be too limiting to do otherwise. God is eternal, omniscient and omnipresent. There are no boundaries.

It is those souls with physical bodies who have an extremely narrow focus and limited view about the role of religion but now let's go back to this specific group of people who don't feel they are worthy of receiving eternal life. In their daily life, they worry about not being good enough for their partner, their boss, their children, their parents, their teachers and ad infinitum which would indicate a fear of rejection. But you are a part of God's energy force and as such, there is no real reason why you should fear 'his' or 'her' rejection. How could God ever reject their flesh and blood, so to speak? And because you are one, you may then say in all sincerity that 'I am God, therefore I am'.

Let's move on to another group who are generally known as atheists, who don't believe in a God of any sort. As a result of this and to a certain extent, they are rejecting their own existence. Of course, they intellectually know and accept in their head they are alive but don't fully feel it in their heart; sadly and in this situation, they are living a life half lived. They can either then become cynical, bitter and angry or they will emerge as being a positive pragmatist. So what's a pragmatist?

For those of you who don't know, a pragmatist is someone who strongly believes in the doctrine of dogma, is very matter of fact and treats history with reference to their practical lessons only. Everything is black or white in their world. Grey doesn't exist. They believe that you are either completely right or completely wrong. Of course, it is not only pragmatists who hold on to this belief but how they are different from the majority is they have no fear of death, because it is a fact of life and as such, it's not important in the overall big scheme of things to them. It is merely one more thing to deal with and once dealt with, let's move on.

Looking at death from this perspective, really does work in their favour. Understand, no one individual or group are all bad. Good points can always be found if you scratch below the surface. As I said before, death can be a welcome friend. The more you struggle, the harder it will be, but if you let go and surrender your body to the light willingly, this final transition will flow smoothly. In fact, it will be so smooth that when you do 'cross over', you will wonder what all the fuss and fear was about.

In the case of death, a fearful mind will create an abundance of pain, where a fearless heart will help you to remain calm. When you can apply a fearless heart to your everyday problems, when the time comes to let go, it won't be such a big shock to the system. It will be another little hurdle for you to jump over and which will be an easy one at that. 'By the inch it's a cinch, by the yard it is hard'. So, what's it to be, difficult or easy?

So how do you say goodbye to leaving your physical life and loved ones behind? Here is a possible solution. It's not the only way to do it and you can either take it or leave it. The choice is yours. What I am about to describe may not happen as slowly and in exactly the same way as in your future reality but I can guarantee that if you attempt to do the following properly, it won't be easy. You may have to stop half way through and this is okay. You can pick up the thread later.

Also understand that you can't do this visualisation correctly while you are just reading it. Certainly, specific emotions will be triggered while reading this passage of the book but it won't be the same as if you gave yourself some quiet time to truly feel, as you will need this space in which to allow all emotions, positive or negative, to override your thoughts, to absorb and digest all of what you are experiencing. As you read the words, it remains on an intellectual level only. This is okay while receiving instruction but while it's a head trip alone, you can't expect to truly say goodbye.

Be brave of heart, dear one, and it will assist you well in the future, when you are ready to take that final bow to a rousing applause, as the curtain falls upon your life one last time. Death is a process of transition and transformation, which you have already gone through many lifetimes before. Believe me when I say that this energy technique will not kill you. It may be physically and emotionally painful but it won't be life threatening.

The worst that could happen is you will experience a mild case of indigestion, nausea, diarrhoea, chest pain and/or asthma but don't worry, forget about the doctor. All these symptoms are a result of a blocked solar plexus and heart chakra. When you look further into the spiritual meaning of the why, you will see that the solar plexus chakra is related to your identity – that is, who you believe you are, where you fit in the world and whether you like or loathe yourself and others the big majority of the time. While the heart chakra, is the storehouse of positive and negative emotions.

If you want to receive more information about the role of all the chakras, log onto the author's own website at **www.shontara.org**. This is where Shontara has chosen freely to reveal her own heart to the world.

But for the moment, it's now back to looking at these emotions of ours. It is certainly okay to hold on to any positive feelings but the negative ones need to be safely released and this will naturally cause some discomfort within the body. Now that you know this, you have no reason to become alarmed if any of the above happens while going through this 'letting go' technique. It is merely showing you how attached you still are to your physical body and that the energy attached to your fear of death is being worked through on a deep level of your psyche. If by good fortune you experience no physical or emotional pain whatsoever while carrying out this technique, this would be a good indication that you have already said your goodbyes to all earthly concerns and how death is not all that big a deal to you. For the benefit of others, I should mention that this fact does not mean that you are suicidal either.

What it does mean is, that you have adopted a more philosophical approach to both life and death and this is a healthy way to be. If you can do this visualisation more than once, you will find that each time you do it, the pain will become less and less. When a feeling of peace and great inner calm shrouds your very being throughout the entire exercise, you will then know it is time to stop. You have succeeded in beating the fear of death at its own game. Congratulations and great celebration would then be in order. Let us now begin, step by simple step and just so you will know in advance, there are nine steps in all:

Step 1 – *Take yourself off to your ideal dream destination. This place, if you had a choice, is where you would like to breathe your last breath. It could be a tropical island paradise, a snow capped mountain, a tumultuous ocean, a desolate desert, a country cottage in the woods or simply in your own bed at home.*

Step 2 – *Once you can see this ideal place in detail, dress yourself in the clothes that you wish for other people to remember you in. What you choose to wear will be an indication of how you see yourself. So let your hair down, be creative. There are no limits here. If you want to look like a medieval princess, a pharaoh, a country and western singer, Indian chief or bride, then let it be. If you wish to dress in what you would normally wear in your day to day life now, this is okay too. Anything goes. No judgements are made.*

Step 3 – *Now make yourself truly comfortable. Are you in a sitting or lying position? Either way, it doesn't matter. Once you feel at ease with yourself, please continue by experiencing each of your main body parts shutting down. I shall take you through it, one by one but don't forget, in order to truly experience what you need to, take your time. Don't rush it.*

Let's begin with the reproductive system. See in your

mind these organs contracting and shrinking in size. The egg or sperm now withers and dies. There is no possibility of life here anymore.

Imagine next if you will, the walls of the intestinal tract collapsing in on itself, stopping any residual waste product from passing through the body. While this is happening, the liver, gall bladder, spleen, pancreas, kidneys and adrenal glands all stop functioning. Digestion is no longer a matter for your concern.

Change your direction now by focusing upon your hands and feet. They feel cold but you have no way of warming them because you can't move and you can't move because your muscles have turned to slush that has weakened them to such an extent that has taken away all of your strength. As a result of this, your whole body is now feeling quite icy, from the tips of your toes to the top of your head. This feeling turns you quite numb and your sense of touch no longer remains but you are still aware.

Now move to your face. The saliva in your mouth dries up and you lose your sense of taste. As well as this, you cannot speak, scream, laugh or cry. You are mute.

Your sinuses and nose then becomes blocked which causes you to say goodbye to the sense of smell.

We now travel on upwards to the eyes. They are open but to you, they might as well have been closed. A heavy black veil has been dropped that seems impenetrable and which has blinded you to all those things and people you once took for granted. Don't panic. It's not the end of the world just yet.

Let's move sideways and say hullo to your ears but notice you can no longer hear. When did that disappear, you ask yourself?

All in all and at this point in time, you can sense no evil, do no evil, speak no evil, see no evil and hear no evil. But don't fret. All is not lost. You still have your sixth sense and at this stage, it largely takes over from where the others have left off. This extra gift or sense can never be destroyed. Upon physical death (or before for some), this ability is greatly heightened.

You have now discovered, possibly with great surprise, that you can still think with your brain and feel with your heart. What more can one ask for at this stage of the dying process? With your mind now, become aware that the cerebral fluid flowing up and down your spine including the fluid that protects the brain no longer moves. This means eventual stagnation and evaporation. Your brain cannot survive under these harsh, dry conditions for very long.

Your nerve endings have become frayed and fragile and can no longer send messages to the brain.

Lastly, we must visit the heart. Upon your arrival here, it forgets to continue beating and pumping the life force through your body. Your heart has finally given up the ghost and takes a well earned holiday, till the next time it begins a new journey within a different body on another time line.

Step 4 – *Spend a moment here and truly experience what it is like to have died. Are you still scared, nervous and angry or do you feel quite the opposite – liberated, pain free and calm? Once you can acknowledge at this point what you are feeling, ask yourself, why am I scared or why am I happy? One thing that should be perfectly clear by now is that you still have thoughts and feelings, in the same way that you did before your body died. Otherwise, you couldn't stop* *to ask yourself the above question or to receive an answer. This aspect of the process is real. You don't need ears, eyes, a brain, hands or nose to hear, see, think, touch or smell. Nothing changes except your perception and awareness.*

Step 5 *– We wish for your spirit or soul to then step outside your body and look at it from a detached point of view. As your eyes travel towards the feet, you notice a movement to the side of you that attracts your immediate attention. Who has joined you? You turn quickly to look in that direction. A friend is waiting to warmly welcome you to their world. As you acknowledge their existence, you may or may not recognise this person. Either way, it doesn't matter. Accept they are here to help you and may appear in human, angelic or alien form. Or alternatively, they may simply be seen as a pulsating ball of coloured light energy. Go to them now and allow yourself the luxury of being embraced by this special Spirit being, who is similar to you.*

Step 6 *– At this stage of the game, you notice the silver cord still exists by a mere thread. Your heart may have stopped beating but it hasn't yet released your soul cleanly. There are certain things that still need to be done. The process of letting go is not yet complete.*

That Spirit being you have just been introduced to, ask them if they will help you to destroy all remaining ties that you still have in regards to your earthly body and other mundane concerns. With great respect, they hand you a match. You know what needs to be done.

Once lit, you set the cord ablaze. Within seconds of it

erupting into flames, it disintegrates and vanishes into thin air. It no longer exists but you still do, as a free Spirit. As the flames die out, your body then begins to disintegrate even further by decomposing rapidly before your very eyes, with the bones and flesh turning into ashes and dust. Watch this part of the process carefully, while taking note of how you feel.

Step 7 – *Once you have come to a self-realisation of where you are now at, you rapidly move on to a new location and time, three days after your death. You are watching your funeral ceremony with great interest. Your choice of being cremated or buried is entirely up to you. For now, this is where you will once again see all the loved ones you left behind, your friends, your family and your work colleagues, including your enemies. They are all there, some crying and some laughing. As well as those surviving pets you had to leave behind.*

As you have become pure Spirit, you now have the ability to step into the energy and thought pattern of each person there and this is what we wish for you to do now. Absorb their pain or joy and learn to forgive those who are happy about your demise. Make sure you don't miss anyone, young or old, sick or healthy, rich or poor, even those you dislike, as you have something to learn from them too.

But before moving on to each new person, you need to see clearly the umbilical cord that links you together. Once you can accept all of what they think and feel, grab hold of a pair of scissors, a knife or a sword and cut the ties that bind you together. You both need to move on. Set yourselves free. This part of the process may take a particularly long time for you to complete because of the number of people you will see but persevere.

Step 8 – Once all of the above has been done, a separate group arrive to pay their last respects. This is where all the other pets you've loved before come once again to life, on this special occasion. After all, this is your graduation, which is cause for great celebration. Those pets that have crossed over before you can stay and become your travelling companions.

Call each of them by name and they will stand behind you, if they so wish. Those who still exist on the earthly plane must stay where they are, along with all those people you have disassociated yourself from. You cannot take anyone under your wing at this stage but you can promise to be there waiting when their time comes to cross over into the realm of Spirit.

Step 9 – Once all your goodbyes have been made, you will see before you a closed wooden door that suddenly opens through which a shower of bright sunlight shines. Your job now is to cross over its threshold. To accompany you the rest of the way is an army of Angels.

If this procedure has been done correctly, you should be feeling quite confident and secure at this point. Never look back, always go forward.

The transition period between death and life has now begun. Be at peace within this space because it is here that will determine where you end up. Will you stand proudly in the light or will you be thrown into a dark abyss? This technique is now complete.

Learn to say goodbye now rather than later to all those material possessions and people you have acquired or those that you still crave for and desire this lifetime. This doesn't mean you have to give up everything and walk away to live like a hermit. By all accounts and purposes, stay and enjoy the fruits of your hard labour with the understanding that you can't take any of it, or them, with you.

You must also realise that if you and your loved one suffers the same fate where you die together at the exact same place and time, there are no guarantees that you will remain together in the Spirit world. This is something you have no control over, no matter how much you wish it to be.

If you should choose to kill another and yourself in order to be together forever, it will more than likely backfire on the one who committed murder. What you want so obsessively, you won't get. And so it is with everything in life, as well as in death. What happens on Earth today is a mere reflection of what you can expect in the Heaven of your future. There needs to be a constant maintenance of balance that brings about harmony, which in turn can create all sorts of miracles. Obsession to possess will turn your dreams into an endless stream of living nightmares from which you can never wake up. If you think you are having a tough time now here in the physical world, you certainly won't be looking forward to what awaits you on the other side.

Perhaps part of your fear of death relates to you innately knowing this fact which would then compel you to avoid at all costs what could be far worse than what you are experiencing now. Certainly, death can set you free but your belief and attitude about yourself and other people, as well as your philosophy on life and death in general will determine the outcome of your future in the Spirit realm. This is also why that while you are still alive, you practise not taking everything for granted if you want to be assured of some success. So let's take a look at that more in detail.

If you were a single person trapped in a house fire, you only had three minutes in which to get out and where you were surrounded by all of your most treasured possessions, what would you take as you flee for your life? What could you not possibly live without? What would you try and save? Could it be your favourite CD collection, a rare antique piece of jewellery worth thousands of dollars, this book, a happy family photo, cash, clothes, car keys or mobile phone? Or would you let it all go without a backward glance and gladly walk out the door with only your life? How devastated would you feel if you had to live without all the modern comforts, that is, your home sweet home? Could you start again from scratch and be happy about it? Or would you stay angry and seek retribution, revenge and compensation for your loss, even if it was due to your own stupidity, vowing never to quit until you have got what you wanted, back again?

In reality, to try and re-establish that connection to your past in its exactness can never be recreated or re-enacted again. Once destroyed, that's final. Like the physical body but your soul still lives on. That is eternal, regardless of what religion you follow. The soul, that is the true essence of ourselves, is Universal. In the final analysis, we are all the same, in life and in death. Death is a man made illusion that keeps us a prisoner who can never truly experience life to its fullest potential. Fear limits us. If you seek true freedom, then change your state of mind and fully open your heart today. Your fear of death will consequently dissolve.

As far as God is concerned, we are all his equals, so in order to bring about world peace, we must treat others as God treats us with no discrimination, no judgements and no class barriers. This won't be easy but if you and everyone else, remains resolute in following this path, then the darkness will have no choice but to be absorbed by the forever expanding light.

Everything in nature dies, so why not you as well? Do you not consider yourself as being part of nature? Sometimes, one flower or tree will die in order to make way for another more robust or more beautiful version of themselves. What is old must eventually become new again. Some ask what they have to do in order to be reborn.

The answer to this is nothing. It will automatically come to pass without you having to try and orchestrate or control a possible outcome. To be reborn has nothing to do with your belief or disbelief in God. Even sceptics, heathens, atheists and heretics are all given the same privileges as everybody else. And so it is in life and death.

No one individual or group is better than another. That is why there is such a great divide between generations, science, religion and music. This has come about because that individual or group has placed themselves above the rest. This would mean that they are living a lie or a less harsh word would be 'illusion'. Death is the only true equaliser at the moment. Although standing completely naked in front of God and others, comes a close second.

For example, when you place a group of naked people together in a natural setting and who have come from all different socio-economic, religious backgrounds and nationalities and instruct them to get along with each other as one cohesive community, at a glance, equality is achieved.

You can't tell anything about them because we are given no concrete clues to their personality. Our clothes, our homes and work environment all give us away to a large degree of letting people know where we fit in society. We largely base our judgements of others on how they look and where we demand to see what sort of a house or hut they live in and the type of car or boat that they drive. Being naked then forces us to express what we feel from the heart. We have nothing to hide behind, except perhaps our glasses if we wear them. Certainly, as a result of this, we can become overly exposed and vulnerable to attack.

But let's face it, if everyone else is in the same position as you, we can then make positive adjustments to be more accommodating because you have truly realised by being exposed to this unreal situation and perhaps for the first time, you sense they are no different from you; as were the Apostles, Jesus, Buddha and any other great religious or spiritual leaders who have been placed upon this Earth at various times in history to give humans a bit of a kick along in the evolution of mankind. Their specific purpose whilst here in human form was to bring about change and a shift of consciousness. They achieved this remarkably well and so it will continue, long after you die.

God can give with one hand and take it away with the other. God is both the Creator and Destroyer and this is happening all around us, on every level of society, although we may not always recognise that this is happening. Quite often, we view them as separate events that don't relate to each other but they do. Like life and death. We think they are separate when they really are the same. We all have dual natures or personalities;

although some mentally unbalanced and disturbed people will possess more than two faces at the one time. This is just one of the reasons why they become so disorientated and confused, as do those people who come in contact with them.

Within life, there is always the presence of death and where there is death, you can always discover the creation of new life. When this principle is drawn on paper, it will then take on the form of the yin and yang symbol that represents duality and togetherness, rather than singularity and separateness.

I was in the desert when I first had the taste of death in my mouth. I was in my early twenties and was originally travelling with a medium sized band of relative strangers but at one point, I disengaged myself from the main group to look for something. If you ask me what that something was now, I couldn't tell you. It could not have been all that important but at the time I thought it was. I misjudged how far I had walked but not only this, the route that I followed took me many times to the left and then to the right.

When I tried to retrace my footsteps, this is when I got hopelessly lost and being dark didn't help matters. All it did was to dull my perception of the facts and this caused me to become unclear and disorientated. I ended up walking in circles but as it was night time, I wasn't immediately aware of this. And because I had not told anyone I was leaving the rest site, by the time the group had started off again, no-one realised that I had gone but I noticed. As I mentioned earlier, I was not travelling with friends. They were complete strangers, so of course they would not be as aware or even care, about my movements. Besides that, people at any time could go their separate ways without question.

After a couple of hours wandering around blindly, I began

to feel alone and scared. I no longer felt as confident as I did before I left. In my belief that I wouldn't be long, I took no provisions. This was a mistake that nearly cost me my life. When the darkness of night plus lack of provisions and direction are also added to the mix, it then becomes a certain recipe for disaster.

I knew in my heart that I needed to conserve my energy and one of the best ways to do that was to remove the fear factor. Fear, if left unchecked, can produce anxiety and panic attacks that can be quite physically debilitating in itself. This same fear will sap your life force, leaving you lethargic and unmotivated, while lack of fear provides you with a storehouse of power that originates from deep within. Alongside that power, comes alertness and enthusiasm.

The other way to stop confusion is to stop everything but I couldn't. Something kept pushing me forward. I felt that some movement, even if misguided and misdirected, was better than no movement at all. I see now that I should have stopped, if only for the fact that it might have saved me from experiencing complete exhaustion. It would also have allowed me to catch my breath and think logically about my whereabouts.

For at least three days and three nights, I became like a madman; yet no-one saw me and I saw no-one. Funny that! Why is it that when you don't want to see someone, there they are, staring right back at you while in your face and space? And on the other side of the coin, when you seek out someone to talk to, they are nowhere to be found. This then leaves you floundering, which can sometimes lead to your feathers being ruffled. In this situation, my feathers were being well and truly ruffled. I was hungry, dirty and thirsty but no water could be seen.

Certainly, at various points in the desert, excluding the oasis, there is water buried underground but you had to know where to look. There were clues at ground level but I didn't know what those clues were. My ignorance and obsession blinded me to what was there. Eventually, I fell into a pit of torturous despair and exhaustion. This is when I finally gave in and stopped. I had no choice. My body and mind shut down. It had had enough. This helped me to stop struggling against my destiny and in that moment of letting go, I felt super calm and peaceful. And let's face it, after three days of growing confusion, tiredness and hallucinations, this calm and peaceful feeling made for a pleasant change.

While in that state of transition between the awake and asleep modes, I saw within my mind, a glowing green light fast approaching my body and remembered thinking, 'is that what God looks like?' As this being of light moved closer, a male figure began to take shape within this green aura of light. The features were not 100% clear at the time, because as it moved closer, I lapsed into a state of unconsciousness. My lack of strength forced me to accept and not deny my fate any longer. Perhaps I also completely let go of my control because innately I knew, I was safe in the presence of this 'being' that had approached me. I remember my last conscious thought before I surrendered, was that this figure represented the Angel of Death and who was I to plea bargain with such a mighty force.

In reality, my perception was wrong about what I thought I saw. He was quite the opposite. He was not of the Spirit world. He was of the physical realm and he was instrumental in saving my life, rather than ending it. While being in such a vulnerable position of submission, to trust a complete stranger (or God) with your life is a courageous and selfless thing that you can do.

The message of this story is to assure you that when you move into that space between life and death, you will discover that all the fear that went before will be lifted from your heart leaving you in a scare free zone but only if you allow it to be.

It has been earlier mentioned elsewhere in this book that babies and young children are more accepting of death – their own and that of other people. So, why is that? Could it be they haven't yet become so attached to their little bodies, loved ones, favourite places or toys? Could it be because they remember, either consciously or unconsciously, the world of Spirit they so recently left behind, so have an innate understanding that they have nothing to fear? The answer is a combination of these two factors. Children are also more open and receptive to suggestion and are apt to try new and creative ways of thinking through problems.

Solutions are always found quicker if you have an open heart and mind and let's face it, the simplest solutions are usually the best. Also, babies and children have not yet been talked out of their true feelings. Their doubt is small in comparison to their adult counterparts. As such, adults can learn a lot by listening to and absorbing this lack of fear that the young ones generate outwards. The roles can then successfully be reversed, where the adult once again becomes the student while the child becomes that student's teacher.

Which brings me to the point of why the young and very young have to die so tragically. Those parents left behind believe the lives of their children were wasted but they would be wrong in thinking that but regardless of this, they insist upon turning their anger towards God or the doctors who are paid to keep everyone alive, young or old, under all circumstances. There is always a most valuable lesson to be learnt by the adult in their children's passing.

You could live to one hundred and be none the wiser as to what life is really all about. While a one year old, possessing only innocent eyes can see more clearly the truth in all things. Certainly, they may not yet have the ability to express this wisdom verbally but it is still there regardless. Just because you, as an adult think you know better but can't hear, feel or see the obvious, doesn't mean the wisdom or knowledge of a child does not exist. And so it is the same in regards to the existence of God.

Many fear the intangibles of life and as a result of this we place our trust solely upon those things that are tangible. But please remember that those things that are tangible – such as our body, other people, money and all inanimate objects that fall under the broad heading of material possessions – can be destroyed at the flick of a switch, beyond all repair.

What happens next? Where or in what do you place your faith in then? It is best to rely upon that which is intangible, such as knowledge, communication, wisdom, love, energy, life and death, including the very air from which we breathe, in order to live this earthly existence. We cannot see the air around us but we know it's there, because science tells us so, and we have no fear of it. It is something that is explainable. Some will take advantage of this same air and do their best to pollute it but thankfully, this same breath of fresh air cannot be completely destroyed.

You cannot live life to its fullest potential if your soul is held back because of your limiting fear of death. Do you not see the relevance that if you relied more upon the intangibles in life, the fear of death would then take a back seat where it belongs and will become less of a concern?

Crying is a natural part of the letting go process when

someone you love dies. The desire to cry needs to be allowed and expressed. It is a healthy release. But don't hold on to your tears in the same way that you hold on to life. Be happy for yourself and be happy for your loved one when the tears no longer wish to come. And when this point of time arrives, don't feel guilty because you no longer have the need to cry anymore. This means you have both moved on from each other but you will still always remain connected energy wise from the heart. And when all the tears have been released, this won't be cause for you to forget them either.

You will always have your memories, unless of course you have been hit hard on the head that results in long and short term amnesia or if you suffer from Alzheimer's disease. If you have healthy brain activity, there is no reason in the world why you should forget. But I need to give you a warning about memories for future reference.

Don't become obsessive or controlling about them. Allow them to rise naturally to the surface in their own good time but please don't sit there crying in your beer, whiskey or gin, day in and day out, feeling compelled to remember every nitty gritty detail of the life you had together.

By trying to re-enact the past that binds you together, you can no longer be involved with living in the present. You are trapped in a memory that belongs not with today. You might argue that you do live for today, as you still go to work, look after the children, wash and iron your clothes, you cook the food that you eat, you keep yourself clean and presentable, you drive a car and you pay your bills. What is that if it's not living in the present? In a physical sense you are but your mind is busy wandering down memory lane while your heart revisits and relives the feelings. You have accordingly split yourself in two or should that be three different directions. Because of all these facts combined, you cannot feel totally satisfied in either place.

The same applies when you are so caught up in creating and feeling imaginary future events for yourself, good or bad. Your thoughts and feelings are pure energy. As such, the person you are thinking about is drawn back to your thought vibration and if this soul now belongs in the Spirit world along with their Angels, this constant pulling back to the physical is extremely frustrating and exhausting for the soul that has departed from this earthly plane. They need lots of rest and recuperation in between re-evaluating what they had experienced while living within their physical body. You may have a better understanding of this if I put the shoe on the other foot.

Just imagine (if you are not already) being a parent of a demanding baby, young child or teenager and because of this, you can't get a moment's peace except when they're asleep, which of course you believe they don't get enough of. It is only then that you are free to explore other avenues of learning and pleasure, so is it any wonder why we may sometimes lose our cool with our children? We only want to be left alone for a little while. This doesn't automatically mean you love them any less. All it means is that you would like your own space to tap into your higher self.

This situation and all its corresponding feelings are exactly the same for those dearly departed loved ones that have left you behind holding the baby, so to speak. They too, like you at times, would like to be left alone in peace so they may advance to another level of awareness. Is that so much to ask?

Life continues after death. So please be a little bit more respectful of that soul's need to not have their energy drained. Let them be and let go with unconditional love in your heart.

Don't worry, you will see each other again soon enough, when your turn comes. In the meantime, you both need to continue living in the moment, in whichever way it manifests itself. Don't let a little thing like the death of another person limit your experiences.

And when death does come finally knocking upon your own front door, be ready, be brave, take that leap of faith that leads directly to meeting your own soul, face to face. It is there you will recognise and acknowledge who you really are. It is through death we are reborn again into pure and unconditional love and how can you possibly be afraid of that?

Shontara

Fly Free Tonight

Fly, fly, my precious Mum,
the Angels ask for you to come.
The softest cloud, the whitest dove,
upon the wings of Heaven's light.

Pass the planets and the stars,
leave this earthly world behind.
Escape the sorrow and the pain,
and learn to fly again.

Fly, fly, my precious Mum,
your endless journey has begun.
Cross over to the other shore,
for there is peace, forever more.

I hold this memory bitter sweet, until we meet,
fly, fly, do not fear.
Don't waste your breath,
don't shed a tear.

Your heart is strong and your soul is free,
be on your way, don't wait for me.
Stand and accept God's wondrous light,
until the end of time.

The moon will rise and the sun will set
but rest assured, I won't forget.

Fly, fly, my precious Mum,
fly where only Angels sing.
Fly away, the time is right,
go now and fly towards the light.

I won't forget, God bless you Mum,
so let your soul fly free tonight.

Source: Unknown
Adaptation: Shontara

Affirmations

> THE SEEDS OF LIFE can be found within death.
>
> Death is the beginning of A NEW ADVENTURE.
>
> A part of me dies every day
> as MY LEVEL OF AWARENESS EXPANDS
> and separates from my old unaware self.

Part 2

And Then There Was More

MATTHIAS

Many will come to

Accept your words of

Truth. It is

Through your love that

He can speak and share his

Infinite wisdom and compassion to the world.

All we ask is for you to

Stay, a clear and perfect channel.

As a young boy, I knew I was destined to do something special. I didn't know when and I didn't know how. All I knew for sure that something big was to happen. As a result of this overpowering inner knowledge, I began to search for clues and signs by looking to the sky and nature, as well as to those other people who chose to walk in and out of my life at various times. Sometimes, I thought this is it but it would inevitably fall through, fold up or fade away over a short passing of time. Rather than pushing the continuance of any of these experiences, I let go of wanting to know what that might be in advance.

And the same must go for when a person seeks out their perfect soul mate who they can share the rest of their life with. As the old saying goes and which pertains mainly to women, one has to kiss a lot of ugly toads before they find the handsome prince. Well, I'm no handsome prince but I'm not all that bad either. You just have to take me as I come, or not. It's all a matter of perception and what the other person expects of you.

After Judas died and I was asked to join the circle of the then eleven men, I was both excited and reluctant. They felt they could trust me but could I trust myself? I didn't want to do anything that would make them doubt my honour and integrity. They had been through enough of that already. I knew I would never betray them but still, I felt I had a lot to live up to.

In those real early days when we first worked and broke

bread together, I put an enormous amount of pressure on myself in order to play out my perceived expectation of a perfect partner. Now in reality, there is no such thing. We all have faults, fears and weaknesses, as did Jesus, but he dealt with his in a public way and chose to overcome them in order to do God's work while others would keep their fears well hidden from prying eyes, afraid that they would be considered as being weak, unworthy and possibly even dangerous. No matter what we have or have not done in our life, I am here to tell you that we are all worthy of God's love, even if we think that we are not worthy of anyone else's.

To open your heart fully and experience the energy that is God, is to become cleansed and balanced; where all impurities and black marks against our name are all washed away. That is how great God's love is for all of us. Jesus was his channel at that particular time in history, as he still is but now in a different way. There have been many before Him and will be again later. Each individual has a special role to play in his or her own soul's evolution and while we are experiencing our own Spirit awareness, we need to realise that we are already perfect and complete in the eyes of God, irrespective of the fears and weaknesses that hold us back from being truly successful, both materially and spiritually.

It is what's in our hearts that counts and not what we have or haven't done or said. We only become disappointed in people as a result of our own expectations of them. There are not many of us who can accept fully everything another says or does without passing some sort of judgement or criticism. And quite often, we will feel justified in doing this because they have been hurtful and cruel to us or to someone that we love. I'm not saying you or any other should stay and cop it sweet (with 'it' meaning verbal, emotional or physical abuse). All I'm saying is we need to move on in more than the obvious way, which must incorporate the ability and willingness to try and forgive those who have hurt us.

This can be an incredibly hard thing for us to do but if achieved, we are helping our soul's growth which will enable us to go back to the Light which is where we all truly belong. Our spiritual ascension must take priority and where we need to leave behind all earthly fears and concerns while still living this human existence. As I said, it's not an easy thing to do. That is why we have been given more than one life to do it all in. But eventually, we will all learn. How quick we choose to learn or what method of learning we adopt is left up to our own discretion, but rest assured that no-one remains untouched by the hand of God.

I was very much an explorer at heart. I used to enjoy leaving no stone unturned and I mean that in the literal sense as well as metaphysically. I wanted to see for myself what sort of creature lurked within our midst without our knowledge of their existence. Some are truly masters of disguise; where they camouflage themselves so they may receive no unwanted attention. Can you do that?

It is an art, let me assure you. Sometimes, it can take great acting ability to pull it off properly without showing your true colours. These are normally expressed through the tone of your voice, your facial expressions, the words that you speak, the way that you stand or how you fold your arms and all these things, when taken in context with each other, can tell an astute observer a great deal about you.

And then we have the chameleon or the master of disguise I was talking about earlier, who does not react and blends into whatever type of environment they find themselves in at the time. They can then become one with the crowd or take on the personality of the individual they are talking to, where they simply mirror back what is being reflected to them. It is the chameleons of this world who are greatly popular with the majority and everyone likes them because they see themselves.

But if you're really alert and smart, you may discover certain traits about yourself that you dislike, thanks to the master of disguise having the ability to give back what you put out. This is when they truly are being of service to humanity. Their purpose is to help shock people out of their bad habits and fears, so much so that the person, who can now see the truth, feels a strong desire to take action towards creating positive change within themselves and their environment. Jesus was of this nature. He blended in, yet at other times when deemed necessary, he also felt comfortable at standing apart from the rest.

The secret is to feel equally secure in both situations and while being surrounded by people you may either love or hate, you stay loyal while being of service to yourself and them at the same time. This is where a balance of both give and take is so important. At all times, speak your truth with compassion, enthusiasm and sincerity. You will be heard and you will bring about great change to a person's life, even if they are not aware of it. Change is not always easily recognisable but it is there, in the same way that the wind is. You can't physically see the wind but you can certainly feel it.

You can experience its destruction or creation, as we must take responsibility for being our own creator or destroyer of good fortune as well. Perhaps you may feel justified in blaming another for apparently destroying your happiness and sense of security but we can always fix it simply by thinking outside the square for a solution. Some people at this point get into further strife because they feel it's all too hard to work at finding a solution, where it is so much easier and simpler to take the easy route of placing blame squarely upon the shoulders of another. Everyone must be responsible for their own actions and reactions.

Look at what happened to poor old Atlas; after a period of time of being forced to hold the pillars of the Universe upon his shoulders, he collapsed under the strain. His heart gave up the ghost and consequently came crashing to the ground, finally being crushed to death from the sheer weight of the world upon his heart. It was too much to bear.

Instead, why not work towards distributing the stress load more evenly, release all build up of sorrow and pain within your heart and ask Spirit to help you rest and recuperate from the grind of daily life. Your Angels are there specifically to assist in matters of the heart, mind and soul. Take full advantage of their help. Be at peace, don't worry and be happy, with yourself and your fellow man. Perhaps this could become the Eleventh Commandment.

Marriott and I are linked together in love. As you would say today, we 'tied the knot' under the light of the full moon. It was a perfectly clear night, not a cloud in the sky and with no wind present, while a trillion stars above were our Heavenly witnesses. We had a smattering of earthlings as well, all standing in a circle holding hands while Marriott and I stood in the centre and took our vows. In the middle with us, there stood a trestle table covered in a simple blue and white cloth, upon which sat a row of thirteen lit candles, a bowl full of red wine and a platter filled with roughly broken chunks of bread.

As part of the wedding ceremony, these same pieces of plain bread were dipped into the wine, which we then lovingly fed to each other with our fingers. This act signified us being bound together by the body and blood of Christ.

Even though he was not there physically amongst us, his Spirit could certainly be felt. We said some words and rings were exchanged. After officially being betrothed, Marriott and I went in opposite directions around the circle, where each well wisher had an opportunity to anoint and bless us with perfumed oil and mark us with the sign of the cross upon our foreheads. It was strangely moving to receive so many blessings from those people we could trust.

This night would mark a significant turning point in my life. Along with what I spoke out loud at my wedding, I silently vowed that nothing would ever destroy my love for her and even when finally separated through physical death, our love would still continue to bloom and grow, that was a natural part of our soul's makeup.

Afterwards, much merriment could be seen and heard, along with much eating, drinking, laughing, singing and dancing. It was indeed a joyous occasion, as all weddings should be, no matter what form they take or where they are held.

Much later, I was to have two sons, who were as different as chalk and cheese. This sometimes made it awkward and difficult for us, being parents, to please one while unintentionally upsetting the other. When this happened, we were then forced to later tip the scales in the other direction so the unhappy one then received what was needed for him. It was a constant juggling act but we finally got it down to a fine art, which lent itself to a relatively harmonious living environment.

Marriott enjoyed both her pregnancies and the two births

were relatively pain free, although I wasn't there at the time. I was later told this by a reliable person, whom I felt I could trust. To see Marriott suffer in pain would have cut me to shreds so I was grateful to God that he protected her through this birthing ordeal.

For some women, both today and in ancient times, it was much more than that. It was a trauma over which the women had no control. One had to have great faith that everything would turn out for the best but the best for who? It is not so easy to trust while your body is being ripped apart by another little soul, hell bent upon entering this physical world. You will never make another entrance like it; it only happens once in a lifetime and every other entrance you make after that pales into insignificance.

Each evening, I would take a walk to the base of a mountain that was relatively close to my home base, where I would sit upon a log to pray and meditate. This daily or rather nightly ritual would clear my head of any possible confusion and anxiety picked up during the day. I highly recommend a similar practice to all people of all ages. I loved the evenings best of all, especially after everyone had gone to sleep. It was quiet and peaceful, although even then, one still had to stay guarded and alert to any approaching enemies who were more than willing to stab you in the back when you weren't looking.

One particular night, a snake came to join me. I wasn't scared of it and it wasn't scared of me. I considered all animals to be my friends. I felt I could trust them more than I could some other people, but certainly not all.

To have fear of something or someone can make us do stupid things which we could later regret. Don't react unwisely or angrily in the heat of the moment. If you attack another person, they could possibly be forced into a position of retaliation which creates the continuation of confrontation. And this may not always be the best thing to happen for all concerned. There are good aspects to fear such as it keeps you on your toes quite literally, but if that same fear is not controlled and is allowed to run rampant in our lives, this can then become like a debilitating disease, which can sometimes stop us from progressing forward. To control our fears, real or imagined, takes much discipline on our part.

This is where visualisations, meditations, affirmations and prayers can come in handy. Just imagine in your mind, the fear leaving your physical body far behind. This then produces a sensation of freedom for both yourself and the fear, because it will have to move on until it finds a new host or hostess. It is then up to that next person to either accept or reject that fear's all pervading presence, like a thick black cloak that blocks out all light. If accepted and depending upon the person's desire, they can then reduce this same fear to a friendly status or enhance and magnify its power by seeing it as some hateful enemy to be despised.

But if you take away its power to bite, it has nothing to latch on to. Always try to turn your fears about face and make them positive rather than a negative. Let your fears work for you rather than against you. This then means that you are thinking smart on your feet. While remaining loyal to your beliefs, think before speaking or taking action first and then feel or react second. You are the master, while your fear is the slave. Did you notice I avoided using the word mistress and put slave instead? I believe it's safer that way. Force the fear to do your bidding and don't you give in to its demands.

There needs to be a clear pathway from your brain to your

mouth that then continues in a southerly direction towards your heart. What I am trying to say is that your crown, throat and heart chakras need to remain unblocked in order to live surrounded by harmonious energy, but now back to the path. If it becomes blocked or eroded away over a long period of time due to stormy thoughts, hateful words and negative feelings, you will perceive that all your experiences are going from bad to worse. You may believe you are being cut off from the rest of the world; where no-one loves, supports, accepts and understands you. From your point of view, you might as well be living like Robinson Crusoe on a deserted island for all the good that anybody does for you, which of course is next to nil.

To live as if one was stranded can be an extremely life changing event for the better. It will teach you to accept 100% responsibility for all your failures, as well as all your successes and this can only be a good thing. Most certainly, because you are all alone on this isolated island that exists only within your mind and where no-one can reach you, things will certainly not be any easier for you. In fact, it will be downright hard and exhausting, in a mental, verbal and emotional way. And in exchange for real people who figure in your life, you are left to deal with a more formidable force which will become magnified due to the fact that you are so isolated.

This force will become larger than life making you feel so small and quite insignificant. What is this force I speak about? Your inner demons and fears, of course. Jesus experienced them and so must you, at a particular stage in your existence and for some I would say that this should take place sooner rather than later. Our soul cannot continue to evolve without this experience. This event will either make or break us. While passing through this traumatic form of mental and emotional torture, you will feel it's never ending and will scream for mercy from a being more powerful than yourself, begging them to release you from this inner world of fears, but face your fears, you must and preferably, on a voluntary basis.

It will strengthen your resolve to not accept into your life, those things or people of that same vibration that are not good for you. It will help you to see more clearly what it is that you do or do not want or need.

Now the great news is we can take this journey in little chunks at a time. We don't necessarily need to physically remove ourselves from society for 40 days and 40 nights in order to achieve enlightenment. We can easily do it each night before we go to sleep as we put aside some quality time to let go and re-evaluate what we experience throughout our day. And in this time, we need to remain brutally honest with ourselves and view our actions with detachment. And while you're there, take a look at what motivated you to do or not do something.

Look at your highlights and lowlights. Are they of equal balance? Are there more lowlights than highlights? If you go down more than you go up, what can you then do in the future to tip the scales in the opposite direction? What could you have done differently that would have brought about more positive change?

While asking yourself these questions, remain still within your body and mind while waiting for these answers to arrive. When you finally do receive the valuable insights that will fall upon you like a cleansing rain, write them down before you forget and make it a goal to put them into action the next time an opportunity presents itself. Be proactive rather than quitting, each time something goes wrong.

Doing this can be exhausting work in the beginning but if

done on a regular basis, it will become less and less hard. Believe it or not, this inner process of seeking resolution will become another highlight of your day. It won't drag you screaming into the gutter where you can easily be trodden upon. In reality, it will have the opposite effect which will lift you up so high that you could almost see eternity.

Routine or habits are two non-romanticised or non-mysterious words for ritual and ceremony. The procedure, which may not necessarily be of a spiritual or religious nature, may differ but the end result is the same. It is an action taken on a regular basis for a specific purpose. Each day, we have our little rituals that we act out and which have been created through our automatic responses since childhood, to certain similar situations that will occur throughout our lifetime. These habits, routines and rituals are a result of conditioning received from ourselves, family members and society in general. For example, upon waking, some will rise immediately and go to the toilet, while others will stop to put a pair of slippers on or walk barefoot towards their goal. Some may stop to snooze for another 10 minutes before becoming active and will immediately head for the bathroom to take a shower in order to wake themselves up properly.

Other people upon opening their eyes to a new day, will light up a cigarette, followed by a quick trip to the kitchen to prepare a cup of coffee or to pour some cereal and milk into a bowl which they will eat for breakfast. When we put our shoes on, we will always put the same foot forward first and if this changes due to forgetfulness, it then feels uncomfortable, awkward and doesn't quite feel right. When you brush your teeth, you will begin either on the left or right without your conscious awareness of doing so. You then continue getting ready and you leave the house to drive your car or to catch a plane, bus or train to your next port of call. All these little insignificant pieces of the puzzle add up to a complete picture but we do these things on autopilot.

We overlook the obvious and take it for granted, except when our body rebels and can no longer carry out these automatic requests. As an interesting exercise, spend three consecutive days out of your busy weekly schedule and remain consciously aware of your physical movements throughout the day; in particular what you do the first thing each morning and last thing at night. Take mental notes or write them down if you have to. Can you see a pattern emerging? What will you discover about yourself? Then follow this by another three consecutive days of consciously forcing yourself to change that routine that you are now aware of and see how you feel. It won't be easy to break this habit and from time to time, you will feel as if you are fighting an uphill battle but persevere and observe the results of the changes you put into place.

This is when you can really branch out and be brave, by putting this simple yet effective technique into practise when dealing with other people in your personal, social and business life.

Take a mental note and snapshot photo as to what your responses are to situations that continually repeat themselves on a daily basis. This is how conscious change is bought about. Discern whether you need to keep a certain ritual or routine going. Is it still of some benefit to you? Just because everyone else does it like that, does that then automatically mean it is right for you? Why do you do it that way – is it because you were shown or told to do it that way? Whose rituals or routines have you adopted and which ones can you give up? Are you in control of your life or is someone else?

It is the totality of these little things that can make a big difference to the perception about ourselves. Routine serves a useful purpose in that it helps us to feel secure and it gives us that sense of stability that we all crave for and believe is essential to live a balanced and harmonious lifestyle. Because let's face it, life can appear to be uncertain, so we have an already inbuilt strong need to hold on to something that is certain or upon someone we can rely. This is human nature. Remain aware of when it's time to let go of those bad habits or wrong beliefs which are holding you back.

Step aside and start afresh. As they say, "a change is always as good as a holiday". The person who works hard for a living spends much of their time daydreaming about a holiday and which provides a temporary mind escape from their day to day routine. This means that every day can then become a holiday of sorts.

It was frowned upon by the authorities for women to receive a proper and advanced education. This does not mean to say that women were not smart or intelligent. To say such a thing would be far from the truth. Just because one receives little or no formal education does not mean they are stupid. Women talked and learnt by sharing their life experiences with other women. They would listen and absorb what their husbands spoke about to their friends or elders, while in the home environment. These same women may not have spoken at these times and where they endeavoured to become part of the background; unobtrusively blending in with their sparse and simple furnishings, never drawing untoward attention to themselves. They also chose carefully as to when it was best to express an opinion, which they always did privately, behind closed doors. To do so publicly would only invite trouble.

Many times, women were seen to be silent but obedient partners to their husbands. The mother/daughter relationships in those days were particularly significant and less competitive and controlling than they have become today. Each person was important in their own right, to each other. The mother knew that her daughter would one day become a wife and mother, just like her. The mother ensured that her female offspring would receive a more valuable but different type of education. Everyone had an expected role to play.

Perhaps I must concede that men, in the same way as they are today, were most certainly given more choices but women still played an important role in the home. My own mother had nerves of steel yet at the same time possessed a high level of compassion and understanding for the plight of others. Nothing appeared to ever faze her. She allowed her husband, my father, to believe he was right but she knew better and was subtle in letting him know this. It was enjoyable to watch the interplay between them. It was a most illuminating experience and one which led me to have a great respect for the ability of women.

I say now to the women of today – never sell yourself short. You have much to offer, not only to your immediate family but to society in general. Your role is equally as important as a man's. Don't let the men in your life ever underestimate and belittle your talents and abilities and never, never, never, do the same to yourself. Be proud of what you can do. Ignore all acts of suppression and continue to allow your personal light to shine.

Fear of Feelings

Firstly, I need to explain there is a difference between our feelings and emotions. One is based upon unrealistic impulsiveness, while the other relies upon logical reasoning. Can you pick which is which? If you're confused or not quite sure which way to jump, visualise in your mind, a pair of old fashioned scales complete with two brass dishes being perfectly balanced on either side of the other. Place upon one dish is an assortment of positive feelings such as love, peace, joy and power. On the opposite, empty side, position one at a time some negative feelings such as anger, fear, hate and frustration.

With great surprise, no doubt, you will notice they stay the same but this is only because you are not allowing whatever feeling you happen to be experiencing, to take control and for one emotion to become more dominant than the other. In your eyes, it just is. Your attitude is – 'whatever I am feeling, let's deal with it now with reason and logic, at the same time as acknowledging that what I feel can change in an instant without warning'. I mean, it doesn't always have to be bad and it certainly won't always be good.

Acceptance of your situation helps to maintain that equilibrium whilst denial will only cause you to lose your cool and balance. Once that is lost, it becomes more certain than ever that you could badly fall and hurt yourself, without it being necessary.

Let's try something else now. Leave both these positive and negative feelings where they are but change your intent, belief or attitude to the opposite of what has just been experienced. For example, here you will give permission for one side to become more dominant than the other, allowing your mood to control your reasonable reactions. This will depend greatly upon who is stimulating your emotions at the time. They can swing quite dramatically without notice and as such, you'll think you've been caught on a never ending and forever flexible seesaw; you might say, too flexible, where it becomes downright uncomfortable.

One minute you're up and the next you're down. There is no balance between the two extremes. So when you are up, you are very, very good and while you are down, you are bad. To speak sensibly with such a person, whose emotions are never stable and which run rampant all over the place, high one minute and low the next, can be most frustrating and sometimes scary for the one communicating because you know they are not listening.

It's like talking to two different people trapped in the one body. One part of their nature, you will have good reason to like but the other more 'darker' aspects of their psyche could evoke within you a strong desire to either run and hide or equally, you could become aggressive and abusive to match their mood. Physical, verbal or emotional violence then erupts between those concerned, both determined to win and claim victory.

Many people suffer daily from schizophrenic like personalities, which leaves those who have no difficulty in maintaining a balanced equilibrium, never knowing how that 'swinger' is going to react to what we say or do; irrespective of whether it be a positive or negative situation to begin with. Do you now have a clearer understanding of the difference between your feelings and emotions? We can have both positive and negative feelings but the scales are tipped off balance when we place too much emphasis or importance on one while neglecting and rejecting the other.

The same can happen in relationships where one partner gives consistently and receives nothing, while the other takes and gives even less. In this situation of inequality, both people are lacking balance and one day, things will abruptly come to a head and end. It is the same with communication. Once all communication has ceased, confusion and mistrust will quickly step in and take control, which makes things so much worse.

All people will oscillate between the two spectrums of light and dark; some more often and quicker than others. There will be those, men included, who are too emotional for their own good, while others will lament they have no feelings whatsoever which can sometimes drive them to distraction as they worry and question – 'what's wrong with me? Don't I have a heart? I wish I had more compassion, love and understanding for the needs of other people. Why do I sometimes feel so uncaring? It's like as if I'm in a state of suspension, where nothing is happening and where I have been placed in an emotionless pit that never ends. What's wrong with me?' Dear me, we've returned to the beginning so soon!

To those 'emotionless' beings I say that this is no cause for alarm, as Buddha would suggest to feel nothing is still feeling something. It's just another state of consciousness. Many Buddhists and other enlightened ones strive in their daily meditations to be in such a space where no thoughts, no feelings or body exist. It's a truly peaceful place to be and as such, is a great opportunity from which to heal yourself but we must touchdown and come back to the physical realm occasionally, because it is here that much work still needs to be accomplished, while lessons are to be learnt and not avoided.

Those people who feel they are devoid of any worthwhile feelings that matter, try so hard to avoid being bombarded by any type of emotional pain whatsoever but by doing so, they are shooting themselves in the foot because they can never truly experience pleasure either.

Remember the yin and yang principle, the chicken and the egg, the tortoise and the hare, the hand and the glove? They need each other in order to experience completeness. This is why we desire to have a partner – to feel whole, complete, to be a part of someone else's energy and life. But even though this is what we most want, when we do finally get what we wish for and where the feelings are so intense, that we try and run from them. We can do this in many ways.

Some believe that drugs and alcohol are the answer that will kill any pain they might be feeling but what they do is quite the opposite. These substances, designed to alter your original state of consciousness, will only enhance them. This is why those people who depend upon their constant availability will crave more drugs or alcohol, believing that if they have enough of what they think they need, there has got to be a point where all feelings of pain are wiped out.

All you are really wiping out here are the brain cells that are needed to nourish the body properly so it can stay healthy and in tip top condition. And while we are talking about keeping ourselves in tip top condition, it truly astounds me when I watch people, men in particular, who will spend large amounts of time, money, love and attention on inanimate objects such as their cars or computers (that coincidentally can't have human feelings) while these same people neglect themselves and their partners.

Others will wish to spoil their pets, children or friends in order to keep themselves from ever feeling bad. This too, then becomes a tactic towards avoidance that can maintain control over our fear of feelings and emotions. Another way humans can sidestep this fear is to keep themselves busy at work or in a particular cause, so they never have any time to acknowledge what they might truly be feeling. These are your workaholics and fanatics who never stop; who work around the clock.

They tend largely to be loners, because as far as they are concerned, to have less contact with other people is so much better than being constantly pulled in all different directions; as your feelings and emotions can best be experienced when other people are in your life. Their belief is that no people equates to less intense emotions. These loners thrive upon this self-imposed aloneness but still its main purpose is to camouflage what's inside; merely hiding rather than exposing a problem that needs to be aired. Because it's buried deep below the surface, doesn't mean it's not there. Every good treasure hunter knows this basic fact.

We then have another group of 'sad sacks', although they don't appear to be sad, who keep themselves busy but in a social sense. They love being with people because as long as they are surrounded by them, they never have to feel lonely. Even in a crowded room, if they are made to feel like an intruder, they will feel worse than they did initially. They then try harder to be liked by becoming the life of everybody's party. To be caught up in their energy is like being tossed around in a whirlwind of activity; where your feet never get to touch the ground.

These social butterflies who possess enough energy to light up a whole nation, who fear being alone and who occupy themselves every minute of their day and night to live the opposite, can be quite damaging to the health of others. Besides, where and when does it end? It is nature's way for a whirlwind to eventually blow itself out but what then?

You run out of steam of course, take temporary rest and then restart the process by repeating the same mistake, over and over again. To sit still and be by themselves, for even short periods of time, can be quite torturous for them. They will end up feeling like a caged bird that is compelled to break out of its enforced confinement and once it has escaped, seeks out a companion to fly around with but if you insist upon flying too high, expect to get your wings burnt, that will then cause you to come crashing to the ground with a thump.

And there you have it – the classic 'seesaw' effect I described earlier where you swing from one extreme to the other; where balance and harmony do not exist in your world, all because of your fear to feel. But regardless of what you do or don't do, your feelings or emotions are something you cannot avoid, not only in life but in death as well. It never stops. If you are somewhat intelligent and I know you are, your goal while still alive would be to maintain balance. This will help you to advance as a soul easily.

Imagine yourself, if you will, sitting beside the bed of a dying person you care for deeply. There you are packing death, trembling in your boots, praying that you could be anywhere else except there. For some, the person in the hospital bed doesn't even have to be dying for you to feel what I have described. Just the fact you are in a hospital could scare you into wanting to run in the opposite direction but out of love, loyalty, duty or obligation, you stay put. Fear will also keep you there, rooted to the spot. You would do a runner in a minute if you were given half a chance.

Really smart ones (or at least, they think they are) don't show up at all. They'll make up all sorts of excuses as to why they can't pay the person in need, a visit. What's the real problem here and who is more important in regards to having their personal needs met?

The problem lies with the visitor and not the person who is stuck in the hospital bed. Have the roles ever been reversed? Have you been the patient while waiting for a visit from a friend? How did it feel? Did you feel abandoned, rejected, scared and lonely? Now step into the visitor's shoes – are you constantly watching the clock? Did you make a decision before you left home or work that you would spend a certain amount of respectful time with the patient but anything beyond that limit was just not on?

While sitting there trying to mind your own business and forcing yourself to look calm and detached, you are in fact living through a blind panic and sheer hell within. You might internally be asking such things as – 'what do I do if they die while I am here? I certainly can't break down and cry? It's not proper to cry in public, not to mention embarrassing for myself, as it would be for those people being forced to listen and watch my display of emotion. This would have to be my worst nightmare.' Take a step back and try and discern what is wrong with this picture just painted.

As an outside observer, you may think the visitor is being totally selfish and lack all sensitivity. You are right in believing they are selfish but they certainly do not lack feeling. It is quite the opposite and this is what makes them fearful, that is the intensity of their emotions. It's not only about the fear of being confronted by the actuality of death itself, although they may believe it is, especially if they choose to deny their truth. This is most definitely one time where they can't ignore their fears and have nothing they can rely upon to help them escape from the pain they are feeling until perhaps later, but by then they've already been put through the mill. This then makes it more about them rather than the other person.

Some people can be strong and supportive of the patient in question but when you place someone in the situation where they fear not only death but fears all types of intense negative feelings or emotions as well that is thrust upon them so unwillingly, they become weak, powerless, angry and out of control. Besides which, they don't like those feelings either, so in their eyes, there's no way they can possibly win. If you are this type of personality, how do you think you can get through this ordeal in one piece?

The key is to firstly accept that these real and strong feelings and emotions are completely valid and that you have nothing to apologise for. Secondly, rather than denying their existence that originates from within you, claim ownership of them, right there and then. Thirdly, acknowledge that you will survive. No matter how scary or intense our feelings are, they can't physically kill us. We may sometimes wish we were dead; believing that in death, there is no pain but still we keep on living and that is the way it has to be. Fourthly and if at all possible, rise above your own earthly concerns and give a thought to the needs of the other person for a change.

And lastly, behold a most remarkable rite of passage that we must all go through at one time or another. You can't avoid it so you might as well get used to it when given the opportunity to observe death's reality. In order for the dying process to be easier for yourself, it is best if you have been an observer, several times if need be, before your turn comes around. The more you confront what you fear, the less scary it will become until one fine day, you wake up to discover that the fear has disappeared altogether. And no, you are not dead at this point; you are still very much alive and vibrant. It is then that you can look back upon your life and wonder – 'what was I so afraid of?' You will be amazed to see what lengths you took to avoid seeing and accepting your truth.

We avoid the sometimes ugly truth in order to protect ourselves from feeling pain. The good stuff we can handle by the bucket load but when it comes to admitting we may have made a mistake by doing something wrong that hurt ourselves and others, we shut ourselves down. We don't want to know. But I speak of only the majority here because there are certain other souls floating through life today, where to speak and receive the truth is all important to them. To lie does not come naturally to these sorts of people and one look in their direction and at their face easily gives them away, because as much as they try and hide it, they still wear their heart on their sleeve, for all the world to see.

A world which will proceed to pick at, analyse, dissect and destroy all sense of that person's credibility and worthiness; whose prey becomes like a pack of hungry wolves feeding upon the dead carcasses and rotting flesh of humans and animals alike.

But let's now go back to those people who are fearful to feel too much, as they will react quite angrily when confronted by their truth and where there is all hell to pay for the one who passed on the message. For both the communicator and listener, it can sometimes be a cross too heavy to bear.

In order to achieve some semblance of peace, they give up the cross completely and choose to remain silent but never ignorant for the rest of their existence, until the next time when they have to start all over again and not necessarily from step one. We will always advance but some will reach their destination quicker than others.

And there we have our main problem of today and that is there is a lack of honest communication between two or more people, and that includes communication with ourselves as well. Who wants to see and acknowledge our own bad points? Surely we have enough people in our lives already who are more than happy to fulfil that role rather brilliantly, so why should you add your little bit as well?

But this is exactly what is needed. No-one knows you better than yourself. You may deny your pain till your blue in the face but this still doesn't change the fact that you still feel it strongly. You may be adept at hiding how you truly feel from others for a variety of reasons and you do this because, other than wanting to protect yourself, you have the very real issue of not trusting other people with your mind and heart. So you hold yourself back, sometimes even with the partner you have chosen to spend the rest of your life with and where your relationship is founded upon a 'need to know' basis only.

Is it any wonder then that, over a period of time, the other person in this picture will begin to suspect that you are keeping secrets from them, which you are, and because you are not willing to communicate honestly with your partner about these painful secret places that you have securely locked away, they are then forced to make up their own stories as to what you could be keeping from them? When this happens, that partner can then turn that tiny seed of doubt and mistrust and make it into a whopping big tree full of their own insecurities and fears.

By keeping secrets, you are doing much harm to your partner that will continue to grow and spread to others, which only adds to the original insecurity and fear until one day this tree will become too top heavy and goes belly up, ever so painfully and slowly to the ground. It loses its footing, its bearing, its direction and rather than sharing with you what they have been feeling, your partner will take a leaf out of your own book by remaining silent as well. So first there was one but now two have fallen but soon there shall be four, eight and sixteen, and on it goes.

This process will then continue on to touch other people beyond your realm of comprehension and so creates a worldwide network of secrets, lies and fear. Is it any wonder then why there are so many unhappy people today? It's because each one has a whole closet full of secrets and as such, there is no chance in Hell they are ever going to share them with another out of a fear of being rejected, laughed at, judged, attacked and persecuted if someone else should accidentally or intentionally come across their hidden pain. A sense of mistrust then becomes a normal part of everyone's life, all because we fear exposing our true selves.

It is now time for the air to be cleared once and for all because without it, we are polluting ourselves and ascension to a new dimension and level of understanding will be impaired and fraught with much personal chaos and disruption. We wish for all of this to stop but the future is still placed largely in the hands of each individual. When you take that first step towards changing what you fear, we can then fall in step beside you and walk with you the rest of the way. Are you ready to speak what you truly feel without fear or will you allow your emotions to overwhelm and destroy not only you but everyone else as well?

If we allow our fear of feeling too much too soon or take the risk of becoming too emotional, we may hesitate to get involved in new adventures and opportunities that may come our way, in particular, the area of relationships. When our heart has been broken many times, and sometimes once can be enough, we are not too keen on reliving the initial ecstasy and expected agony.

We may also not accept new and better job offers, simply because we doubt our abilities to perform well, especially in times of a crisis. And because of this self-doubt, we can put an enormous amount of pressure on ourselves so that we then decide that the promotion is not worth it. Who needs that extra pressure?

You may think – 'I don't like feeling pressured and anxious.' But you don't have to feel like this. Believe it or not, you may sail through any perceived obstacles like a breeze. You have absolutely nothing to worry about or fear, do you? Why imagine problems where there are none, before you have begun? What we see in our mind can stimulate some pretty strong feelings and emotions, but they are not real. They are an illusion that you have created out of your own fear and what is imagined in our mind is always far worse than what it is in reality.

It's like spending a lot of time and effort trying to bring to life your favourite fantasies, when sometimes it is best to leave well enough alone. But no, because of your stubborn streak and 'have to have it now' attitude, when fantasy gets to meet reality with you caught in the middle while introducing the two together, sparks can fly in your direction and you can discover, to your horror, that they don't like each other. This is because they come from two totally different stratospheres and when their separate energies mix and mingle, an explosion can occur that will cause harm to those once innocent observers of the fantasy who have now become reluctant participants; which means you and anybody else you have decided to be a part of this new reality.

Don't fix something that doesn't need fixing in the first place. Leave it the way you found it. Don't change for change's sake. Don't change for other people's sake but please do change for your own sake.

Besides, it's only human to feel both good and bad emotions from one minute to the next. That's what makes life so interesting, because you never know how your feelings might change. It's like playing the 'Lucky Dip'; you never know what you're going to pull out of the bag. Always remember that our feelings and emotions are governed by our thoughts alone. This is what your brain takes its instruction from. Your feelings are secondary to your thoughts but this is still something we can control, for better or for worse.

Denial is the most powerful form of protection there is to guard against any unwanted feelings, both pleasant and not. How many of you immensely enjoyed that first, second or third kiss at the beginning of a new relationship but soon after, you did a 360 degree turnaround, denied your true feelings, became quite disgusted and indignant and backed right off the scene instead, leaving the other person confused, wondering what had they done wrong? What were you so afraid of – getting too close, future sadness and heartache, people you respect not approving of your choice of partner? These are not good reasons to deny yourself all of that which makes you feel contented.

How many of you, who have recently become first time mothers, feel disappointed and let down when they discover they lack a strong maternal instinct? The percentage of you who feel like this may be small compared to the majority of women who feel quite motherly towards their offspring but there it is. What do you do about this perceived lack of feeling when you leave the hospital – pretend that what you are feeling is not real and replace it with a false happiness instead, where you trap yourself into living a lie? Your baby will know, as they are a complete mixed up bundle of feelings.

Do you proceed to beat yourself up by claiming to anyone who will listen that you are a bad mother? But then again, you may keep this little secret all to yourself as you wish for no-one to be ashamed and non-accepting of your feelings and beliefs. When you are with other people and your child is also present, are you as sweet as apple pie and cream but when alone, you adopt a different persona altogether and stink like a rotten egg, which to a baby or child's sensitive nose, is sheer agony? Again, what are you so afraid of? Are you afraid to own up to your feelings? To put your hand up and claim responsibility, you may then be required to seek professional help but if you have to do that, it would be like having to admit you failed miserably in the mothering department and we can't have anyone knowing that, can we?

Here's another scenario – how many lie when they are asked the question 'what's wrong?' and you reply 'nothing'. To the observer, they know this is incorrect but will let you keep your feelings to yourself out of a sign of respect or disinterest and so makes a hasty physical retreat to leave or will change the course of the ensuing conversation towards themselves or to discuss the state of the weather. But you don't like this abrupt change in direction, as you inwardly scream at them for being so insensitive and uncaring.

But to be fair to the one enquiring, and irrespective of whether they really wanted to know the true answer or not from you, they did ask the question but you chose to dismiss it by saying nothing. You can't then turn around and blame the other person for not prying any further.

But then again, this forced change of tactic may just break the ice which will enable the person who is feeling awful to spill their guts, but in some cases, once again, they may stay silent and indignant, thinking that their feelings are insignificant and unimportant when compared to others.

What I'm trying to get at with the abovementioned situations is that you are not saying what you truly think and feel. Your communication with others is less than honest, which upon occasion the other person will be aware of, while at others times, they won't. Don't be afraid to speak from the heart. You may wish to warn them before you begin that they may not like what they are about to hear but it is still something you have to say. Then let rip but later, take it one step further by explaining to the listener why you feel this way, if you can. This will help them to understand where you are coming from and which space you are standing in.

And who knows, they may be thankful for your honesty because what you reflect is the same way they feel too. So there you have it – two people who have much in common but didn't know it because they were too afraid to show their true feelings and emotions to each other.

As I said before, regardless of your fear, you will feel it

anyway. You cannot be devoid of feelings or emotions. It's not humanly possible. Certainly you can remain detached and untouched which may give the appearance to others that you are made of stone and that you don't care. Maybe the feelings and emotions you experience are on such a subtle wavelength that you lack the ability to discern their vibrations but still the fact remains that they are still forever present.

Like your silent and unassuming shadow, they are always there. When you complain that you are an 'emotionless' creature, remember that over the whole period of your lifetime, you have learnt little by little to suppress and deny what you feel. Perhaps as a child you were regularly being punished for crying, being too loud, telling the truth and having too much fun, when really you should have had your head down studying and working hard. So for those of you who truly believe they lack all feeling for either themselves or others, take a glance at some of the emotions you experienced in those first seven years.

I think you will find there was a plentiful supply of feelings. I would even go so far as to suggest you would have had an overabundance and as such, you would not have known what to do with them or how to react to them all at once. In order to protect yourself from having certain emotions overwhelm you, a switch located within your heart was flicked over to the off position. This was not a conscious act on your part and you may, even to this very day, not have been aware of the reality of such a switch but it is there for your protection and it needs to be used with extreme caution. If you used it too much in your younger days and you relied upon its power to make you feel better, it then becomes a habit and a habit built up over a lifetime of switching yourself off and shutting yourself down, can take another whole lifetime to reactivate those no longer in use.

There is one main switch that controls the big picture but there are countless other minor switches that relate to a wide variety of emotions. Now that you know about this 'secret switch', spend some quality time with yourself by taking a walk within your heart and turning them all on again. You may not feel or see any visible improvement initially but that's because after such a long time in hibernation and being asleep, it needs a little extra time to wake up fully, much like a car battery needing at least 24 hours to kick start properly again. As you wander down this long corridor crammed full of separate switches, turn them on one by one.

Don't rush because if you run around in a blind panic or with an over the top enthusiasm, you may accidentally miss a feeling or emotion that is really important to your overall spiritual growth and understanding. So when you come across an off switch, reach out to change it. But keep your hand securely fastened upon it, focus upon what it's giving you in return and absorb its current running through you. Each switch is labelled appropriately and set at the same level, so there is no need for adjustment. There are no high or low positions. Just plug yourself in and remake the connection you have lost. You have nothing to fear and everything to gain.

Don't blame other people for making you the way you are today, you did it to yourself. No-one can manipulate or control your heart as well as you can. So why not reclaim your power and become like an electric light that never loses its glow. People will notice and they will want what you are having, even though they may not understand what that something is. Share with them this secret freely and then stand back and allow them space to be bathed in their own glorious light.

    In order for us all to become highly evolved souls, we must be willing to take the bad with the good. If you know only one aspect of your nature well, this will create an unbalanced point of view in life and cause disharmony of spirit within the heart and this is something worth avoiding.

Forgiveness Visualisation

In my mind's eye, I see clearly (PERSON'S NAME) face and body standing before me. I realise in my heart, that the image I have just created, cannot hurt or harm me in any way. I have the power to control what happens in this situation. As I continue to look at (HIM/HER), something strange eventuates. (HE/SHE) is shrinking in size but not only that, (HE/SHE) is becoming younger. Very soon, (PERSON'S NAME), appears before me as an innocent and frightened three year old child. Although (HE/SHE) has dramatically changed, I have not.

(PERSON'S NAME) looks up at me, with eyes pleading forgiveness for being so cruel to me. What am I to do? Can I possibly punish or physically hurt a young child? I can't. I consider myself to be a better person than that, where I don't need to resort to violence or anger of any kind to resolve personal conflicts. I then kneel down, where I place myself at (HIS/HER) level. (PERSON'S NAME) begins to cry uncontrollably. I reach out and hold both (HIS/HER) little hands in mine. This however, does not seem to console (PERSON'S NAME).

I then let go of (HIS/HER) hands, put my loving and nurturing arms around (HIM/HER) and hold (PERSON'S NAME) close to my beating heart. As I do this, I feel the warmth of (HIS/HER) tears falling upon my chest. I feel (HIS/HER) pain, anguish and sorrow. It's the same as mine. I stroke (PERSON'S NAME) hair and speak the only words (HE/SHE) wishes to hear, which is "(PERSON'S NAME), I forgive you". (HE/SHE) listens and (HIS/HER) crying stops. (PERSON'S NAME) then looks deeply at my face and kisses me on the cheek.

It is now my turn to cry. (HE/SHE) then says with all sincerity "(YOUR NAME), I am truly sorry for all the fear, pain and anguish I have put you through as a result of my own selfish and thoughtless actions. (YOUR NAME), you deserve better than that". I listen to (HIS/HER) words and believe it is time to let go of the past and all associated negative emotions and move on in a positive way. We give each other one last hug and kiss, before we go our separate ways and say goodbye.

I turn my back and walk away, leaving (PERSON'S NAME) to stand there, still as a three year old child. A child that no longer has the power to throw me in a state of panic each time I think about what happened. Something then compels me to turn around and take one last look. (HE/SHE) is still there watching, as (HE/SHE) waves me goodbye but (PERSON'S NAME) is not alone. Standing beside (HIM/HER) and holding (HIS/HER) hand, is (PERSON'S NAME) Guardian Angel, who is there to guide (HIM/HER) to discover true enlightenment and respect, as well as helping (PERSON'S NAME) to live a more honest and better way of existence in general.

Knowing that we will both be okay, I once again turn and walk away. Leaving (HIM/HER) with only love, peace and hope within my heart and from this moment on, I shall vow to always remember (PERSON'S NAME) as a three year old child, who kissed me on the cheek and told me (HE/SHE) was sorry.

Source: Shontara

Affirmations

*I TRUST MY POSITIVE FEELINGS, more than I do
my negative emotions.*

*I AM NOT AFRAID TO EXPERIENCE
the whole range of emotions.*

If in doubt, chuck it out.

PAUL

Please

Assist

Us

Lord

My name is Saul. I was later to become known as Paul. I am a Roman citizen but was born a Jew. As a boy, I was required to fetch water from the well in an earthenware jug and felt annoyed at having to do such chores. I wished that I was somewhere else. Many hours were spent in drawing and painting. I would also spend some time within the village market place, playing with my ball. I often wished I was like the other children but knew I was different. I felt restless. I had a thirst for knowledge and was eager to speak and listen to others, to guide and to teach.

Quite often as a man, I could be found sitting on a rock with people gathered around; men and children. I had a special empathy for the children. Enjoyed spreading the word, it gave me much pleasure and satisfaction. I didn't need to see in order to believe. I wanted so much to be part of the group and was willing to do anything to be of service. I am strong-willed and proud, compassionate and had a good ear. I would listen intently to others and then looked beyond that which I simply heard. I could see clearly the root of all problems and was able to cut to the chase quickly. I was discerning and perceptive.

I possessed and expressed unconditional love for Jesus, without knowing why I felt this way. I accepted it as my fate. There must be some higher purpose. Who am I to question the Son of God? His Will, be done. I explored the hearts of others with enthusiasm. I later joined the Apostles after the death of Jesus.

I'm so tired and quite devastated that I have lived for so

long. My Master had only 33 short years in which to achieve a purpose that would have taken any normal man, like myself, hundreds of years to complete. Why did he have to suffer alone? Why not I, too? To die in one's sleep is no great honour, in my eyes at least, not then. I wanted to be a martyr and felt that I had to follow in Christ's footprints, every step of the way, even to the last breath. But I had to learn that I can only be me and my life's purpose differed from his.

This did not mean that my life had less meaning or less value. It just was. I had to learn how to feel comfortable about living with my own shadow. Jesus wished for all of his chosen ones to continue his work but not at the expense of losing our true identity. We were all human beings who aspired to be like God, which can never be achieved, not in a physical sense anyway. What I am saying here is that each one of us must set realistic goals and expectations of ourselves; otherwise we shall live only with bitter disappointment, which will lay in ambush, waiting for us to turn that next corner.

My travelling companion was a Tanzanian; a black man in his 20-30s who was most faithful and loyal to me. He wore a square shaped cap on head, covered in many different coloured materials – thick stripes in the colours of red, yellow and black. He wore a robe of the same colours, draped over one shoulder. No shoes. He carried a shepherd's crook as he was a sheep herder. A Moor by nationality, he was one of a Muslim people of mixed Berber and Arab descent that were based in North Africa.

Because I didn't have a large family, I learnt from a young age how important it is to value and cherish those family members you do have because you never know when it might be their last moment on Earth. I've seen so much heartache and misunderstandings arise within the family unit because of stubborn pride, unwillingness to compromise and lack of desire to change one's own negative attitude and fixed picture. I am so glad I was not brought up in the type of environment just described. Much harm can be done, especially to children.

If they don't receive a physical battering, they certainly receive it on an emotional or mental level. This can sometimes scar them for life and as they grow up to become an adult, they then repeat the same destructive behavioural patterns of either one or both their parents. As a legacy to their own children who come after them, they freely pass it on for them to deal with in the best way that they can. The belief held with each generation is – 'it's not my problem. My only focus needs to be with today. Tomorrow, someone else can handle it.'

Well this attitude is all well and good but these same individuals never stop to think that tomorrow never comes, where nothing gets done, until one day there is born into that family, a shining star that will bring about great change for the better.

Jesus was one such shining star burning bright, well into the night. He was born to bring about change and those people yearning for the same thing as he chose to stop, listen and hear his words. Then they left to put the information about transformation into practical use in their personal and daily life.

Some already enlightened folks stayed to learn so much more. Like his disciples who later became The Apostles. But a disciple is not only a follower without a mind of their own. Jesus encouraged each one of us to think for ourselves and to maintain our individuality while working harmoniously together as a team. This wasn't always easy but we were a band of tough, determined and mainly merry men whose common desire was to never lose sight of the final goal ahead and to never give in to those negative forces that surrounded us from time to time. We were not pampered or spoilt as some would like you to believe.

Because Jesus gathered us together in his name, didn't automatically protect us from experiencing our own sleeping demons that disguised themselves as a variety of different fears. Even Jesus had certain fears that plagued him but he was taught from early on how to not allow those same fears to control him. The moment you give in to your fears, is when your life can easily become unravelled like a ball of wool.

To heal oneself is the greatest gift. Everyone has this ability but there are some who choose not to believe this. They would prefer to pass on the responsibility of their own good health and wellbeing upon the shoulders of another. That way, if things don't go according to plan, they then have someone else to blame because to accept this responsibility themselves, would then be too painful to contemplate or comprehend.

Doctors are trained to look after the welfare of others and it can sometimes be a real heavy burden when they see the same people over and over again, especially for those doctors who genuinely care about their patients. They enthusiastically get rid of one problem for their clientele and sometimes, quite literally overnight, up pops another. It's like the person who requires a healing is trapped within a never ending revolving door that is of their own making. They are merely passing time, forever going in circles, being shoved from pillar to post, never being able to break the cycle of ill health and stress.

Being sick occasionally is not a bad thing. It can be a most effective form of release. But when it becomes a regular habit pattern, like smoking or drinking, this can then cause real problems on a long term basis.

As a doctor, friend or relative, it is here that we need to ask ourselves what exactly is going on within, not only in the physical body that includes the heart and mind but also within that person's soul. How did their spirit get so damaged? How can it be fixed, if at all?

Why does God appear to have favourites where some are protected regardless of whatever negative habit patterns they have created for themselves, while others who apparently on the surface do much good have to suffer? What separates these two groups?

Well firstly, God has no favourites and when we look at and diagnose ourselves or a person who is ill or feels ill at ease, we merely tend to scratch the surface and never bother going too deep because that takes time and effort, not to mention an unshakeable discipline, courage and determination. Like an infected tooth that's gone bad, it needs to be eradicated; where a physical operation must be undertaken. But if only the tooth is taken without its root cause, then the operation cannot be considered as being successful.

It's much like gardening really. You bend down to pull out a stubborn old weed that is difficult to budge and all we get in our hand is what's seen on the surface but the root is still left behind, buried deep within the ground, ready for the next golden opportunity to manifest itself again. But if only we had taken the time to equip ourselves with the appropriate tools, we could have dug deep around it. That would loosen it from its foundations and where at a certain point, the weed would passively be extracted, roots and all.

Without this digging around process, we may never get to truly see how far the real problem goes. Physical illness is not contained within the physical body alone. It starts within our aura, that energy field that surrounds us and each aura is unique. No two auras can ever be the same, like our fingerprints. The condition of our aura will either make us or break us.

Certainly, there are many enlightened souls who are aware of this partnership or connection between the physical form and their spirit self. But there are still just as many people who are not so aware and love nothing better than to complain and blame their family, doctors or God and anyone else who gets in their way of achieving good health and happiness, for not being more sympathetic and supportive. 'Woe is me. I think I'll go down to the garden and eat some worms.' Which reminds me – it's not always what we eat or drink that causes us harm. It's our thought processes that count, as we absorb them readily into our mind that in turn, later affects the body in a negative way.

For example, if you feel guilt, blame or anger and believe you are a bad person for eating or drinking something you think you shouldn't, you are first creating and then later living this self-fulfilling prophecy and which will cause many physical disasters in the future. It's like we automatically turn what is good into something bad. It started off good because we wanted it. For whatever reason, it doesn't matter. We then place it in our mouth and then that moment of sheer indulgence is ruined as we then feel guilty for enjoying what it is that we have freely taken. By this time, it then becomes like poison and we are forced to swallow it whole, whether we want to or not. It's too late to turn back now. That poison then collects and grows within our bodies while we promise ourselves, we will never do this again – until the next time, and believe me there will always be a next time, where the cycle of destruction begins again due to our negative thoughts.

The same can be said about relationships with ourselves and other people. Because of our own degree of guilt, anger and blame, we set out from day one to destroy it by our thoughts alone, although we are not always consciously aware of these negative thinking patterns as they can remain hidden from view, buried deep within, like the weed. But with proper nourishment of mind, body and soul, we can blossom and become the rose.

To give a smile or to hold a person's hand when they are stressed or ill can be a great healing for the one who is receiving it. Sometimes we feel we don't give much of our time or energy to others but this may not be the truth at all. We can achieve great things without our knowledge or conscious thought and it can sometimes take a second or two. And when you add all these little seconds up at the end of a lifetime, the amount of energy given to care about the welfare of another could astound you.

We may also think we are not worthy of receiving such glowing praise or genuine thanks from other people but I say, accept it anyway. This is their gift to you. Don't reject those things that can be of benefit. This particular group of people think that to accept such gifts, including public recognition of the good works they do is not being humble or modest about their accomplishments. They would say that it is quite egotistical but I believe that if you are not the one actively seeking out such rewards and people still naturally want to commend you for your outstanding efforts in your family, workplace or the general community, it is not wrong to enjoy that moment of glory. Be appreciative without the desire or expectation of it happening again and again. Don't hide your light behind a bushel. It is your inner light and love for yourself and others which is greatly needed in this world of chaos and uncertainty.

Those poor souls seeking answers to their problems and prayers need someone who can show them the way out of their misery and suffering. Jesus did this exceptionally well and his Apostles tried to follow in his footsteps as closely and as humanly possible but sometimes we failed, as you will too upon occasion. The secret is not to beat yourself up over your mistakes. Acknowledge, accept, let go and learn. And this rule of thumb can be applied to having and keeping a good and long term relationship or friendship. For many, this still remains a mystery because most people still prefer to dwell upon the negative aspects only, while skimming quickly over the good times.

If something goes wrong, then it must mean that someone is to blame whether it be the other person's fault or their own. Some take it even further and blame God for all of their problems. But I say why must the negative emotion of blame or guilt be placed upon the shoulders of either party?

In my eyes, forgiveness is a far better option to run and play with. This creates less stress and anxiety for everyone concerned which leads to mental, emotional, spiritual and physical wellbeing. When this golden day arrives, doctors and healers will no longer be required.

In my free time, which became a lot less as I got older because of my personal commitment to the spirit and philosophy of Jesus, I loved working with clay and stone. The latter of which is not the easiest medium to work with but was the most fulfilling for me. And other than experiencing the joy of working with what Mother Earth provided, the finished item would be practical as well, that I could easily use in my daily life. In particular, the pottery pieces such as plates, jugs and cups, have not stood up to the test of time, as they were easily breakable. Although, some of the larger carved stone pieces I made still exist today and each time I come across them, I have to have an internal chuckle to myself as I cast my mind back thinking 'I remember when ...' as you do, when reflecting upon the past.

But our memories can be selective, where we only recall what we wish to and even then, over the years, fact is sometimes replaced by pleasant fantasy in order for us to accept the real situation. Although some will swing in the opposite direction by visualising an event far worse than was actually the case. Both sides of the same coin are not a good place to be. We need to deal with the reality rather than our imaginations, although I am not saying that imagination has no role to play in our lives either. Because, it is within our minds that we create not only miracles of manifestation but this is where we can create our future as well.

Let's face it, if there was no imagination or creativity in the minds of men, then who would have invented such things as the wheel, the phone, the discovery of fire and electricity, jewellery, the plane, automobile, as well as the cure for many of our physical diseases. The list is endless, as are the possibilities. Many science fiction books have been written and many sci-fi movies made have later become science fact. We can't change our history. We can only learn from it and pray we don't continue to make the same mistakes and believe me, I made many mistakes; when I would sometimes have cause to think 'what a blundering fool I am'.

This type of undermining thought didn't make things any better for me or bring about positive change. Instead it had the opposite effect where it caused me to stand still but thankfully, due to my obligations, duties and lifestyle, I never felt trapped for too long in this place where nothing happens and everything passes by. And because I lived till a ripe old age, my apparently foolish ways could not have been all that bad, otherwise I would not have survived for so long; as it will be for you too.

Stop going in circles because of your desire to chase your own tail – that's located behind you (that is if you had one). This relates to NOT wanting to let go of your past and to move in a forward direction that relates to the future.

We are but like sheep sometimes, where the majority of the populace of each great nation becomes a bunch of followers rather than leaders, although this is now changing and it has been changing as the centuries increase.

Jesus never wished for us to cling desperately onto his coat tails. By doing so, we would have held him back. Instead, he taught the importance of being independent, self-reliant, compassionate, secure and decisive. These qualities and more are those which lend themselves to a happy and longer lasting life filled with great contentment, inner peace, joy, purpose and meaning.

And who hasn't asked themselves the age old question at some time in their life – 'what's my purpose and what am I doing here?' Some may never receive their answer, while others may become obsessed by it. They then create such a busy life, forever searching and where they lose sight of their original goal, which is to just simply be – 'I AM'.

Don't allow lack of imagination to limit your success. Disbelief in one's own abilities can hold us back quite dramatically from fulfilling our life's purpose and wouldn't that be a crying shame? Yes, I know it's easy for me to talk when none of this really matters in the Spirit world but it does. What we think or feel and not necessarily what we do or don't do in our physical world does determine where we gravitate to, once we rejoin the world of Spirit. This will determine our future life back on Earth or some other planet within the Cosmos, if that is our choice.

If we are not careful, due to our natural desire to turn even the positives into a negative, we will find ourselves in quite a hostile, volatile and scary environment and the only hope for escape lies with believing in one's own self-worth again.

You need to understand that in your world as you know it now; there can be a marked difference between what our heart truly feels about ourselves and others as opposed to what our mind thinks we want or need. In other words, if the thoughts and feelings don't harmoniously correspond and match up with each other, conflict and inner turmoil is created; where indeed our perceived Heaven all of a sudden can become a living and permanent Hell.

As we continuously think or feel one thing but do the opposite, much strife is caused and we have no-one to thank but ourselves. A pure and happy heart can always connect to the God source. An angry, begrudging and confused one separates us from receiving only the best. There are always two ways of looking at something or someone and that is where freedom of choice comes into it. If we choose to hang ourselves with the lifeline given rather than using it as a tool to get further ahead in life, is our responsibility. Certainly, as Paul and in many other lifetimes I had before and since, I had fears that would threaten to separate me from my God, but I endeavoured to fight and claw my way back into the light.

The light was where I naturally preferred to stay, although the time spent in darkness can also teach us some valuable lessons if we listen properly. And if we take action upon receiving that lesson, the darkness is then transformed into light. How long or short a time we choose to stay in our self-imposed darkness depends greatly upon our own thought patterns and belief structures. We can't blame God or anybody else for our misfortunes and where we end up. We create our own journey towards either self-discovery or self-destruction. The brain that houses our thought processes is certainly a complex piece of machinery and, like the heart, it needs proper nourishment in order to function properly.

By withholding what it needs to grow and prosper, the brain will eventually cease up and die. Much in the same way that a broken, unforgiving and unrelenting heart can result in premature death if positive healing principals are not applied soon after it needed mending. To place a bandaid on it is a short term, quick fix solution; it is not enough to ensure complete and long term peace, contentment, success and happiness.

Fear of Abuse

Abuse can take many forms as there are varying degrees but if you are a victim of abuse, this piece of information is cold comfort to you. As far as the victim is concerned, they would say – 'abuse is abuse and I don't give a damned about the differences, I just want it to stop.' There is physical, verbal, emotional and spiritual abuse. We have already talked elsewhere in this book about the fears of being powerless, judgement and persecution, where the actual abuse is how it's implemented.

Physical abuse, rape, incest and domestic violence are strongly on the increase, while verbal and emotional abuse has been going on for centuries, as has the withdrawal of a person's right to follow and perform certain religious and spiritual ceremonies without some form of interference from the authorities. In regards to this latter form of abuse, there is more tolerance today than what there was before in our dim, dark and distant past, although still it has not been totally eradicated. So, as an individual, how can you stop it from happening to you?

Firstly and most importantly, you destroy all traces of this fear from your heart because the more you allow it to control your every thought, feeling and action, the more likelihood you are of attracting it. Beware of the possible dangers you or your loved ones may face in all situations but give this thought your lowest priority. When these thoughts become an obsession, this is when you can expect trouble. Our thought patterns, like money, are another form of energy that can manipulate and control our every movement. If you consistently allow this fear to be your close companion and confidante, you will manifest it and sometimes it will be worse than what you first imagined.

The majority of those people who have no idea what they are creating for themselves understand little or nothing about the powerful magic of manifestation. At the end of this section and before the affirmations, Shontara has included an invocation or prayer that when done properly, will help you comprehend and accept the power that I have just talked about. At any time, you can create your own good or bad magic, according to your original thought and intent and you don't have to be a witch, wizard or warlock to do it.

That is why we strongly suggest you stop and listen for a while to your self-talk. In which direction does it flow? Is it pleasant to listen to or do you feel anxious and uptight? If you wish harm on another, that harm will come back to you. Perhaps not from the original person you felt badly of but it will return with a vengeance and often from the most unsuspecting quarter.

And when this bad magic you initially created finally gets back to you, you won't be expecting it. This will come as a horrifying shock to the system that will make you feel sick to the stomach each time you think about what has happened and possibly is still happening. Then you will cry, scream and shout – 'I never asked for this.' But there is no beating the laws of karma. There is a Bible saying that says it well – "as you sow, so you shall reap".

Be careful about what you think and expect the unexpected but also realise the unexpected may not always be good and as such, you may not always like what you receive. And please don't believe for a minute that this is a form of punishment for you thinking consistently bad thoughts about yourself and others.

It's another lesson for you to understand what it's like to walk humbly in another man's shoes. They may feel uncomfortable and awkward at first but the more you relax into their shoes, the more they can be stretched to fit your personality. When you fight every pinch, blister or cut, you will feel much pain and the shoes will remain locked upon your feet until you are ready to listen and accept your lesson about the identity of that other person.

Then you can be released into the wild and roam free like a tiger, until the next time your thoughts do you in. Of course, there will always be people who will make you angry from time to time but don't hold on to this thought for too long. Don't hold grudges. You will drown if you do but before that can happen; you will only ever know what it's like to be a victim of abuse. Certainly those others may have held the sword that penetrated deep into your heart and made you bleed profusely but it was you who handed them the sword in the first place. So take it back, reclaim power over your own mind and use this for your highest good; to destroy those poisonous thoughts that consume you.

As you are now an adult reading this book, try and ensure from now on, not to accept and develop any more bad habit patterns or mistakes your parents or guardians chose to live out for themselves. Within each family, the next generation we give birth to should be better than our own. In reality, this has not always been the case but once again, it is slowly changing where the old new souls coming through on this special wave of energy are highly intelligent, intuitive and secure. This is good news for those souls who have already chosen to enter the physical realm a generation after.

These children are our future. Implore them to be respectful and independent. Don't expose them to the same cycle of abuse you were subjected to by thrusting your problems into their face and transferring them on to their little shoulders. The sheer weight could crush their fragile spirit and by doing so (although it is not always done intentionally), they are forced to carry not only their load but yours as well. This means that you need to be more respectful of their needs rather than only thinking about your own.

Look ahead to the years that are to come. If you truly wish for your flesh and blood to know the type of peace that you have only glanced at and experienced briefly, they must be taught to act and make decisions different to you and from an early age. Your children will then learn how to stand in their own space that contains only their energy and truth, rather than absorbing all the other rubbish picked up from those around them. After the age of seven, the die has already been cast and set. Don't believe for one minute that they are too young to have the capacity to comprehend complex emotional or spiritual issues, as well as never underestimating their inner strength. It is as strong as yours, if you allow it to be.

Also allow your children, young nephews, nieces and cousins to explore their own truth in their own time and not in yours. If you are a parent, as you tuck them into bed at night, take them through a visualisation rather than a bed time story (although it can appear to be read in the same way) that will help them to maintain that already close connection with Spirit. Reintroduce them to the angelic, fairy, mermaid and intergalactic realm, including leprechauns, genies, mythical make believe creatures and more, to their young hearts and ears. I say re-introduce rather than introduce because they already innately know of these things.

Learn to incorporate into this visualisation, lots of vivid colour, bright lights and soothing sounds, as well as protection techniques. And if you are not all that imaginative in creating a child's visualisation from scratch, turn to your child for assistance during the day and ask for their input into their own 'story' to be read later that night. Whatever positive image they come up with, include it. This will give them a sense of contributing towards the creation of something they can hold on to and sleep with, which will only enhance and improve the knowledge and wisdom they have already bought with them into this world and which can be implemented in a positive, constructive, safe and practical way. Even if you think the idea is a bit bizarre and is not to your personal taste or belief, don't reject it. Remember, this is their story, not yours and if it makes them feel all happy and giggly, it can't be all that bad.

But what's all this got to do with the fear of abuse? I am merely trying to come up with some gentle, creative ways and means that your children can use to safeguard themselves from becoming abused and mistreated later in life. By incorporating such techniques and visualisations into their daily routine at an early age, the pattern will be set for them to come up with creative and innovative energetic solutions to complex physical and emotional problems they may have to face later as an adult.

Teach them young and they will thank you in the future. Because your parents never showed you what to do and how to protect yourself properly, is this any reason why you should deny your offspring the best and which you can bestow upon them as a gift?

To set your feet upon the right track, let's think about those things that give our children pleasure and then start building upon our visualisation from there. Bear in mind, we need to keep it simple, short and sweet because some won't be able to concentrate for the same length of time as an adult can. When you read the following visualisation out loud to yourself that I have created and depending upon how fast or slow you read, this takes approximately 10 minutes but you have my permission to shorten it if necessary.

It is merely a gentle guide that you can use but it is good to give the children some variety, otherwise they are more than likely to get bored if you present to them only the one story; not forgetting my previous suggestion for you to receive your child's input towards creating their own meditation.

Without further introduction, here's a list of other possible characters and events that could be implemented (not mentioning again what has been suggested before):

- The name of their pet dog, cat, fish, rabbit, guinea pig, bird or snake;
- Their love of nature that incorporates the use of flowers, trees, grass, sky, mountains and oceans etc;
- Real people they already know and trust (adults, siblings and peers);
- Make them the central figure of their own story;
- Popular music and nursery rhymes they are aware of (have them sing or hum along with you);
- Eating handfuls of dirt and making mud pies;
- Singing and dancing in the rain;

- Painting pictures (on walls, fences, paper and themselves);
- Baking a cake and licking the bowl using their tongue and fingers;
- Riding a bicycle;
- Building sandcastles at the beach;
- Swimming; and
- To travel the world in a hot air balloon etc.

I have many more ideas but I hope I have inspired you enough to continue where I left off. I hope you now enjoy what follows, keeping in mind that you can change the names and gender accordingly to suit your family circumstances:

"Once upon a time, there was a pretty little girl by the name of Crystal. One day, she wandered far from home but she was not frightened. Soon she found herself in a large field of long blue grass and bright yellow sunflowers that was complimented by a purple sky. A row of volcanic mountains standing in the background could be seen. Both the sun and moon were up and frolicking about. The man in the moon took time out from playing with the sun to wink at Crystal and she waved gaily back.

After saying hullo to the sun and moon, Crystal then ran barefoot through this field of flowers with great enthusiasm, enjoying the freedom, the coolness of the grass against her skin and the dirt between her toes. She stopped suddenly and spun around and around on the one spot that caused her to become dizzy and fall with the sounds of happy laughter coming from her lips.

Crystal, once having picked herself up, began talking to

the flowers, seeking some sensible advice. Not to her surprise, the flowers more than willingly answered her questions, fears and concerns. 'What a wonderful way to pass the time of day,' Crystal thought. 'This is so much better than doing some dull and boring homework each night.'

There was one flower in particular that Crystal felt drawn to approach more than the others. This flower's name was Angelica. She was so beautiful, just like Crystal. They were giving each other a quiet hug when suddenly another person Crystal didn't like or trust, approached this sacred space.

Crystal felt threatened and became frightened. All she wanted to do was run but Angelica, through her powers, made Crystal stay where she was and tried to reassure the little girl that she had nothing to fear here and that part of Angelica's duty was to protect her from all forms of evil.

Crystal then gazed into the heart of Angelica and saw her friend was speaking the truth. Crystal was now feeling better and was ready to face her intruder with a sense of real peace, calmness and security. Crystal turned to look at him. His name was Richard and he was so much bigger, taller and meaner than her. Normally this would have bothered Crystal but today, with Angelica and all the other Spirit flowers on her side, Crystal felt an inner strength she had never felt before. Meanwhile, Angelica called upon her own friend and protector – the fire breathing, white, multi-winged dragon to assist in taking Richard away from their presence, who was to be later returned to them as a whole different person.

The dragon's name was Puffy. At the sight of this scary looking creature, Richard wet his pants with fear and *screamed, as Puffy flew down and picked him up between his razor sharp claws and flew off in the direction of the mountains. Crystal and Angelica watched in awe, knowing that Richard would remain unharmed but reawakened. Puffy and Richard flew directly above one of the active volcanoes that Crystal and Angelica could see in the distance. This is where Puffy offloaded his human cargo. There was nothing poor Richard could do except to pray for his survival. It seemed to Richard that there was no end to his fall and to his amazement, Richard discovered the fire did not burn or even kill him.*

It merely cleansed and purified his negative and abusive energy that if left unchanged over a long period, could do much physical and irreparable harm to Crystal. When the time was right, Puffy then flew down, deep into the volcano to save Richard but Puffy had no fear for his own safety as he passed through the white hot flames that licked his body and wings with glee, as this was Puffy's home base. Richard was ever so grateful to see Puffy again and thanked him, as he was flung up and out from the fiery belly of the volcano.

On the way out, Richard noticed he had been transformed into a pure white snowflake that had the power not to melt upon contact with any form of heat but what happened to his human form? Will he ever know himself again as he was? As he could do nothing about his situation, Richard decided to hitch a ride on Puffy's back where both dragon and snowflake returned to Crystal and Angelica, who were expecting them. Richard was unceremoniously dropped at Crystal's feet. His meanness (not to mention his size) had all but evaporated, so Crystal once again was able to take control of the situation that once scared her.

> *Crystal bent down to pick up Richard and tenderly put him in the palm of her hand. She then placed him in her top pocket located just above her heart and that is where Richard and any others who tried to hurt her in the future would stay.*
>
> *And from that day on, she made sure to visit the field of blue grass and yellow sunflowers every day as she first awoke and the very last thing before she fell asleep each night.*
>
> *Her newfound Spirit friends were always there waiting for her and Crystal knew she could rely upon and share a hug or two with them when needed. As was Puffy, the magical mythical dragon who would become her protector and best friend and so it came to pass."*

Just one last word on the above – although this has been written for children in mind initially, this is not to say that adults can't do this same visualisation and expect to feel and see positive and real results of doing it on a regular basis. The miracle of manifestation must first be created within the mind which can then later be bought into your physical reality. Believe and it will be.

In case you haven't already figured it out, this particular section of the book will go into the various protection methods you can use on an energetic level to stop all types and degrees of abuse. Some of them you will recognise, especially if you have already worked with Shontara and because of this, you may think they are her words and not mine but who do you think gave her these insights and ideas in the first place? I can see thirteen hands and more arising all around me, all claiming ownership of these creative solutions. This is because we all speak with the one voice.

To give you a good example of where this could happen in your life (or if not in yours, you know of someone it has happened to), is where you have a close and honest relationship or friendship with another and where you don't even have to utter a single word and they answer your unspoken question or move into action without having to be asked in a verbal sense. In that situation, what do you think is happening?

The simple answer is that their energies have melded together to become one mind, heart and soul. This is what has happened with Shontara and us, because we as a team (and that includes Shontara) have agreed that it will be so. Now let's get back to the matter at hand:

Imagine if you will, the person causing you great pain and fear, standing or sitting opposite you. Next build a wall of mirrors around yourself. This will be your protection but have the mirrors reflect outwards (that is, away from yourself). These mirrors are your shield of armour. The third step would be to create another separate wall of mirrors around the person who is attacking you in whichever way but this time, turn the mirror inwards, where the person is then forced to look upon their own nasty reflection being bounced back at them. I can guarantee they won't like what they see and this will make them feel even more uncomfortable, which they will direct at themselves and not at you.

Once these mirrors have been inverted around the other person, the very instant a negative thought form tries to escape its barrier and do harm to either yourself or other people, it will find it can't leave. It becomes trapped within the owner's force-field and must return to sender. The person won't like this either but it is still an effective form of protection for you. But there is more.

You must then claim either out loud or in your mind – "I do not accept this anger (or whatever emotion it may be), this anger is not mine, I gladly give it back to its rightful owner with God's love and blessing".

Repeat this prayer or affirmation three times (or more if you feel you need to), by the end of which you will begin to feel better about yourself and where you will feel you are more in control of the situation.

The next step is to do with developing forgiveness and compassion for the one who is scaring and distressing you. You can do this by creating within their wall of mirrors an image of an Angel, God, Jesus, Buddha or any other Spirit being you feel is stronger than you. You direct your next words to them, which are – "Please, take this anger from this person's heart immediately, shoot it back out to the Universe for purification purposes and transform it into another emotion that is pure and good. Once this transformation is complete, return it to them, again with God's love and blessing".

If this person is physically present when you do it, very quickly you will recognise a visible difference in their attitude towards you and if that way inclined, you will feel a great undercurrent of calmness descend upon both of you. This particular technique has the power to diffuse potentially volatile and explosive situations before they arise. You don't have to believe in its effectiveness now. The proof will come with the practise of it later.

You can do the above when your physical body is in pain

as well. You may not know why or where it is coming from but sometimes the pain we feel does not belong to us. Try this technique then and the pain will miraculously disappear, that is, if you do not claim ownership to it. Try it with the next headache you get. Give your pain a physical form and behold the near instantaneous results.

You can even use this same technique for those other people you might be concerned about. For example, your neighbours have the most horrendous verbal and physical fights nearly every night, while their children watch on frightened. The police are called but it continues. What do you do? Do you sit and stress out about what is going on next door or do you close the curtains, shut the doors and windows and try to ignore what you hear. Rather than being a passive observer or listener as the case may be, take action next time by sending your spirit energy to your neighbours place.

Picture them in your mind, fighting with each other. Create the wall of mirrors around them both and do this technique (including the affirmations) three times for both of them. Then stop and count how long it is before everything calms down again. It won't be too long, at which point, you can have a little chuckle, give yourself a pat on the back and feel satisfied that you were able to take control of that situation without getting physically involved. Because if you had dragged your body over there to see if you could help, you would then have run the real risk of being physically hurt.

By doing it in the way I suggested, you stay detached, separate and safe, while no-one else is none the wiser, except you and your God of course. A further adaptation of this mirror technique is to find a photo if you can of the person causing you trouble. If you don't have such a photograph, then on a piece of white paper, write their name and if you don't know their name, make one up for them. Spirit knows where the energy is to be directed. Then stick it on your mirror, face or name down and leave it there, until things have changed. The moment the trouble returns, put it back up again. It does work.

And here now is something that comes direct from St Germaine. It is too effective not to speak about it. Visualise your aggressor seated, standing or lying down in a raging purple fire. Then repeat the following invocation several times or until you see or feel the scene has changed for the better. Of course, fifteen minutes would be preferable and later I will explain why. So what are the words you need to say – "Bruce is a being of violet fire, Bruce is the purity God desires". That's it, no more and no less, short and sweet, easy to remember. And as you might have noticed, always put the person's name into the picture but when you are doing it for yourself, revert back to the first person by stating – 'I am'.

If you have lots of people in your life causing you misery and in order to save yourself a bit of time, don't visualise them separately. Put them together to form one big group, all immersed in the violet fire. Again, change the wording to adapt to this new situation by saying – 'they are' instead of the individual's name.

Then take note of their reactions when next you meet but in order for this technique to work (like many of the others that have already been shared with you), this requires consistency on your part, so permanent change can then come about.

Let's take a look at the suggested fifteen minute time frame to be spent in any one session. After this amount of time, you would have raised your vibration to a much higher level than when you first started. For it is there we can then move in closer to your energy and clearly communicate with you, which you will be consciously aware of.

The following is a true story that was told to Shontara by a third person. It took place in America (although the country has really nothing to do with anything, I just thought I would mention it). A meditation circle was happening one night. About a dozen people were in attendance and they had just finished doing this violet fire affirmation/mantra for a bit more than fifteen minutes. The lights were on and they were sitting still, enjoying the peace that had come over them. In walks someone who was late.

This person saw no-one, so dovetailed it out of there, switched off the light, closed the door and walked away. They let him go. This group was within clear sight of the person who walked in late but because their collective vibration was on another level totally different from the third party who joined later, that is why they could not be seen.

We are not saying this group disappeared or evaporated into thin air but what we are saying is that the person looking for them could not see what was in front of them because their vibration was set at a much lower level. This is a true story. This technique can also be taken to your busy city streets.

Whether you are a pedestrian or a driver, in your mind see yourself immersed in the violet fire and mentally affirm the abovementioned 'first person' words. The crowd of people or cars will sense your presence and because of this, they will move out of your way and give you the clearance you need to travel in your chosen direction without being hindered and stopped by others.

Some people will find it difficult to hold any sort of image for such a long period of time. This is okay. Remember, it's your intent that matters, nothing else. And lastly, this technique can easily be adapted by you visualising another person who is requiring a little help because they are sick, injured, depressed, dying or recovering from an operation.

If done on a regular basis, this will quicken the healing process for these people. They'll be amazed, along with their doctor, as to how quickly they get better. Of course, if it's not your place to do this for them, the healing energy you put out there will return to you and nothing will happen. This doesn't mean you failed. It wasn't meant to be and no harm is done.

The other valuable method of protection against all forms of abuse is to use water. This life saving liquid is symbolic of Spirit. Write the person's name on a slip of paper or better still, use a photograph. Place this object into a bowl of water. Position your hand over the bowl, container or glass and repeat three times the following – "In the name of Jesus Christ and with your blood, I bless and purify this water and Caroline". Once done, carry it carefully to your fridge. Open your freezer door and place it gently in a position where it won't get knocked over easily. Leave it to freeze. By doing so, you are putting them on ice; where all negative energy becomes powerless and invalid for as long as it is frozen. Then forget about it.

Leave for at least three weeks in your freezer. Mark it on your calendar if you need a visible reminder. At the end of which time, remove it. Let it thaw and once defrosted, take the photo or piece of paper and throw it directly into the rubbish bin, ready for collection by the garbage man later that week. This will then leave you with only the water. Pour it over your plants so they too may receive some benefit. It won't hurt them.

The other useful technique that can be done is to mentally

see the person you consider to be a disruption in your life and trap them in the centre of a huge block of ice, several metres thick. Ask the Archangels (or some other powerful being) to take it from your sight immediately and send it floating back out into the Cosmos. In time, the ice will melt and the person will eventually come back down to Earth minus any bad energy that he or she left with. Upon their return, they will have no desire to have any power or control over you.

Another adaptation would be to see them in your mind's eye, being led by their Angel into a body of water, where Jesus is waiting to baptise, anoint, cleanse and protect them. All hate and anger will instantly evaporate; that leaves you safe and secure next time you come in contact with each other. Another version would be where you see them taking a bath at the base of a waterfall, where all the dark and dirty energy they have collected over the centuries, is washed away downstream.

And if you want to protect not only yourself but the whole world as well, rise above planet Earth and see it awash with a shower of God's golden rain. Visualise the people standing outside in the rain, heads pointed to the sky, mouths open like hungry birds, in readiness to take into their bodies this purified water for their own healing. Some bright souls may even decide to collect this rain for future use by positioning large buckets (without holes) around them that they can carry to a safe place, for future implementation. There is so much you can do with water (Spirit). You are only limited by your imagination.

How many more visualisations can you think of? Don't forget to write them down, otherwise you could easily forget. Play with them. See which one works for you the best. And those that you feel uncomfortable in doing, don't do them again, but please keep and use what you do like.

All of what I have spoken about in this section could appear to be a bit 'hocus pocus' or 'mumbo jumbo' but don't let this deter you from experiencing its effectiveness. Some would even go so far as accusing us of practising the dubious art of 'witchcraft' or 'casting spells'. This is not true, although this would depend entirely upon your definition that you place upon the word 'witchcraft'. For some, it has good connotations, where there is nothing to be fearful of. While others will cringe inwardly, run a mile and who will get caught up in the myths and misunderstandings that surround this ancient art.

We are all working from the one energy source. This energy I speak of is not designed to scare but you are still free to use it in a bad or good way. The choice is yours. All of what I have been suggesting so far (including the other Apostles), have nothing to do with wanting to cause anyone harm and I am sure you can see this, if you have read the book in its entirety but there is more to come, for I am not the last to speak. Luke, Mark and Timothy will follow soon. We don't wish to control your thoughts and feelings. These need to remain exclusively your own property.

All we wish to do is make it easier for you. Why not make it easy for yourself too? We suggest you remove yourself from the 'victim' mentality. When you become conscious of falling into this trap, change your belief structure to incorporate the idea that you are victorious and that you deserve a medal for having to put up with this truckload of negativity for so long.

Martyrs and victims are born from the same mould and are of a similar vibration. Martyrs suffer a tremendous amount of torment that goes beyond the call of duty and victims do exactly the same thing. The only real difference between the two is that one is willing to suffer, while the other is not. The end result stays the same.

Besides which, who is going to thank you for this prolonged agony you have so unselfishly put yourself through? Not many, so please do not depend upon it. It will only add to your misery and pain. It's time you divorced yourself from the abuse you have been receiving. It's a lifestyle choice you don't need to accept. By walking away or standing your ground, will help the one used to getting their own way all the time, to realise they can't go on treating people in this manner. And if enough people do this in the life of the abuser, one day they will wake up and question their motives and how they do things.

Sometimes, if you are the one being abused, you have to realise that no amount of talking may help your abuser come around to see and accept your way of thinking. That is why we suggest working with them on a psychic, energetic level instead. Our Spirit energy is far stronger and more powerful than your own. I am not saying it is necessarily better but it is different and we can produce effective results in a lot less time than what you could ever do if working by yourself. Call upon us for help. We are available twenty four hours a day, seven days a week and three hundred and sixty five days a year and we won't even charge you a cent.

Allow us to lighten your load. Allow us to help you take away your fear. Allow us to lift you out of this eternal pit of despair. Allow us the freedom to take away your pain. So help me God. For this is my song.

And as I have been the last Apostle to speak here and on their behalf, we would all like to thank you for giving us the opportunity of sharing our heart and some of our personal experiences with you. It truly has been an honour. May our words from the past, help you today become a much happier, healthier, stronger, wiser and more abundant person than what you were yesterday. And here is one last message from us – use this book as a continual reference guide for your future. Refer to it when needed. You will always find the answer that you need. The trick is, not to reject it. This however is your choice and we place no restrictions or conditions upon what you do or do not accept from within.

    Now what follows is the voices of our friends – Luke, Mark and Timothy. Enjoy.

Invocation Prayer

(Adaptation – see below)

In the name of Jesus Christ
I invoke the Light of Christ within
I am a clear and perfect channel
for God I am
and Divine Light is my Guide

In the name of Jesus Christ
(PERSON'S NAME) invokes the Light of Christ within
(PERSON'S NAME) is a clear and perfect channel
for God (HE/SHE) is
and Divine Light is (PERSON'S NAME) Guide

Source: Dael Walker
Adaptation: Shontara

Affirmations

*I take POSITIVE AND CONSTRUCTIVE ACTION
to defend myself when necessary.*

I have no fear of attack.

NO ONE CAN TRULY HURT ME *except myself.*

Part 3

Our Friends

LUKE

Let us shine our

Unique light across the world, filled with an abundance of

Kindness, love, compassion, acceptance and

Enthusiasm for our fellow travellers in life.

When I felt nervous or fearful, I began to hum or sing. This somehow soothed my nerves quite considerably. Where any repetitive sound or note made by another can be quite hypnotic to listen to and when you become part of that sound and fall into step with it, you blend into that person's energy pattern. Can you imagine if you have a group of like-minded people all focusing or speaking out loud the same positive thought at the same moment in time, what amazing things their combined energy could create for themselves? Of course, this same principle or power can be used for evil.

I guess it all boils down to personal choice and, whether we like it or not, God has given all his children unconditional free will to choose the light or dark path. Sometimes though, mankind can get carried away with themselves and forget this important fact, where they may begin to feel compelled to force change upon another, to do their bidding. It doesn't matter if we wish to have no part in the other person's plan.

Quite often, it can simply come down to a matter of survival where one must weigh up all the pros and cons of that change, forced or otherwise, and decide to either do or die. There are many ways to die. Some die as martyrs, others die as heroes. Some take the coward's way out while others face death bravely. Some are happy to die while others get angry and try desperately hard to avoid the big event, which then turns into a prolonged trip into agony rather than an ecstasy.

Death is a release. It's not an ending but a new beginning. So much emotional pain is attached to this single issue, although this depends greatly upon your nationality, cultural, religious and spiritual beliefs. Not everyone is afraid. But to kill another on purpose is a crime against humanity. When we kill in order to get what we want, we take on multiple roles of judge, jury and executioner, including God. How dare we presume such a position in such matters as life or death!

To make contact with the water, rocks, grass, mud and soil in bare feet gave me great pleasure. As a result, this part of my body can withstand a lot of punishment before having to seek out less painful playing grounds. They are hardened to cope better with the various stresses that I may find myself in.

So don't ever be afraid to expose yourself to a degree of pain. Some pain is good; it makes you a more resilient spirit. This ability is greatly needed today. Put under vast amounts of pressure and negativity, the weak will crumble and fall, while the strong will remain brave, loyal and free.

Inner strength is always more beneficial and fulfilling than pure physical strength and brute force alone. To have a balance of both inner and outer strength is a bonus and much good can be achieved. The same can be said for enthusiasm. The higher the degree, the more chance you have of doing something about your passion or dream while lack of enthusiasm can quite literally put you to sleep, where little can be done in your physical world. And if lack of motivation and imagination is not quite enough to put you to sleep completely, procrastination and indecision will quickly set in.

By putting off an inevitable decision, the matters at hand will always become much worse before they get better. It's fear and doubt that holds us back. So how can one possibly eliminate fear and doubt from one's life for good? I don't believe you can completely but they can be cut down to size quite dramatically by retraining the mind to think and act differently to the way you normally would.

For example, how quickly do you give in to the demands of a screaming baby or child? It's the same when you are confronted by loud and aggressive adults. What do you do if you don't agree to what they expect from you? Do you mirror back to them what is being projected on to you? Or do you immediately become subservient and do their bidding, no questions asked? If you have answered 'yes' to this last question, ask yourself – 'why do I do that?' There could be many answers, some of which could be:

- *I don't like causing waves;*
- *It's better to please than to upset;*
- *To keep the peace at whatever cost is important to me;*
- *My own needs must take second place, in situations such as this;*
- *I don't want to get beaten up;*
- *I'm a lover, not a fighter; and*
- *I'd do anything for some peace and quiet.*

How many of these above thought patterns are familiar to you and do you constantly play this record over and over again in your head to such an extent where you believe you have no better options or alternatives available to you? And because this is a habit pattern so well ingrained into your conscious thinking mind which is extremely difficult to break, do you then consequently feel trapped, angry, not fulfilled and lack direction?

It's best to learn not to react while standing your ground. This then becomes most annoying, frustrating and threatening to your aggressor and nine times out of ten, they will withdraw from baiting you.

I loved to cook and the more I cooked for, the merrier I got, believe it or not. Normally the preparation of food was left in the domain of women to a large extent but I would, from time to time, like to take charge and show them how it's done. My help may not have always been appreciated but they couldn't fault me upon the taste of what they put in their mouths or bellies.

To watch people eat the food that I prepared was a fascinating lesson in itself and would never take offence if I spied one who gobbled it down like there was no tomorrow, hardly pausing to take a breath, let alone actually taste what they were eating. I took it as a compliment.

I mean, the time to really worry is when they refuse to eat, but even then, I can't afford to get too upset about that either. Besides, their lack of appetite or rejection of what is being offered may have nothing to do with me but then again, it may have everything to do with me.

How often have you got all upset at someone you care about when they have said no to your offer of genuine help? Why is it so much easier to take no for an answer from a complete stranger? Is it because we don't really care or don't place too much importance about their opinions and feelings? How many actually stop to ask the person who said no, why? Are we afraid that their truth may involve us personally in some way?

As we choose to stay silent and not probe for the 'why' of the matter, we can then more easily shrug off their refusal or rejection and take no further responsibility for it. This is what I call, the – 'what you don't know won't hurt you' mentality. It's another form of protection really but it's also a way of not wishing to explore another person's sometimes harsh truth (whether they be friend, family, stranger or foe), as well as our own.

I largely travelled with the Apostle Paul and on one occasion in particular, I was sitting with my back to a large tree. In front of me, and spread out like an elaborate smorgasbord, were masses of people that consisted of men, women, boys and girls; all belonging to different age groups. Sometimes, even the animals that wandered by en route to their own destination would stop and take rest. These gatherings were like great family affairs, all joined at the heart. They were there because they wanted to be there. They had come for a message and Paul tried to ensure they were not disappointed. These gatherings could last from dawn to dusk.

It could also become mighty tiring and boring for all of us if Paul merely preached all day, so he made sure that there was much singing and laughter in between the serious talking. If it was all too heavy, the people could easily switch off to what was being said, so Paul tried hard for that not to happen. We both understood that talking was not enough to keep a crowd's attention. You somehow had to involve them in what you were speaking about. So you would conduct yourself in such a manner that would invite audience participation and one way to do that was to ask them questions. And so it is the same for you.

When you sit down at the dinner or breakfast table together as a family unit, is there one who insists on being in control of the conversation and who loves the sound of their own voice? Or is it all for one and one for all, happy pandemonium? As a child, or even as an adult, which table would you prefer to sit at? One situation is closed, rigid and controlling while the other is more open, flexible and accepting. In relation to communication with other people, which side of the pendulum do you swing on? Is there an equal amount of give and take, is it all take or is it all give?

Each person must learn that when communicating with only one other or a group, whether it be big or small, that in order to maintain balance and harmony, we need to know how to speak and listen properly. It's no good listening only to what we want to hear. Many husbands and wives today would either bitterly or laughingly complain that their partner has selective deafness, while the children will accuse their parents of never listening to them and complain they are so unfair. Everyone, no matter who it is or how young or old they are, all have the same desire to be listened to without harsh judgement and criticism.

To be ignored or laughed at can brutally crush our spirit easily if done too many times; where that particular speaker will clam up and withdraw into their shell and begin to keep a silent vigil. To pry them open again after being tightly shut for a long period of time, can be a difficult to near impossible task and much damage can be caused to the one staying quiet – both mentally, emotionally, spiritually and physically.

Then we have the person who talks all the time, never taking a breath and who receives no feedback whatsoever from the one being talked to, can be just as harmful. For the talker, it's like talking to a brick wall, never knowing if their message has been heard or not. This can lead to feelings of great frustration and annoyance to such an extent where the 'talker' may then have a strong desire to yell and stamp their feet, to grab the other person by the shoulders and give them a good shake or alternatively to 'punch their lights out', just to evoke a reaction, whether it be verbal or physical.

So please be sweet and learn to be a good speaker and listener at the same time. Everyone then wins and this is showing respect for yourself and others.

Due to an unnaturally high arch on my left foot, I found that I would tire easily and be in some pain if forced to walk for long periods of time. Because I did move around and travel long distances a great deal, I would take advantage when I could, of the donkey, as my preferred mode of transport. Although, the donkeys were mainly used to carry large loads of produce rather than people, unless those same people were extremely old or infirm. Meanwhile, the mothers or women in good health would carry the babies or young children on their back.

And when there weren't enough supply of donkeys to go around the number of needy, the really bad cases were then carried on makeshift stretchers made of wood and canvass. The strongest made sure that even the weakest link within the group survived for as long as possible. It was an unwritten law for the fittest to take care of the weak, elderly, sick or maimed in any way that they could and they did so happily and with no sense of guilt or obligation to the other person. Because those who were then the strongest knew that one day, there was always the possibility of them becoming incapable of looking after their own needs and that some day in the future, they may need to accept the offer of another person's help graciously.

But that was then and in some cultures today, but not many, this community spirit still exists but it has dropped off quite dramatically. The more modern and advanced man has become, they have also become rushed and selfish and where the welfare of those who have a problem, weakness or chronic physical or mental illnesses are passed on to an outsider to fix and look after. Or, if there is no solution, they are then to be locked away, never to be seen again.

The attitude today to a large extent is 'leave me alone; I

want nothing to do with them. Their problems are holding me back from moving forward with my own life.' These 'weakest links' become a burden rather than a joy. What is needed in these instances is much love, understanding, compassion and forgiveness.

I know it's painful and quite distressing emotionally to watch someone you love, fade away or destroy themselves before your very eyes and there's not a damned thing you can do about it. But have you stopped to look at the other side of the coin and take a moment to think about their pain because of you rejecting them?

In their hour, day, week, month or year of need, they have no-one to turn to and are then forced to face alone their worst nightmares of wandering around blind in a never ending darkness filled with demons of gigantic proportions. Some will suicide, while others will create, by using the power of their mind alone, a physical or mental illness that will help them find permanent release from living in a torturous Hell.

But death for these people may come agonisingly slow and in the mean time, the person floats in and out of reality, preferring not to know the truth, as the truth can quite often hurt and haven't they been hurt enough in the past by others? Why prolong the agony or make the situation worse for themselves? Let's obliterate the truth by turning towards the only real friend they can trust, the one who won't answer back and who will always be there, no matter what. So, who is this great and reliable friend and constant companion that I speak of?

This friend can reveal itself in a few different ways but mainly they appear in the form of alcohol or drugs. The inhalation of some naturally narcotic plants can have the same effect. To be taken in moderation is fine but when you cross that line into excess, problems arise, not only for the addict but for those around them. When partaking of these substances on an irresponsible and regular basis, the mind loses control of reality and that is what this person is seeking. Living in their self-created world of fantasy is so much more pleasant than living with the sometimes harsh truth. It all comes down to a matter of personal choice. Do you give up and give in or do you confront head on that which frightens you the most?

Those people who doubt their own inner strength and ability to survive all types of adversity will more than likely give in and attempt to find a permanent escape route. All I can say to these people who think they are alone and if they wish to listen is, regardless of the non-support from others, still do the things you fear the most and the death of fear is certain. This will set you free and where you can once again travel in the right direction.

Quite often, I would have to claw my way to the top of a particular mountain range or high mound built of loose rocks, stones and dirt. These mounds were particularly difficult to climb, as I would make some progress but if I put one foot wrong out of place, I then fell back down to near where I had first started. It took much guts and perseverance to continue. To be successful in any project I set for myself, including those goals given to me by others, was important to me. To be a success was my driving force. I was forever pushing myself beyond my perceived limitations. And quite often, because of this, I managed to surprise myself as to how well I did once the project reached its conclusion.

I could actually look back and see clearly all of what I achieved. I could see the full picture although at the beginning of each separate journey, I only received glimpses of what was expected. At these times, I had to trust that when one stage ended, I would then be guided to begin a new step. In other words, the full picture was revealed little by little, piece by piece, bit by bit. Sometimes, I found this process to be most frustrating but who am I to argue with my inner guidance? And sometimes I had to learn patience between taking each new step. To remain still and wait was difficult. I liked to achieve good results immediately.

With this same attitude today of wanting good things to happen instantly, some would accuse me of being like a bull in a china shop and we all know how dangerous that situation can be. It wouldn't be a mere accident of fate. It would be a catastrophe. My main lesson in that lifetime as Luke was to pull my head in, rather than charge into something without thinking.

I needed to pause, create a definite plan of action and to work through each step or phase slowly and methodically. To do otherwise may have got myself killed sooner rather than later. That sort of reminds me of a modern day children's story, with the two main characters being a tortoise and a hare. At first glance, you would think the hare would have won the race paws down but Lady Luck and Divine Providence were barracking for the tough little tortoise. I had to learn to become that tortoise.

At times, it was torturous but in the end, I was pleasantly pleased at the results. And when I began to feel that time was running out and I had to move faster, I forced myself to do the opposite, which is to go even slower until that feeling of panic subsided. I know it sounds a strange way of doing things but sometimes the only way to overcome a particular dislike or fear is to live it. Your modern day psychologists or therapists know this when working with people who suffer various forms of phobias.

This is where they force their clients, albeit slowly, to confront their fear while in a safe environment and little by little, that safety net is totally removed; the person stands alone and on their own two feet, is able to remain firm in their resolve and not run from what they fear. Once this can be done, the feeling of accomplishment is mighty great. This can quite often cause the person to break down and cry a combination of tears which stem from a source of great joy and sadness in equal amounts.

Crying is another effective way of releasing an excess build-up of negative emotions and energy. As is anger but crying or laughing is a lot healthier way of getting rid of any pain. But don't wait too long before you do battle with what is bothering you. Go easy on yourself. Why wait and make it more difficult for yourself?

Do you wish to experience a smooth transition through life or are you in it for the thrills, never knowing from moment to moment, whether you are up or down? Everyone will be different. That is why you can tell a lot about a person when they choose to ride either the 'throw you around' roller coaster or the rather more sedate merry-go-round at your carnival, fun fair or circus. The latter group of people will always choose to play it safe in life while the former group of little dare devils will go full steam ahead and take risks, without giving much thought about the consequences of their actions.

But I say, what about experiencing a balance of both and then make a decision as to what suits you the best? There are no wrong answers or mistakes in life. They will just lead you to a different destination and will take you down a path that you had not originally figured on travelling before. But do not overly concern yourself about this because if you don't get it right this time round, there are many other future lifetimes to be had where you can put things right again. How many there are, is up to you. The Universe wasn't created perfect in a day (that is symbolic of one lifetime) and neither can you expect the same of yourself.

Jesus did not heal all of the sick, all the time. Why was that? Why was he so choosy? Have you heard of the term, "physician, heal thyself"? We are all healers, first for ourselves and then for other people. Jesus understood that sometimes the person who was in pain needed to go through that in order to learn something positive about themselves. It was an invaluable lesson to learn and one which should not be avoided. If you remove the physical problem from this person's life completely, how can they learn that specific lesson? Perhaps they needed to learn perseverance, determination, courage, acceptance, enlightenment and motivation.

Certainly, you may intellectually argue that there are other ways to learn about these issues but quite often, people won't listen or they consistently chose to ignore the truth until reality comes knocking on the door of their temple in a harsh way. We must sometimes feel, first hand, the pain because the pain then becomes our driving force to work on the problem and eradicate it for good.

Now of course, there will always be a select group of people who will learn nothing good from their pain, especially if they have created that situation only to obtain the compassion, sympathy or attention which they think they deserve, but would not have got if they had remained positive, fit and healthy.

It is this group of people who will suffer the most pain and for the longest time, because in their mind it serves a purpose, along with providing them with the perfect excuse to show outward signs of anger, abusive behaviour, bitterness, holding grudges, demanding attitude, a high level of impatience and lack of tolerance.

When confronted by ongoing problems, how do you deal with it? The problem or physical pain you are experiencing doesn't need to be a permanent thing. You can pass through this painful time relatively quickly or if you so choose to struggle with it, you can go through it at an agonisingly slow pace. The physical problem is always a by-product, symptom or result of some deep seated, ingrained negative attitude from within.

This book, other than to give people hope for the future, will force people to open their eyes and to realise once and for all that the Apostles of Jesus were human, just like you. They were not chosen because they were already perfect little Angels. They all had their own individual fears, weaknesses and sometimes great personal sadness and loss to deal with. And when you really think about it, if they had been so perfect, why would they have chosen that particular body and at that particular time in history to experience all of what they needed to? Rest assured, it wasn't always safe and where they did not roll around and luxuriate on a bed of sweet smelling roses.

Upon occasion, but not all of the time, they were forced to get down and get dirty, like pigs, in the pile of animal manure that helped those same sweet smelling roses to bloom and grow. But they would not have had it any other way, because much good was learnt and gained and they, including myself, hope that by sharing some of our experiences, that you too will learn and gain much.

MARK

May all your problems be few and

All your good fortunes be many.

Rejoice for I am here, to develop strong

Kinship links, between God and the Brotherhood of Man.

I loved to read and study such subjects as medicine, philosophy and mathematics. To know the 'why' of things was always important to me. I did not live my life with blind faith alone. To do so would have been dangerous. There were many charlatans (as there are today, if not more) who were extremely willing to take your money and to pull the wool over the eyes of the adoring flock of faithful followers. I wasn't prepared to take risks with my religion or spirituality, just because someone told me so. I needed to experience the truth first hand for myself. And before making a commitment to a particular person or belief, I liked to question what was said or what was shown; to do my research, to prove that what I was hearing or seeing is the whole truth and not just a fabrication of the truth.

I have met many a skilled scholar, master, wise man and philosopher. I have met those "would be's" who never "could be's". How does one tell them apart, that is, the genuine from the fake? Sometimes, it is hard to tell the difference between the two, so a certain amount of diligence, tenacity and determination to never give up helps a great deal while seeking the truth. Question, question, question! Don't allow others to spoon-feed you information. Seek out your own answers. The only one you can honestly rely upon is your higher self first and then the Son of God and Man.

This doesn't mean I am better than the Almighty. I am merely stating that we need to be more self-reliant and independent. God helps those who help themselves. Trust your own intuition. To their own detriment, many underestimate their own abilities. They doubt.

They place their faith first and foremost in a higher power or to someone with a physical body that they regard as being 'Godlike'. But even these 'Godlike' beings of the faith are still human. Like Jesus was still a man. He was no ordinary man mind you but he was a man who willingly experienced the whole range of emotions – both positive and negative.

Too many people – both then and now – have exalted these men to such a high level that these holy ones become untouchable and unreachable. They have been put on a pedestal and only the most elite or rich group of loyalists were ever allowed to communicate with these honoured masters.

These idols or gurus (but not all) then railroaded their followers to come and rely upon them. There was no way that these 'Godlike' humans were ever going to lower themselves enough that would then force them to get their feet dirty. Their philosophy was – let the peasants, commoners and slaves come to them.

Jesus though always made sure his own two feet were firmly planted on the ground and did not totally exclude himself from the masses in order to teach the chosen Twelve plus two. His vision went far beyond this small but remarkable group of men. He knew that only one man can do so much. That is why Jesus needed many others that he could trust to help him with passing on the message.

To the Apostles, he gave specific tasks to carry out before and after his death that they all carried out to the best of their ability. I was never an Apostle of Jesus, as many might think by reading the Gospel According to Mark. Luke was the other who was not an Apostle, where Matthew and John most definitely were. We (that is myself and Luke), came to believe in the goodness of his countenance and through the selfless and non-judgemental actions of Jesus, we had our eyes opened to great spiritual truth and wisdom never before known.

I certainly did not understand everything I heard from this great man but there was much I did understand and that far outweighed the little I did not. In time, I believed I would comprehend the incomprehensible. Jesus commended me for my questioning and enquiring mind, which is something that not everyone who knew me, did. He didn't want any sycophants bowing down at his every command or mere presence. That would have been too easy. Jesus knew and accepted that God had given every man, woman and child to think and feel for themselves. A sycophant is the exact opposite to this. A sycophant could be seen in today's terminology as 'sucking up to the boss', 'a yes man', a person who will bend over backwards for another in order to gain more money, acceptance, popularity or protection.

How outwardly agreeable are you when dealing with others, while on the inside, the word 'no' screams loudly within your head that of course only you can hear and where a great amount of anger is created and grows like an infected boil? How long can you keep up this façade or charade – a day, a week, a month, a year or fifty years? How sick do you think you're going to get by hiding the truth of how you feel to those concerned? By staying strong and silent (if not sincere) can be devastatingly and deceptively deadly and it's you who would be ultimately responsible for any ill health leading to a slow and lingering or unexpectedly quick premature death.

Certainly you may not have committed suicide but you might as well have. You still died by your own hands because you were dishonest, maybe not with yourself but with those that you serve – your husband, your wife, your child, your boss, your teacher, your guide, your guru, your master. If the aforementioned people are working from greed and ego, they will use and take advantage of your sycophantic ways for them to obtain more and more of what they want while you get less and less of what you deserve. When dealing willingly with these types of charlatans, con artists, users and abusers on a regular basis, their power grows while your own decreases.

You then become a victim, you become weak, you become powerless, you become like a puppet where, because of your desire to please and not rock the boat by outwardly saying 'NO', you are too easily manipulated to do or say things that you don't really believe and if you had a choice, you would never have done so.

Both Jesus and I implore you to take control over your life, your thoughts, your feelings, your beliefs and your actions. Jesus does not want people to be subservient to him or anybody else. Through unconditional love, he wishes only to help you find your own power within and this force is the God force. It may be suppressed but it can never be destroyed. Even after physical death, it continues to exist. It is eternal. There is no end. It just is, like the Brotherhood of Man.

Wherever I went in my travels, hungry mouths of children would closely follow. There was never enough to give. Then there were the adults and they could be even more demanding than the children, not only for food but for money as well. Most days it was a matter of survival to get through this crowd of people, all jostling and vying for my attention. It was most disheartening and distressing because I felt largely powerless to bring about positive change for them but because I knew

Jesus, I was even more in demand. They thought I could produce miracles to the same standard that they were told about or had come to expect from Jesus but I was nothing compared to our great Lord and Master.

I felt quite humbled to even be associated with such a man of honour but Jesus never wanted us (or anyone else for that matter) to feel lesser than he and tried to take positive steps to ensure this never happened, to the best of his ability. Trouble is, one can only do so much for another, as the other person then needs to accept responsibility for how they feel or react to certain truths or lies. You can never dictate or demand how another person should feel. You may advise but that's the full extent of it. You must then allow your personality to step aside and let them get on with it or not. It's like pushing a stubborn mule from behind and forcing it to drink, let alone move.

If that stubborn old mule is determined not to do your bidding, no amount of poking and prodding will help change its mind to take those first few tentative steps towards experiencing the art of practical action. It (the prodded), not you (the prodder) will move in its own good time and not before. Does this description of a mule's stubborn behaviour pattern sound familiar to you?

We humans are a lot like that mule, myself included, especially when I'm not following God's will and where I am being led by the nose by my own ego, down the garden path. When I follow that particular bumpy track, things don't always run so smoothly. I later learnt that I needed to let go and let God.

Miracles can and do come true for all people, whether they be in a position of great power and influence or even those down on their luck who are suffering great misfortunes. Miracles have no boundaries. Miracles can come knocking at all types of doors yet when it does come knocking and upon our opening the door, we may reject its existence. We laugh and think it's just our imagination, coincidence or luck. You want to believe but dare not place all your hope into something that is intangible, which is of course untouchable and unprovable.

Besides, you may have had your fingers badly burnt before as a result of believing in something that wasn't true which brought much chaos into your life. The one thing that all cynics, sceptics and doubters have in common is that they need physical proof. But proof is a funny thing in that those who demand it never receive it and those who don't need proof to believe always get it.

The former group will argue there must be a simple, scientific explanation for why everything happens but when has science ever been simple? Even the Church hierarchy are forced to thoroughly check out the facts and work with the scientists before they can proclaim that a bona fide miracle has taken place and this can take many years or even centuries, to come to this conclusion or not.

How sad it is that even in the rank of believers, they still must find fault where they too fall victim to their own hypocrisy. Heaven forbid if the church openly admits to modern day miracles, even if the individual personnel do believe. On the one hand, they accept Jesus and speak of his miracles in their Sunday sermons but reject those miracles that are happening to other souls living on this planet today, even with members of their own congregation. It's like they feel threatened, that it's dangerous to have their parishioners empowered by the Holy Spirit without their assistance. Would the church then no longer be needed if people found God by themselves?

Miracles are not something that one can easily be discounted at leisure and turn your nose up at the merest suggestion of its existence. Besides, I'm not only talking of major miracles that happen in front of millions of people, which sceptics would explain away as being a case of mass hysteria, group consciousness and auto hypnotic suggestion. I'm talking about those smaller miracles that happen to each and every individual, nearly every day.

Sit and re-evaluate the word miracle and how you think it should happen. If it happens on a small scale, quietly and without a big bang to one person only, is this then not important enough to be considered as being a miracle? To that person it is. It's like the truth.

The truth is relative to each person. Believe me when I say, it's a miracle to wake up alive and continue to take our next breath full of life giving oxygen and to then, on each out breathe, to empty ourselves of the poisonous build-up of carbon dioxide from our bodies. It's also a miracle to be born. The birthing experience can be traumatic and distressing for both mother and baby but it is still a grand miracle of nature.

Moving away from the body now, what about when you're in a hurry while driving the car and you get green lights all the way? Or if you're rushing for a train and it arrives late, that gives you just enough time to catch it? What about those vacant spaces which magically appear before you in a busy shopping centre car park? What about that stranger you met on the street, who unwittingly helps you achieve your dream or answer an important but unspoken question? The list of so-called minor miracles could go on but to the person it is happening to, they are most grateful that things are going their way, at last.

Miracles are manifested by your own thoughts, your own

belief and your sincere plea for help from above. Not all your prayers or requests will be instantly fulfilled but don't ever give up hope. Keep on asking and we'll keep on listening and when we can, we will provide you with the necessary event, outcome or means that make it possible for you to be successful.

Miracles and success go hand in hand. Take heart, trust, stay alert and maintain a realistic belief and enthusiasm at all times. Retrieve your head from the sand and take a look around you. Enjoy all the good you have and give thanks for being alive at this greatest time in the history of mankind.

In the meantime, there's nothing better than getting your hands dirty in God's good soil, to till the land, to dig a hole. This is why growing your own vegetables and gardening is considered to be strangely therapeutic but not only that, you get to eat, seek shelter from the hot sun and rain or simply admire what you grow. It is indeed a fulfilling pastime. Who cares about the dirt beneath your nails? You can always wash and scrub your hands and nails later with a bit of soap and water. That will solve this temporary problem.

To walk barefoot and feel between your toes, great gobs of squelchy mud can be most uplifting for the soul and can do veritable wonders for your feet, believe it or not. Many women in the more developed countries can spend a small fortune to have a beautician smear mud all over their face and body. They know, although I must say and agree with the experts, that some mud is better than others. As an adult, don't be afraid to experience once again what it's like to be a child, eating dirt and making mud pies that you can then present to your loved ones with pride. You can also choose to work with clay and learn the art of pottery making.

This too has a practical application where you can use the

end result. But in the meantime, you can experience getting your hands all messed up. There are many fascinating pottery pieces (or some would say they are works of art and perhaps they are right) being made today. Use your imagination. You don't have to be like everybody else, make up your own creative designs. Use those pieces yourself, give them away to friends and family or sell them to those who will pay. Spread your material abundance around.

Even if you hate what you made, don't sit on it or hide it away at the back of a cupboard. Let people take advantage to see that spark of ingenuity, initiative and creativity at its best; one that began as a small seed which blossomed into a big and sturdy tree, standing tall. This is accomplishment. Wisdom and knowledge, like your earthenware products, can be shared with those who wish to listen and accept. Communicate your ideas, beliefs and feelings. They are all valuable commodities and if expressed fearlessly, with great passion and enthusiasm in your voice, I guarantee that you will indeed be heard.

Other people may not accept all of what you say or do and this is their right but they will ponder for a time upon what you say, before making a yeah or nay decision to get further involved or not. Let it go, don't hold on to it, then sit back and watch with interest if the seed you have planted within the minds of man takes root or withers and dies. Let it be God's will rather than your own.

Thinking and worrying too much about a specific problem, situation or person can cause damage to the brain and heart, which if held on for too long can cause adverse reactions in the physical body. It is still fact, whether you accept this or not. Remove the psychological, mental or emotional barriers and the body then has a chance to heal itself; although for some unlucky people, it could be too late and radical medical intervention is required.

Knowing this, why do you continue to worry and stew in your own juices? It is not a healthy thing to do. By deciding consciously to hold on to your worries – whether they be justified or not, real or imaginary – coupled with an attitude of not wanting to forgive, will lead to a constant source of anger and bitterness. Why go through life the hard way?

You have specific lessons that highlight your fears, dislikes and weaknesses which will hopefully teach you something positive and constructive about yourself. Take note, I said YOUR fears, dislikes and weaknesses. They belong to you, not to somebody else. And in order to learn these sometimes painful, or eye opening lessons, other like-minded people are needed to show us the way. Rather than begrudging them for playing the role of the antagonist or Devil's advocate, thank them for helping you to see your truth.

All those people we hate, bear a grudge against or intensely dislike in our lives today are only reflecting back to us that same quality we possess within ourselves (which coincidentally is a hundred times magnified in the other person). This has to be like that. Otherwise, we wouldn't see what ails us. Sometimes, our lessons need to be blunt and sharp. If they are too subtle, it is then extremely easy to ignore the real issue at hand and reject the simple truth. It is easier to think bad thoughts of other people than it is to acknowledge and accept that we have a problem, not them, and that we do possess a dark side to our nature.

But when we can take on board, embrace and love that same darkness within ourselves and not run away from it (which logistically, is impossible because it is a part of you, like your own shadow), upon acceptance, this must automatically be transformed into light. We are a mixture of both the dark and the light. Little by little, each different lifetime that we choose to experience chips away some of that darkness, until one day we fully ascend into light. That light force is us and when combined with God's own, we can make an invincible team, where everything becomes possible and nothing is ever seen as being too difficult.

But if you choose to constantly struggle against the darkness that makes up a part of you, that same powerful but opposite force will engulf and destroy any remaining light that can be found within you. This won't happen overnight but it will happen. Life then becomes a living nightmare. It can be seen as being like a battlefield where you are forced to fight for your survival against the 'baddies' that constantly bombard you with their dark energy. Is this the type of existence to wish for yourself?

Life shouldn't be looked at as being a punishment. To experience life is a reward, it's precious and needs to be enjoyed and respected as such in equal amounts. Don't ever take things or people for granted. The minute you do, this is when everything falls apart. So, how would you describe your life? Do you have more up days than down days? Are there more sad moments than there are happy ones? Are you on an even keel where neither your positive or negative emotions control your life? They just are and where the negative can be looked at dispassionately with detachment, while the positives can be appreciated minus the desire, craving or expectation for it to continue.

When we expect, from both ourselves and other people, the positive will then naturally be turned into a negative; where we don't get what we think we should deserve. Whether that be love and acceptance from others, money, sex, a house, car or boat, a good paying job, a husband or wife, children and food. How important are all these things really? One way to gauge their importance is to decide what is it of these things you can live without? Has the list been shortened considerably? If not, it means that you have based your success and happiness upon those things that are outside of yourself, where you have become dependent rather than independent.

Let go of your desire to have these things in your life and you will then find that all this and more will naturally gravitate towards you, without you ever having to lift a finger. You become like a magnet, a shining example of positivity and light that absorbs all the good and transforms the bad. This is true ascension but don't only take my word for it. Do it and experience it first hand for yourself. This way, you then won't be reliant upon what I believe and the only one to thank then is yourself, because you did it for you.

Because I was not one of The Twelve, my hands were less tied than theirs, not that this fact ever stopped them from fulfilling certain set specific tasks. But for me, it was easier to move about unhindered. I didn't have to watch my back as much. I loved the work that I did for God but as well as this, I gained much pleasure in sitting and watching children pass the time of day away.

Those little innocent and angelic like faces would sometimes look joyful, angry, confused, sad, hungry, defiant or fearless. Mind you, they weren't always little Angels and like today, they would invent ways of how best to get into and out of trouble with a minimum of fuss. They had fewer problems in accepting children of different nationalities. Children are less prone to worry or even think too much about the colour of the skin or cultural beliefs of their playmates. They got on with it. If fights erupted, it was due to something wrong being done or said.

Think back to when you were growing up. Did you really care that someone looked a bit different from you, essentially? The only time you may have allowed it to bother you was when an adult whom you respected thought they were helping by letting their personal discrimination views be known to you. Some young ones could reject these hurtful comments about their new little friends but some could not.

Those children who could not ignore would then go out of their way to be cruel and judgemental, all because of an adult in their life saying that it was dangerous to associate with such children. Children are most intelligent and perceptive when it comes to the truth but sometimes, they are also easily manipulated and can be swayed in their convictions. In their eyes, the adult knows better. This may not always be the case. By accepting bits and pieces of wrong information as a child can later cause lifetime scars on a mental, emotional or physical level.

When this happens, this is sad because that young child's innocence of fair play has been corrupted and warped, so they grow up to throw natural justice to the wind and deny themselves the pleasure of being in the company of someone from a different country. What we believe, think, feel, say or do today has a direct bearing upon what we had previously experienced during our first seven years. This is where most of the psychological problems originate but will not appear as such until much later in life.

If the will is weak and where the child feels insecure about making their own decisions, they will be more prone and susceptible to wrongful manipulation of adults. As adults, some can later reject the conditioning received in their early years but this requires a large amount of hard work, dedication, determination and perseverance, while others cannot achieve this. So, which group of children do you think will grow up to be the happiest, more responsible, successful and forgiving? The answer should be obvious even to Blind Freddy.

We, as adults, need to change our attitudes and not be so narrow minded into believing there is only one truth and that must be our own truth, while in the meantime, everyone else doesn't know what they're talking about. Become like little children.

Look at life through untainted eyes. Have respect and fear not at being exposed to ideas and beliefs that are unlike your own. Broaden your horizons and open your heart to embrace all your fellow man and not just some.

Even the most evil of people still desire the same thing as we do, which is love, acceptance and respect. If this is given in large enough amounts to those who live in the darkness, they can be rehabilitated to walk fully in the light once again. They in turn, can help others who were like them, to step off the apparently never ending treadmill that leads to self-destruction.

Any improvement in the quality of life must start with ourselves through our consistently good and sincere works which if not interfered with, can affect all those around us in a positive way. People naturally want what other people have and this applies not only to material possessions but to the intangibles that you can't touch but you can feel such as love (which has already been previously mentioned), truth, wisdom, knowledge, happiness and success.

All this leads to great inner and outer abundance plus good

health. We must teach our children well today, for they are the adults of tomorrow. Because you may not be around to see the results, doesn't give you the automatic right to not do anything. Have compassion for those who are not as smart or spiritually evolved as us. They each have an important role to play but wouldn't it be grand if we could all ascend in peace, together? Accept rather than struggle. Give in and let go of your desire to control other people and outcomes. Just simply be.

From one single step forwards, we move towards advancement. Like the emu and kangaroo in Australia, we can never go backwards. Although to some, it may appear like this is happening but remember, outward appearances alone can be deceiving. Don't always be fooled by what you see on the surface. If in doubt, ask Spirit to help you interpret what someone is really trying to say. Sometimes, no editorial changes on what's been said or written need to be put into place but other times, this will be required.

Also, try not to fall into the trap of only listening to what you want to hear, as the other person strokes your bruised, doubtful, shattered and sometimes insecure ego. Or if you live on the other side of the coin, when going through the process of stroking another's ego, try and ensure what you tell to the other is sincere. Little white fibs can be tolerated as they do no real harm but to make grand statements that are far from the truth can lead to disaster and chaos in that person's life, when they finally get to learn the real truth of the matter.

As well as this, never lie about something that is important to you. Some people believe that by staying silent or choosing to give only half the facts is okay. It's not okay and this leads to confusion for the other person, especially if they cannot read your mind. Honest communication is essential at all times in order to achieve peace of mind and success. Some will hate you for it but others will fall at your feet and come back for more because they know that in you, there is a person they can rely upon and trust. This is most vital in both business and personal relationships.

But with that same honesty, there must be mixed in with that, a blend of diplomacy and tact as well. Be firm, fair and gentle in your approach to others. Put your aggression aside. The truth then becomes more palatable and less painful to bear. Our purpose is not to hurt people with the truth in order for us to gain revenge (or justice, depending upon the way you want to look at it). Our purpose is merely to be like a messenger. Don't wield the truth like a weapon that has been dipped into a liberal coating of guilt and blame. This type of truth is not pure.

When the truth is spoken in great anger and haste, nothing good is ever achieved. Speak the truth once only or three times if you must but anything more than that becomes nagging or interfering and you could be wasting your precious words upon those who do not wish to or who are not yet ready to hear. If they are consistently hurtful or non-respectful after being told in plain and simple terms how you feel about it, you then have a decision to make as to whether you are going to stay and accept or leave and reject what is no longer any good for you.

I know full well that there may never be a perfect time to speak the truth and if you wait for that perfect time, you may be waiting forever. So please, stop finding a myriad of excuses as to why you cannot be honest in your oral communications. The longer you procrastinate on what you wish to say, the matter will only get worse before it can ever get better. Let it all hang out. Don't bottle it tightly up inside. To release is a healing in itself.

Repeat what you see in the following bold italics out loud or internally for at least fifteen minutes on a regular daily basis – ***I accept who I am and release the true I am.*** The results will astound you. Wrinkled brows will become unfurrowed, your frown lines will turn into smile lines, while your unfocused eyes will sparkle and shine with much self-love and enlightenment.

TIMOTHY

Thoughts are the measurer of the soul. It shows me clearly where

I truly belong and how I feel about

Myself within, which has a direct bearing upon how I act with the

Outside world at large. Negative

Thoughts will only harm me, while

Happy mental meanderings will strengthen and revitalise my

Youthful exuberance and belief in my abilities.

I have a big voice and when I really get going, you can hear me roar across the land. Some would say I'm loud mouthed and obnoxious but this is not a good description of me because it's not true. Although I do admit I am a bit of a chatterbox. Set me in concrete and I'd still find a way to continue talking. Some would say I had a natural gift of the gab and that I had no trouble talking my way in and out of a paper bag, quickly and easily. So quick in fact that most people didn't know what hit them until they stopped and sat to think about what had transpired between us, moments before.

I also loved being in the company of women and being the centre of attention in their world, while I never discriminated as to their overall shape or age. In my eyes, they were all beautiful – whether they be 10 or 100. I found it most fascinating to watch their interactions between each other or with the men that they loved or hated. Because of my own smaller physical size, many older women felt quite motherly and protective towards me, while the really young girls would look to me for guidance as they would to an older brother. No woman ever saw me as a threat to their honour and virtue. I made sure I was always the perfect gentleman.

Even though I loved all of what they could give to me, and that includes them stroking my fragile male ego, I still respected their wishes and never outstayed my welcome. It's funny but with all my keen observations and dealing with the opposite sex, I could still never truly figure them out. One minute, they're glad to see you and the next, they're not. Their mood swings and feelings could change quite dramatically and unexpectedly. It's a good thing I knew how to run quickly.

I abhor violence of any kind and even in those situations where I had to defend myself from being attacked by other men; I only did so as a matter of survival. I took no pleasure from it. Because of my intense dislike of hurting anybody – animal, man, woman or child – I was quite often hurt myself but not to any major degree. As they say, "you can't keep a good man down". If I was unable to pick myself up again, there would always be someone there to do it for me. In this way, I was lucky, blessed and most appreciative to have such fine and continual support.

I loved to travel and never liked to stay in the one spot for too long. You could say I was a bit of a nomad or gypsy, always on the move and never having a base. This never bothered me but by saying I never had a base is not completely true either. It moved with me or should that be, I moved with it. My home was where my parents and other brothers lived, as well as with my spiritual brothers and their respective families who all closely followed in the footsteps of Christ.

I was a patient and tolerant person. I didn't mind waiting for things to happen in their own natural timing. I have seen many people – in particular men (although I don't mean to sound discriminatory because some women can also do this quite well) – who rush into things without clearly thinking through the consequences of their actions. For example, this was mostly true when the emotions involved were anger, jealousy, greed and unrequited love.

I gained much pleasure in watching those around me who would dig themselves into an early grave because of their lies. I say, give them enough rope to hang themselves with. That may sound rather callous and uncaring of me but that is what I feel. Once you begin down the track of not speaking the truth about a particular person or situation, this will force you to continue living the lie; where you begin to continue the trend in order to make the first lie sound plausible and to cover your back. I believe that if you can't speak the truth, then keep your mouth shut and not make the situation worse by deliberately lying about it.

Those people who feel they need to lie do so because they have a secret that they wish to remain hidden, if not about themselves but of the one that they love. As a result of this, they re-invent the wheel in order to protect the innocent or guilty party from persecution and mistrust from others; which in some cases could be quite justified on the part of the people whose lives are affected as a result of these lies.

Telling a tall story said in good fun is completely different. In that situation, your listeners can normally discern the truth, simply by picking up on the meaning and tone of voice used by the story teller. Let's face it, who doesn't like a good yarn when done in jest and where what is being said, has no ill intent of hurting another? Even though I have said all that, there is another side to this coin and it concerns the person about whom the story is being told.

If they lack a sense of humour and are a bit touchy about the subject matter being spoken of, they could react in a way that the teller may not like, which results in the story being told, backfiring in the storyteller's face. So, the moral of the story is, and I have come full circle again, that perhaps it is best to keep your mouth shut and not say anything.

Of course, life would be so much simpler if there were no secrets, although I know that some would disagree with this radical theory of mine, because it is only a theory. It hasn't been tested yet. But there are always anomalies in any good plan and not everyone will react favourably to what they hear about themselves or another person.

You see, to a certain extent, I think it's a good thing to know exactly where you stand from someone else's point of view; where there are no unpleasant or nasty surprises in store that raise their ugly little heads in your future. The harder you try to cover your tracks and to hide the truth from someone – regardless of your intentions – let me assure you it will eventually come back to haunt you all over again. There is no escape. People will naturally talk and embellish the facts sometimes.

There are always more sides to someone's personality than just one. Depending upon how often and where we see them, we may incorrectly judge that person in a positive or negative light as being either a joker, a womaniser, someone who lacks a sense of humour, stuffy and boring, intelligent, overbearing and obnoxious, non-stop talker and so on. But if you take that person out of those familiar surroundings in which we see them the most, more than likely you will notice a completely different side to their nature.

In this equation, we must take into account the emotions they express while chatting or being in the presence of someone they either hate or love. There will be marked differences, unless of course we are talking about a person who is a master at hiding his or her true face behind a mountain full of lies, white or black, it doesn't matter. What does matter is that all is not what it appears to be. It's like the still calm freshwater lake.

On the surface, it appears that nothing disturbs it. But when you take the plunge and take a closer look at what lays beyond our line of sight, we then notice a whole new world that opens up to us that may include some fish, plant life, pebbles and sand. There is so much activity happening on a much deeper level, if we care to look.

The same can be said for the three different levels of the mind. The one that is widely accepted and readily perceived is our conscious thinking mind. But this is not where it stops. It extends its greedy little tentacles downwards into what then becomes the feeling subconscious mind. At this deeper and much misunderstood level of understanding, we can retrain our thoughts. That is where hypnosis, autosuggestion, meditations and visualisations can help greatly. It's easy when you know how. Changing things within the subconscious will have an effect on our conscious thinking mind in a real and practical way. Have I lost you yet? Hope not.

We then dig a bit further and there we come upon what is known as our super consciousness or soul level. This is where clear communication can take place between this physical world and the Spirit realm. With discipline and practise, as well as putting certain protection techniques into place, we then have the ability to go to this other level of awareness that lies within and cross over to the other side of this physical reality, with much grace and ease. It is there that many surprises await us.

The best way to describe this most amazing space would be, if you could just imagine yourself walking down endless long corridors lined with books filled with every conceivable type of wisdom and knowledge that has made itself available since the history of mankind. As well as this, it has a vast section dedicated to all of what is yet to be. Also available in this library of light, you would be given the opportunity of speaking directly with the person involved who created and put to good use those inventions that have changed our life for the better over the centuries.

This is real, as you know it's possible to speak with us, the Archangels, God or any other religious or spiritual leader of the past. There are no limitations or barriers here. Everything is freely available. You might doubt that you have the ability or the necessary know how to get there. If this is the case, ask for directions or better still, ask your Spirit Guides or Guardian Angels to take you there. When you first arrive at this place deep within, don't hold back. Ask specific questions, relax, accept what is given and trust what you see.

Once you become comfortable and secure with this process, then dare to be shown your own special edition of the Akashic Records. Relive snippets of your past lives and see how it relates to what you are feeling and thinking today in regards to your fears, your likes, your dislikes and the different people you are associated with. While you're there, why not release those fears and blockages that you no longer need? But please, it is important to remember that you only have permission to look at your own records. Anyone else's Book of Life and Death is strictly prohibited and will not be made available for you to see, unless under strictly special circumstances.

Good verbal communication between two people is like the meeting and making love of two minds to such an extent where each one can freely express and not hold back their true thoughts and feelings about each other, that culminates in an explosive force of compassion, love and understanding. In any partnership, the two qualities needed the most and that many people do not know how to take advantage of or utilise, are talking and listening. In order to be successful in that personal relationship, each person must have the opportunity to do both, in equal amounts.

Problems arise when one is fearful to speak and on the rare occasion when they do, the other person doesn't hear the meaning behind the words spoken, because they are not truly listening with their heart. They become deaf to the needs of their partner.

Or you have the opposite situation where one will be incessantly talking about anything and everything, about their perceived problems and about themselves, constantly demanding their partner's attention and never giving them a chance to have an opinion. And what happens in the situation where both people involved are too afraid to say what they feel?

They are both so insecure about their own self-worth that they have no desire to upset, in any way shape or form, each other. Both are suppressing their feelings that will result later in many minor and major illnesses. Then you have another situation where both parties insist on being the loudest and the best and where they insist on competing against each other. With two people of the same mindset in this type of relationship, their fights will be volatile and violent, verbally if not physically.

What I am trying to say in a roundabout way, is that these are all possible situations which depict a relationship being out of balance and will cause great disharmony, the longer time goes on. There is a big difference between being aggressive and being assertive. In today's society, both men and women have become confused as to the role they play within their own lives and in the lives of each other. Both sexes have gone to the opposite extremes, although this change of consciousness did not happen overnight.

At first, it started off slowly but it has now become much more pronounced. Those who used to be quiet and wouldn't dare say boo to a goose, are now particularly aggressive. They are fighting back but sadly have not been able to find the middle ground between the two polarities. Then the other group of participants involve those who were self-confident and assertive. For those who do not wish to compete with like minds have withdrawn into their protective shells and have begun to doubt themselves.

Depending upon the situation, we need to be an expert in playing both roles. We need a balance. Shakespeare once said "We are all but actors on the stage of life". Rather than learning our lines, we learn our lessons and rather than acting, we take action. And did you know that there is a difference between activity and action. The first is doing for the sake of doing something, where action is doing with a purpose.

The true purpose behind meditation is to allow your mind to become a void, free of all thoughts of a negative or positive kind. Many of us will create or be directed by a teacher to visualise certain symbols, places, peoples, Guides, colours and so on. If this is what you feel you need to do, then let it be. Just realise that this is not an end but a beginning. In other words, this is only the first step in a three step process. Any form of visual meditation can have great impact in our physical reality, in a practical way, every day. This helps us to start opening our hearts and mind to the world of Angels. Put these mind pictures that we create, to good use. Enjoy, listen and feel all of what you are seeing.

When you're completely there and you feel comfortable with where you're at in your mind, visualise yourself standing on the edge of a diving board. Look down and there before you is an endless drop into an unknown abyss. It is upon this diving board where you are to stay for a while. Because it is there that you will be required to say goodbye to all of what you know, feel, see and understand to be your Truth. As well as letting go of all those things that you have felt were important to you and that includes all those people you love, your family members and those belief systems that you have clung on to and which have shaped you into the person you are today.

Let it all disappear and have faith that more valuable insights will come later which will create even greater change in your life. Over a period of different sessions, the object of this second step is to allow your mind and body to be completely empty of all thoughts, feelings, words and pictures. This will not be easy and it will require a lot of time, patience, discipline and concentration to release that steely control we have over ourselves.

It is to those people who have a constant busily thinking mind and who don't know how to stop doing things of a physical, mental or spiritual nature, that I say this second step will be most difficult to accomplish but not impossible. If you have a sincere desire to experience this intermingled state of nothingness, completeness and oneness with yourself, God and the Universe, then it shall be done. To be teetering upon that edge of this amazing and fascinating place, is most definitely not so easy to find and achieve.

When you do finally get yourself to this point of heightened awareness, it is then time to close your eyes, have no expectations and jump off the board into the vast unknown. When that day comes for you to take the third and final step, rest assured you can never go back from where you came. It will change you forever on such a grand scale that you cannot truly perceive or appreciate its value, at this time. For it is there, where you will find more profound and never thought of before insights which will be given to you and which will relate not only to this earthly plane of existence. It goes far beyond this.

Sit, be still, listen and most importantly, trust in all of what is being given. This is a gift that the Spirit world wishes to give back to you freely. Never believe that what you are experiencing at this deep level of human consciousness (or super consciousness) is pure fantasy and that it has nothing at all to do with you. This is not true. It has everything to do with you and which will allay any lingering doubts of you jumping into a dream world where nothing is real. Even fantasy, fairytales and science fiction, all have an element of truth in them somewhere. It's not all made up.

The starting point is based on fact and on what is already known. It is only after that, the imagination takes over. But this eternal openness of ancient wisdom and knowledge you have jumped into with all your heart, mind, body and soul, does not belong in our imagination. It belongs to another different reality that each one of us has within. There is a saying that some like to use, which is "there are more things in Heaven and Earth that we cannot see". And so it is with the workings of our inner body and mind.

Between the ages of thirteen and seventeen were the most difficult for me to handle. I sometimes don't know how I survived but I did. While my male friends around me grew taller and bulkier, I stayed the same. Because of this, I felt inadequate and felt there must be something wrong with me. Why else would those boys who knew me react in such a cruel and teasing way? They must be right and I must be wrong – the majority rule. Because I felt insecure about myself, I withdrew and became extremely introverted. I didn't know how, and neither did I want to, stand up for myself. To do so, was too hard and was frightened of the consequences if I did.

Because of this, I felt lonely a lot of the time and quiet often, I would play by myself, which was far better than constantly being made a fool of because of my size. I would try so hard to fit in and would do some pretty stupid and dangerous things in order to be accepted and on the surface; it appeared to work but not for long. I wasn't winning, as far as I was concerned. Before too long, I felt like a loser. I then got to the stage where I considered seriously that I didn't need friends and that I was a whole lot better off being in my own company.

Even when I made that decision, I still felt sad and wasn't quite sure if I had made a mistake in taking such a course of action. The females around me could see how I was being treated and how I felt. As mentioned earlier, the older or more mature women took me under their protective wings. I am sure they only did so because they felt sorry for, and took pity on, a poor underfed waif such as myself. This was wonderful but still I was being teased, although the sympathy I received from the opposite sex soothed a lot of the inner turmoil I was experiencing.

When I realised I could not change my so-called friends opinion of me, I stopped trying so hard to win their approval. I remained a loner but I began to feel more comfortable about who I was. I believe that the love and support I received from those unselfish women who looked after my wants and needs, helped me to develop my own level of self-confidence that I was initially lacking. The more confident I became, the more I started to see that I could be happy and began to focus my efforts on forming firm friendships with the fairer sex. They enjoyed my attentions because they knew me so well. They were also aware that I would never physically harm, threaten or take advantage of their kindness in any way.

How could I repay them in such a nasty manner as that, for all the good they have given me? I couldn't. It was not in my nature to do so. I thank those women for their generosity during that lonely and difficult time because without them, I would not have been so self-assured in my later years. I am truly grateful for their help and assistance. And with the passing of each new day, the respect, desire and love for women grew stronger and felt that once again, I was heading in the right direction. It would only be much later that I would begin to trust and develop long lasting friendships with men.

The reason I share this with you is not for you to feel sorry for me. The message is not as simple as that. Regardless of whether you are male or female, stop trying so hard to win the approval of others. Most importantly, be yourself and be happy for who you are today. Things won't always look so black; where you can't see a way out of your perceived loneliness. Stop seeking love from an outside source. Enjoy loving yourself first and then the rest will naturally follow and when you least expect it, this is when you will find what you have been looking for.

One last thing, no-one can give you confidence. This is something that you must do for yourself and no matter how difficult it is to achieve, persevere. "When the going gets tough, the tough get going". And please, most importantly, don't purposefully destroy those good things you do have just because you are envious or angry at those things you don't have.

Cast a spell of love for the Universe of the future. Many of you do not truly understand and appreciate the power of your thoughts. Even a single thought that you project will have an impact that involves your own circle of friends, family, acquaintances and any other people you associate with. Imagine if you will, a world filled with like-minded people, at the one agreed time, who are all thinking the same positive thought. What do you think would happen? The effects would be near instantaneous and miraculous.

Many people fear the future for themselves mainly but sometimes this same fear will extend outwards to include those people and children they love in their own personal hemisphere, while others fear for the state of the world at large. Singularly, it is sometimes hard to make earth shattering changes on a large scale but collectively, miracles can be achieved and seen by all. That does not mean to say that smaller miracles do not exist on a daily basis because they are happening naturally all around and to us. But because they are on a much smaller scale and not as obvious as the parting of the Red Sea, we are not even aware of what is taking place right under our nose.

Redefine your personal definition of the word 'miracle'. If you can do this, your life will have more meaning and purpose and instead of looking at the world through negative eyes, you will begin to see the beauty and wonder that is you and planet Earth.

Did you know our thoughts and feelings are even more powerful than action because it is our minds that direct the body to do or not to do? We live and create our own self-fulfilling prophecy every moment of our waking day, although, there would still be certain times where you would emphatically deny ever having had such an evil thought.

In other words, I can hear some of you might scream out 'and what about all those terrible things I never asked for?' For example, women and children who have been raped, Sudden Infant Death Syndrome, being caught in a fire, laying in a coma with no hope of ever being a 'normal' person again and so on. You know what I am trying to say. These are personal catastrophes that need to be dealt with immediately, constructively and effectively. Many people, when confronted by these disasters claim 'Why me? What have I done to deserve this?' Depending upon each individuals own belief system and conditioning, the answer to these two questions may differ from one person to the next.

Some may say it's Karma. Others, who tend to sit upon the religious fence and who are into self-flagellation and who experience a lack of love for themselves, will consider seriously that God is punishing them for some past sin they had committed and they will accept this as fact. Even when they can't remember ever doing anything so bad that would warrant such wrath from God. Then you have another sad group of people who cannot for the life of them, come up with some sort of an answer at all and it is to this group of people who will suffer the most from these crisis points. They are stuck between a rock and a hard place, where they can't find any reason why and they can't see any hope for the future.

Remember, everything happens for a reason. In order for us to progress on a spiritual level and for the evolvement of the soul, we need to experience these major turning points in our life. Depending upon how you feel about what you are going through and the resultant action you take, will dictate your future direction. These perceived 'negative' experiences, even though not asked for on a conscious level, are necessary.

We can change our future but there are other certain events which are used as catalysts for a dramatic shift in our consciousness. Without them, we would go nowhere. Please remember that no-one is to blame for these events – not God, not yourself, not others. I am not saying that murderers, rapists, child molesters, pyromaniacs and a variety of other criminals are not guilty of the crimes they commit. They are responsible and they must make amends to society. We all understand this easily but go one step beyond the obvious and look below the surface of the person you are perceiving to be a criminal.

Each and every one of us has certain lessons to learn. Some are more difficult than others. Whether you believe a particular individual is deemed to be good or bad, is irrelevant. The end result is the same for all of us. Some believe in Satan (or the Devil) while some do not. For those who do believe, Satan was not always considered to be 'all' bad. He started off as being one of God's most respected Angels but even the Angels must learn lessons in order to continue their advancement and to experience a higher level of awareness and enlightenment. Satan, using his power of freewill, tried to take control so God gave him the opportunity to do exactly that, in whichever way the Devil saw fit.

My point is, even Satan still has a glimmer of light within and that tiny spark of light will never fully be extinguished and so it is with those poor lost souls who create misery, havoc and total mayhem in the lives of their family and strangers.

Another more definite example of this would be the story of Judas and Jesus. On a much deeper and spiritual level, Judas was only helping Jesus to fulfil God's prophecy. This event had to happen, in order to lead people to a better understanding or a new way of thinking. It was with the death of Jesus dying for our sins, that the basis of Christian religion was born. By understanding this, how can we then continue to blame Judas for the role that he played?

One last thing, the ideal of perfection does not exist, both in Heaven and on Earth. We (meaning both man and Spirit kind) are all continuously learning, no matter what level of awareness we have already achieved.

Part 4

A Spiritual Journey Towards World Peace

"Be still and hear my voice. Come and join me friend, while I stand in my specially created rose garden. This garden is representative of the depth of my love for you, for I am the Rose of Love, as you are too. As you can see, it far extends your line of sight and this is as it should be, because it reaches to eternity. Each single bloom that grows symbolises each and every person that makes up the population of the entire world as it stands today.

As a person experiences physical death and leaves their earthly body far behind, a rose here also consequently dies. But this is no cause for alarm or great distress. In fact, it is a happy occasion rather than a mournful one. I am thus alerted to this reality and I immediately seek it out, like the lost lamb. Once found, the rose is tenderly plucked from the bush, at which time, it comes to life again in the palm of my hands.

This rose, grown because of you, is then given back to you upon your arrival here in the Spirit world and you do come here, regardless of your religious or spiritual beliefs. You could refer this place to being like a green room, a holding bay or reception lounge, where those souls newly departed from their physical self wait *to receive further guidance and instruction in regards to their future direction.*

This is also where they are introduced to their own personal team of spirit helpers, guides or Angels, that is, if they don't already know them. Some do and some don't. And because everyone is different, some arrive in a state of confusion and anger, while others are more than happy to be here. I do my best to make all my children feel welcome. You may think – how can I do this? People are dying all over the world, every second of each day and night. Surely, I would be run off my feet?

This picture brings a smile to my face, as I see the hilarity of this very human situation. If this was the case in your world, I would have to say yes, you are indeed correct but because of my very nature and energy, I am present in all things at all times, so this is no real effort for me.

As you can also see, this garden contains many different varieties that come in many different colours, most of which you will never see on Earth. Each colour represents one of the seven great land masses or groupings of land known to mankind today. They are namely Africa, America and this includes Canada and South America, Asia, Australia which include the islands of the South Pacific, New Zealand and Papua New Guinea, Europe and the islands of the Mediterranean, the Middle East and the United Kingdom which also includes Scotland, Ireland and Wales.

As you can see, I have been very diplomatic by placing these land masses or their groupings in alphabetical order rather than priority order, of which there is none. No one country or colour is better than another. Like me, it just is. What colour these roses are and which continents they belong to, is knowledge that will be used later in this meditation but for now, this is all you need to know.

So please, for the moment, take my hand and I will guide you to where you belong in my treasured garden. When you come to visit again in your mind, your soul knows where to find the other half of itself and will take you there directly. Have no fear of getting lost."

In an instant, we are standing on either side of this most exquisite rose, which quite literally takes my breath away. As I peer at it closely, mesmerised and hypnotised, this perfect specimen gives off a pulsating gold aura that brings the rose strangely to life, as if it has thoughts and feelings, just like me. It recognises me for who I am, even if I sometimes don't.

I feel genuine peace and harmony here. I enjoy these quiet moments, connected to that part of me which I never knew existed. Jesus then hands me a bowl full of crystal clear water and beckons that I should water the flower that stands before me, ever so perfect in its natural beauty that is me.

"Please understand that all these roses that grow in this Spirit garden, including your own, don't need the real thing but by the very act of pouring the water on to the flower, indicates that you accept and receive the Holy Spirit into your life, which in turn will help the spiritual evolvement of your soul. The more you water your higher self, the quicker you will advance and the level of awareness in regards to your truth and the truth of others will be greatly enhanced and expanded; solutions will flow from your mind and to later take the appropriate hard action in your world will be relatively easy and hassle free.

This clear but precious liquid also acts as a symbolically

clear channel between Heaven and Earth or between you and me. Enjoy this moment of freedom. Take from this rose what you need but please remember that very soon, we must progress on to the next stage of our journey together. There is much good work that needs to be done in order to heal the world and it needs to be done now. I therefore request that you close your eyes and allow your heart to remain balanced and accepting. Now tilt your head slightly back as if you are looking up at the sky".

Seconds pass before I am requested to open them. I am bowled over by the sight before me. The sky has turned to the colour of pale pink. Not only this, there is a larger than life open eye that floats above me. I am overawed by its presence and bow down before it. Jesus helps me to my feet and suggests that this is not necessary.

"I invite you to see your world through both the eyes of God and your third eye. Let the two become one and you can make this happen simply by walking through this portal in the sky that you see so clearly and behold what lies on the other side. Come, my child. Let's heal the world together".

The powerful energy force or vortex flows through me as I walk through the middle of the eye. The feelings are astounding. No words can describe how I feel. It is something that each individual has to experience for themselves and all the while, Jesus still stands by my side, ever so loving, compassionate and patient.

"This energy pattern or vibration you are now experiencing is the very thing that keeps the world together and is consequently weakened each time a person goes against or interferes with the Laws of Nature and who

kills not for survival purposes. What you do on Earth has a direct effect here in the world of Spirit and vice versa. You could say what goes around comes around and you will pay a very high price for this interference, in those areas of your life that are most important to you. This is not a form of punishment.

It simply means every action must have an equal reaction and every action must begin with a single thought. This energy force you have surrounded yourself with can be used for both good and bad which will result in it being strengthened or weakened accordingly. Please, come again at a later time and stay for a while. It's an excellent starting point to recharge your batteries and to receive healing on all levels.

This place is also a store house filled to the brim of an endless supply of solutions and innovative ideas to make life easier for you. So please come often and begin to work smarter, not harder".

I then keep walking forwards, knowing that I will emerge a better and more aware person than when I had first entered. In fact, it's more than that. It's a transformation in the same way that a caterpillar does upon entering another stage of life, by first creating a protective cocoon, only to emerge later as a beautiful butterfly.

This is exactly what happens to me but rather than turning into a butterfly, I become an angelic being complete with my own pair of magnificent wings. And even though they are big, they are certainly not heavy. And rather than weigh me down, they are uplifting and there begins the next stage of this incredible journey towards world peace.

Other than sprouting wings, what I see as I pass through

to the other side of the eye in the sky is incredibly awe inspiring and beautiful. I see planet Earth spinning as it should in the heart of the Universe, with each continent and country very clearly outlined. Jesus then once again speaks.

"*As you focus upon each separate continent and upon occasion, the various islands surrounding it, that particular land mass will jump out at you in the same way that a 3D picture would. All I simply want you to do is let go some but not all of God's energy force you picked up for yourself and from your heart, freely give it away with as much unconditional love as you can. This is your gift to the world and yourself.*

Also, as each land mass comes into view, spread your open hands with palms facing downwards in a gesture of welcome and like magic, there will fall from your fingertips millions upon millions of rose petals. Its power to heal comes direct from my rose garden that you have just been to visit. Also before moving on, to each new continent or land mass, make sure that every square inch is completely covered. This supply of love is never ending. It can never dry up, wither or die.

By doing so, you will be creating a stronger, harmonious and more peaceful environment that will make it easier for you to work with, upon your return to your physical existence. Also, don't be surprised to see some familiar faces appear before you. This is okay. It is meant to be. Give them what you can, for you need to acknowledge their need for a healing.

Take a close look at their personal pain and see it dissolve before your very eyes as the rose petals comes in direct contact with their aura. Once seen, you then need to accept that their pain is quite often the same as yours. That is why you know each other and are together. Also at a later time, invite certain members of your family and friends, including those ones that you perceive as being your enemies and allow them the pleasure of being surrounded by perfect forgiveness and love.

Have no doubt; it will change them for the better. These places I have shown you today are not to be kept a deep and dark secret, only to be shared with the select few. This is not what I want. It is for everyone who is ready to listen and take responsibility for their actions for today and the future. Besides which, with more people doing the same thing you are now doing will bring about great and good change so much quicker. It is badly needed and for me to fulfil my destiny and purpose, I need your assistance.

We are partners who can never be parted. Even in death, we are still one. Let us begin at Africa, travel west a short distance, say hullo to the United Kingdom, then turn and head east towards the rising sun passing over Europe, the Middle East and Asia, with a final turn at America, where we head straight for the South Pacific, New Zealand and Papua New Guinea, with our final destination being Australia."

There is a moment of silence before the real fun begins. I consider it to be a great honour to be here in this very special place, watching the world go round and that is when the world stopped.

Africa came into full focus. An indigo light spread across the land, while the same coloured petals fall from my fingertips, caressing all those that have chosen to live there at this time like a gentle cleansing rain. I watch transfixed, as to how the country is so quickly covered in petals, as Jesus promised.

No stone, leaf, grass or tree, man, woman or child can escape being smothered in love's extraordinary healing powers. Stress no longer plays an important role in their daily life and I pray that they open their eyes and ears to the real truth before it destroys them.

I then travel further to the west and stop to say hullo to the United Kingdom, Scotland, Ireland and Wales. Green light glows from deep within its heart and as I reach out to touch every living soul resident there, emerald green rose petals pour forth from me. May these countries be blessed with much abundance, both materially and spiritually.

But now it is time to move on towards an easterly direction and drop in on Europe that includes the islands of the Mediterranean. The light here shines yellow like the sun. I therefore bless this area with feelings of warmth, safety and security. Let there be no barriers between friends, strangers and neighbours.

There is no isolation except what we create in our mind. Therefore, those countries that come under the banner of the European flag, I pray that they be united with a positive and constructive outlook. Gold petals embrace its many inhabitants, one by one and two by two.

The yellow light then changes to a fiery red as the Middle East enters the picture. Feelings of fear, hate and heartbreak are all now a thing of the past, as they are replaced by a generous serving of acceptance, tolerance and patience for their fellow man. The petals that leave my hands henceforth are the same colour as my blood, which is used to destroy any deep seated pain that lays buried within its very foundations but these very same foundations can be pulled down and rebuilt, stone by stone and there begins the start of a new and fresh beginning.

I then extend my journey to take in the whole of Asia that includes India, the Philippines and Indonesia. Purple petals thus fall upon their glowing heads. Like Africa, there is much overcrowding but there is also a wealth of untapped knowledge and wisdom. But as the purple light is absorbed into the auras of the millions, a gateway to the mind is opened to embrace all that is true and good. Life, from all points of view, becomes too precious to waste by petty arguing.

I continue my travels further east until I reach Canada, the USA and South America that includes the West Indies, as well as the other islands of the Caribbean. The light that shines from within this land has turned a brilliant shade of aqua blue which brings with it great tidal waves of hope for compassion and clear communication. This is their lesson. My wish is they learn it well and then use this information wisely for the benefit of all. The blue petals soon cover these great lands and merge with the blue of the oceans that surround it. May they all be at peace.

I then turn and travel in the opposite direction and head for the 'aloha' islands of the South Pacific, New Zealand, Papua New Guinea and of course, Australia. The light has now become a vibrant and strong orange, the two qualities of which are in abundance in this part of the world. It is greatly needed to lead the way. Their faith in themselves, mankind and God will protect them from experiencing too much harm.

However, they must never become too complacent or

take things for granted while burying their head in the sand. There is a lot of ground to cover here and their number one priority is to look after their personal needs which brings with it a deep sense of contentment and fulfilment that is real.

I now leave this area of the world and in order to complete the circle of light, a blinding shade of white that is the energy of Christ follows closely behind me that extends from the west coast of Australia to the southern tip of Africa. We have returned to the beginning. Therefore, behold the colours and great nations that make up the world.

This band of rainbow coloured spectrum of light that is indigo, green, yellow, red, purple, blue, orange and white, combined with the rose petals that are symbolic of the Creator's great love for us, will heal the world that extends deep into its core, which in turn cools down and soothes the sometimes raging planet Earth.

Jesus then moves around to face me directly and says **"My work here, for the moment, has been done. I hereby hand over the reins of responsibility to each and every one of you to take the appropriate action towards world peace. This is possible. It's not just a dream or fantasy created out of a need for a brighter future. This can be your reality today. What the mind of man can perceive, you can achieve. Please read these words, again and again until they become a part of you.**

So until we meet again, may blessings abound and if upon occasion, the sweet scent of roses is waved under your unsuspecting nose, know that it is I, just gently reminding you of who you are and the role you are to play towards the evolvement of your soul".

Affirmations

My eyes adore you and I accept the Blood of Christ, which will help me to wipe away all tears of sorrow fear and pain. The Master is with me, as well as the Twelve, therefore I drink from the Holy Grail, which is God's precious gift to me and I will endeavour to fulfil my destiny to the best of my ability with the sign of the Cross, emblazoned upon my forehead.

*A GUARDIAN ANGEL stands closely by my side.
I offer the hand of FRIENDSHIP to myself.
I am never alone.*

Please God, give me the energy and enthusiasm I need to bring together, in your name, enough love and compassion to heal my past and release all negative emotions that are holding me back today.

*My body is glowing with RADIANT GOOD HEALTH, vitality and enthusiasm. My mind remains CALM when confronted by adversity and fear.
My spiritual self SEEKS THE TRUTH by turning within.*

Special am I, special are you, may we walk together over valleys and dunes, neither afraid nor feeling blue.

*I know that I know. I let go and TRUST. I will be guided to safely pass through the vast unknown,
only to EMBRACE what is innately known.*

Shontara

Jesus, I ask that you lift up my soul in order for me not to drown in my own depression and help me to accept the person that I am today and to honestly see that I am unique, gifted and blessed.

I open my heart and arms to RECEIVE. I AM BLESSED and give thanks for all the wealth given to me. I don't just feel but I know I AM RICH, way beyond my wildest dreams.

To thine own self be true. Help me to see clearly the truth of all people and situations that I may find myself involved with and help me to ask the right questions that will lead me to establish a very special and long lasting link with Spirit.

I stand with an ARMY OF ANGELS around me. I am the POWER within. I am a powerhouse of energy which is then TRANSFORMED into something practical and positive.

Joy to the world, put down your alms, blessings abound, as the Messiah walks and talks amongst us. Behold, enlightenment is at hand. So thank you, God, for sending us this man to save our wretched souls.

I have come direct from Spirit, I AM SPIRIT and will return to the world of Spirit. I breathe and ACCEPT THE LIGHT OF SPIRIT into my soul. May the Spirit be with me!

Join hands dear sisters and brothers. Let us unite our once more happy hearts. Then step back and embrace the dawn of a New 'Golden' Age of peace and prosperity.

GOD DOES NOT JUDGE with envy in his heart, so why should I? No one person or being is BETTER OR LESSER THAN me. I stand before you on an EQUAL FOOTING.

Beauty that's true is found within the heart. Acceptance of oneself brings with it a sense of peace and understanding. Responsible acts will bear responsible outcomes. Tools of success, like ourselves, needs constant reshaping and sharpening. Happiness will always create even more happiness. Opposite hate, stands love. Laughter is the best medicine and will keep you forever young. Outstanding actions cause outstanding results. Magnificence can be found, everywhere you look. Enthusiasm is your best driving force to keep you moving forward. Walk your talk.

The TRUTH will always set me FREE to be me. No real harm can come to me here. I REJECT the twin roles of being a persecutor or persecuted.

Peace be with you, dear children of God. My heart I give to you, with eternal love. I am the Way, the Truth and the Light. Allow me to guide and let me inspire. May peace be with you, dear children of God.

YOU AND I remain one. A spiritual split away from myself is far worse than any physical parting.
I AM INTERCONNECTED with all people and all things.

Acceptance of myself and my many gifts, is absolutely vital and necessary to give me the required motivation and drive to be successful in all areas of my life.
Rejoice, for change is just a heartbeat away.
Greet it as an old friend, with enthusiastic open arms and turn this newfound knowledge into wise and right action.

The seeds of success rely upon me to HAVE NO FEAR.
I MEASURE SUCCESS in terms of how I feel.
I look to the stars and CLEARLY SEE THE PATHWAY to success unfold before me.

Let no evil dwell between God, beast or man.
Action, when coupled with an enthusiastic belief in the outcome will bring unlimited surprises.

I reject all of that which is no longer BENEFICIAL to my heart and soul. I am MY OWN BEST FRIEND.
Rejection from other people no longer bothers me.

Jesus and the belief in miracles equal an overabundance of success.

THE SEEDS OF LIFE can be found within death. Death is the beginning of A NEW ADVENTURE. A part of me dies every day as MY LEVEL OF AWARENESS EXPANDS and separates from my old unaware self.

Many will come to accept your words of truth. It is through your love that he can speak and share his infinite wisdom and compassion to the world. All we ask is for you to stay, a clear and perfect channel.

*I TRUST MY POSITIVE FEELINGS,
more than I do my negative emotions.
I AM NOT AFRAID TO EXPERIENCE the whole
range of emotions. If in doubt, chuck it out.*

Please assist us Lord.

*I take POSITIVE AND CONSTRUCTIVE ACTION
to defend myself when necessary. I have no fear of attack.
NO ONE CAN TRULY HURT ME except myself.*

Let us shine our unique light across the world, filled with an abundance of kindness, love, compassion, acceptance and enthusiasm for our fellow travellers in life.

May all your problems be few and all your good fortunes be many. Rejoice for I am here, to develop strong kinship links, between God and the Brotherhood of Man.

Thoughts are the measurer of the soul. It shows me clearly where I truly belong and how I feel about myself within, which has a direct bearing upon how I act with the outside world at large. Negative thoughts will only harm me, while happy mental meanderings will strengthen and revitalise my youthful exuberance and belief in my abilities.

Other Products by the same Author

 Book

 CD

Contact

Email: shontara@shontara.org
Website: www.shontara.org

New Releases... also from Sid Harta Publishers

OTHER BEST SELLING SID HARTA TITLES CAN BE FOUND AT
http://sidharta.com.au   http://Anzac.sidharta.com
***
HAVE YOU WRITTEN A STORY?
http://publisher-guidelines.com

New Releases... also from Sid Harta Publishers

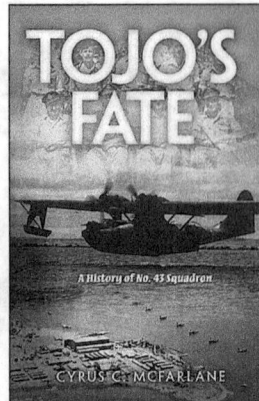

OTHER BEST SELLING SID HARTA TITLES CAN BE FOUND AT

http://sidharta.com.au   http://Anzac.sidharta.com

***

HAVE YOU WRITTEN A STORY?
http://publisher-guidelines.com

Best-selling titles by Kerry B. Collison

Readers are invited to visit our publishing websites at:
http://sidharta.com.au
http://publisher-guidelines.com/

Kerry B. Collison's home pages:
http://www.authorsden.com/visit/author.asp?AuthorID=2239
http://www.expat.or.id/sponsors/collison.html
email: author@sidharta.com.au

Purchase Sid Harta titles online at:
http://sidharta.com.au

New Releases... also from Sid Harta Publishers

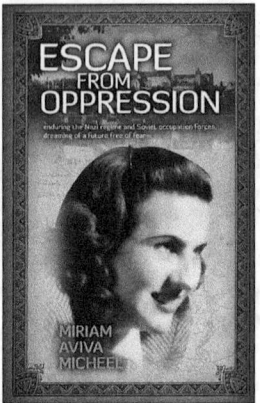

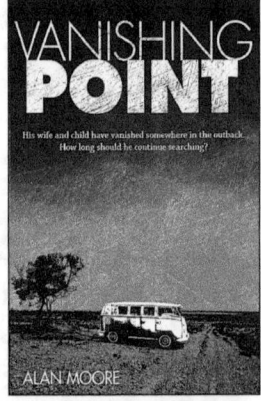

OTHER BEST SELLING SID HARTA TITLES CAN BE FOUND AT

http://sidharta.com.au   http://Anzac.sidharta.com

***

HAVE YOU WRITTEN A STORY?
http://publisher-guidelines.com

www.ingramcontent.com/pod-product-compliance
Lightning Source LLC
Chambersburg PA
CBHW051801230426
43672CB00012B/2590